Angel Sanctuary

story and art by **Kaori Yuki**
vol.10

Angel Sanctuary

Vol. 10
Shôjo Edition

STORY AND ART BY KAORI YUKI

Translation/Alexis Kirsch
English Adaptation/Matt Segale
Touch-up & Lettering/James Hudnall
Cover, Graphics & Design/Izumi Evers
Editor/Pancha Diaz

Managing Editor/Annette Roman
Director of Production/Noboru Watanabe
Vice President of Publishing/Alvin Lu
Sr. Director of Acquisitions/Rika Inouye
VP of Sales & Marketing/Liza Coppola
Publisher/Hyoe Narita

Printed in Canada.

Published by VIZ Media, LLC
P.O. Box 77010
San Francisco, CA 94107

Shôjo Edition
10 9 8 7 6 5 4 3 2 1
First printing, September 2005

www.viz.com
store.viz.com

PARENTAL ADVISORY
ANGEL SANCTUARY is rated T+ for Older Teen and is recommended for ages 16 and up. This volume contains violence and mature situations.

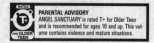

Angel Sanctuary™

story and art by Kaori Yuki   vol. 10

The Story Thus Far

High school boy Setsuna Mudo's life is hellish. He's always been a troublemaker, but his worst sin was falling incestuously in love with his beautiful sister Sara. But his troubles are preordained—Setsuna is the reincarnation of the Lady Alexiel, an angel who rebelled against Heaven and led the demons of Hell in a revolt. Her punishment was to be reborn into tragic life after tragic life. This time, her life is as Setsuna.

Setsuna left his body in what he thought was safety while his soul went searching for his beloved Sara's soul in the depths of Hell. But while Setsuna wandered, his mortal body was accidentally killed. With no where else to go when he tried to return to Earth, Setsuna's soul has taken up residence in the body of the Angel Alexiel!

Setsuna has found out that Sara is in Heaven, but before he can crash the pearly gates, he has to rescue his friend Kurai from a hellish marriage. Kurai was tricked by the licentious demon the Mad Hatter into believing that Lucifer has the power to bring Setsuna back to life...but he'll only do it in return for Kurai's body!

In Heaven, Sara has woken up in the body of the Elemental Angel Jibril. She's blind, confused, and being chased by Sevothtarte! She's determined to restore her brother's soul, but to do so she needs the help of the randy Angel Raphael and the hotheaded Angel Michael.

Contents

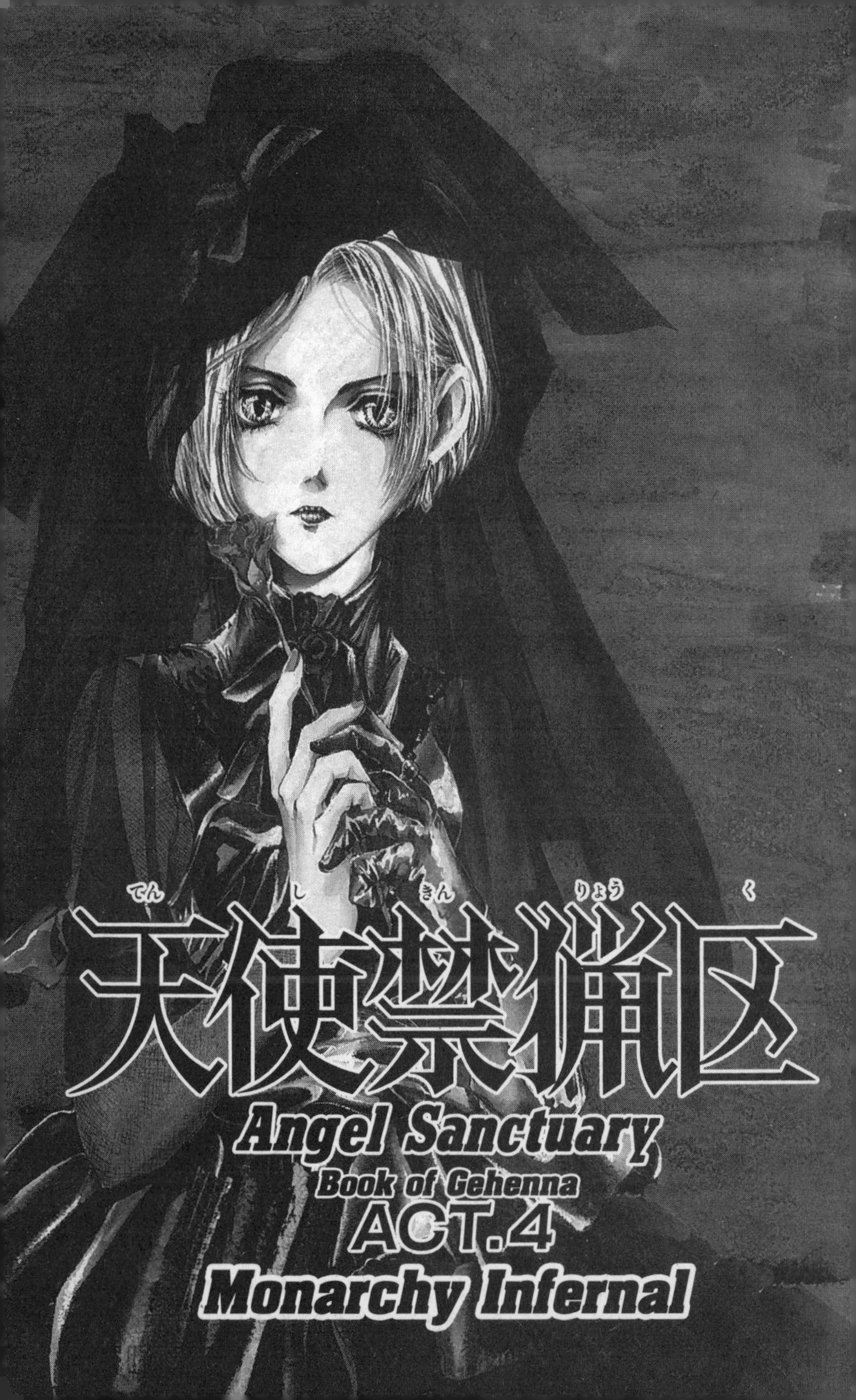
天使禁猟区
Angel Sanctuary
Book of Gehenna
ACT.4
Monarchy Infernal

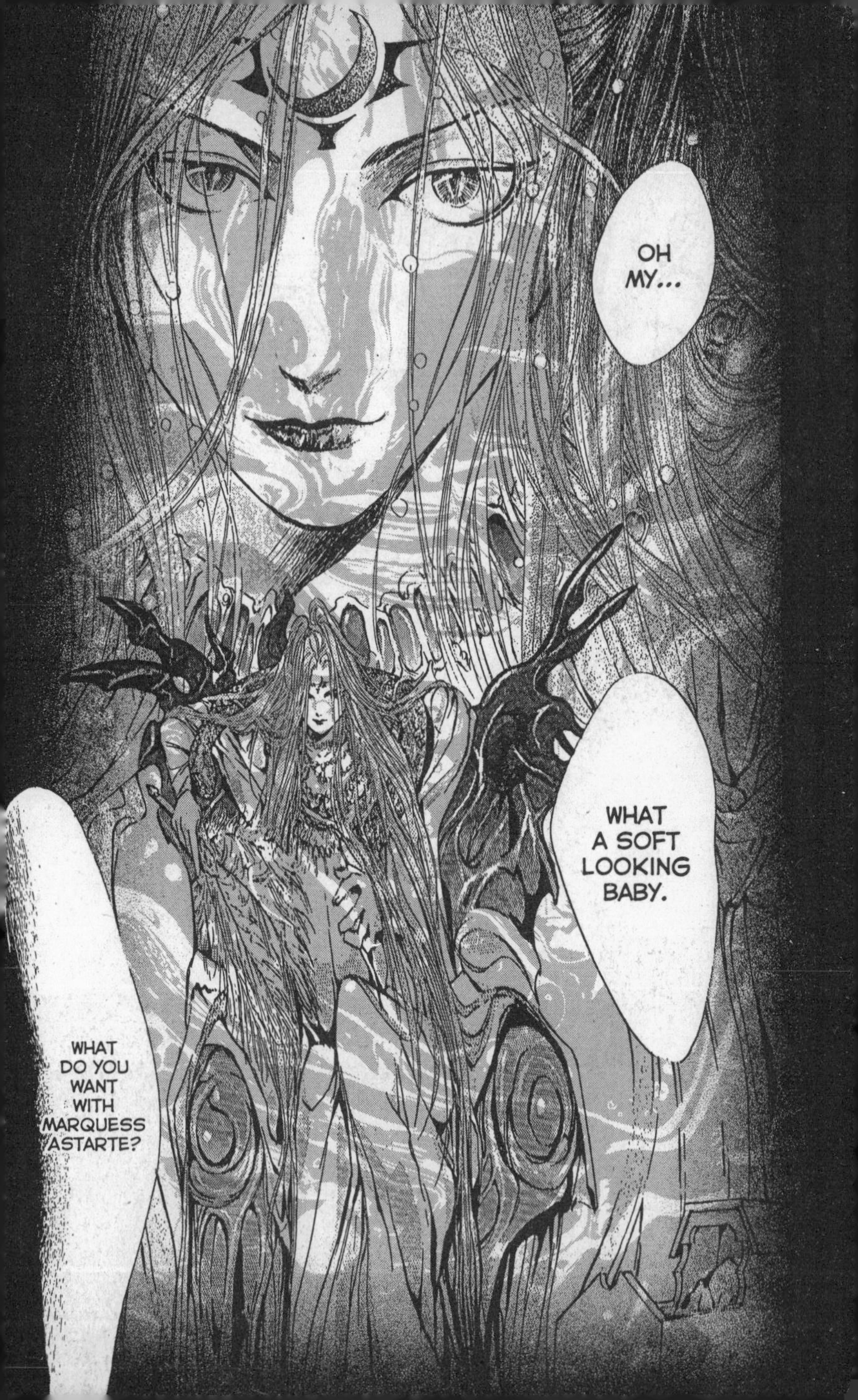
OH MY...
WHAT A SOFT LOOKING BABY.
WHAT DO YOU WANT WITH MARQUESS ASTARTE?

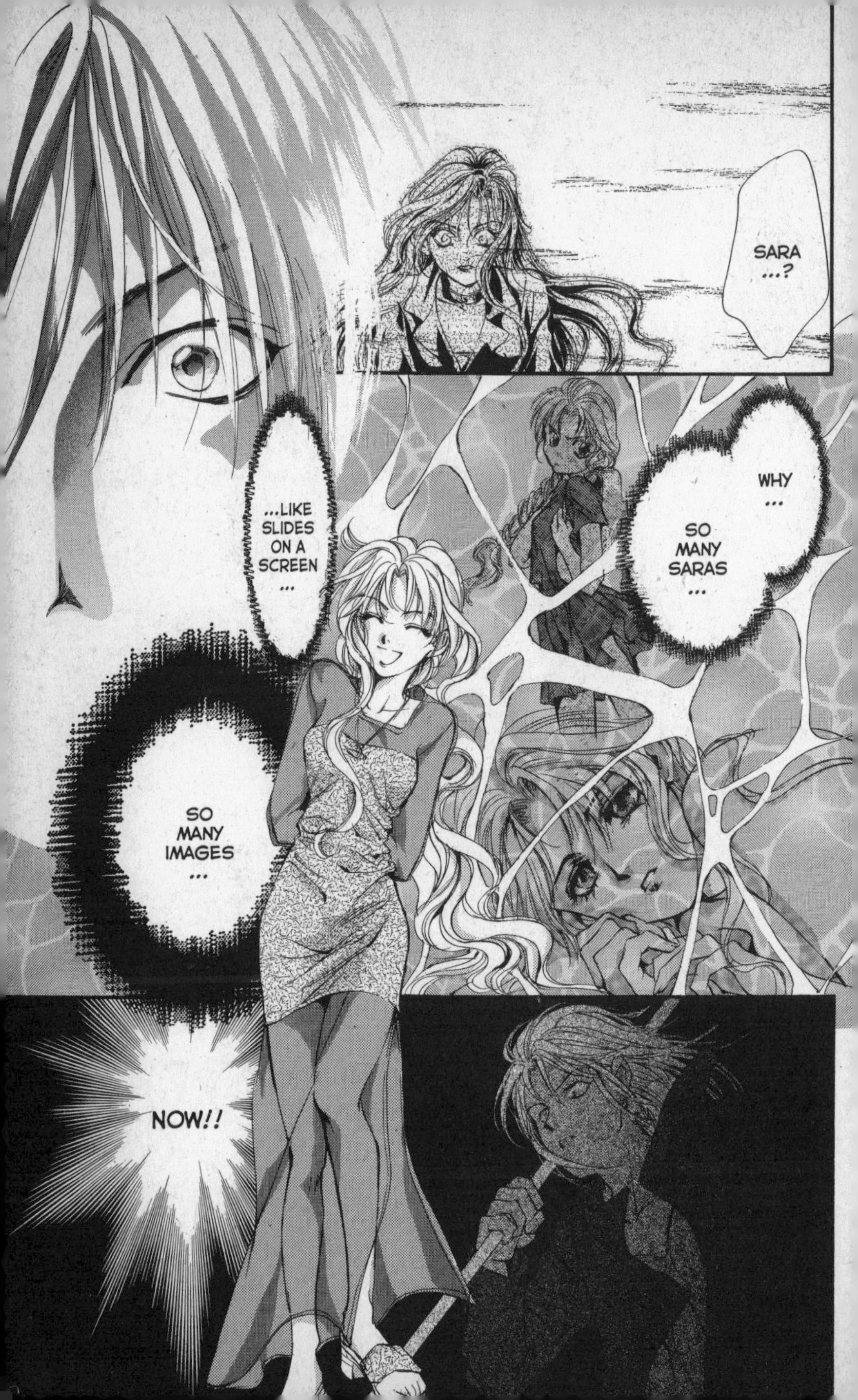
SARA ...?
WHY ... SO MANY SARAS ...
...LIKE SLIDES ON A SCREEN ...
SO MANY IMAGES ...
NOW!!

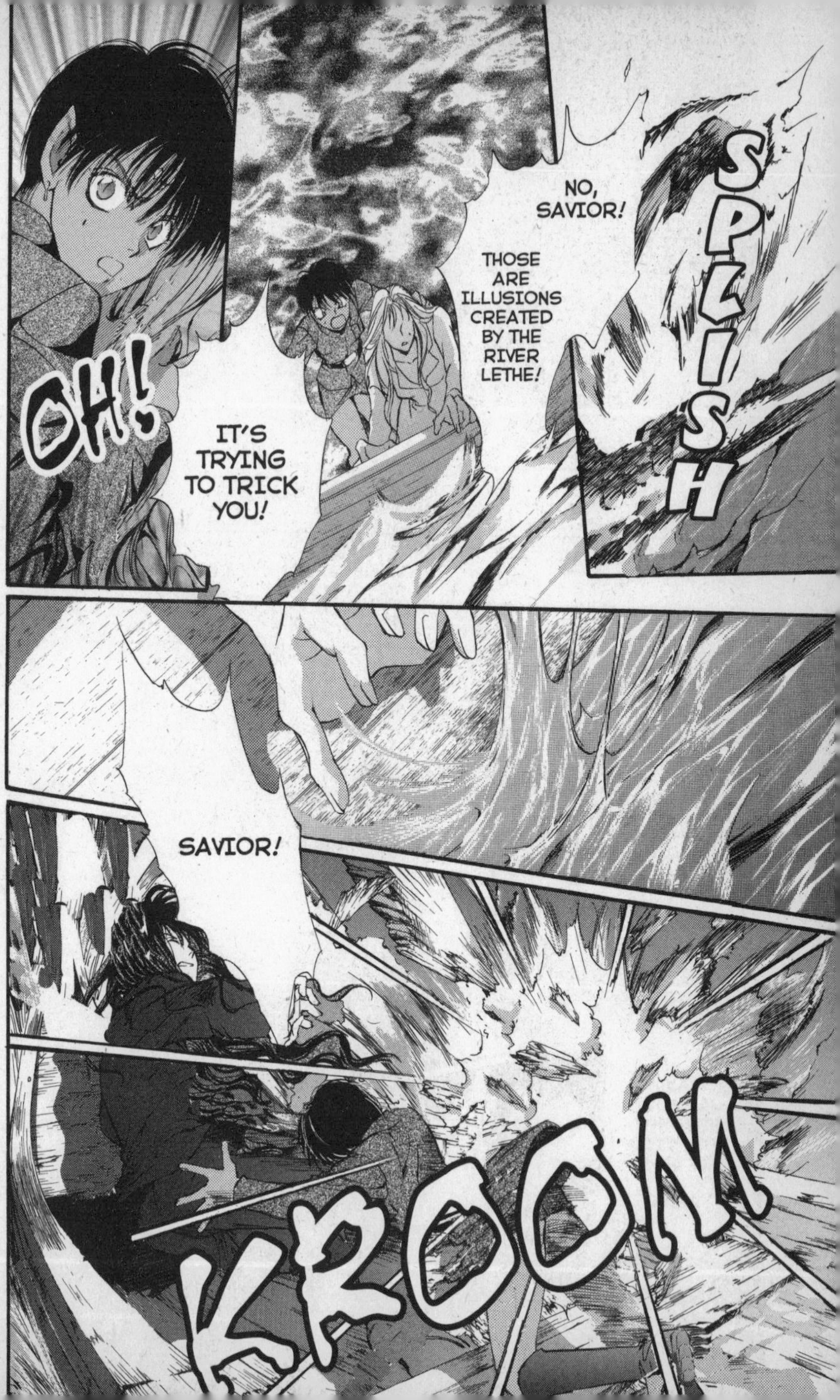
SPLISH
NO, SAVIOR!
THOSE ARE ILLUSIONS CREATED BY THE RIVER LETHE!
OH!
IT'S TRYING TO TRICK YOU!
SAVIOR!
KROOM

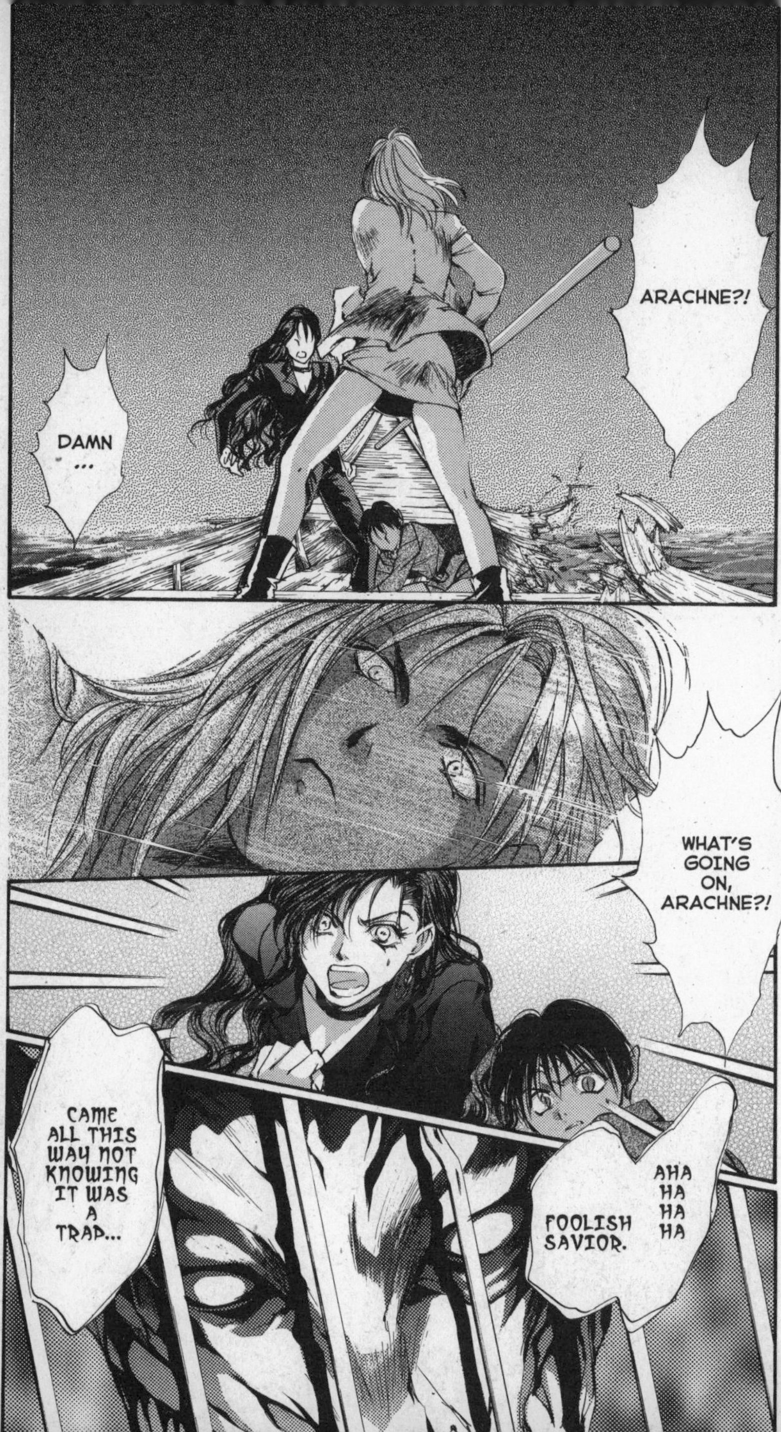
ARACHNE?!
DAMN ...
WHAT'S GOING ON, ARACHNE?!
AHA HA HA HA
FOOLISH SAVIOR.
CAME ALL THIS WAY NOT KNOWING IT WAS A TRAP...

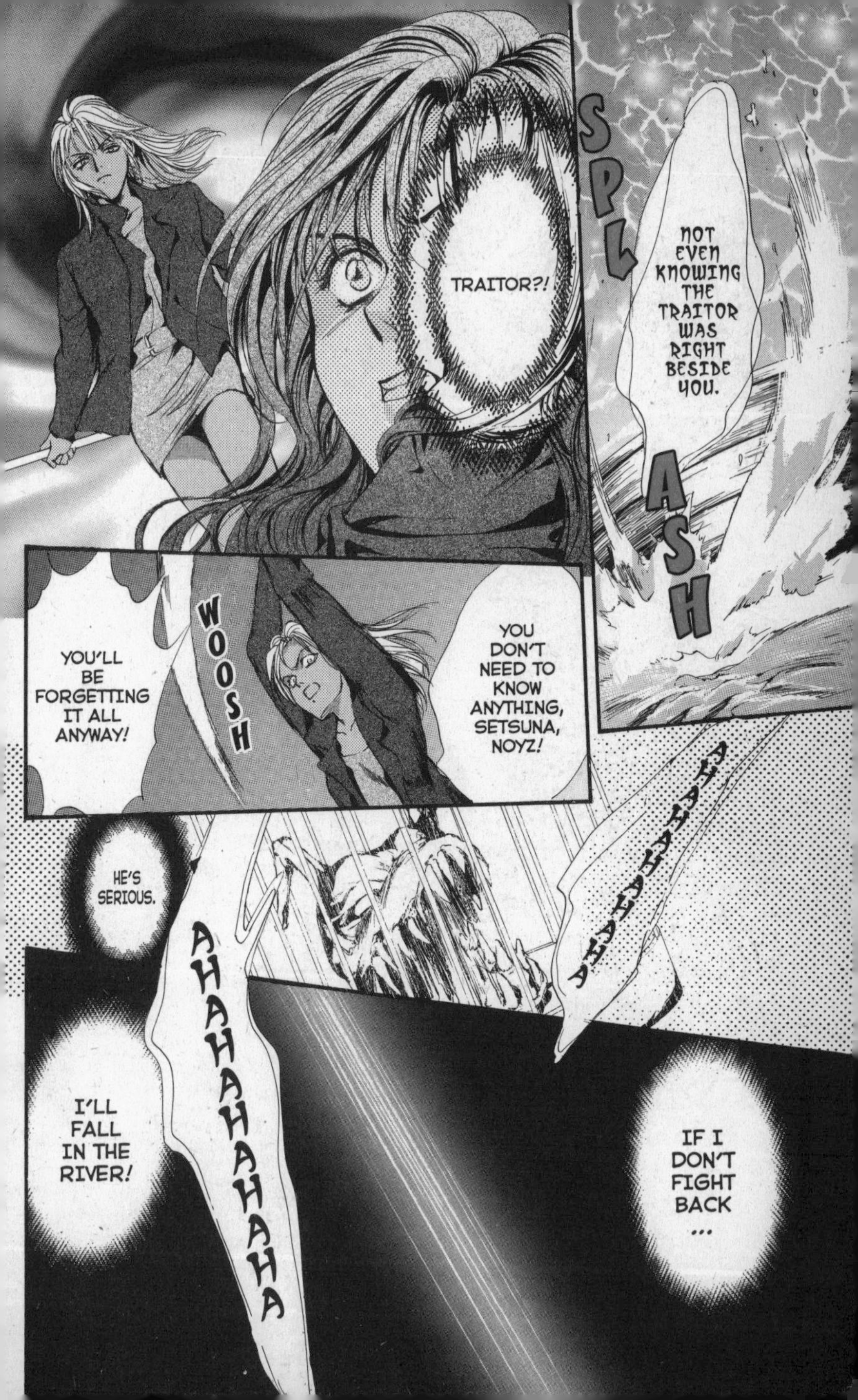
not even knowing the traitor was right beside you.
SPLASH
TRAITOR?!
YOU DON'T NEED TO KNOW ANYTHING, SETSUNA, NOYZ!
WOOSH
YOU'LL BE FORGETTING IT ALL ANYWAY!
AHAHAHAHAHA
HE'S SERIOUS.
IF I DON'T FIGHT BACK...
AHAHAHAHAHAHA
I'LL FALL IN THE RIVER!

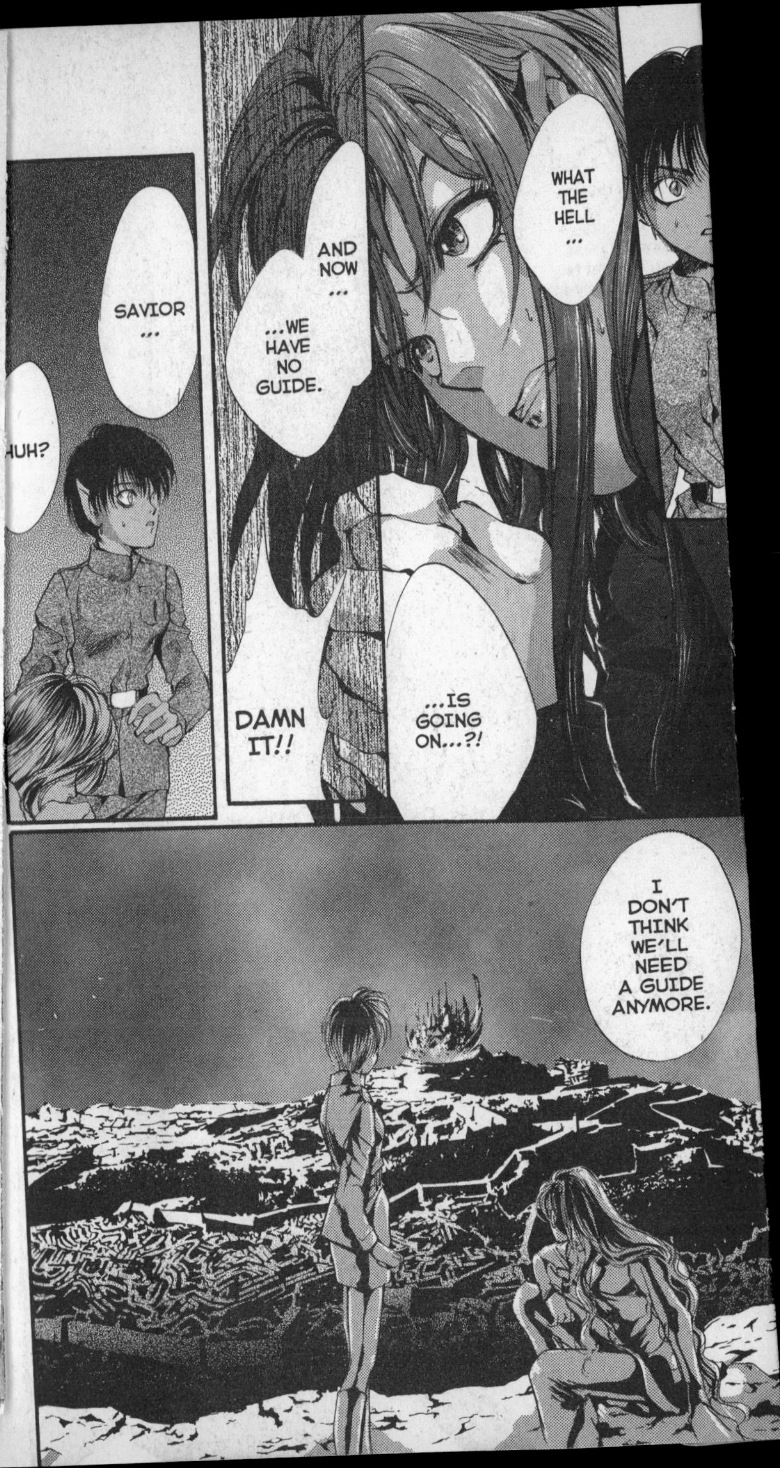
WHAT THE HELL ...
AND NOW ...
...WE HAVE NO GUIDE.
...IS GOING ON...?!
DAMN IT!!
SAVIOR ...
HUH?
I DON'T THINK WE'LL NEED A GUIDE ANYMORE.

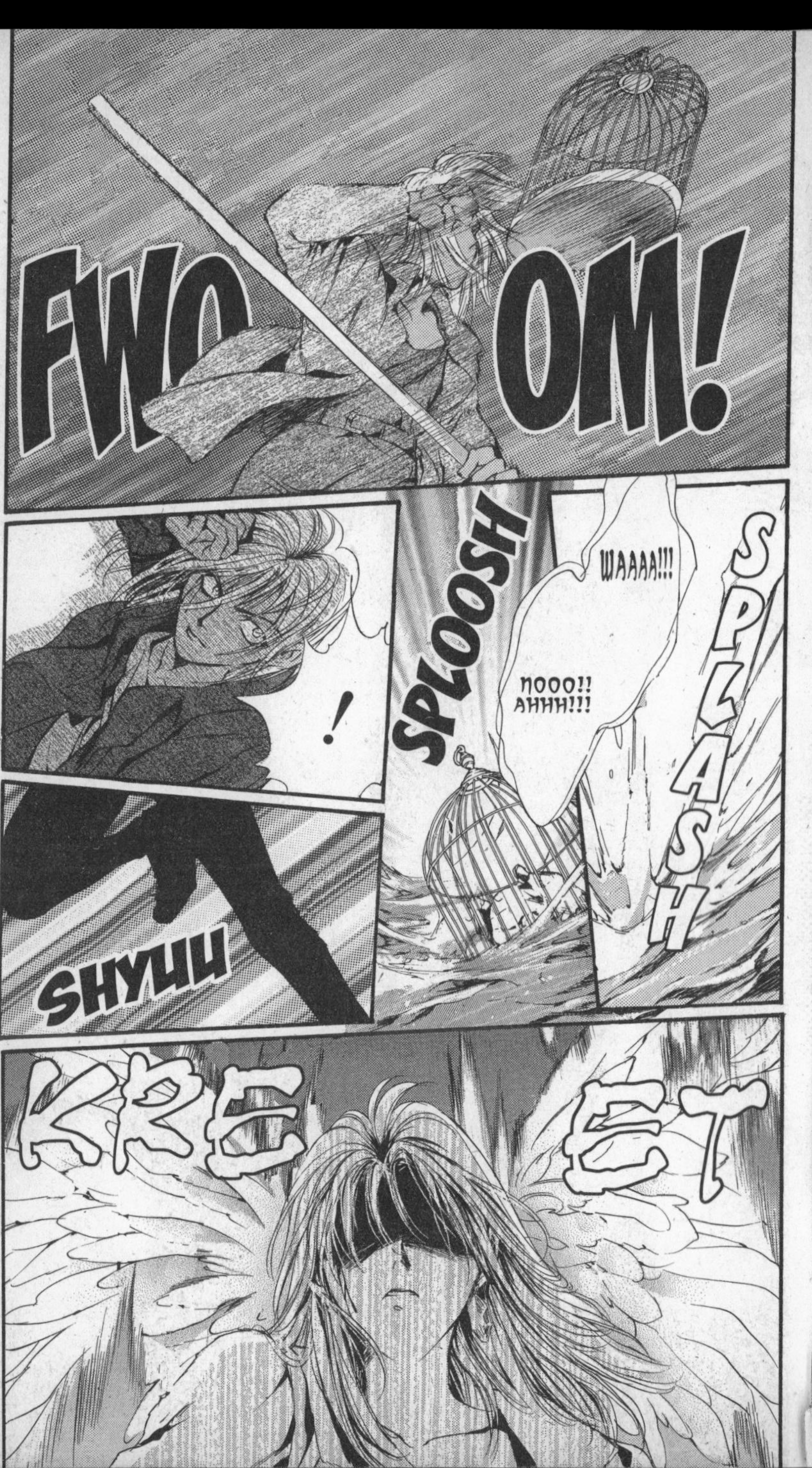
FWOOM!
SPLASH
WAAAA!!!
NOOO!! AHHH!!!
SPLOOSH
!
SHYUU
KRE ET

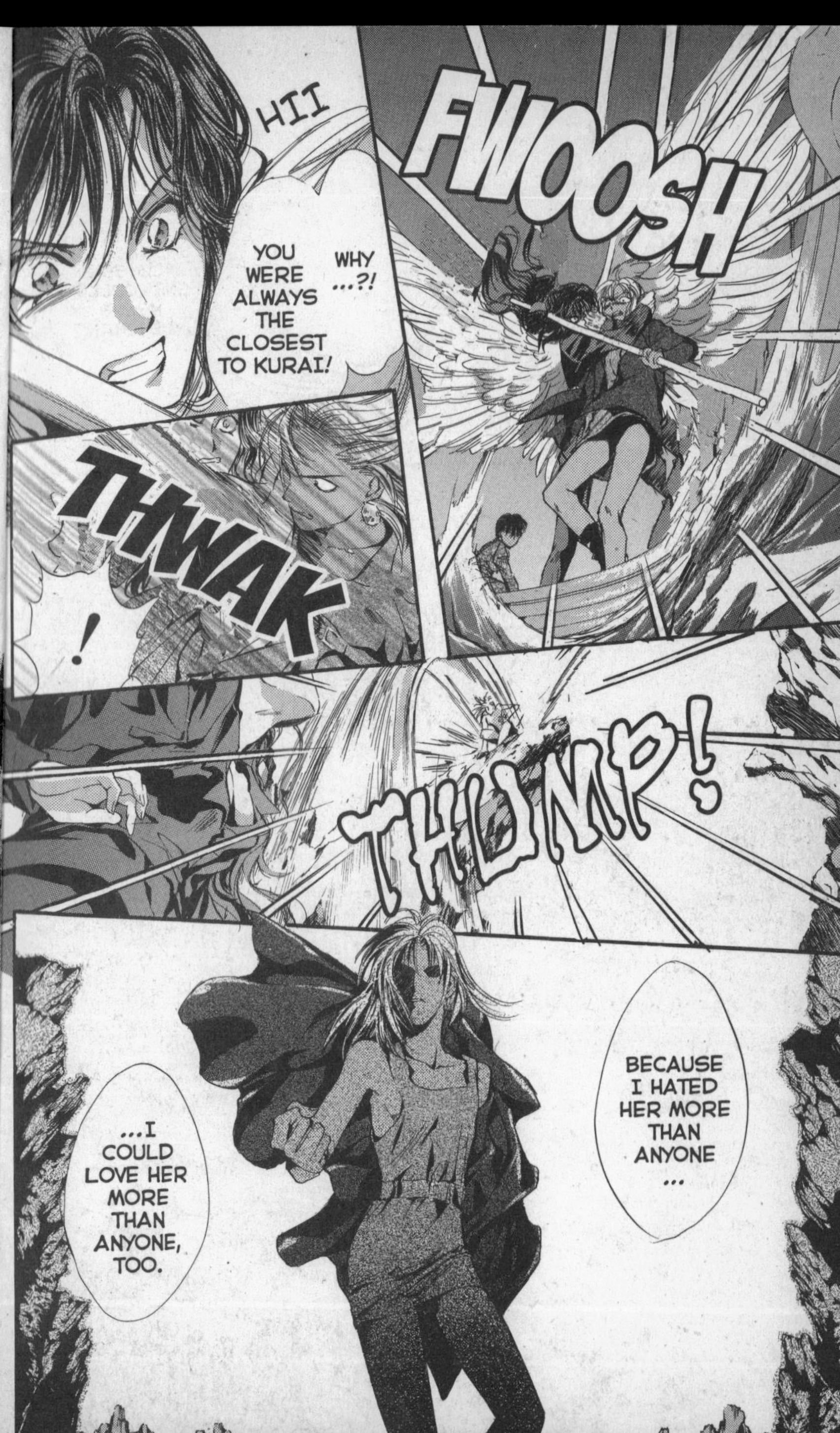
FWOOSH
HII
WHY ...?!
YOU WERE ALWAYS THE CLOSEST TO KURAI!
THWAK
!
THUMP!
BECAUSE I HATED HER MORE THAN ANYONE ...
...I COULD LOVE HER MORE THAN ANYONE, TOO.
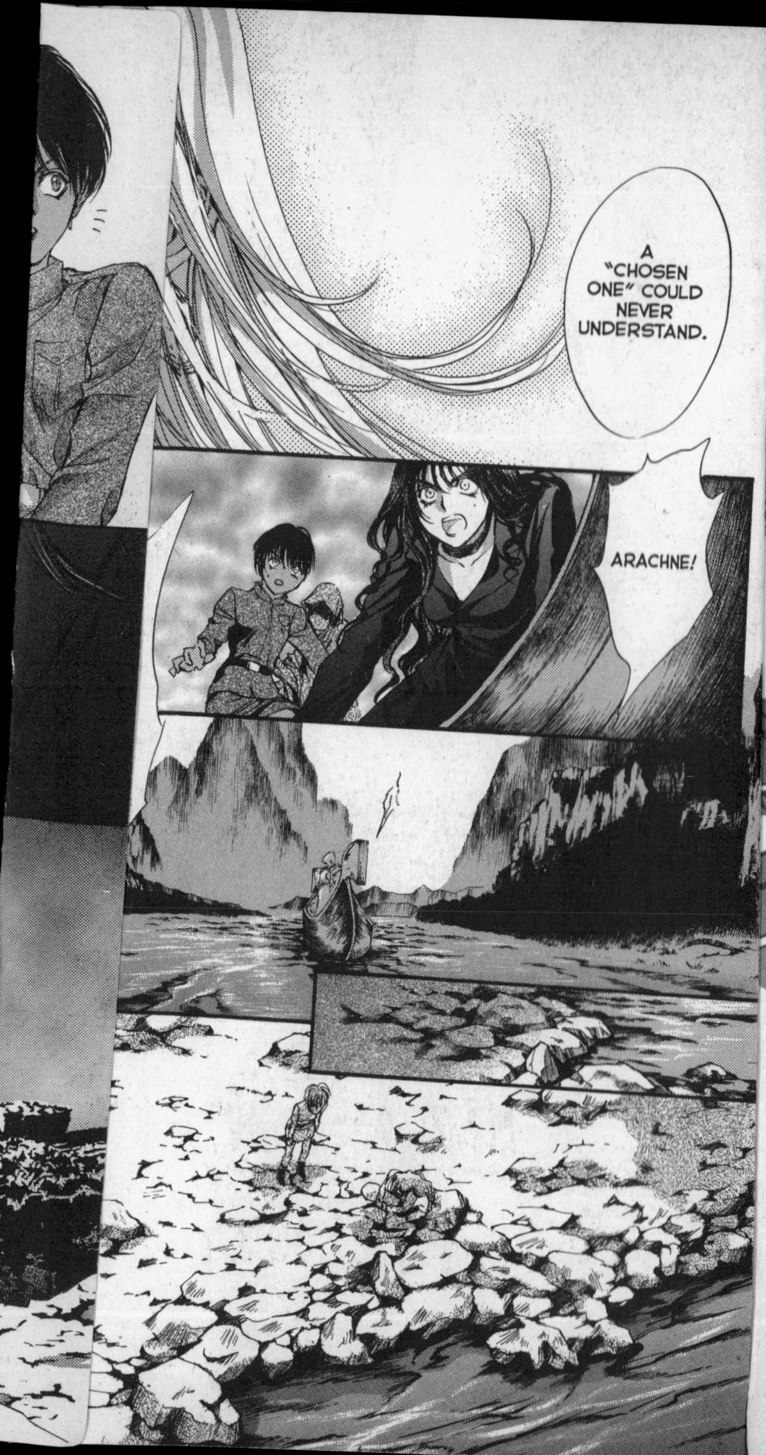
A "CHOSEN ONE" COULD NEVER UNDERSTAND.
ARACHNE!

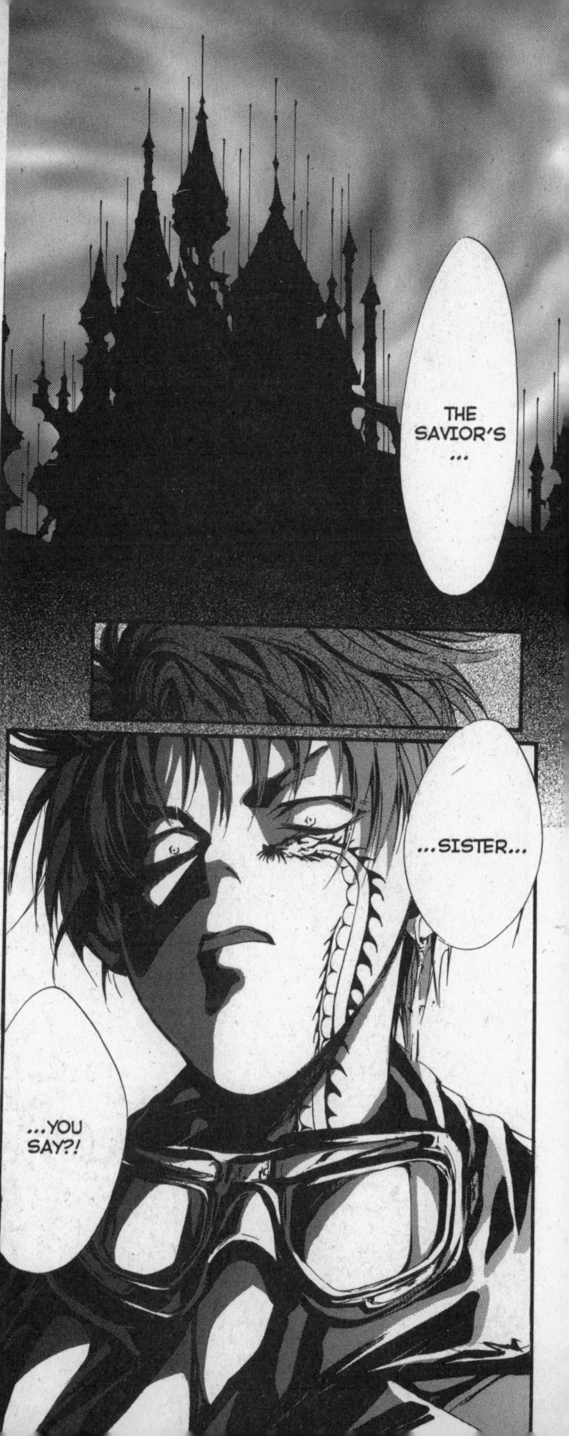
THE SAVIOR'S ...
...SISTER...
...YOU SAY?!

Hello, long time no see (is it?). Angel Sanctuary is finally at book 10! I'm so happy, my first time ever time with double-digits! It's amazing! I can't believe I've continued this twice a month, paaaaaiiiiinful serialization for so long. Everyday, starting with Angel Sanctuary and ending with Angel Sanctuary. Hey, why am I complaining? Oh, I thought I'd do some devil profiles, enjoy.

Belial
Former Virtues angel, current Mad Hatter. Represents "Pride" from the seven sins. Beautiful and especially evil even among the fallen angels. (So wonderful...) His influence caused the corruption of Sodom and Gomorra.

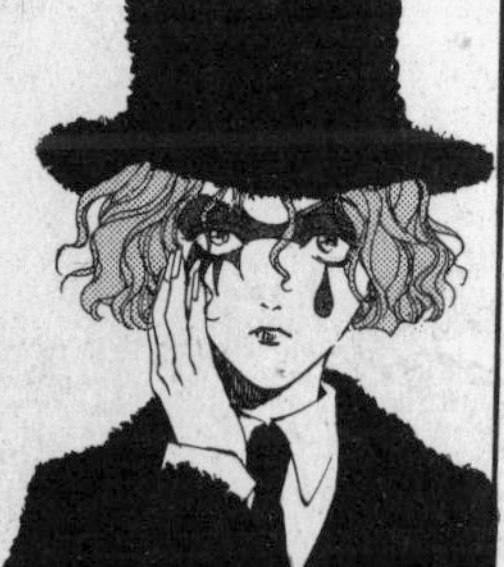

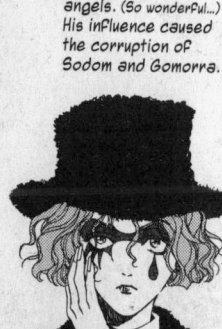

Too bad I won't be able to draw him for a while.

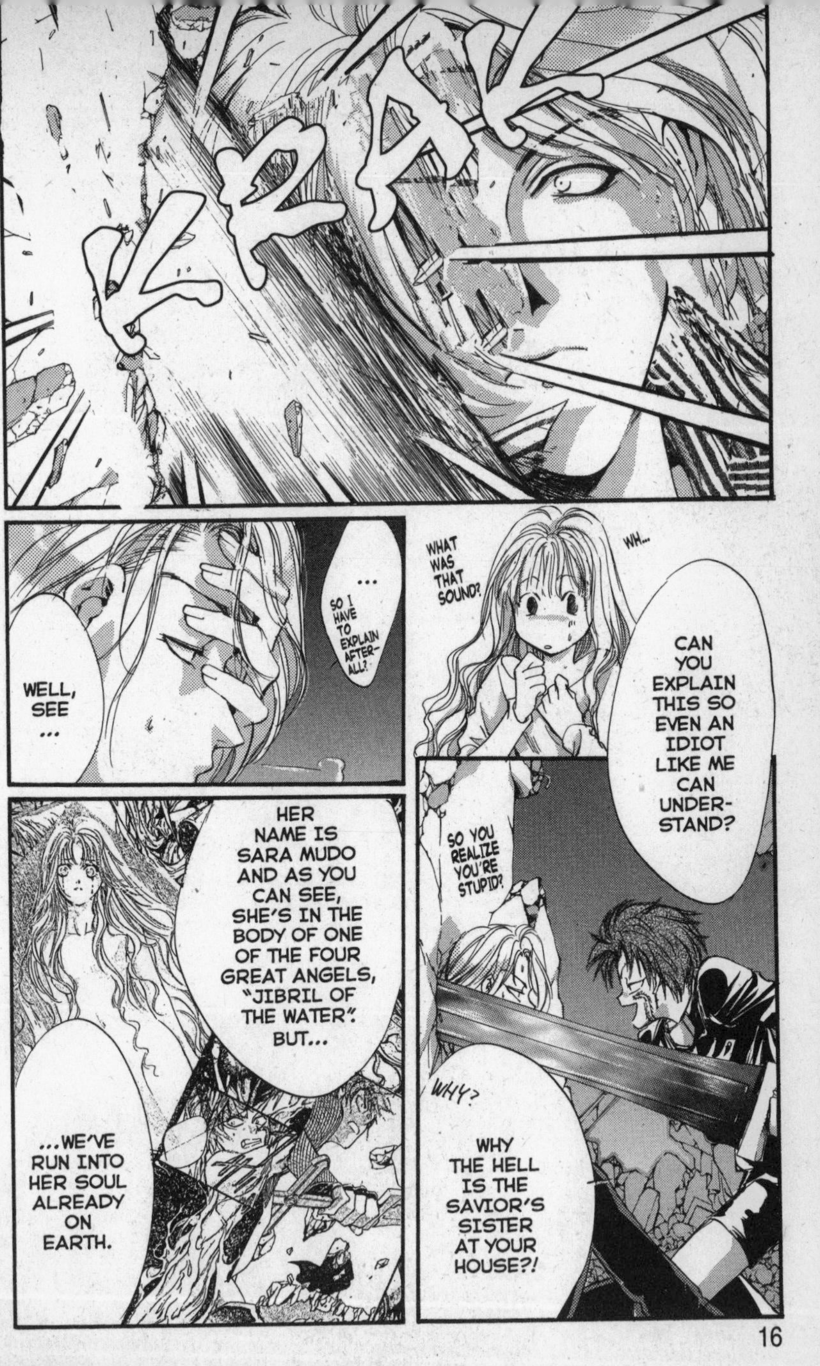
KRAK
WH...
WHAT WAS THAT SOUND?
CAN YOU EXPLAIN THIS SO EVEN AN IDIOT LIKE ME CAN UNDER-STAND?
...
SO I HAVE TO EXPLAIN AFTER-ALL?
WELL, SEE ...
SO YOU REALIZE YOU'RE STUPID?
WHY?
WHY THE HELL IS THE SAVIOR'S SISTER AT YOUR HOUSE?!
HER NAME IS SARA MUDO AND AS YOU CAN SEE, SHE'S IN THE BODY OF ONE OF THE FOUR GREAT ANGELS, "JIBRIL OF THE WATER". BUT...
...WE'VE RUN INTO HER SOUL ALREADY ON EARTH.

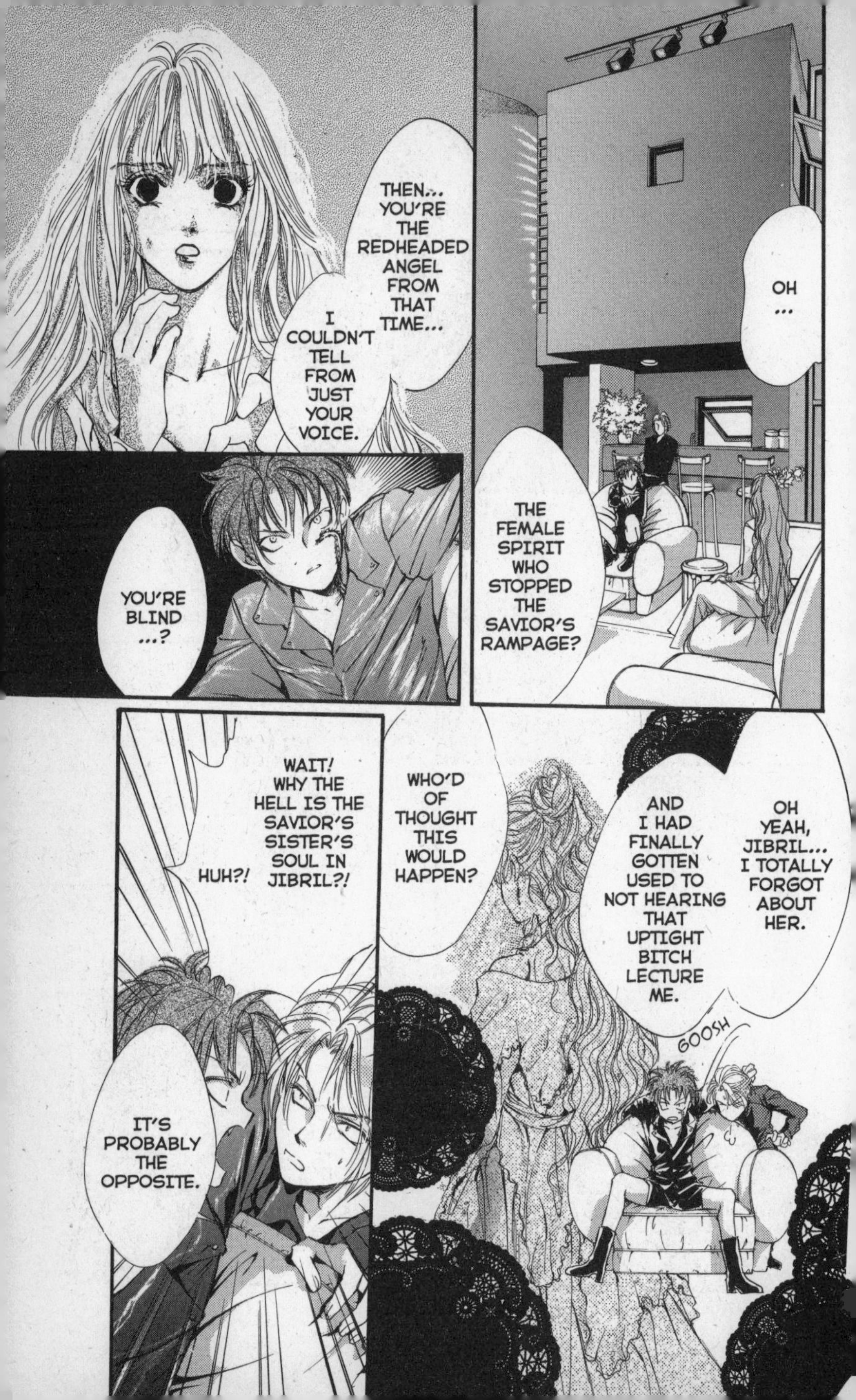
OH ...
THE FEMALE SPIRIT WHO STOPPED THE SAVIOR'S RAMPAGE?
THEN... YOU'RE THE REDHEADED ANGEL FROM THAT TIME...
I COULDN'T TELL FROM JUST YOUR VOICE.
YOU'RE BLIND ...?
OH YEAH, JIBRIL... I TOTALLY FORGOT ABOUT HER.
AND I HAD FINALLY GOTTEN USED TO NOT HEARING THAT UPTIGHT BITCH LECTURE ME.
GOOSH
WHO'D OF THOUGHT THIS WOULD HAPPEN?
WAIT! WHY THE HELL IS THE SAVIOR'S SISTER'S SOUL IN JIBRIL?!
HUH?!
IT'S PROBABLY THE OPPOSITE.

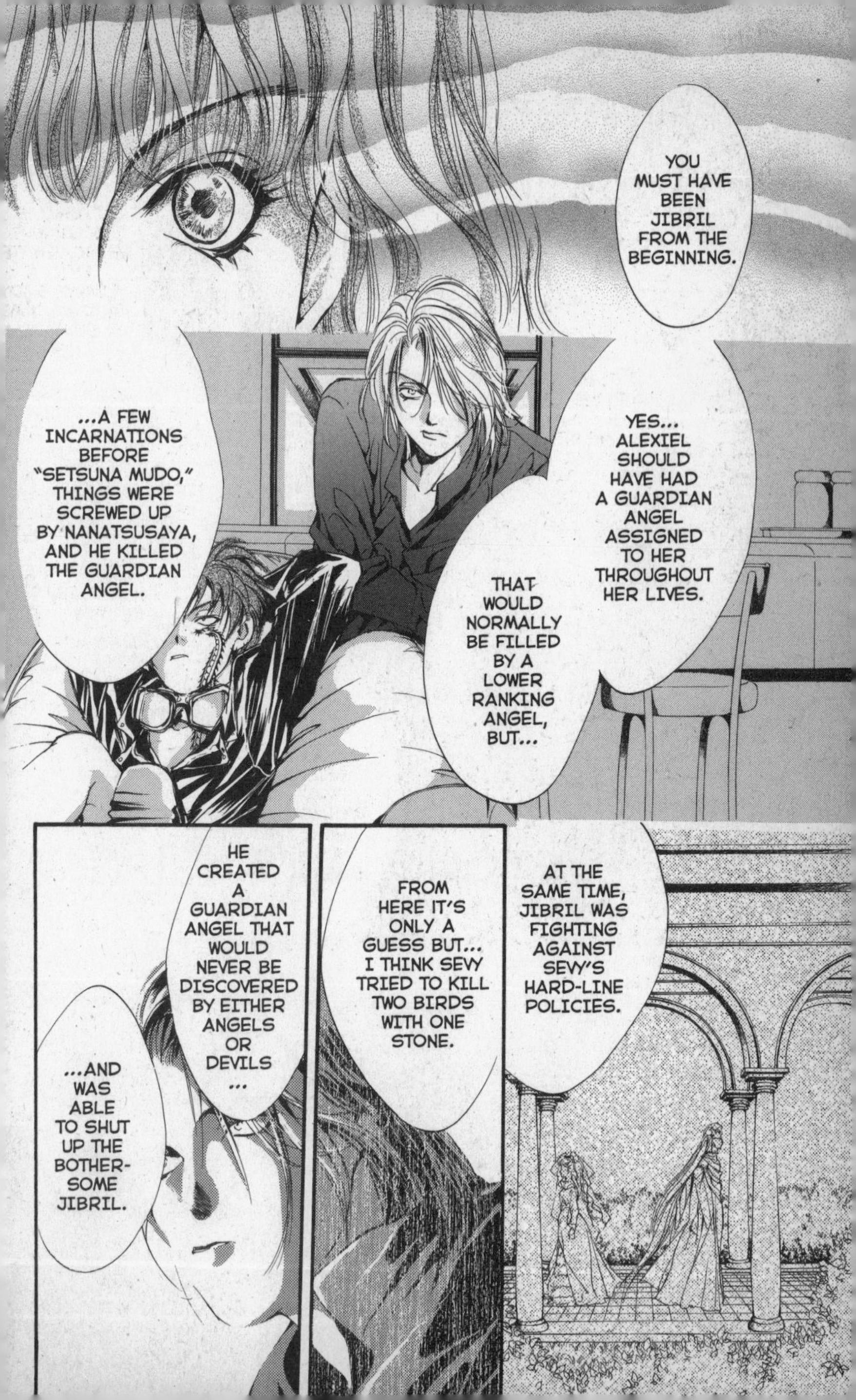
YOU MUST HAVE BEEN JIBRIL FROM THE BEGINNING.
YES... ALEXIEL SHOULD HAVE HAD A GUARDIAN ANGEL ASSIGNED TO HER THROUGHOUT HER LIVES.
THAT WOULD NORMALLY BE FILLED BY A LOWER RANKING ANGEL, BUT...
...A FEW INCARNATIONS BEFORE "SETSUNA MUDO," THINGS WERE SCREWED UP BY NANATSUSAYA, AND HE KILLED THE GUARDIAN ANGEL.
AT THE SAME TIME, JIBRIL WAS FIGHTING AGAINST SEVY'S HARD-LINE POLICIES.
FROM HERE IT'S ONLY A GUESS BUT... I THINK SEVY TRIED TO KILL TWO BIRDS WITH ONE STONE.
HE CREATED A GUARDIAN ANGEL THAT WOULD NEVER BE DISCOVERED BY EITHER ANGELS OR DEVILS ...
...AND WAS ABLE TO SHUT UP THE BOTHER-SOME JIBRIL.

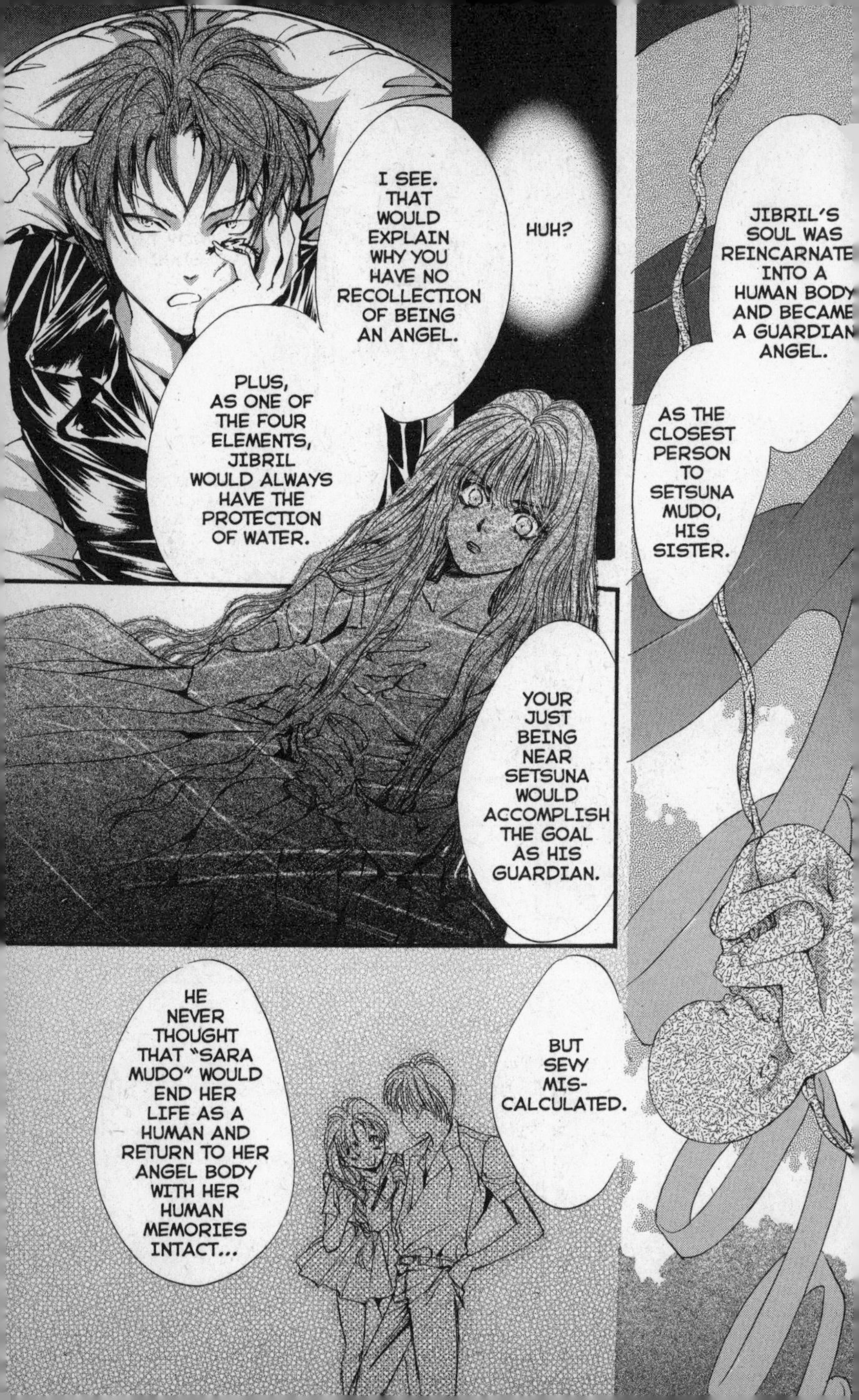
JIBRIL'S SOUL WAS REINCARNATE INTO A HUMAN BODY AND BECAME A GUARDIAN ANGEL.
AS THE CLOSEST PERSON TO SETSUNA MUDO, HIS SISTER.
HUH?
I SEE. THAT WOULD EXPLAIN WHY YOU HAVE NO RECOLLECTION OF BEING AN ANGEL.
PLUS, AS ONE OF THE FOUR ELEMENTS, JIBRIL WOULD ALWAYS HAVE THE PROTECTION OF WATER.
YOUR JUST BEING NEAR SETSUNA WOULD ACCOMPLISH THE GOAL AS HIS GUARDIAN.
BUT SEVY MIS-CALCULATED.
HE NEVER THOUGHT THAT "SARA MUDO" WOULD END HER LIFE AS A HUMAN AND RETURN TO HER ANGEL BODY WITH HER HUMAN MEMORIES INTACT...

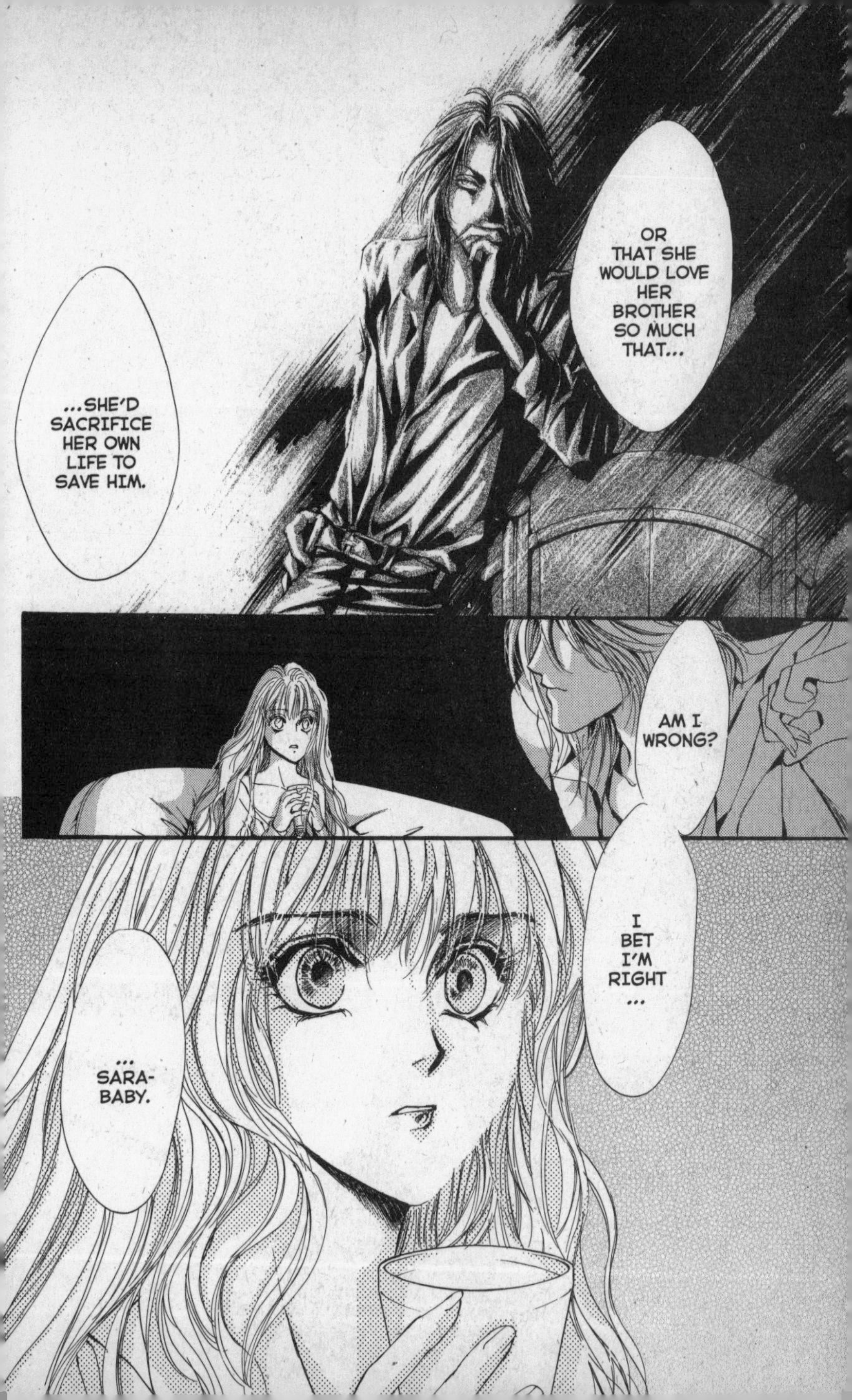
OR THAT SHE WOULD LOVE HER BROTHER SO MUCH THAT...
...SHE'D SACRIFICE HER OWN LIFE TO SAVE HIM.
AM I WRONG?
I BET I'M RIGHT ...
... SARA-BABY.

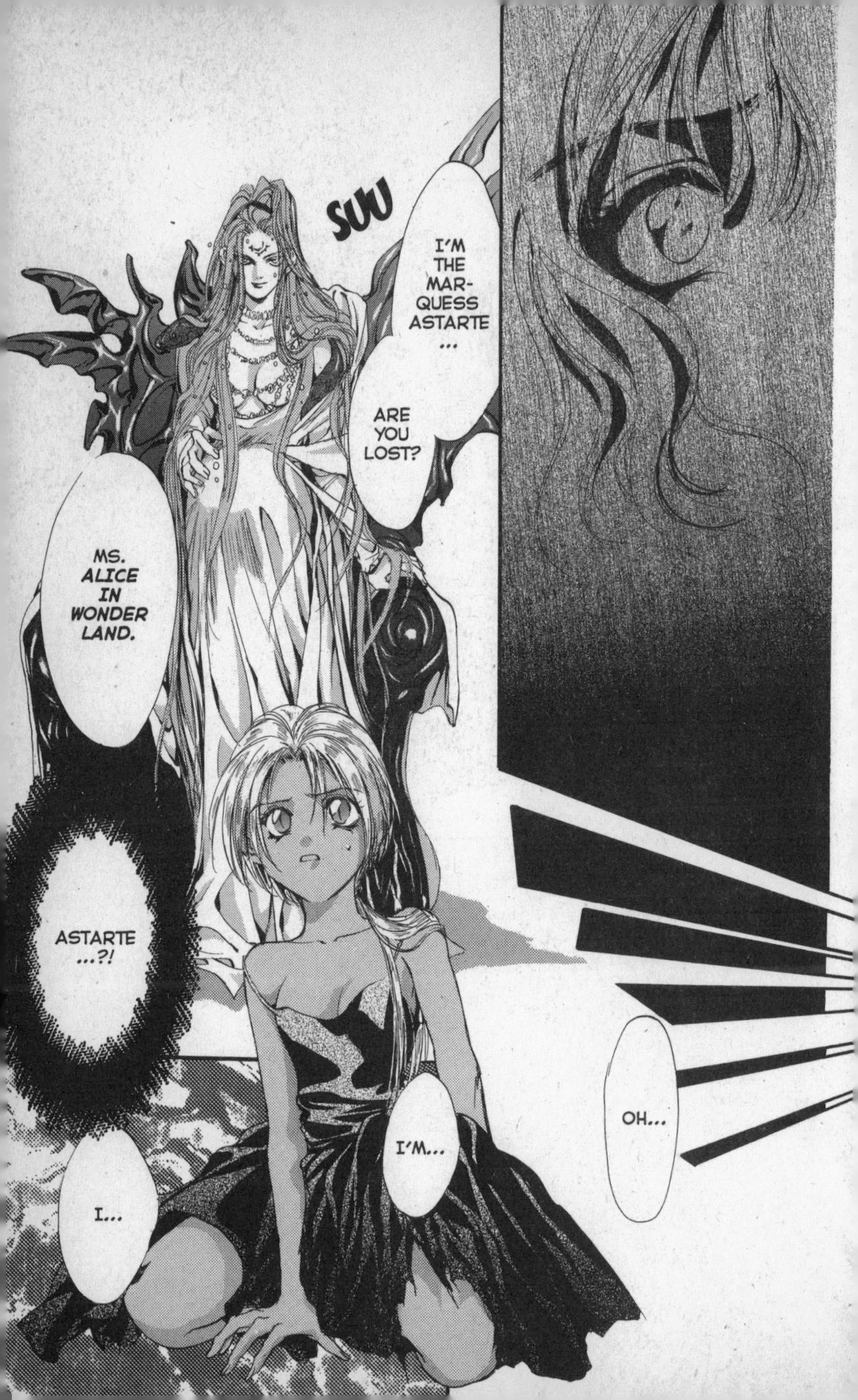
OH...
SUU
I'M THE MAR-QUESS ASTARTE ...
ARE YOU LOST?
MS. ALICE IN WONDER LAND.
ASTARTE ...?!
I'M...
I...

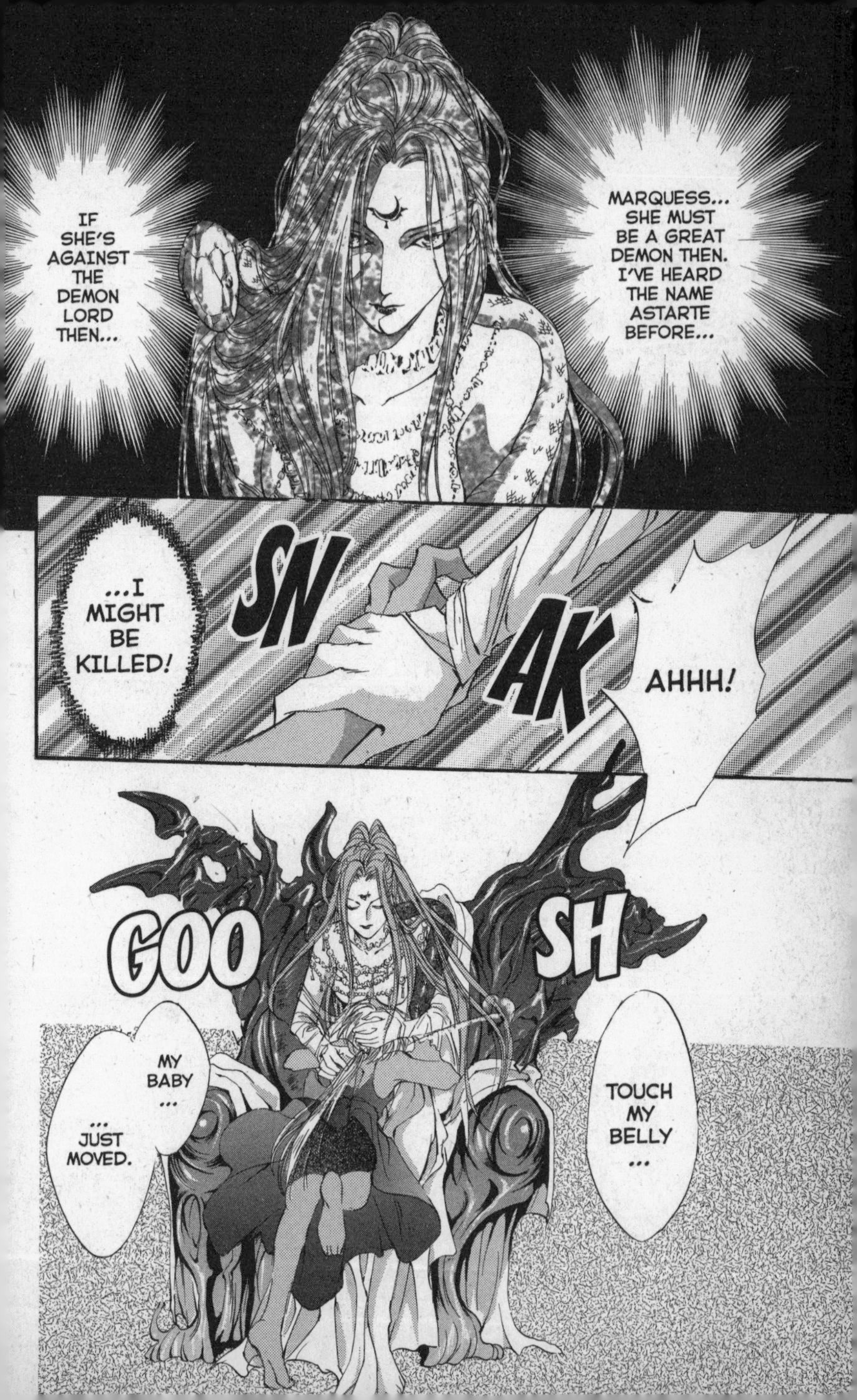
MARQUESS... SHE MUST BE A GREAT DEMON THEN. I'VE HEARD THE NAME ASTARTE BEFORE...
IF SHE'S AGAINST THE DEMON LORD THEN...
...I MIGHT BE KILLED!
SN
AK
AHHH!
SH
GOO
TOUCH MY BELLY ...
MY BABY ...
... JUST MOVED.

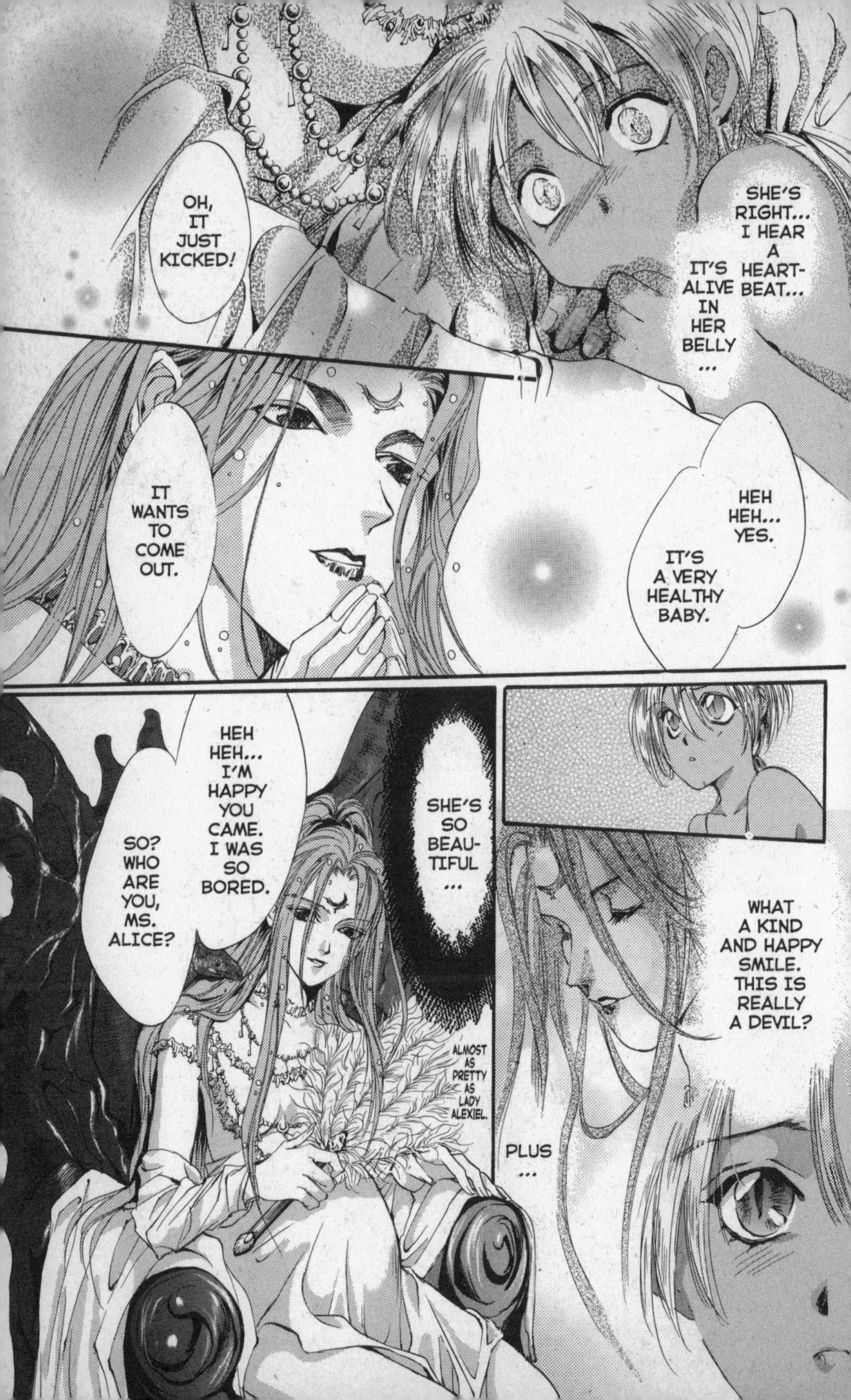
SHE'S RIGHT... I HEAR A HEART-BEAT...
IT'S ALIVE IN HER BELLY...
OH, IT JUST KICKED!
HEH HEH... YES.
IT'S A VERY HEALTHY BABY.
IT WANTS TO COME OUT.
WHAT A KIND AND HAPPY SMILE. THIS IS REALLY A DEVIL?
PLUS...
ALMOST AS PRETTY AS LADY ALEXIEL.
SHE'S SO BEAU-TIFUL...
HEH HEH... I'M HAPPY YOU CAME. I WAS SO BORED.
SO? WHO ARE YOU, MS. ALICE?

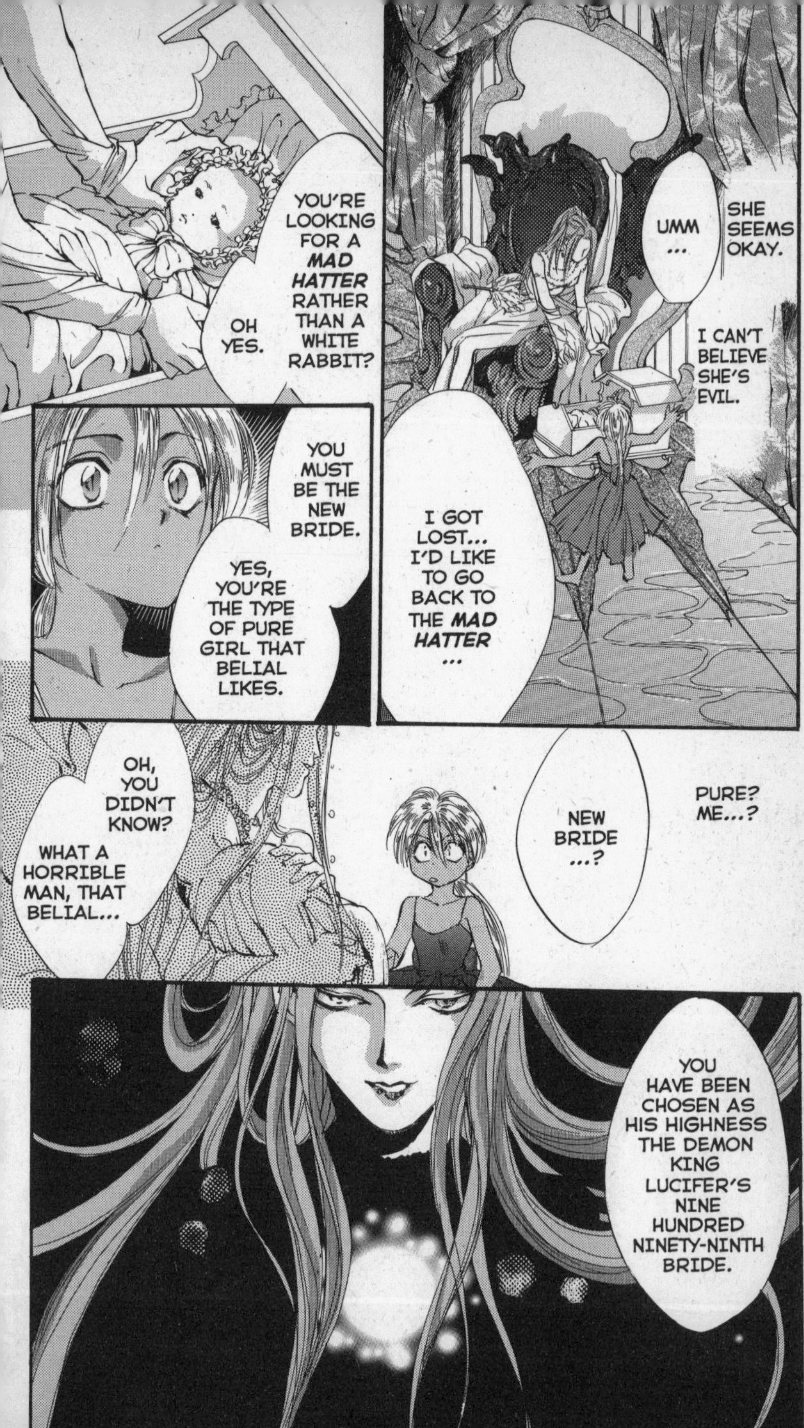
SHE SEEMS OKAY.
UMM ...
I CAN'T BELIEVE SHE'S EVIL.
I GOT LOST... I'D LIKE TO GO BACK TO THE ***MAD HATTER*** ...
YOU'RE LOOKING FOR A ***MAD HATTER*** RATHER THAN A WHITE RABBIT?
OH YES.
YOU MUST BE THE NEW BRIDE.
YES, YOU'RE THE TYPE OF PURE GIRL THAT BELIAL LIKES.
PURE? ME...?
NEW BRIDE ...?
OH, YOU DIDN'T KNOW?
WHAT A HORRIBLE MAN, THAT BELIAL...
YOU HAVE BEEN CHOSEN AS HIS HIGHNESS THE DEMON KING LUCIFER'S NINE HUNDRED NINETY-NINTH BRIDE.

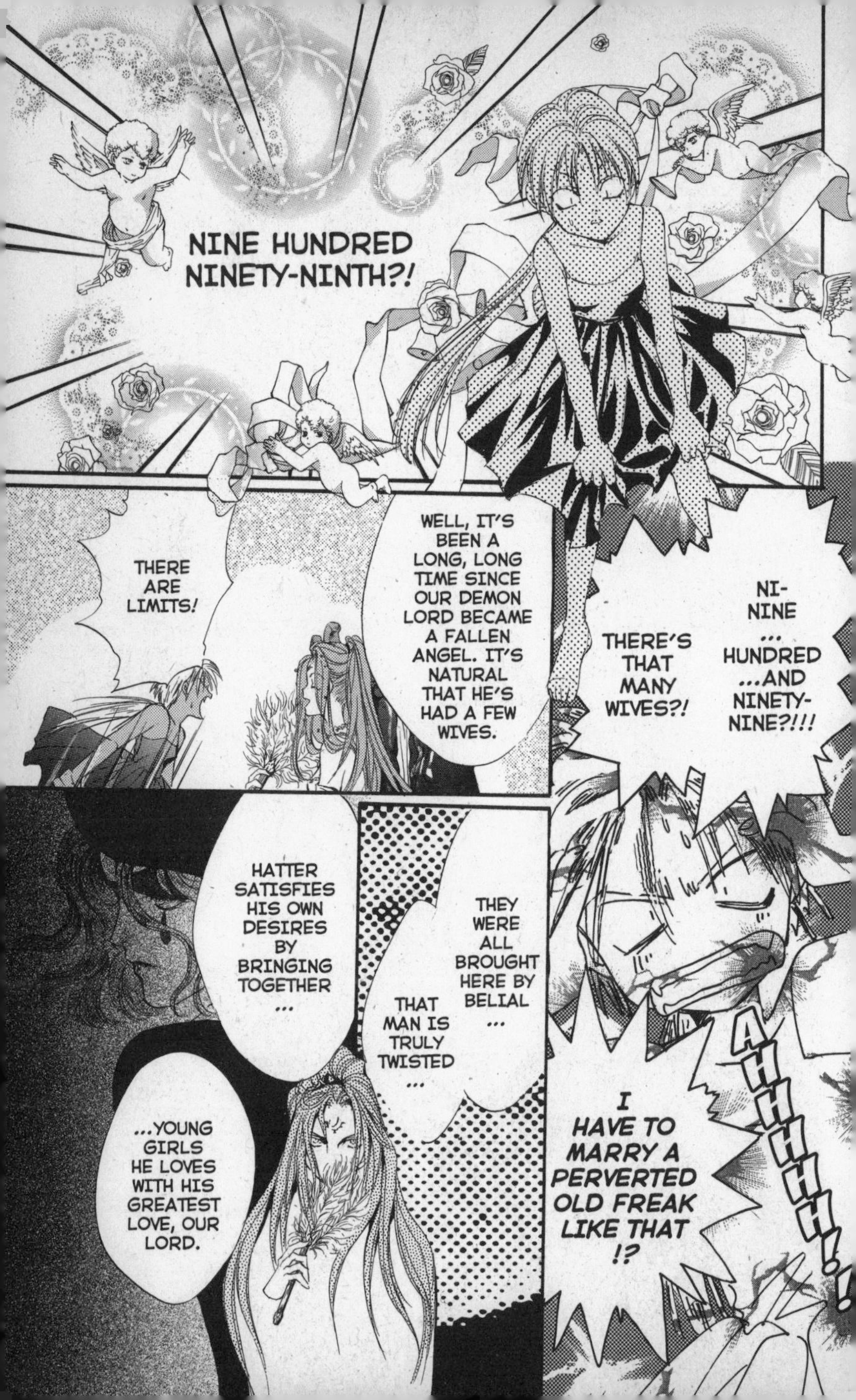
NINE HUNDRED NINETY-NINTH?!
NI- NINE ... HUNDRED ...AND NINETY- NINE?!!!
THERE'S THAT MANY WIVES?!
WELL, IT'S BEEN A LONG, LONG TIME SINCE OUR DEMON LORD BECAME A FALLEN ANGEL. IT'S NATURAL THAT HE'S HAD A FEW WIVES.
THERE ARE LIMITS!
AHHHHHH!!
I HAVE TO MARRY A PERVERTED OLD FREAK LIKE THAT !?
THEY WERE ALL BROUGHT HERE BY BELIAL ...
THAT MAN IS TRULY TWISTED ...
HATTER SATISFIES HIS OWN DESIRES BY BRINGING TOGETHER ...
...YOUNG GIRLS HE LOVES WITH HIS GREATEST LOVE, OUR LORD.

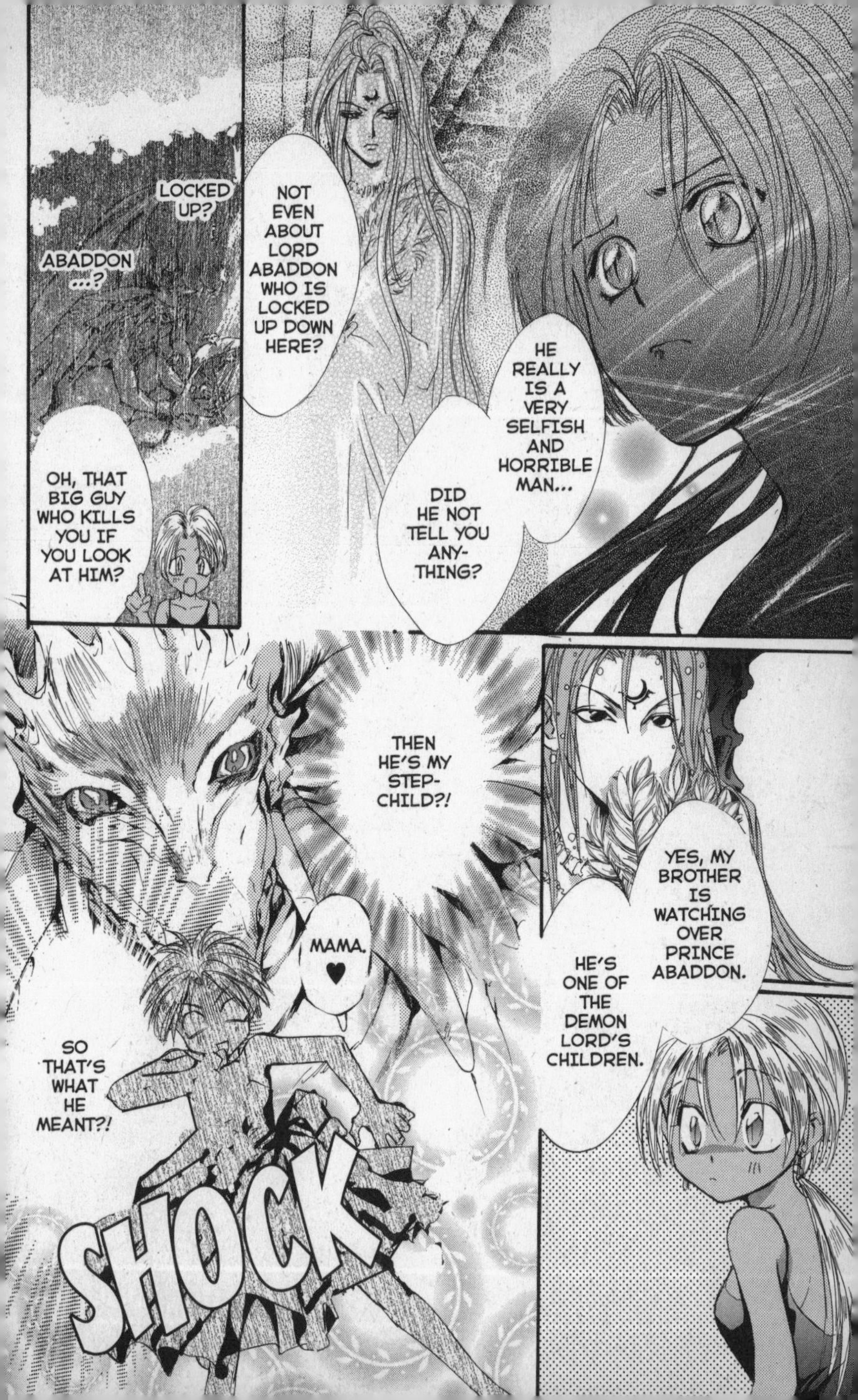
HE REALLY IS A VERY SELFISH AND HORRIBLE MAN...
DID HE NOT TELL YOU ANY-THING?
NOT EVEN ABOUT LORD ABADDON WHO IS LOCKED UP DOWN HERE?
LOCKED UP?
ABADDON ...?
OH, THAT BIG GUY WHO KILLS YOU IF YOU LOOK AT HIM?
YES, MY BROTHER IS WATCHING OVER PRINCE ABADDON.
HE'S ONE OF THE DEMON LORD'S CHILDREN.
THEN HE'S MY STEP-CHILD?!
MAMA. ♥
SO THAT'S WHAT HE MEANT?!
SHOCK

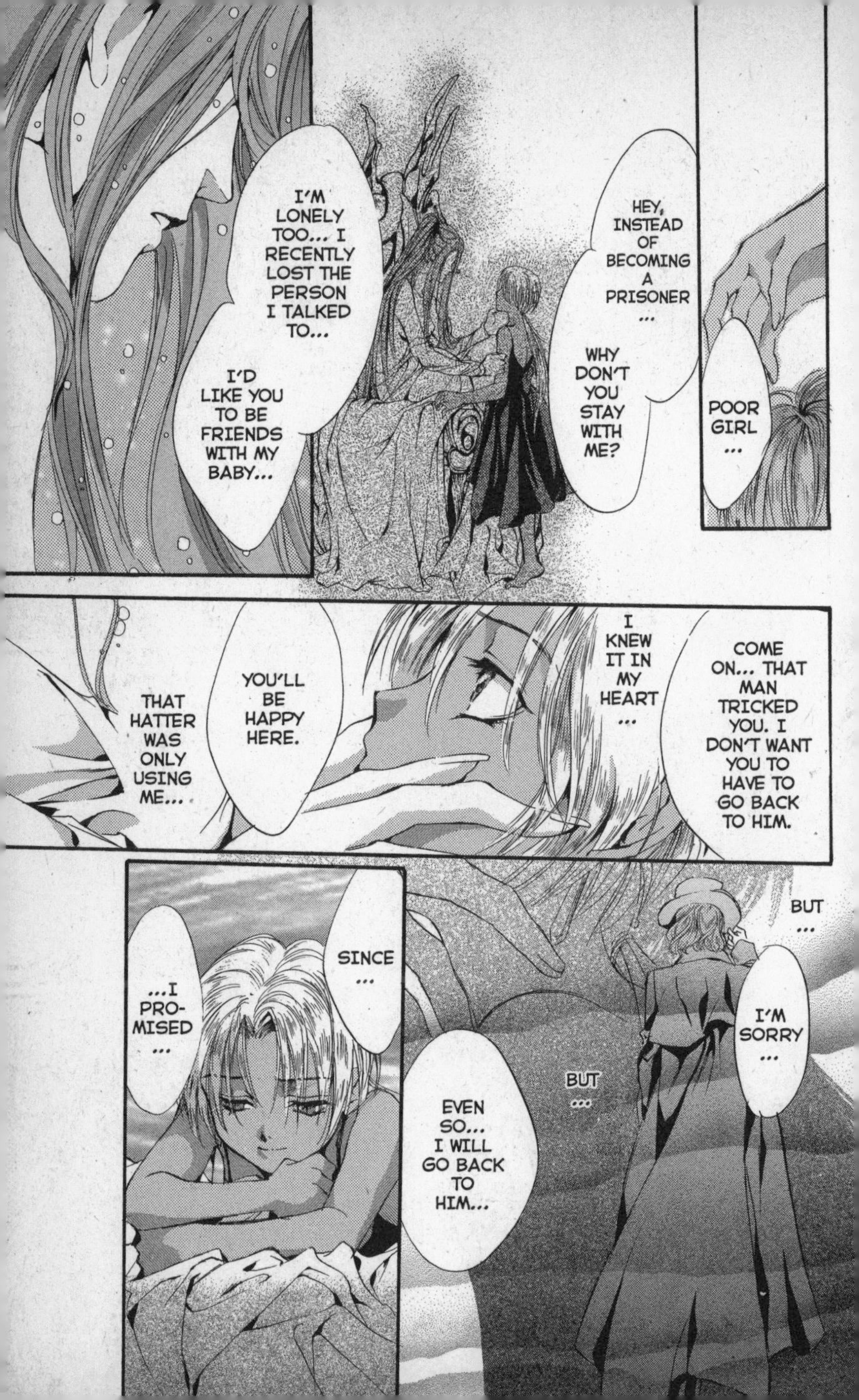
POOR GIRL ...
HEY, INSTEAD OF BECOMING A PRISONER ...
WHY DON'T YOU STAY WITH ME?
I'M LONELY TOO... I RECENTLY LOST THE PERSON I TALKED TO...
I'D LIKE YOU TO BE FRIENDS WITH MY BABY...
COME ON... THAT MAN TRICKED YOU. I DON'T WANT YOU TO HAVE TO GO BACK TO HIM.
I KNEW IT IN MY HEART ...
YOU'LL BE HAPPY HERE.
THAT HATTER WAS ONLY USING ME...
BUT ...
I'M SORRY ...
BUT ...
EVEN SO... I WILL GO BACK TO HIM...
SINCE ...
...I PRO-MISED ...

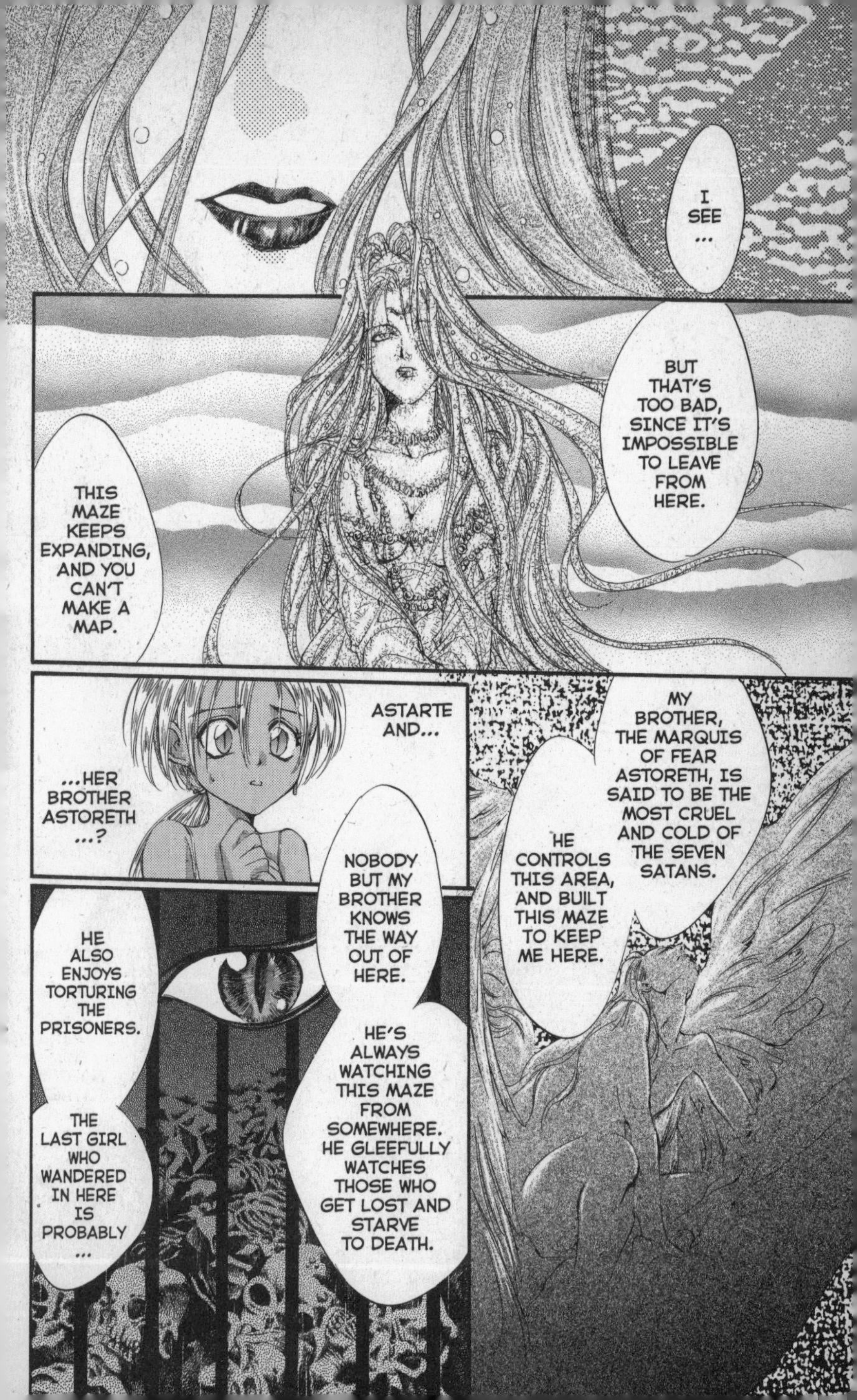
I SEE ...
BUT THAT'S TOO BAD, SINCE IT'S IMPOSSIBLE TO LEAVE FROM HERE.
THIS MAZE KEEPS EXPANDING, AND YOU CAN'T MAKE A MAP.
MY BROTHER, THE MARQUIS OF FEAR ASTORETH, IS SAID TO BE THE MOST CRUEL AND COLD OF THE SEVEN SATANS.
HE CONTROLS THIS AREA, AND BUILT THIS MAZE TO KEEP ME HERE.
ASTARTE AND...
...HER BROTHER ASTORETH ...?
NOBODY BUT MY BROTHER KNOWS THE WAY OUT OF HERE.
HE'S ALWAYS WATCHING THIS MAZE FROM SOMEWHERE. HE GLEEFULLY WATCHES THOSE WHO GET LOST AND STARVE TO DEATH.
HE ALSO ENJOYS TORTURING THE PRISONERS.
THE LAST GIRL WHO WANDERED IN HERE IS PROBABLY ...

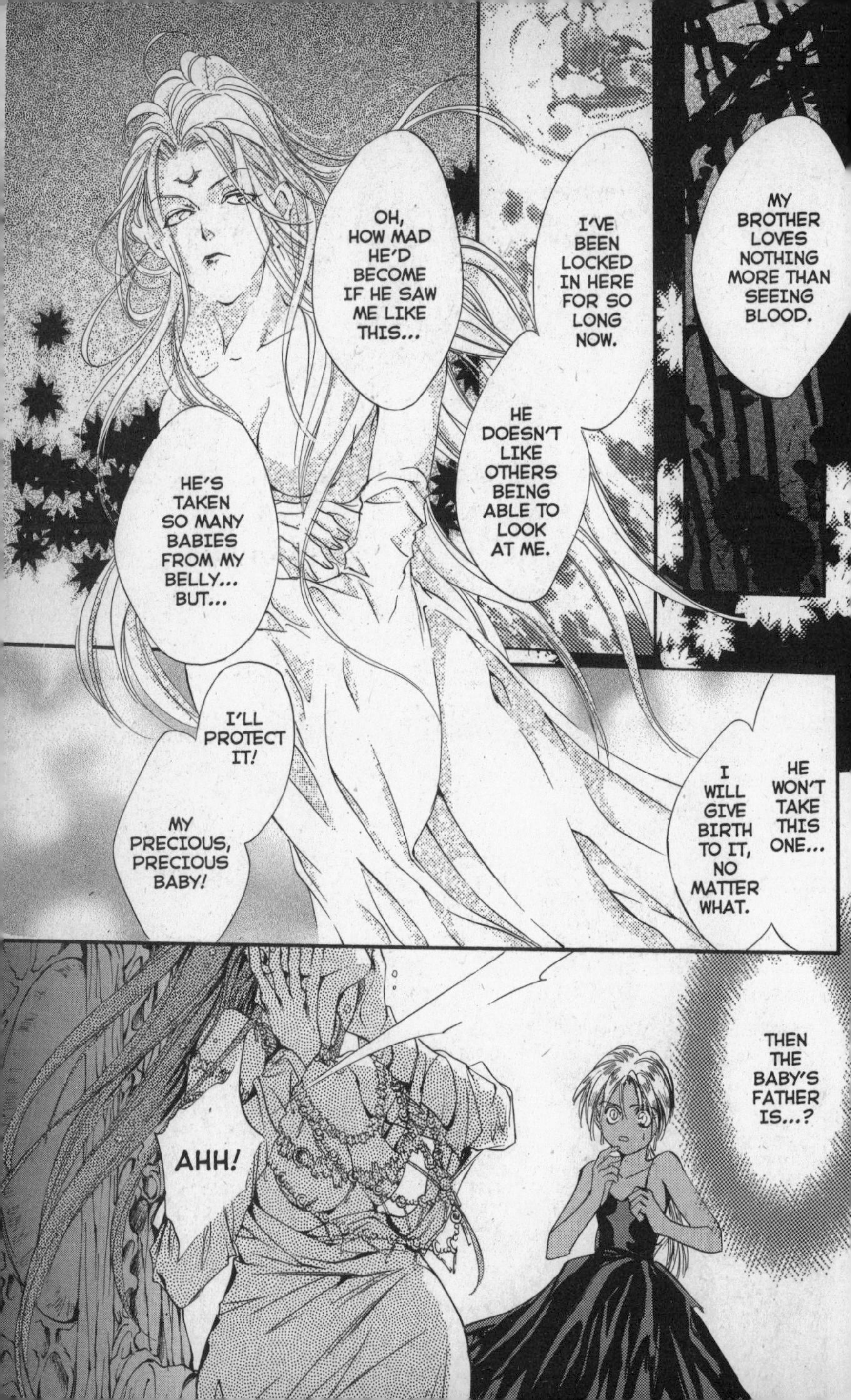
MY BROTHER LOVES NOTHING MORE THAN SEEING BLOOD.
I'VE BEEN LOCKED IN HERE FOR SO LONG NOW.
HE DOESN'T LIKE OTHERS BEING ABLE TO LOOK AT ME.
OH, HOW MAD HE'D BECOME IF HE SAW ME LIKE THIS...
HE'S TAKEN SO MANY BABIES FROM MY BELLY... BUT...
HE WON'T TAKE THIS ONE...
I WILL GIVE BIRTH TO IT, NO MATTER WHAT.
I'LL PROTECT IT!
MY PRECIOUS, PRECIOUS BABY!
THEN THE BABY'S FATHER IS...?
AHH!

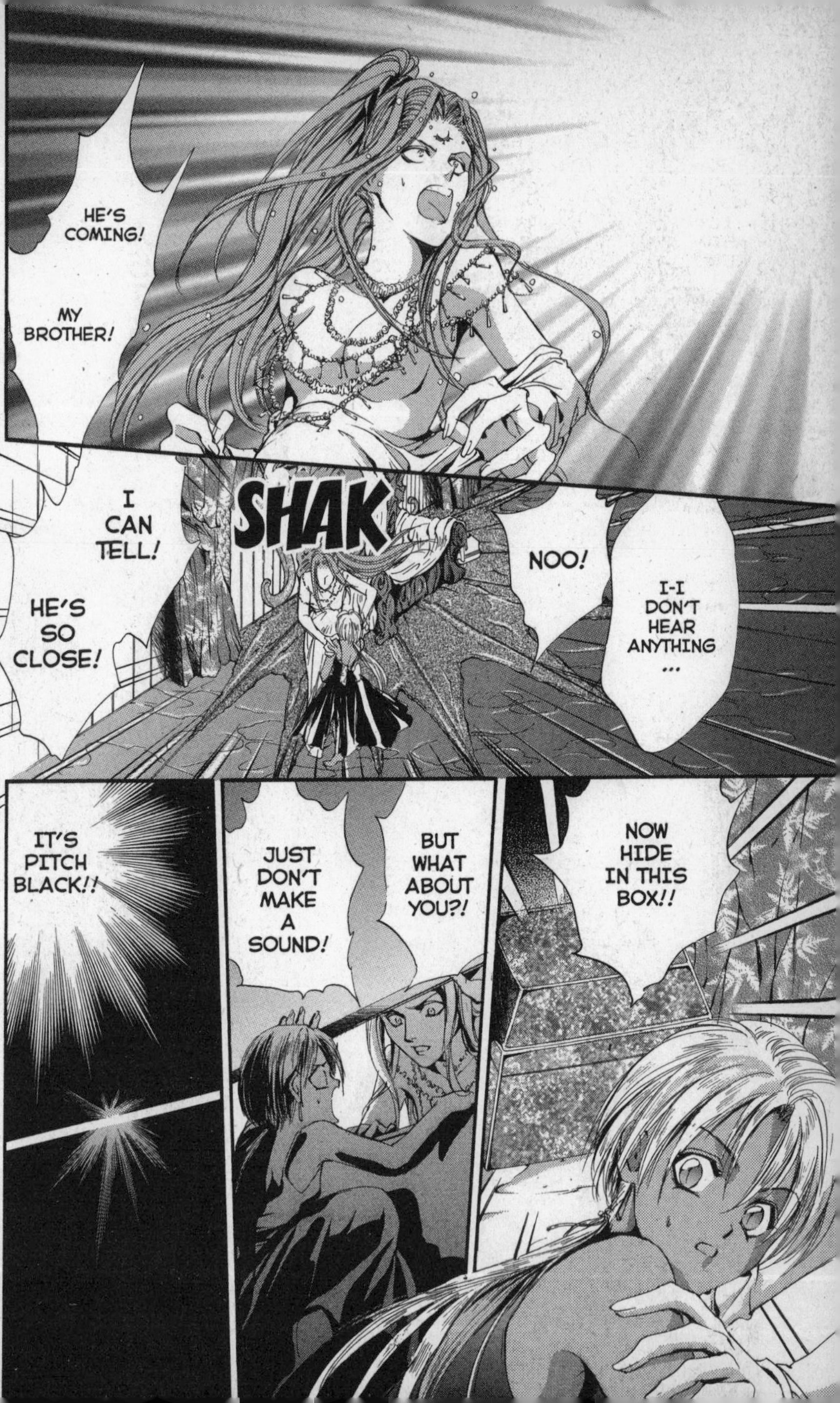
HE'S COMING!
MY BROTHER!
NOO!
I-I DON'T HEAR ANYTHING ...
SHAK
I CAN TELL!
HE'S SO CLOSE!
NOW HIDE IN THIS BOX!!
BUT WHAT ABOUT YOU?!
JUST DON'T MAKE A SOUND!
IT'S PITCH BLACK!!

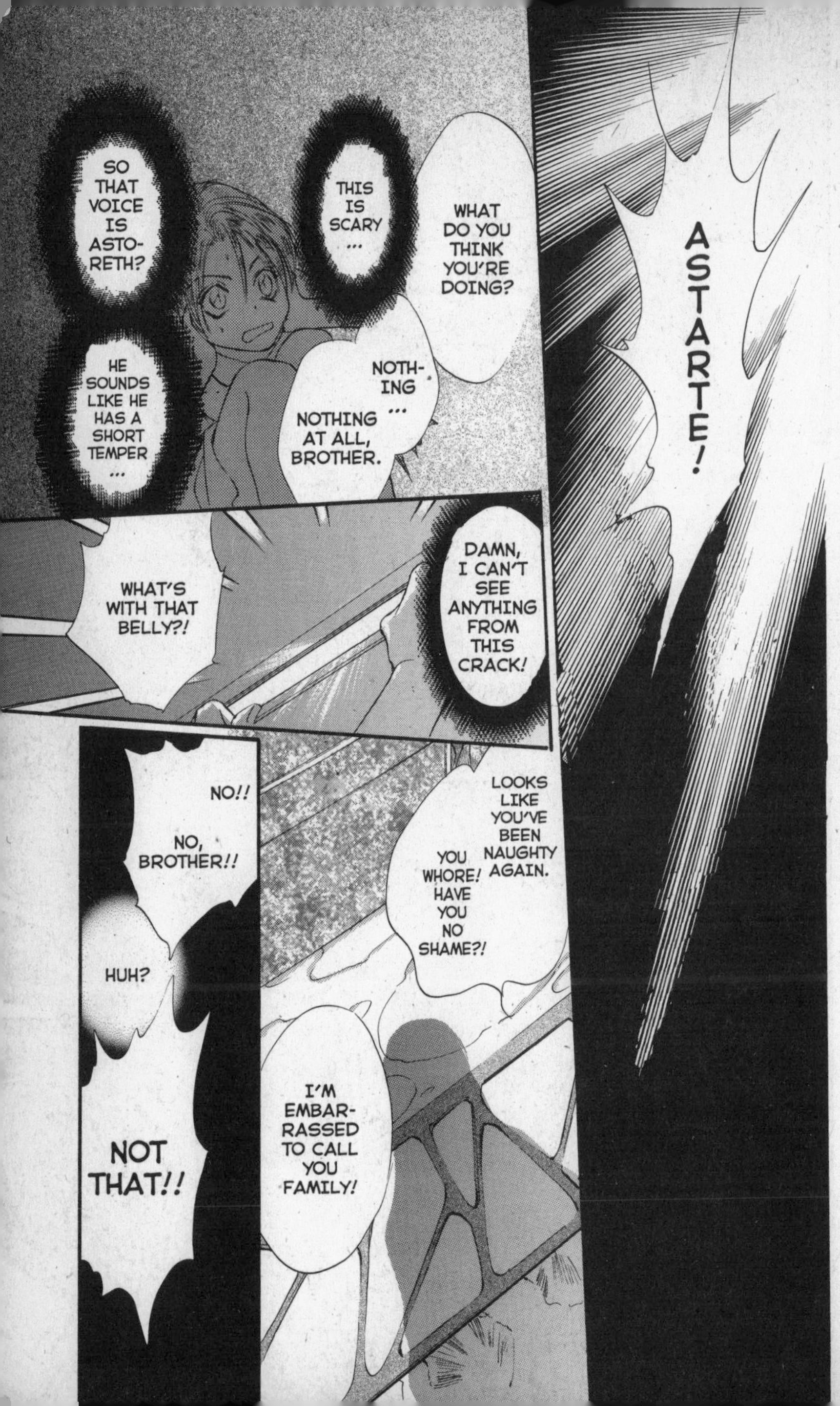
ASTARTE!
WHAT DO YOU THINK YOU'RE DOING?
THIS IS SCARY ...
SO THAT VOICE IS ASTO-RETH?
NOTH-ING ...
NOTHING AT ALL, BROTHER.
HE SOUNDS LIKE HE HAS A SHORT TEMPER ...
DAMN, I CAN'T SEE ANYTHING FROM THIS CRACK!
WHAT'S WITH THAT BELLY?!
LOOKS LIKE YOU'VE BEEN NAUGHTY AGAIN.
YOU WHORE! HAVE YOU NO SHAME?!
I'M EMBAR-RASSED TO CALL YOU FAMILY!
NO!!
NO, BROTHER!!
HUH?
NOT THAT!!

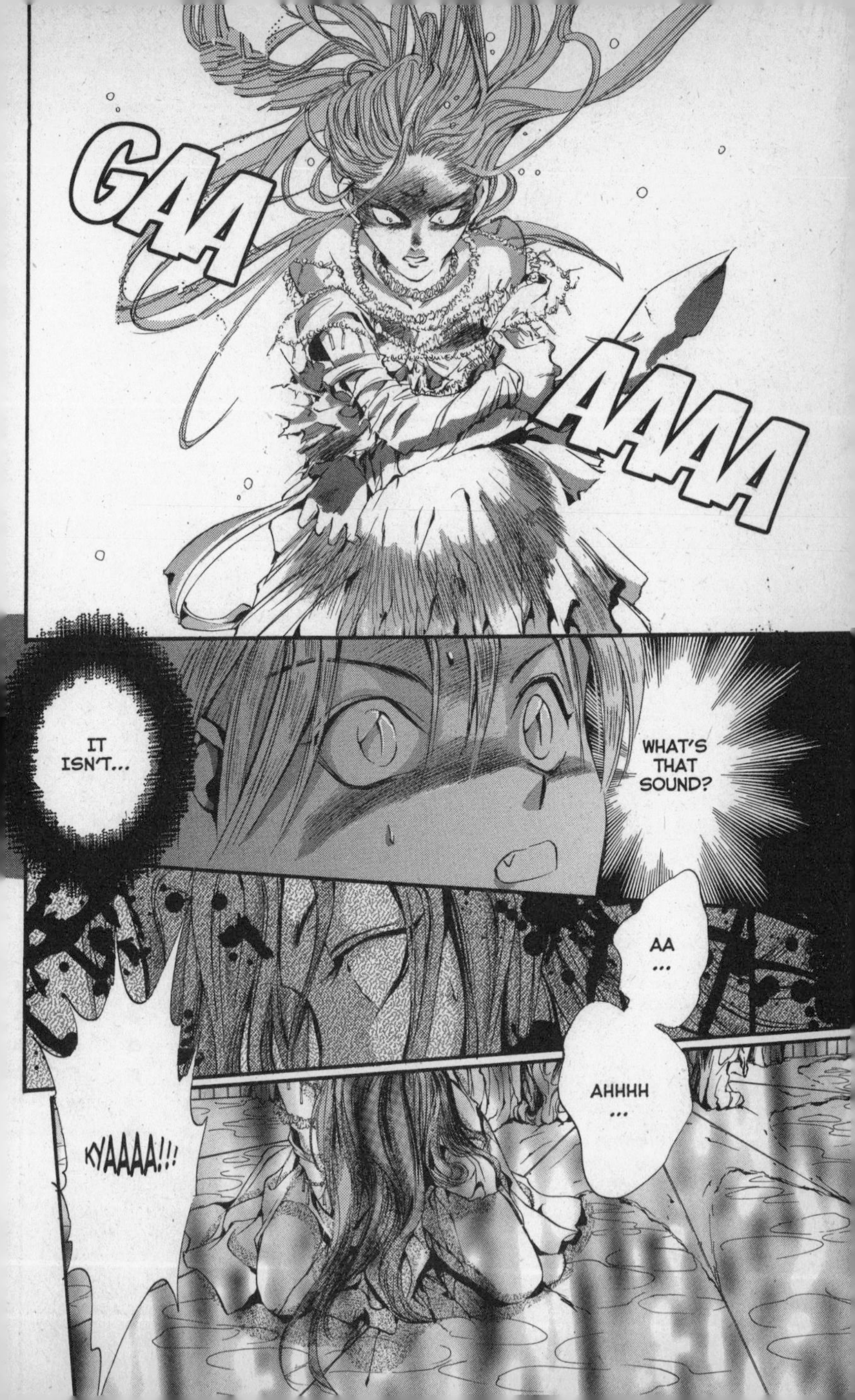
GAA
AAAA
WHAT'S THAT SOUND?
IT ISN'T...
AA ...
AHHHH ...
KYAAAA!!!

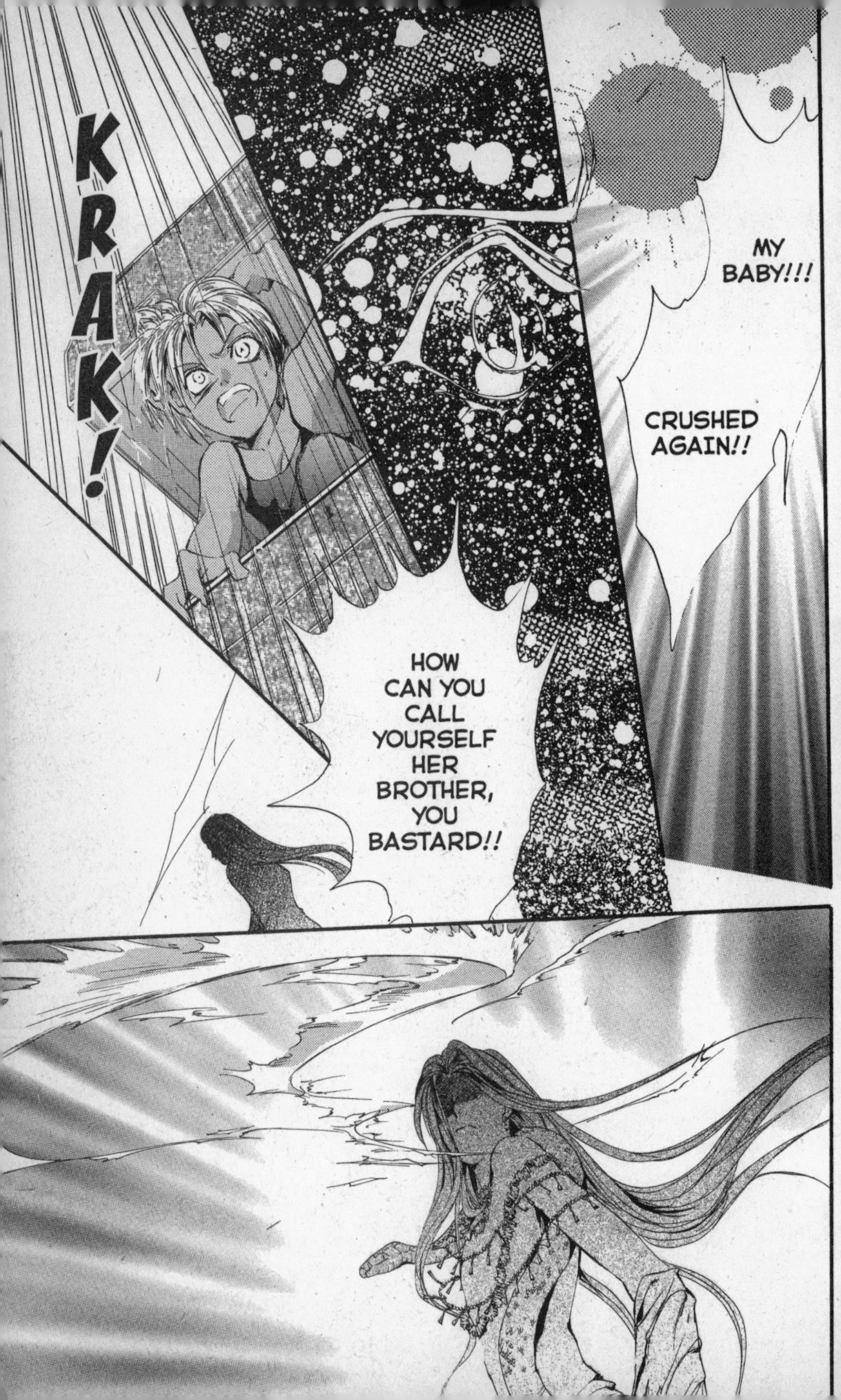
MY BABY!!!
CRUSHED AGAIN!!
KRAK!
HOW CAN YOU CALL YOURSELF HER BROTHER, YOU BASTARD!!

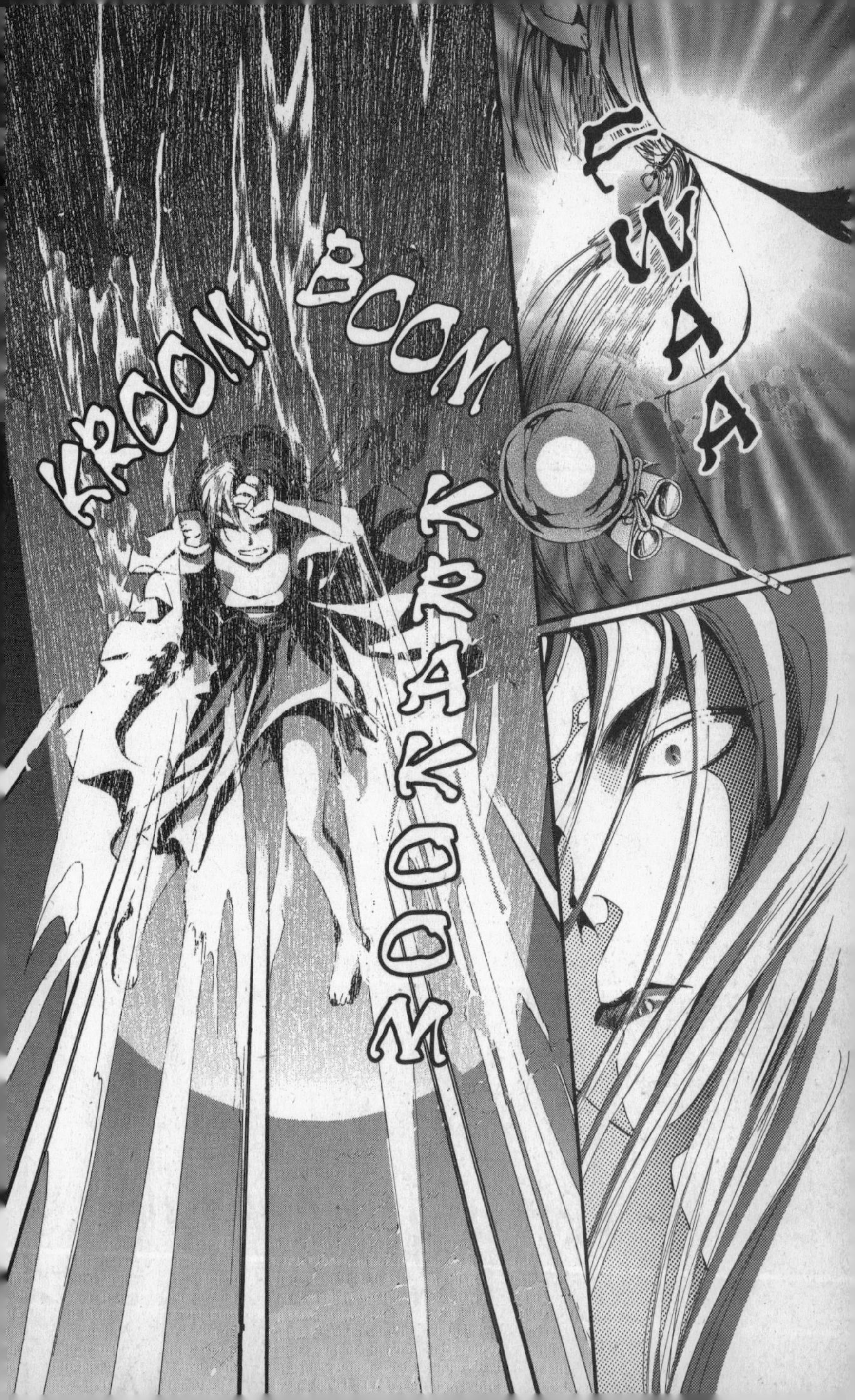
FWAA
KRAKOOM
BOOM
KROOM

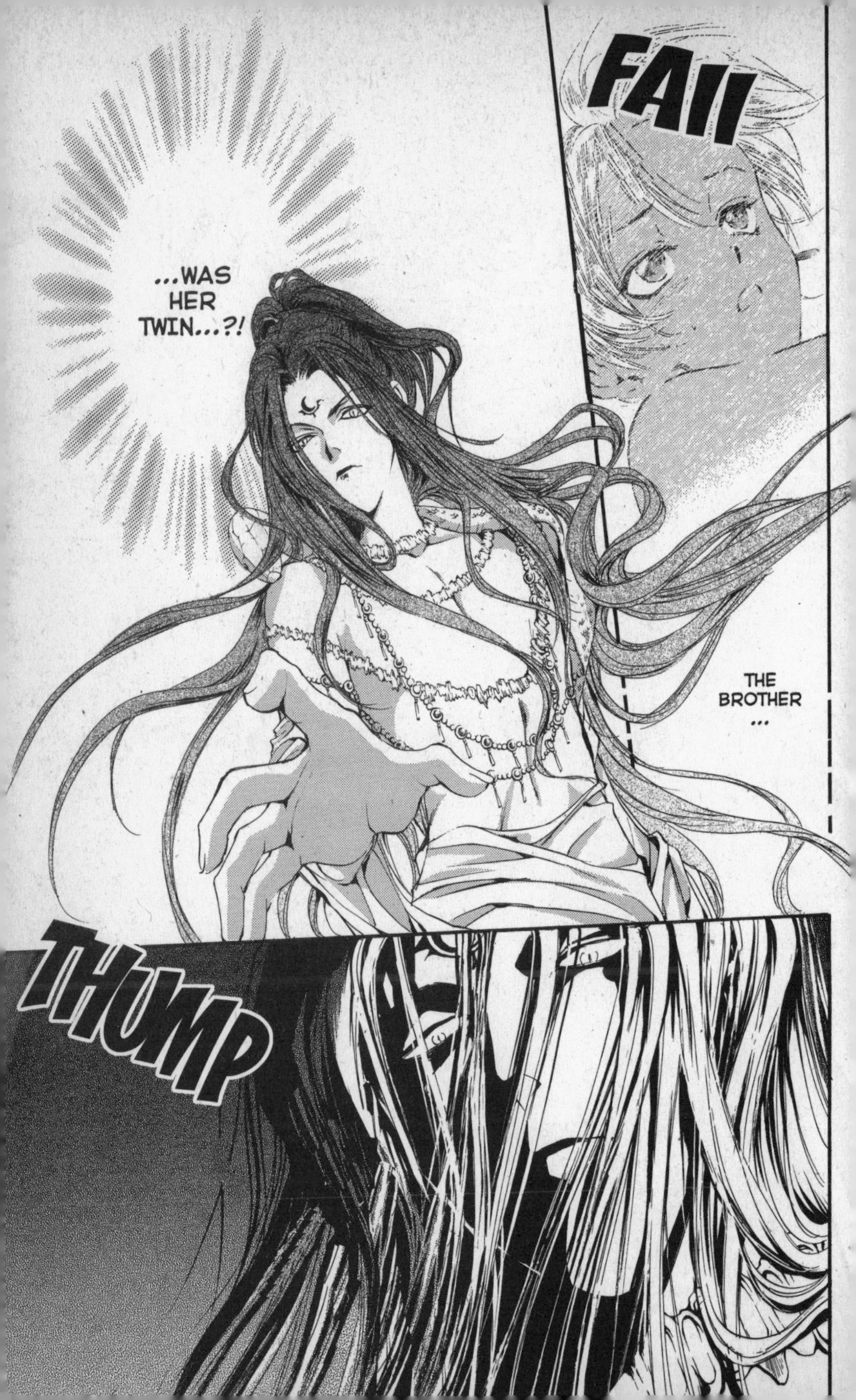
FAI
THE BROTHER ...
...WAS HER TWIN...?!
THUMP

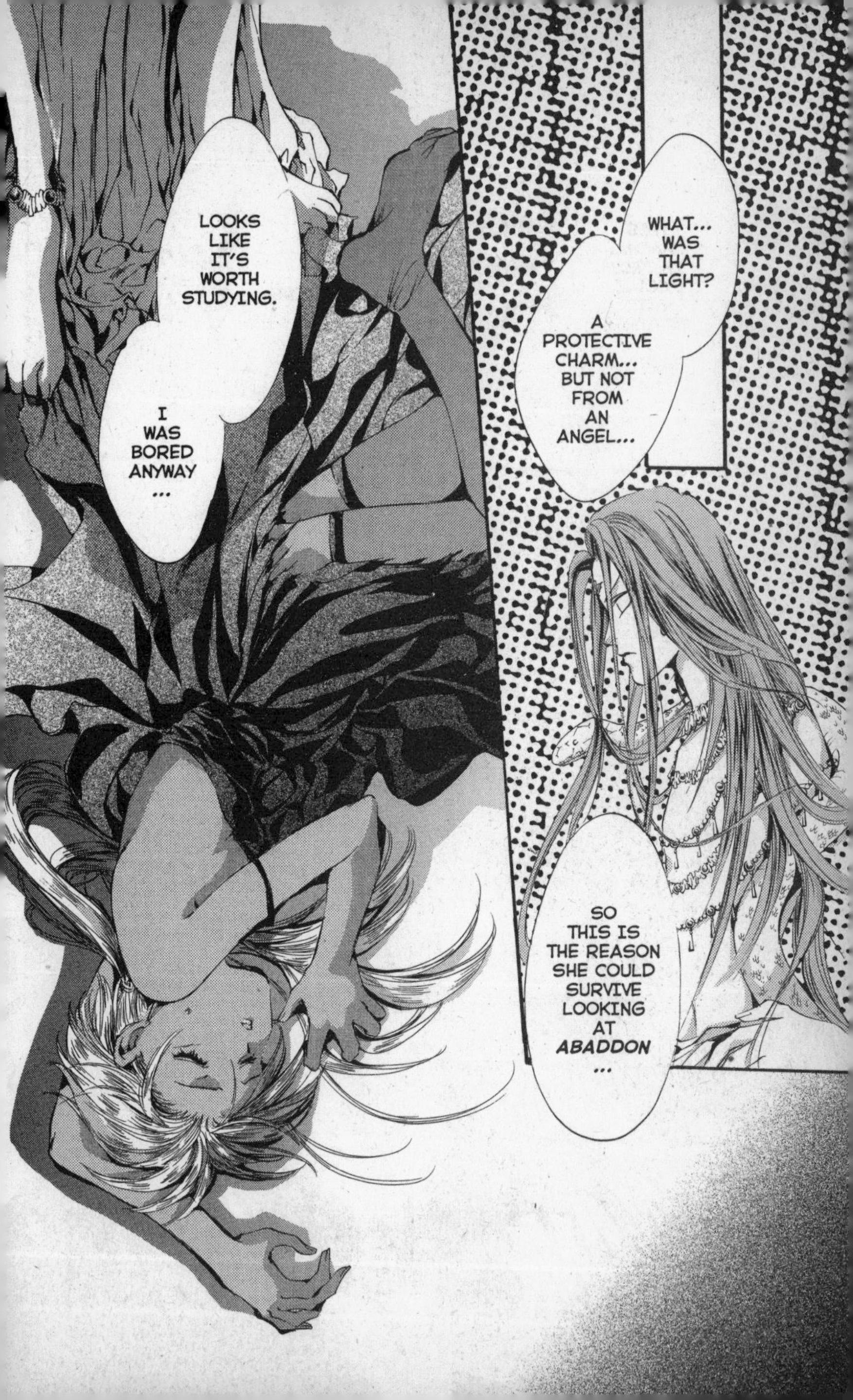
WHAT... WAS THAT LIGHT?
A PROTECTIVE CHARM... BUT NOT FROM AN ANGEL...
SO THIS IS THE REASON SHE COULD SURVIVE LOOKING AT *ABADDON* ...
LOOKS LIKE IT'S WORTH STUDYING.
I WAS BORED ANYWAY ...

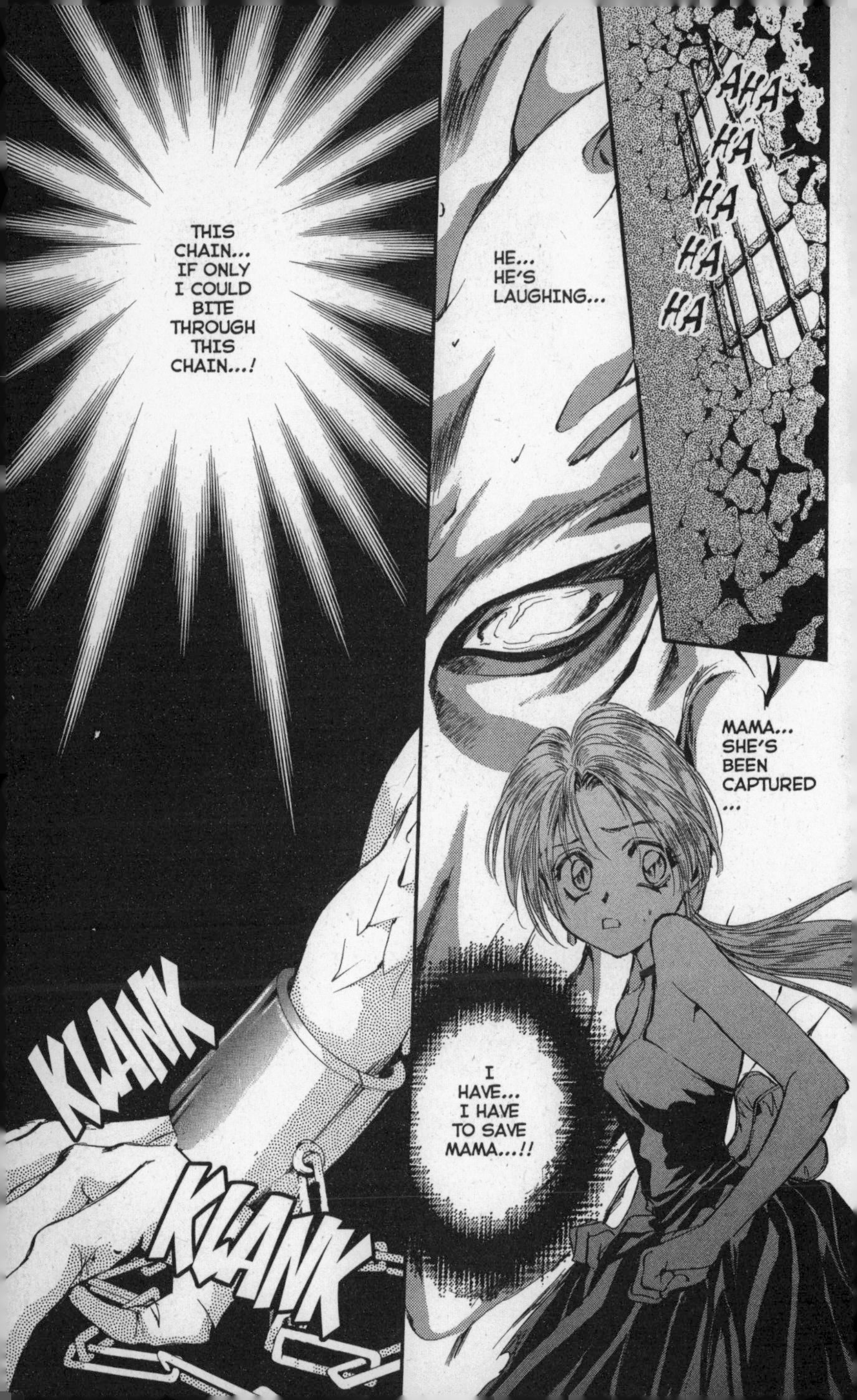
AHAHA HA HA HA HA
HE... HE'S LAUGHING...
MAMA... SHE'S BEEN CAPTURED ...
I HAVE... I HAVE TO SAVE MAMA...!!
THIS CHAIN... IF ONLY I COULD BITE THROUGH THIS CHAIN...!
KLANK
KLANK

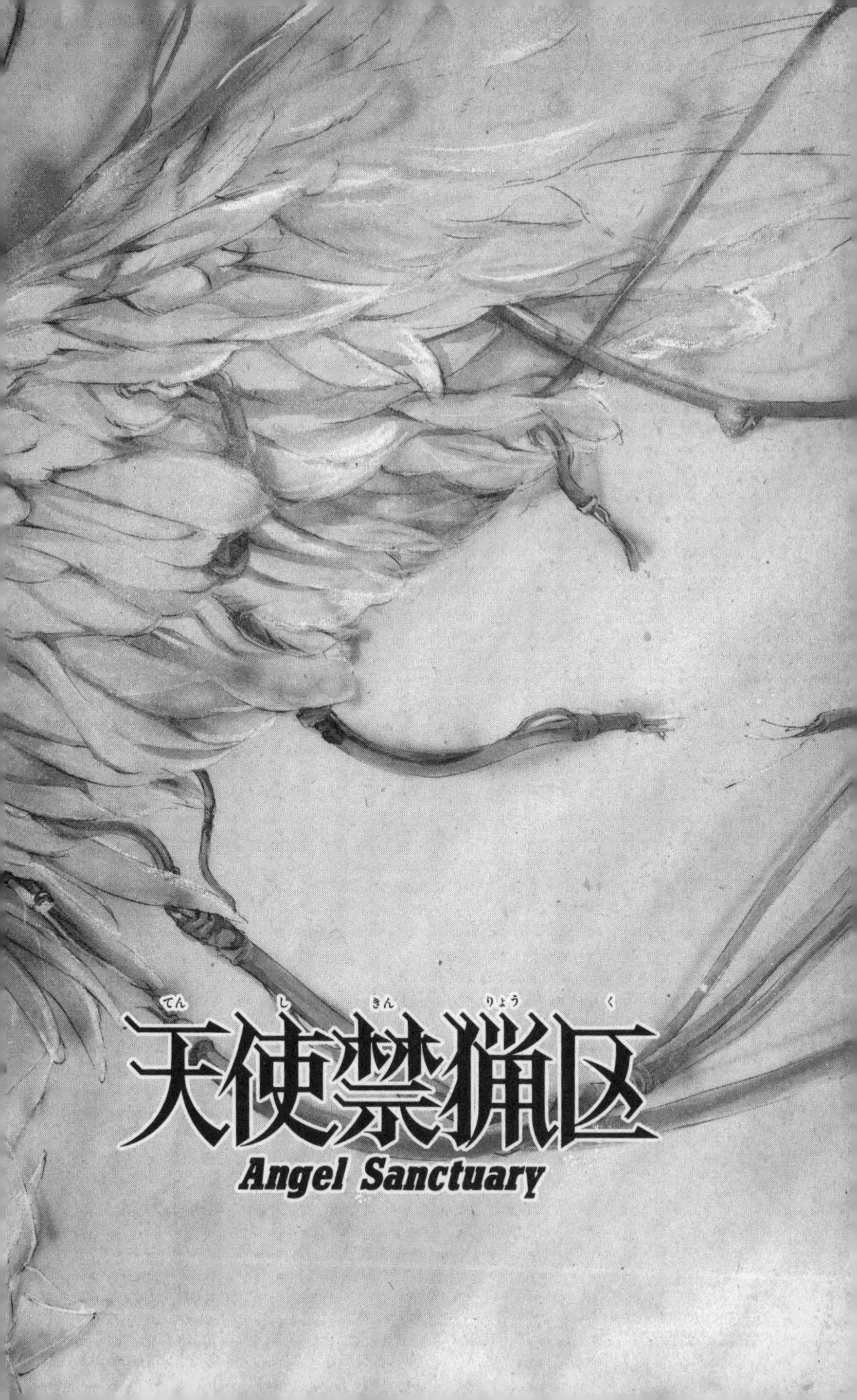
天使禁猟区
Angel Sanctuary

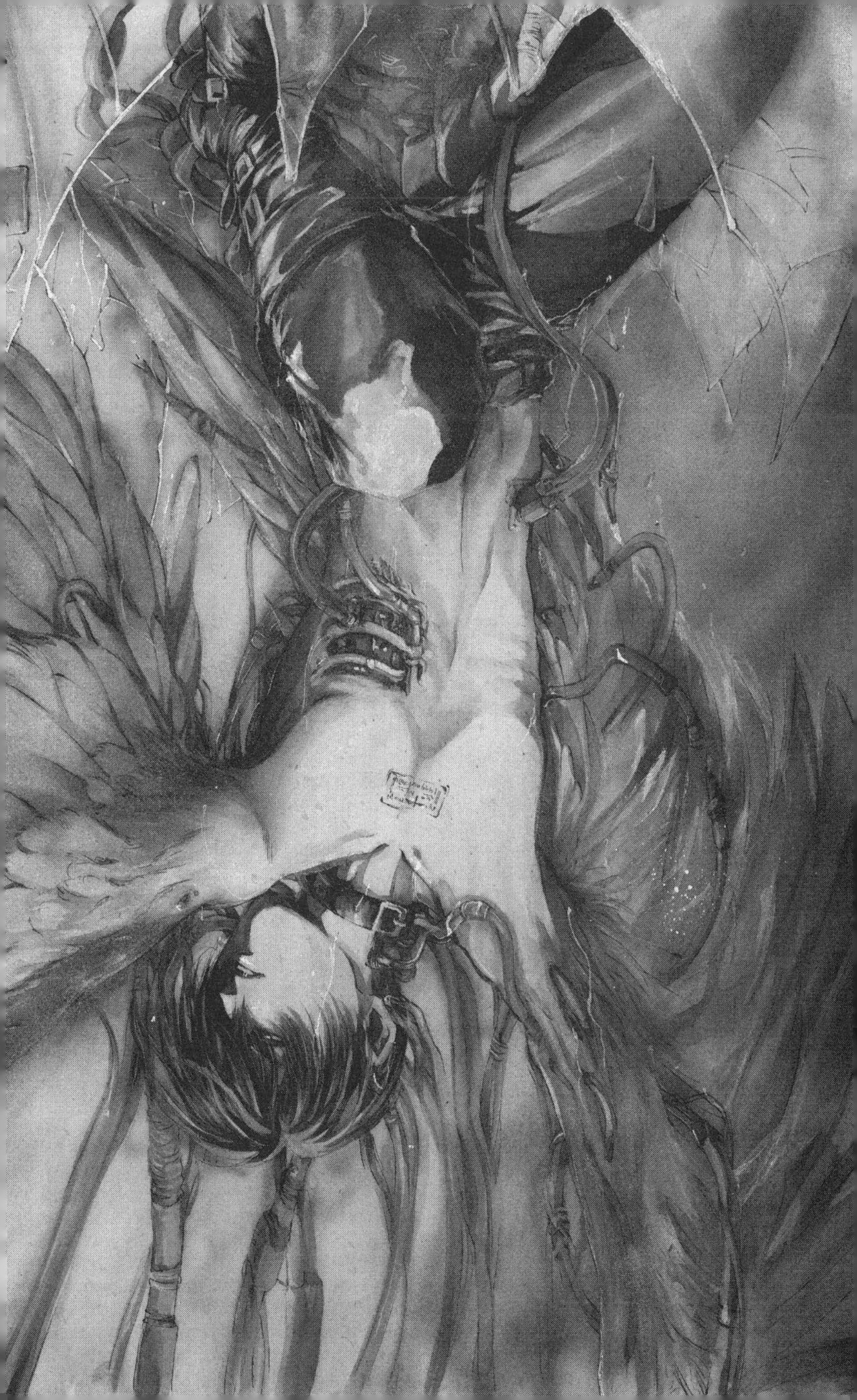

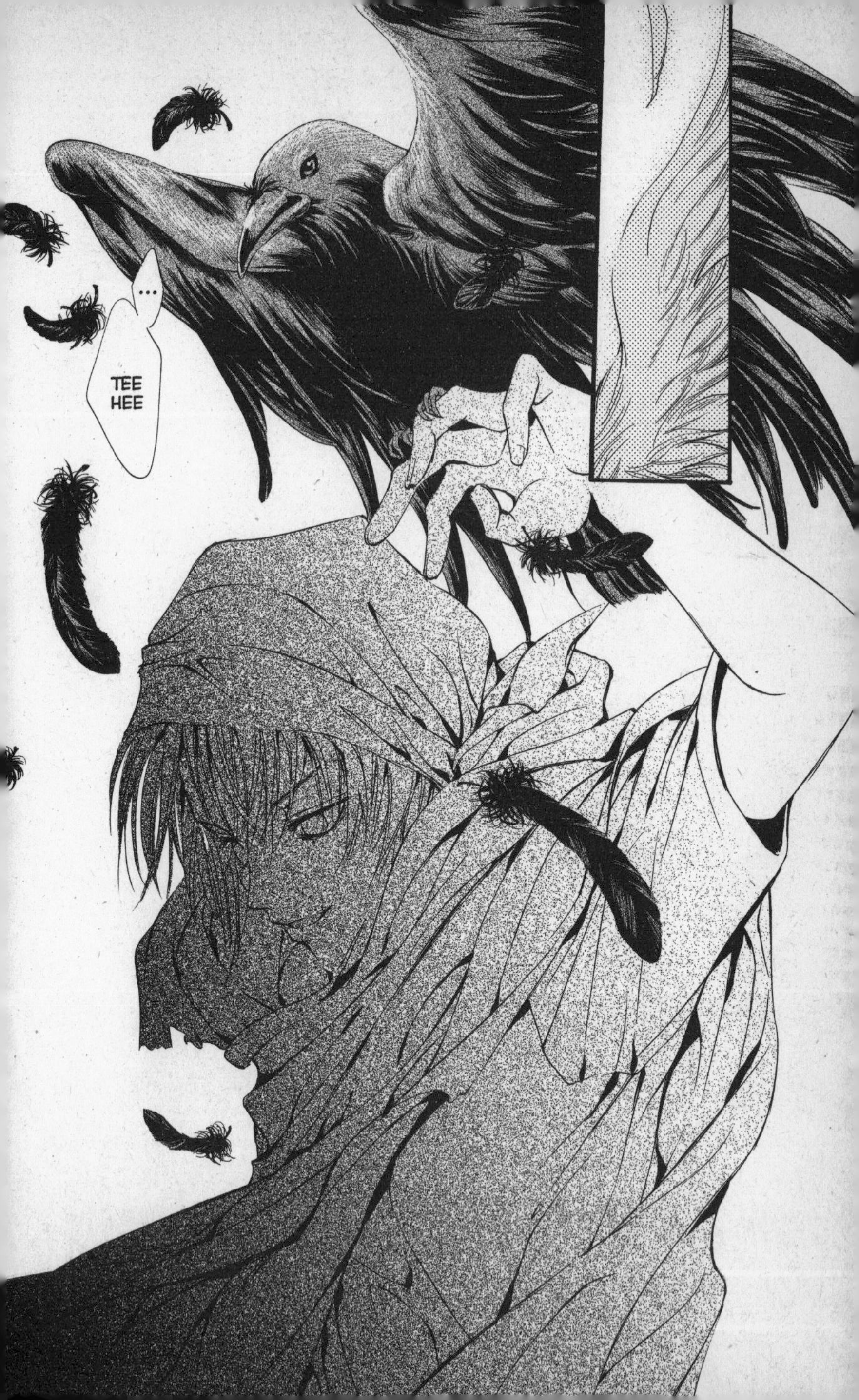
...
TEE HEE

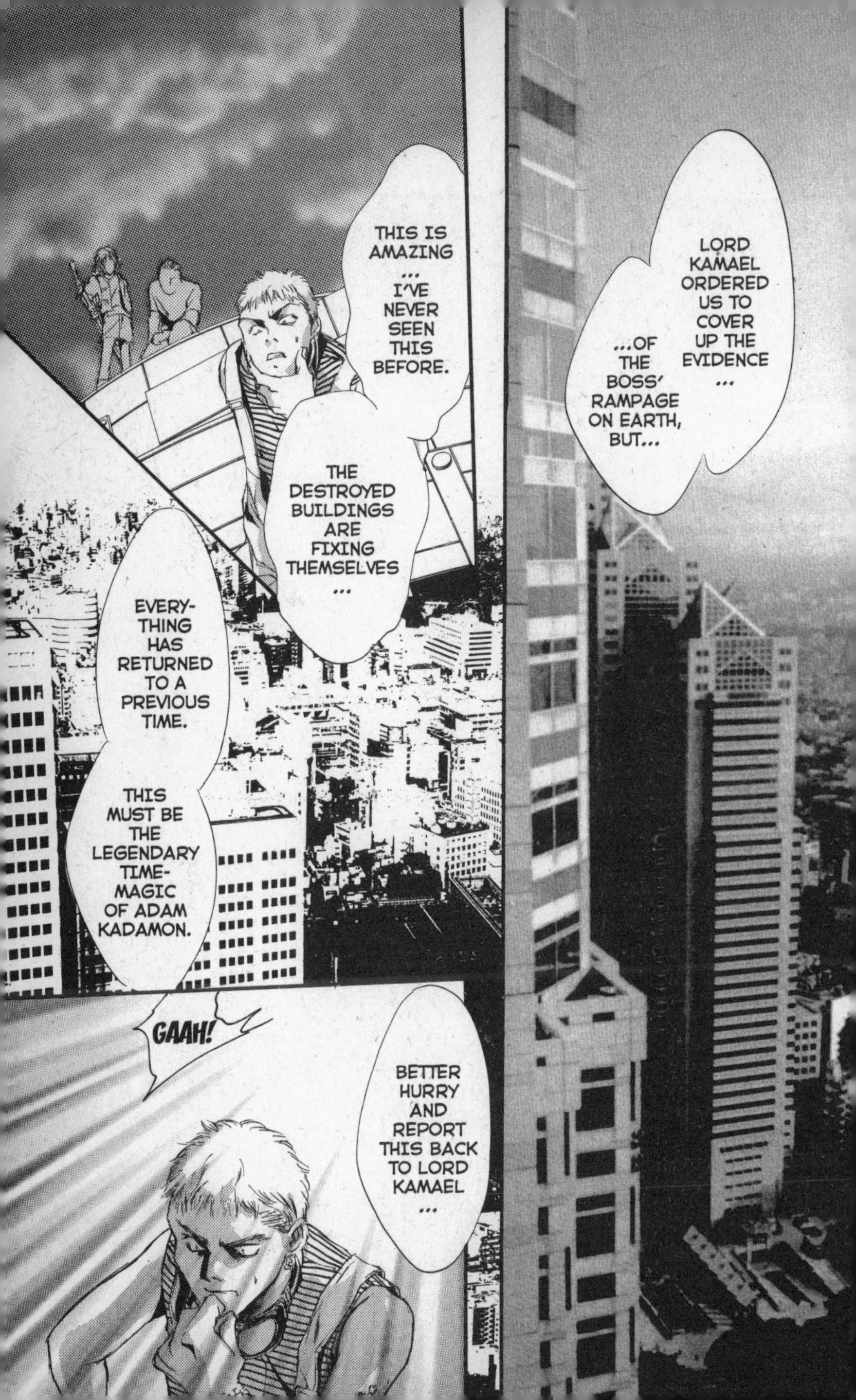
LORD KAMAEL ORDERED US TO COVER UP THE EVIDENCE ...
...OF THE BOSS' RAMPAGE ON EARTH, BUT...
THIS IS AMAZING ... I'VE NEVER SEEN THIS BEFORE.
THE DESTROYED BUILDINGS ARE FIXING THEMSELVES ...
EVERY-THING HAS RETURNED TO A PREVIOUS TIME.
THIS MUST BE THE LEGENDARY TIME-MAGIC OF ADAM KADAMON.
GAAH!
BETTER HURRY AND REPORT THIS BACK TO LORD KAMAEL ...

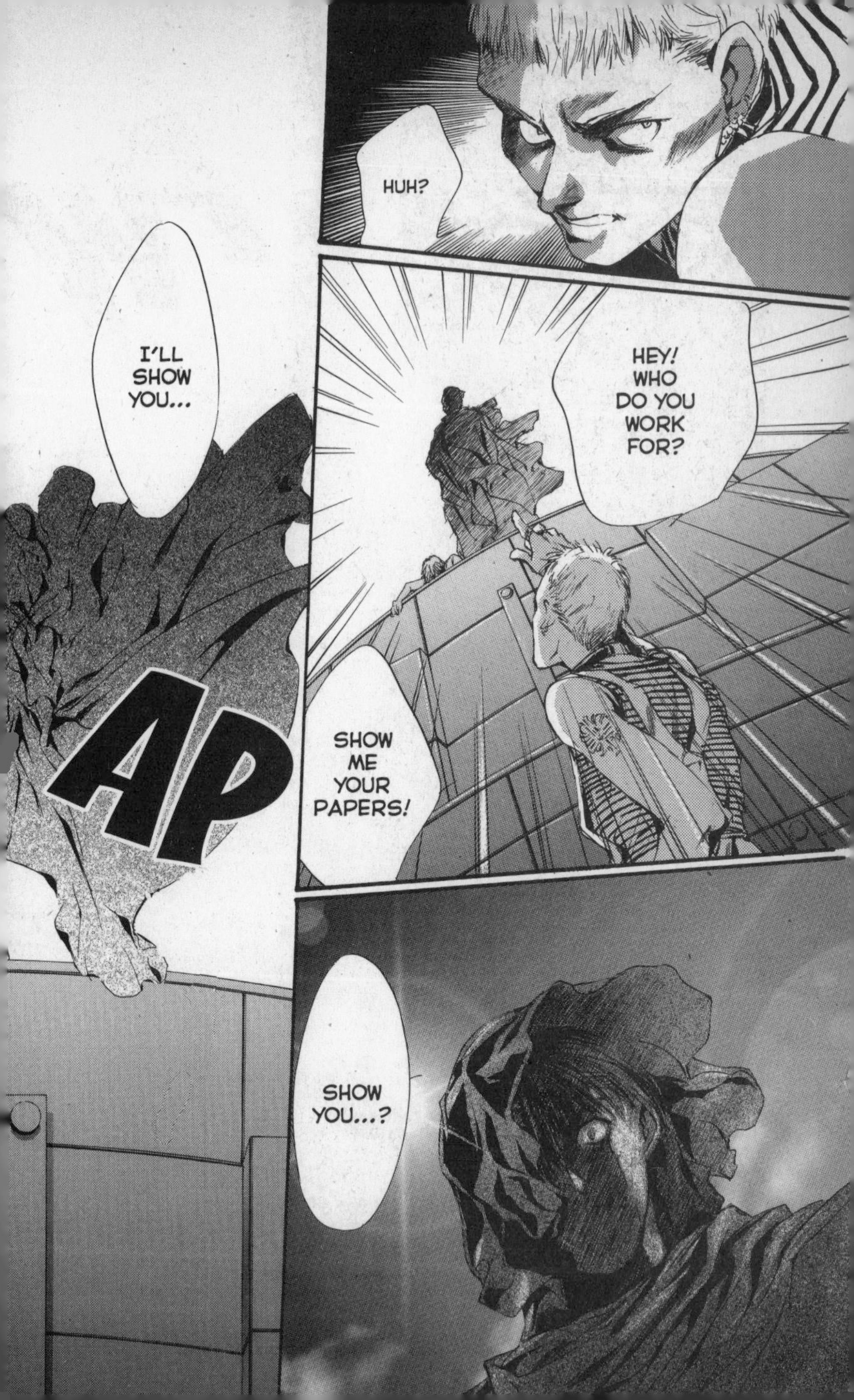
HUH?
HEY! WHO DO YOU WORK FOR?
SHOW ME YOUR PAPERS!
SHOW YOU...?
I'LL SHOW YOU...
AP

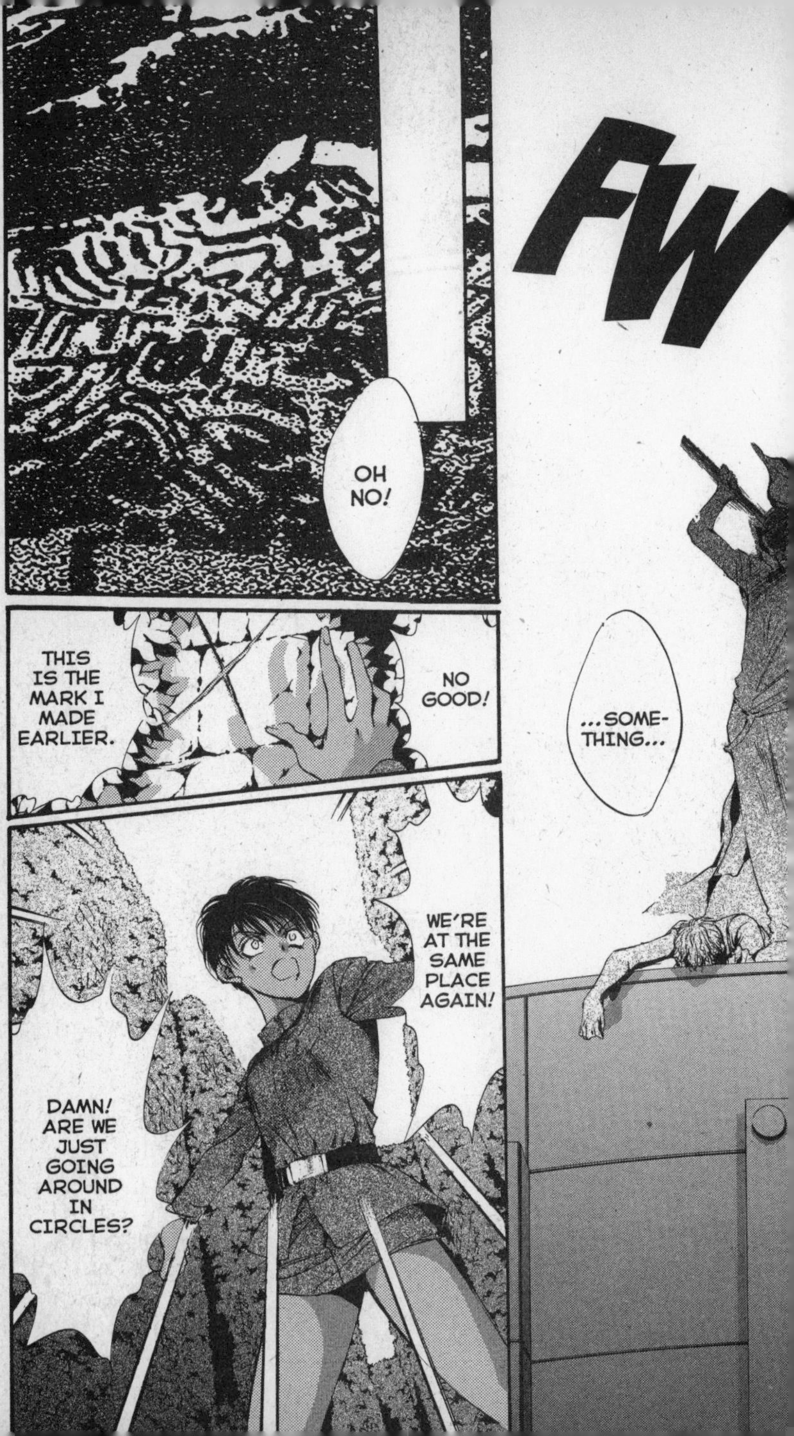
FW
...SOME-THING...
OH NO!
NO GOOD!
THIS IS THE MARK I MADE EARLIER.
WE'RE AT THE SAME PLACE AGAIN!
DAMN! ARE WE JUST GOING AROUND IN CIRCLES?

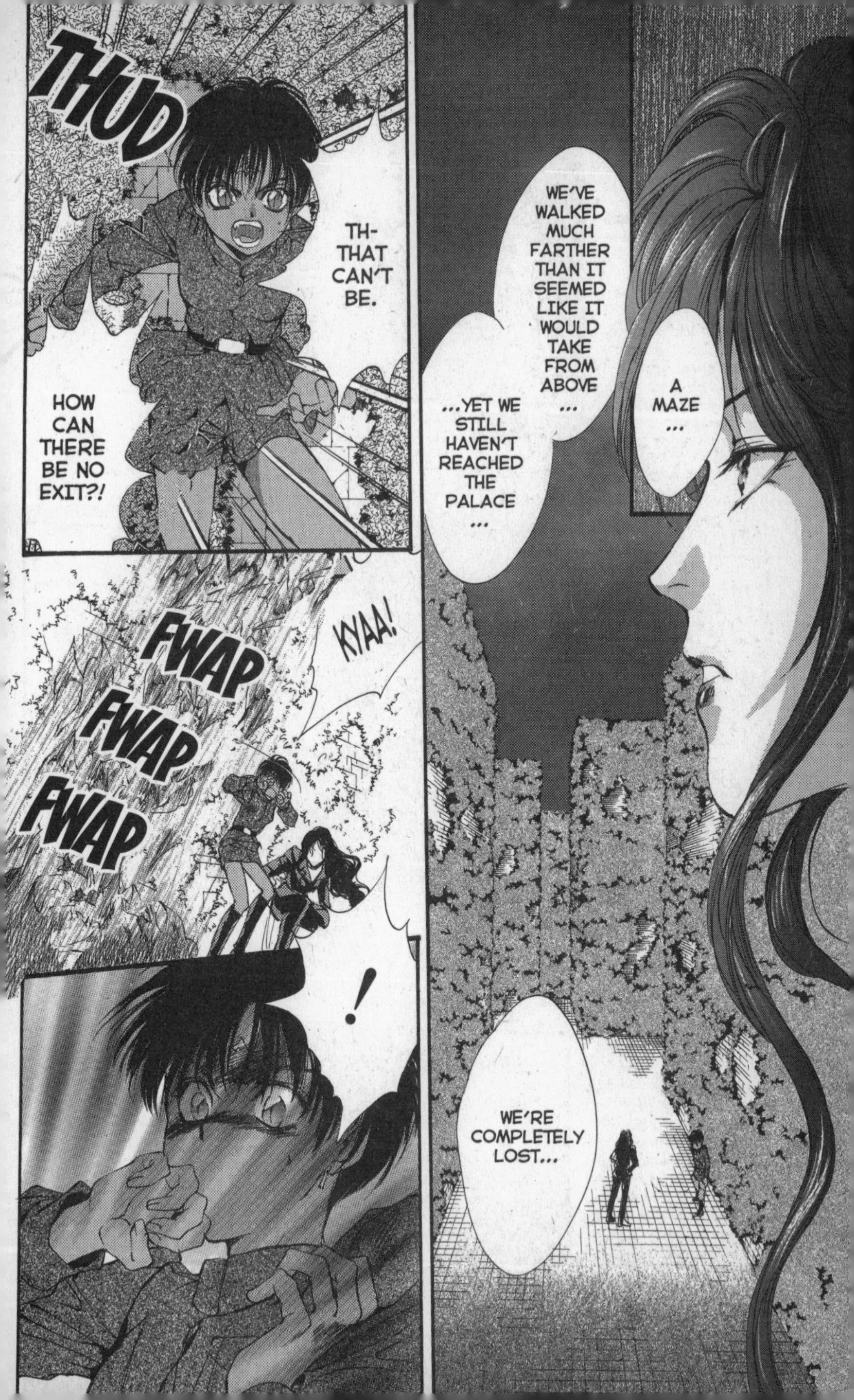
A MAZE ...
WE'VE WALKED MUCH FARTHER THAN IT SEEMED LIKE IT WOULD TAKE FROM ABOVE ...
...YET WE STILL HAVEN'T REACHED THE PALACE ...
WE'RE COMPLETELY LOST...
THUD
TH- THAT CAN'T BE.
HOW CAN THERE BE NO EXIT?!
KYAA!
FWAP
FWAP
FWAP
!

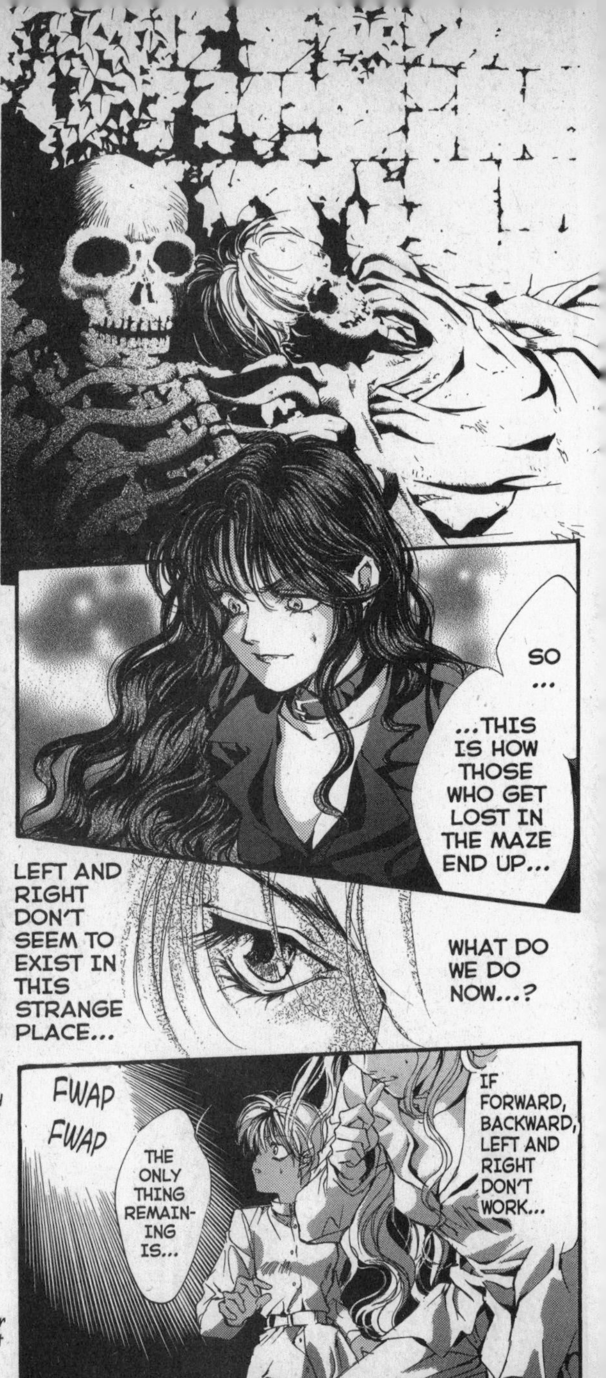
SO ...
...THIS IS HOW THOSE WHO GET LOST IN THE MAZE END UP...
LEFT AND RIGHT DON'T SEEM TO EXIST IN THIS STRANGE PLACE...
WHAT DO WE DO NOW...?
IF FORWARD, BACKWARD, LEFT AND RIGHT DON'T WORK...
FWAP FWAP
THE ONLY THING REMAIN-ING IS...

Barbelo
The Queen of Darkness, the deadly sin of "Wrath." Other than being the daughter of Pistis Sophia, nothing else is known about her. I created her because I felt there needed to be some more female Satans. Though she only appeared in one panel.

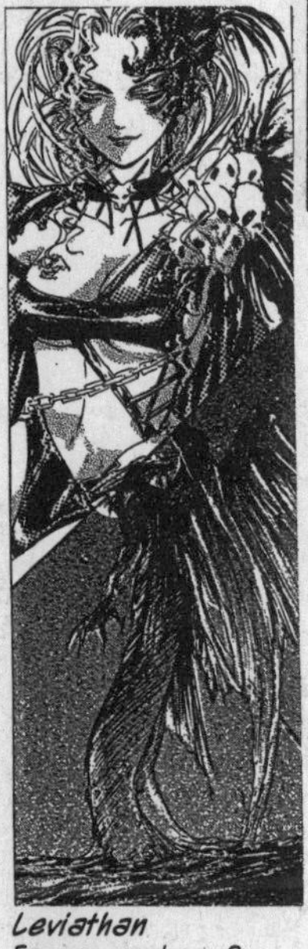

Leviathan
Former member of Seraphim, now the Sea Dragon King. The deadly sin of "Envy." Some say he's based on a pre-Biblical snake goddess. His body is covered in hard scales, and metal weapons are useless against him. With that size, how could he be a former angel...?

Well, there's probably other theories about him, like that he's not an angel.

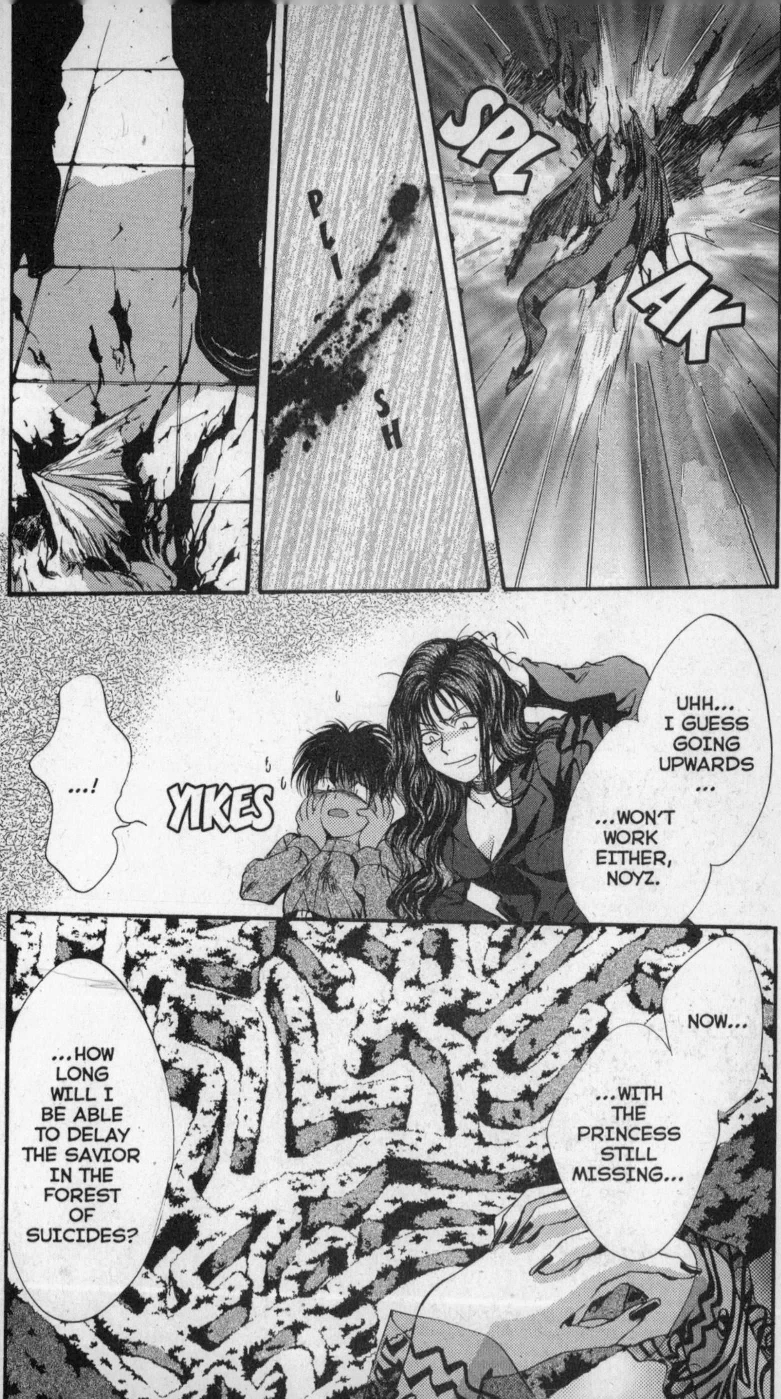
SPL
AK
PLI
SH
UHH... I GUESS GOING UPWARDS ...
...WON'T WORK EITHER, NOYZ.
YIKES
...!
NOW...
...WITH THE PRINCESS STILL MISSING...
...HOW LONG WILL I BE ABLE TO DELAY THE SAVIOR IN THE FOREST OF SUICIDES?

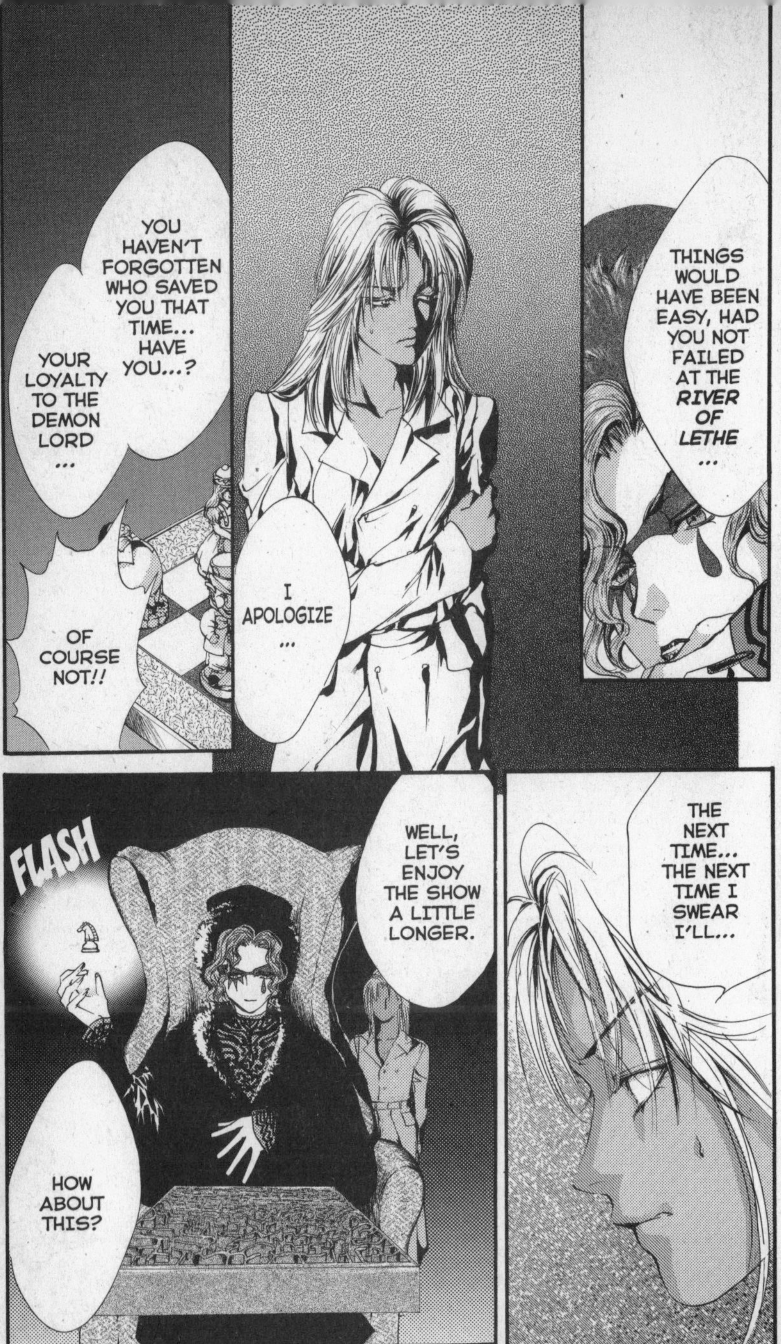
THINGS WOULD HAVE BEEN EASY, HAD YOU NOT FAILED AT THE *RIVER OF LETHE* ...
I APOLOGIZE ...
YOU HAVEN'T FORGOTTEN WHO SAVED YOU THAT TIME... HAVE YOU...?
YOUR LOYALTY TO THE DEMON LORD ...
OF COURSE NOT!!
THE NEXT TIME... THE NEXT TIME I SWEAR I'LL...
WELL, LET'S ENJOY THE SHOW A LITTLE LONGER.
FLASH
HOW ABOUT THIS?

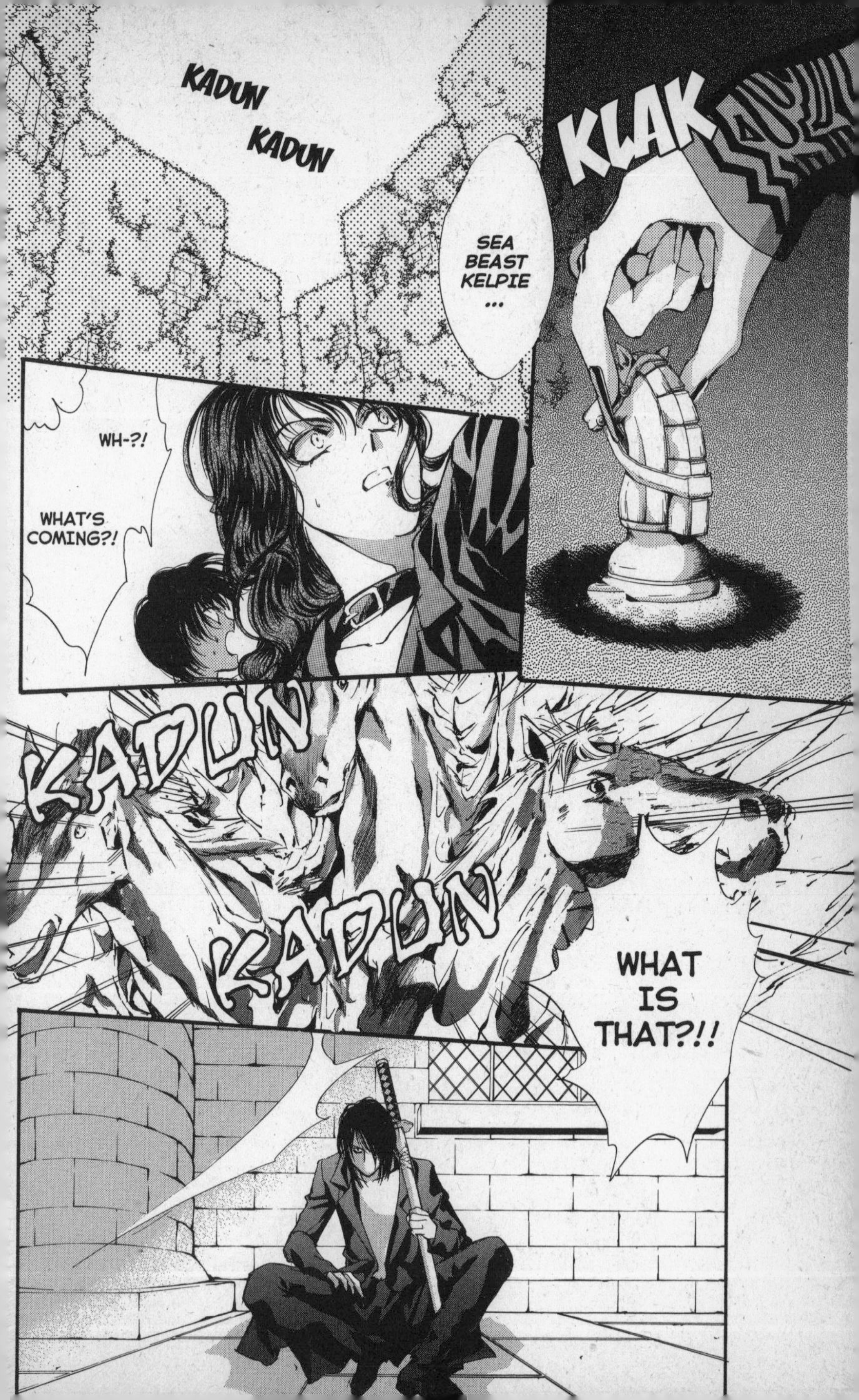
KLAK
SEA BEAST KELPIE ...
KADUN
KADUN
WH-?!
WHAT'S COMING?!
KADUN
KADUN
WHAT IS THAT?!!

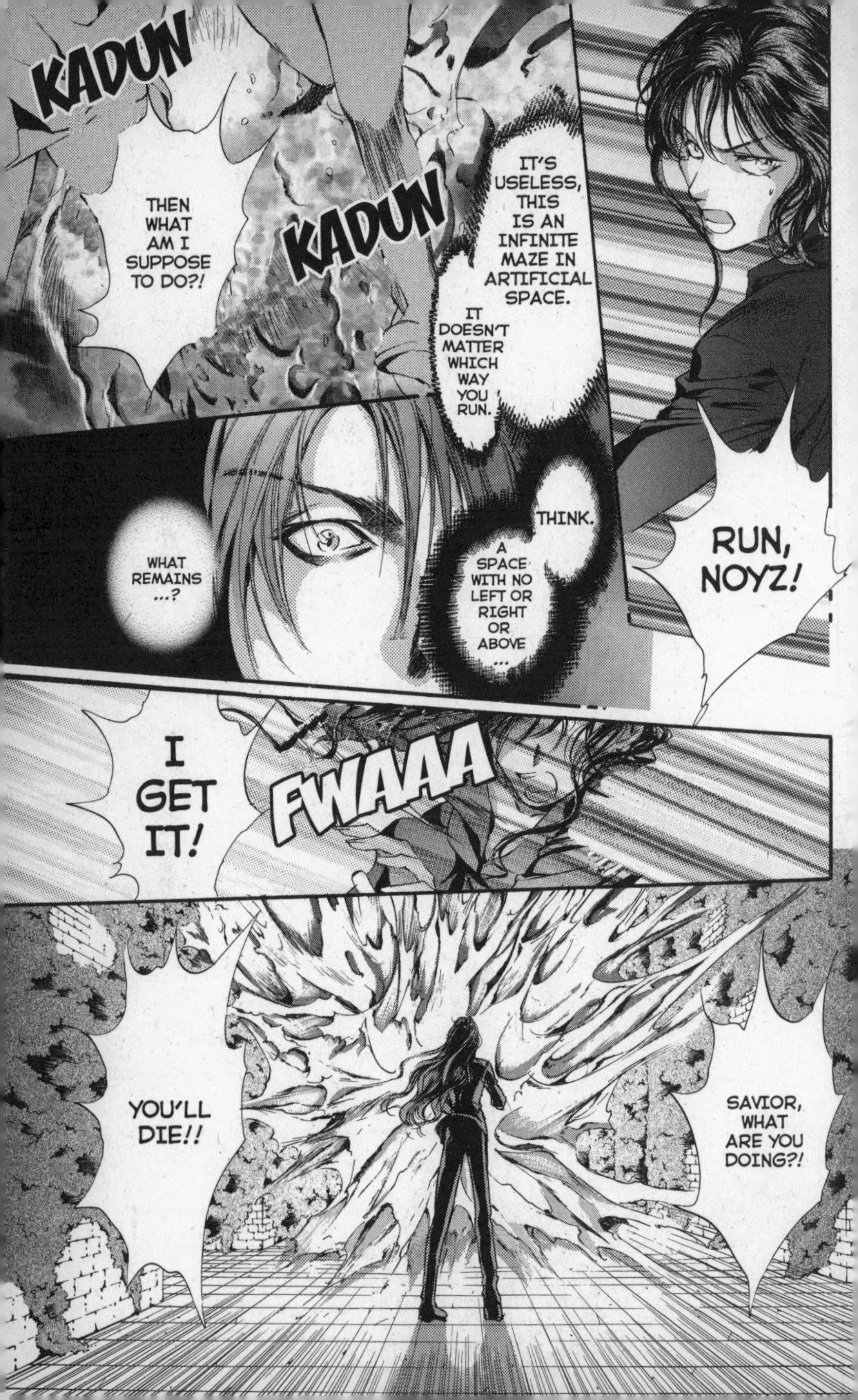
IT'S USELESS, THIS IS AN INFINITE MAZE IN ARTIFICIAL SPACE.
IT DOESN'T MATTER WHICH WAY YOU RUN.
KADUN
KADUN
THEN WHAT AM I SUPPOSE TO DO?!
RUN, NOYZ!
THINK.
A SPACE WITH NO LEFT OR RIGHT OR ABOVE ...
WHAT REMAINS ...?
FWAAA
I GET IT!
SAVIOR, WHAT ARE YOU DOING?!
YOU'LL DIE!!

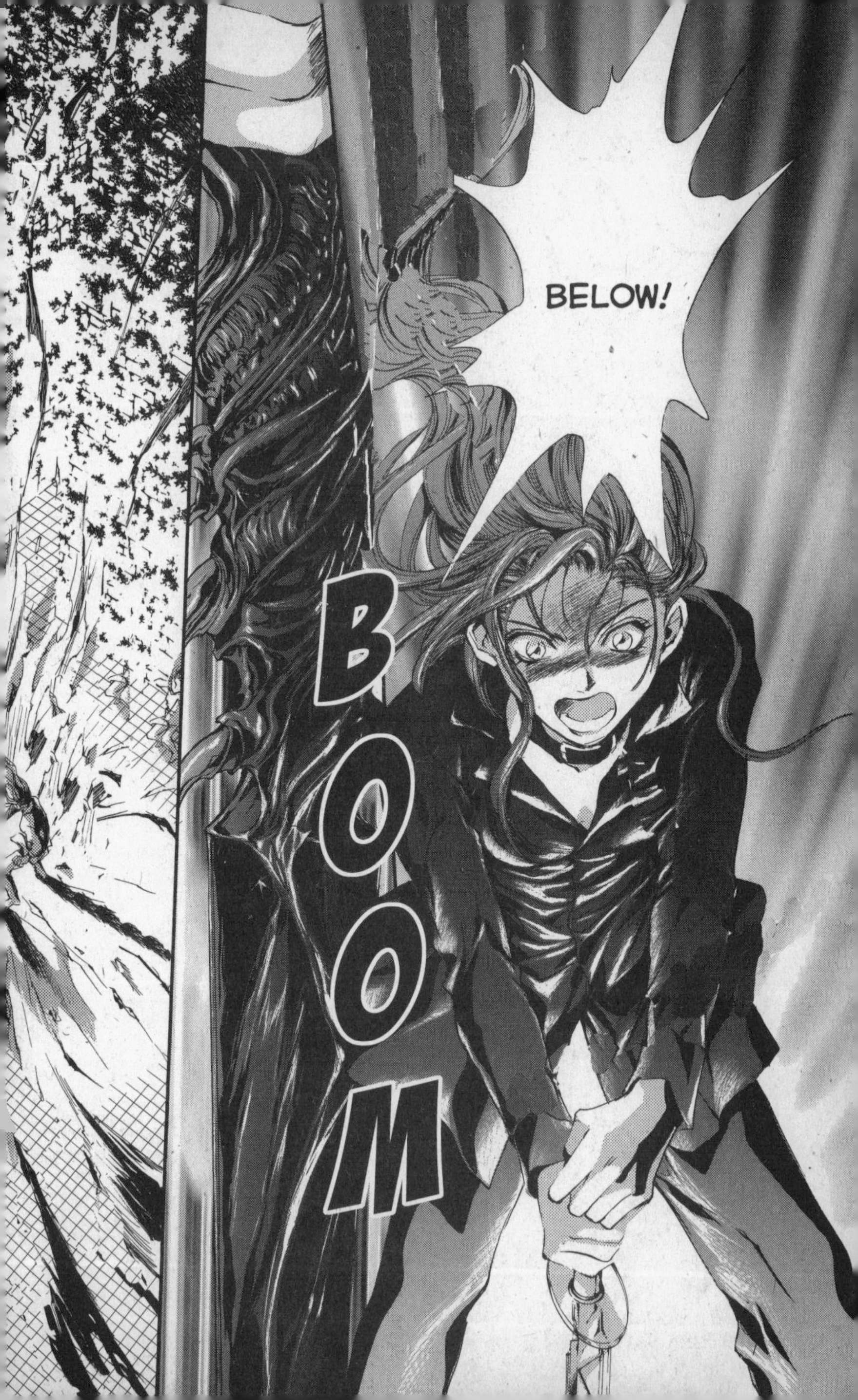
BELOW!
BOOM

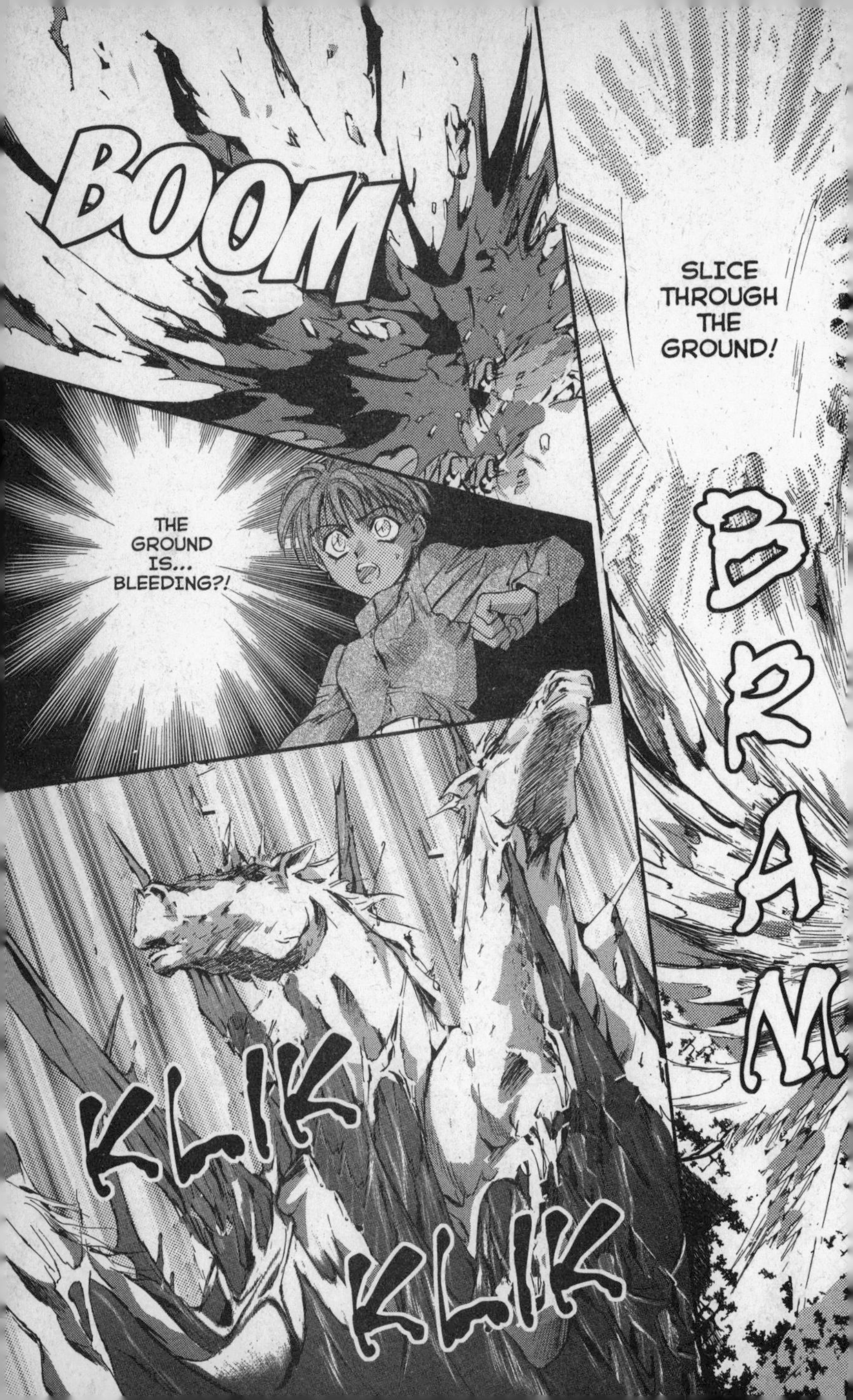
SLICE THROUGH THE GROUND!
BRAM
BOOM
THE GROUND IS... BLEEDING?!
KLIK KLIK

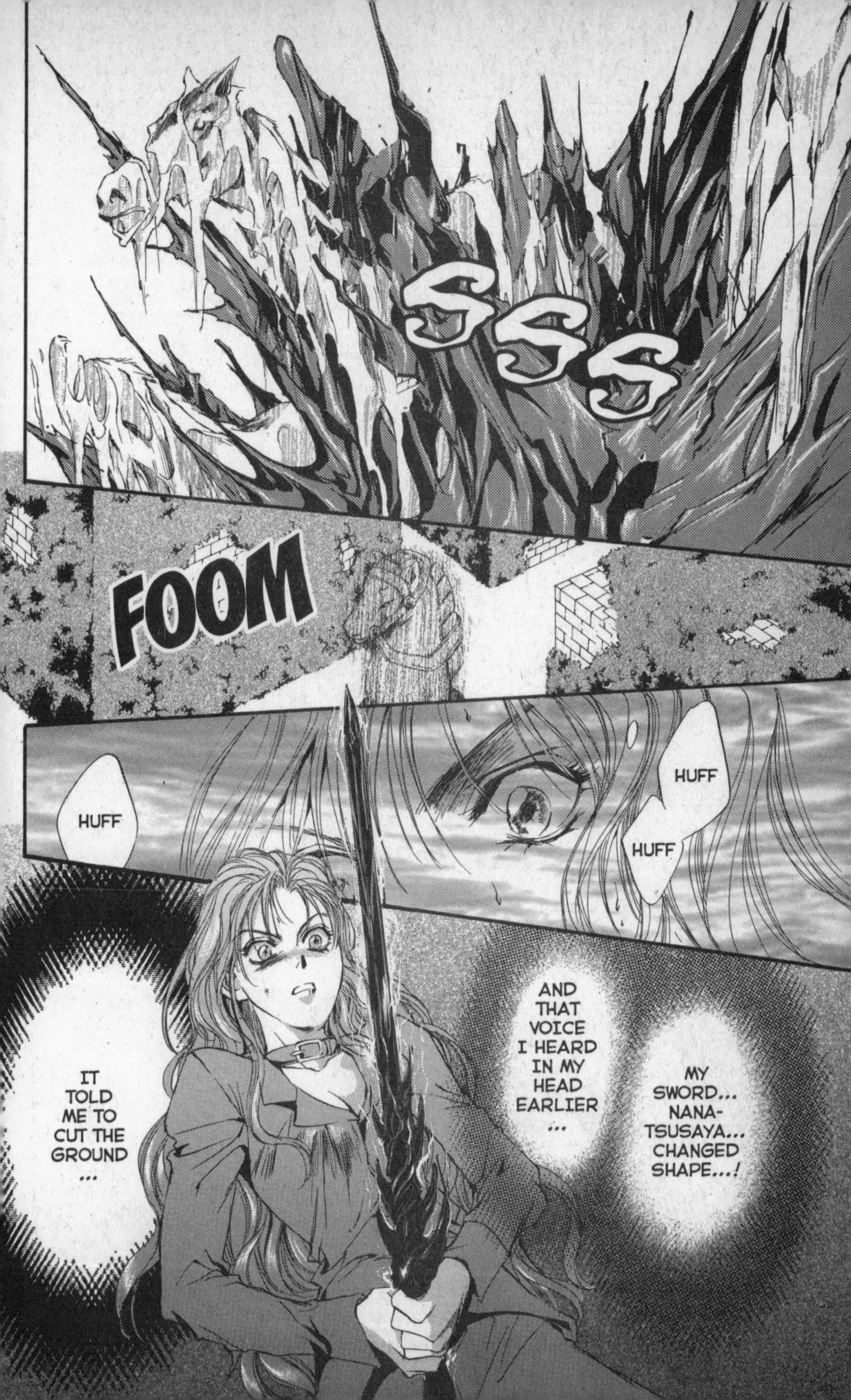
SSS
FOOM
HUFF
HUFF
HUFF
MY SWORD... NANA-TSUSAYA... CHANGED SHAPE...!
AND THAT VOICE I HEARD IN MY HEAD EARLIER...
IT TOLD ME TO CUT THE GROUND...

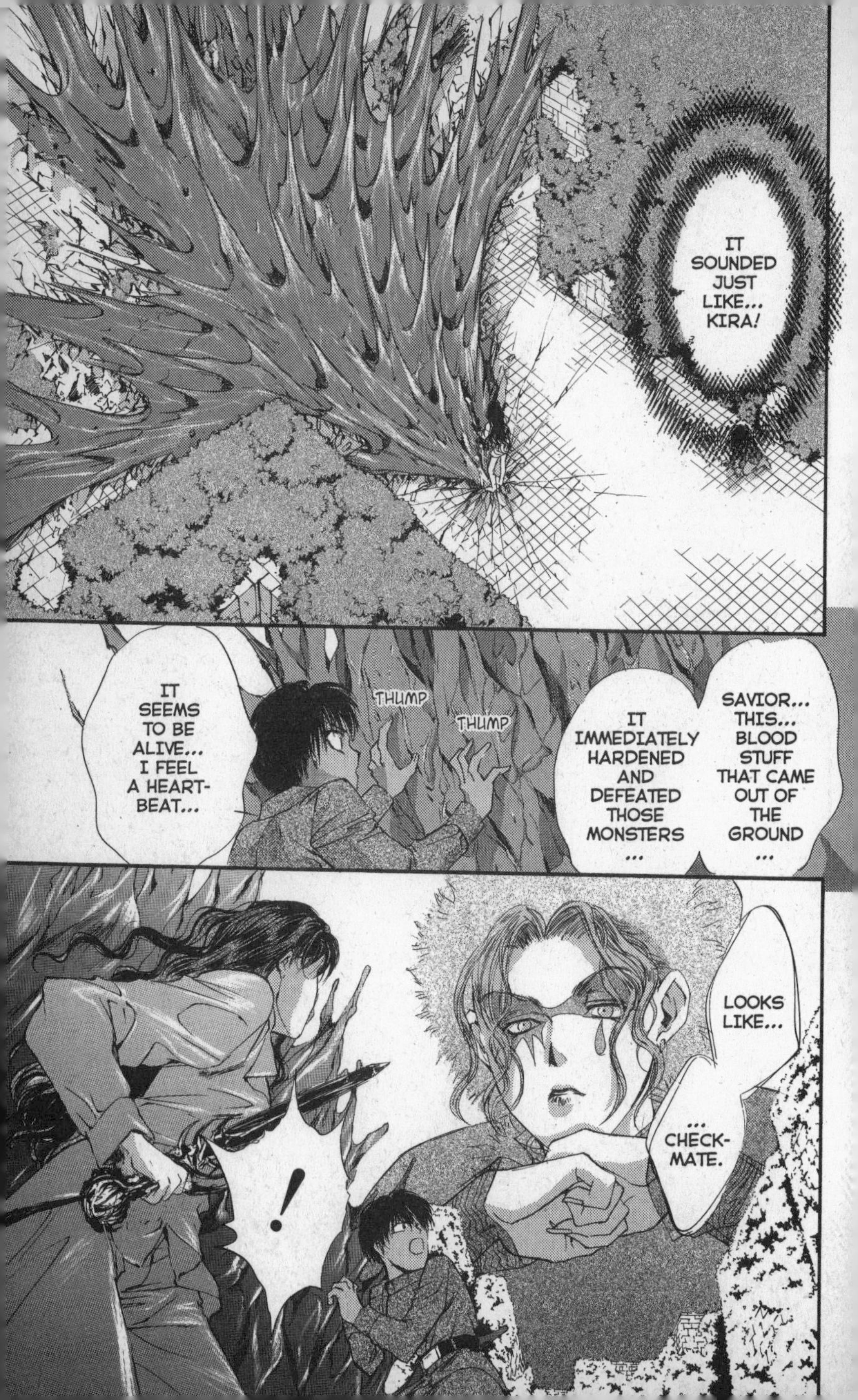
IT SOUNDED JUST LIKE... KIRA!
SAVIOR... THIS... BLOOD STUFF THAT CAME OUT OF THE GROUND ...
IT IMMEDIATELY HARDENED AND DEFEATED THOSE MONSTERS ...
THUMP
THUMP
IT SEEMS TO BE ALIVE... I FEEL A HEART-BEAT...
LOOKS LIKE...
... CHECK-MATE.
!

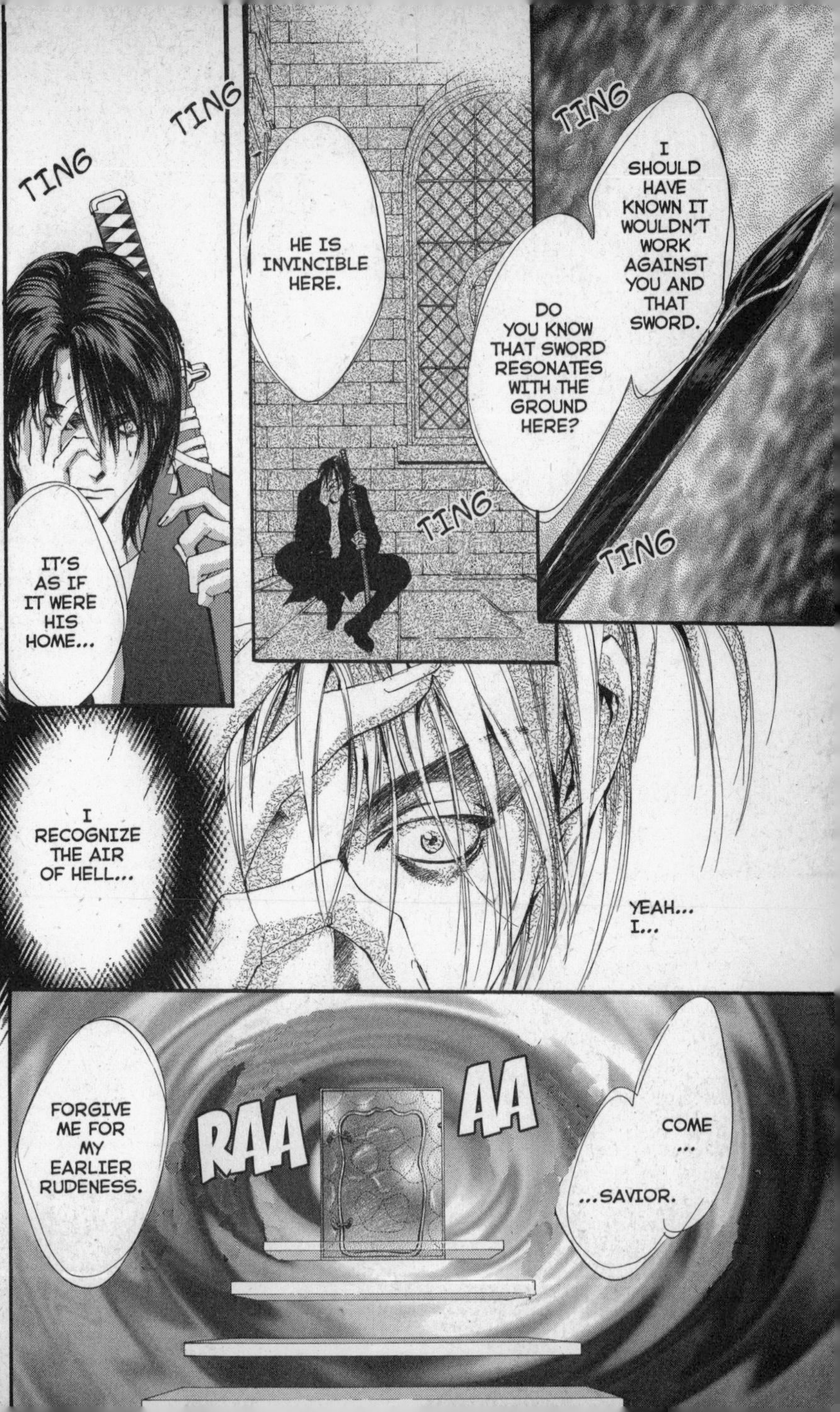
TING
I SHOULD HAVE KNOWN IT WOULDN'T WORK AGAINST YOU AND THAT SWORD.
DO YOU KNOW THAT SWORD RESONATES WITH THE GROUND HERE?
TING
TING
HE IS INVINCIBLE HERE.
TING
TING
TING
IT'S AS IF IT WERE HIS HOME...
YEAH... I...
I RECOGNIZE THE AIR OF HELL...
COME ...
...SAVIOR.
RAA AA
FORGIVE ME FOR MY EARLIER RUDENESS.

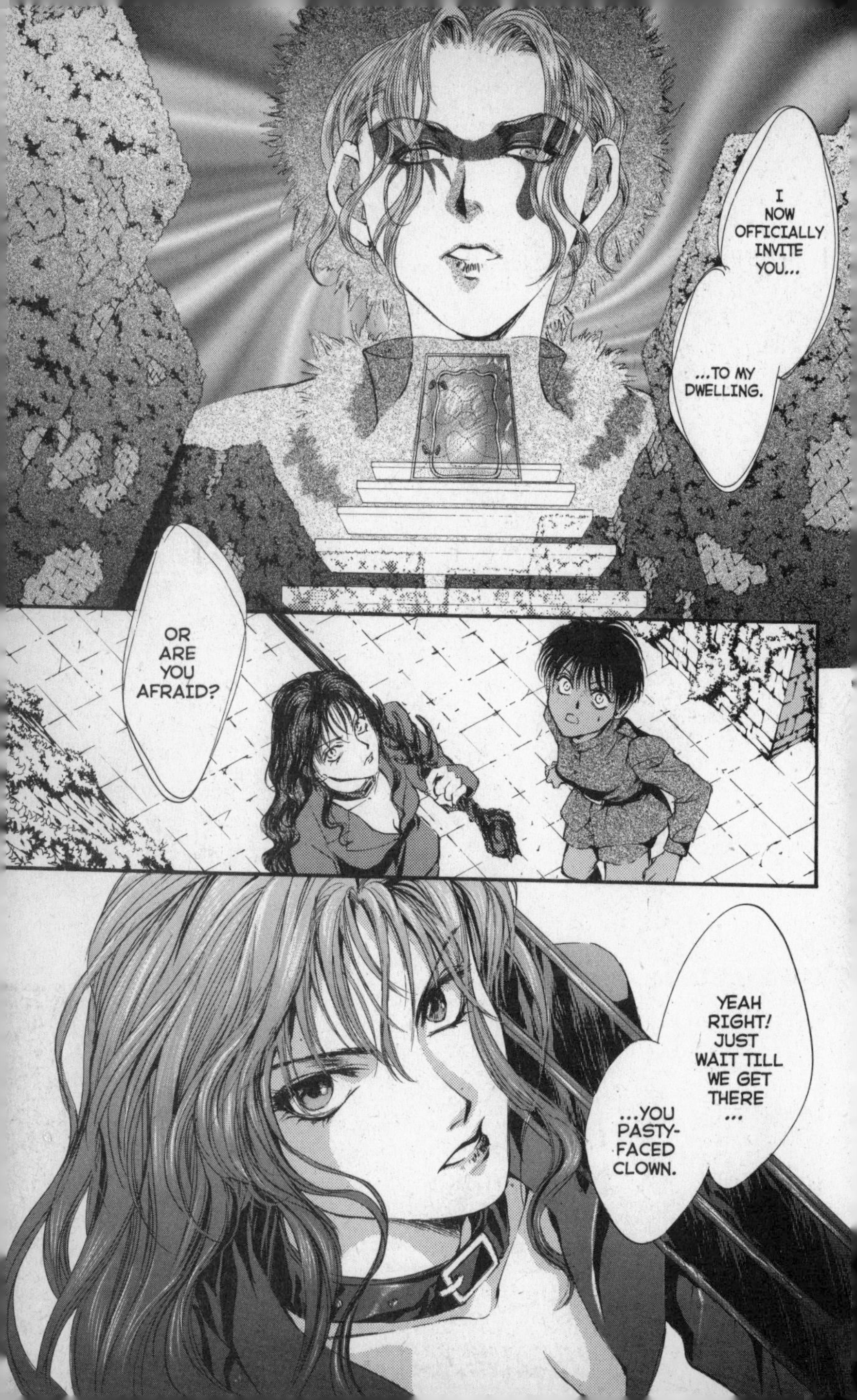
I NOW OFFICIALLY INVITE YOU...
...TO MY DWELLING.
OR ARE YOU AFRAID?
YEAH RIGHT! JUST WAIT TILL WE GET THERE ...
...YOU PASTY-FACED CLOWN.

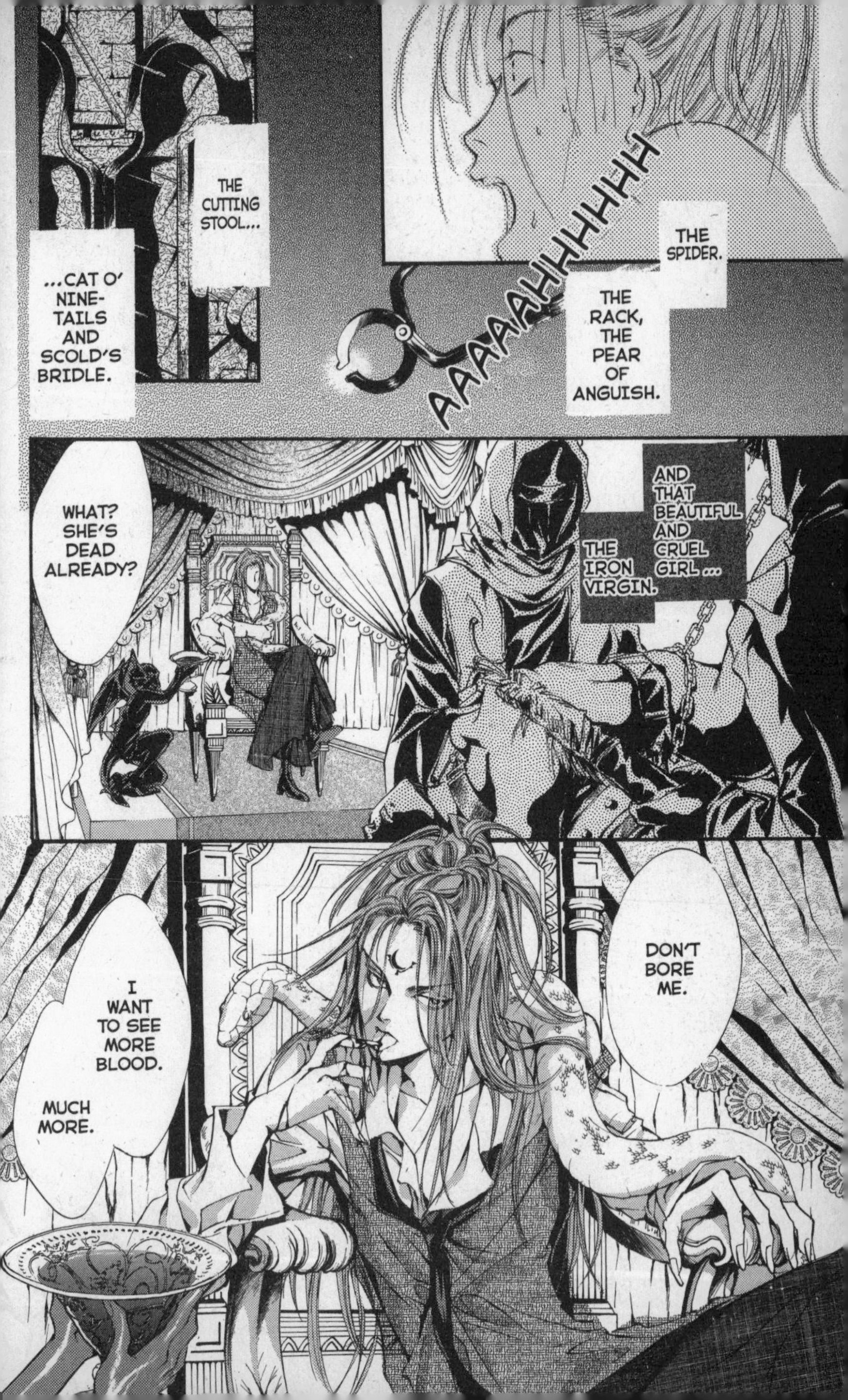
THE SPIDER.
THE RACK, THE PEAR OF ANGUISH.
AAAAAHHHHHHH
THE CUTTING STOOL...
...CAT O' NINE-TAILS AND SCOLD'S BRIDLE.
AND THAT BEAUTIFUL AND CRUEL GIRL ...
THE IRON VIRGIN.
WHAT? SHE'S DEAD ALREADY?
DON'T BORE ME.
I WANT TO SEE MORE BLOOD.
MUCH MORE.

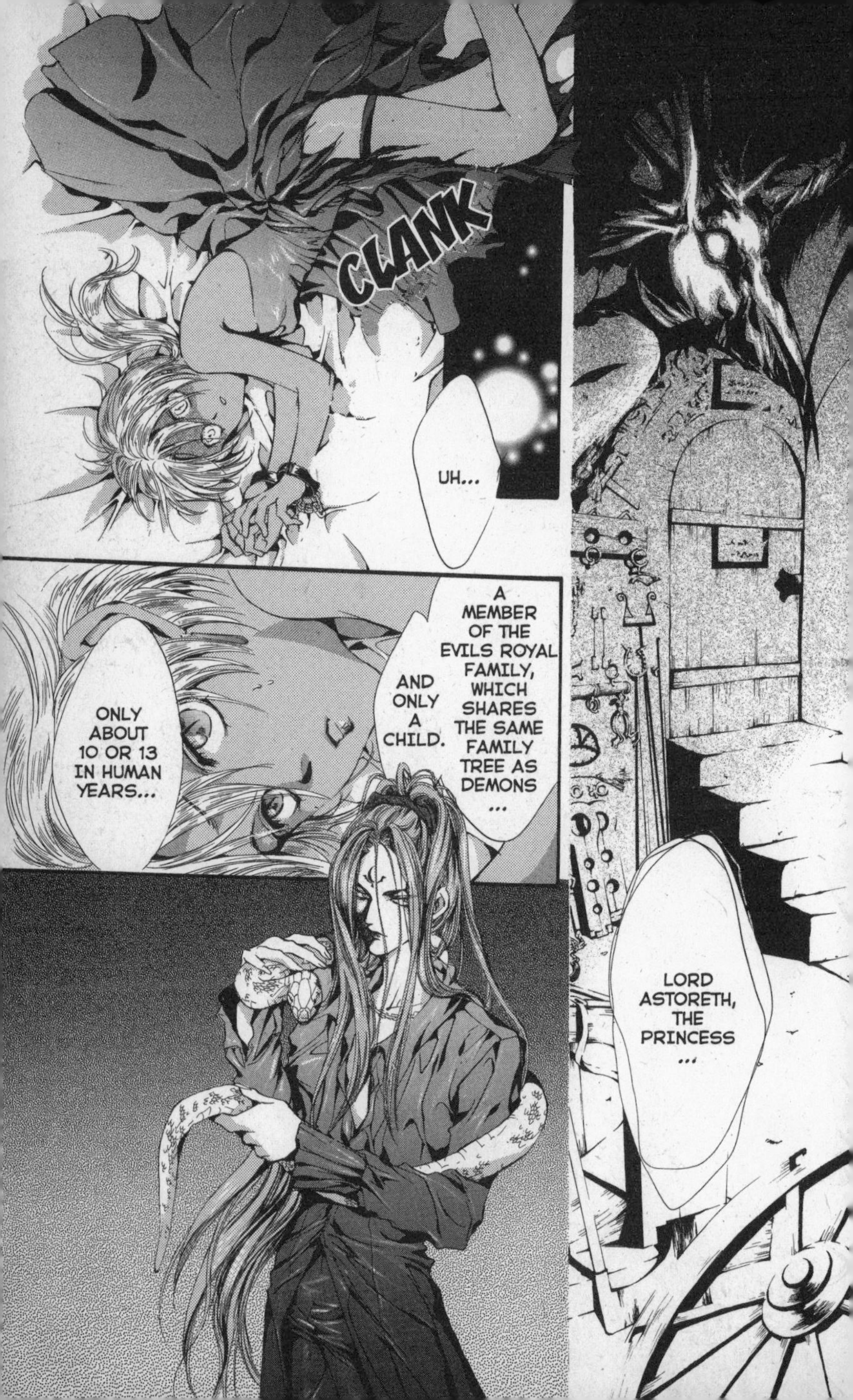
LORD ASTORETH, THE PRINCESS ...
CLANK
UH...
A MEMBER OF THE EVILS ROYAL FAMILY, WHICH SHARES THE SAME FAMILY TREE AS DEMONS ...
AND ONLY A CHILD.
ONLY ABOUT 10 OR 13 IN HUMAN YEARS...

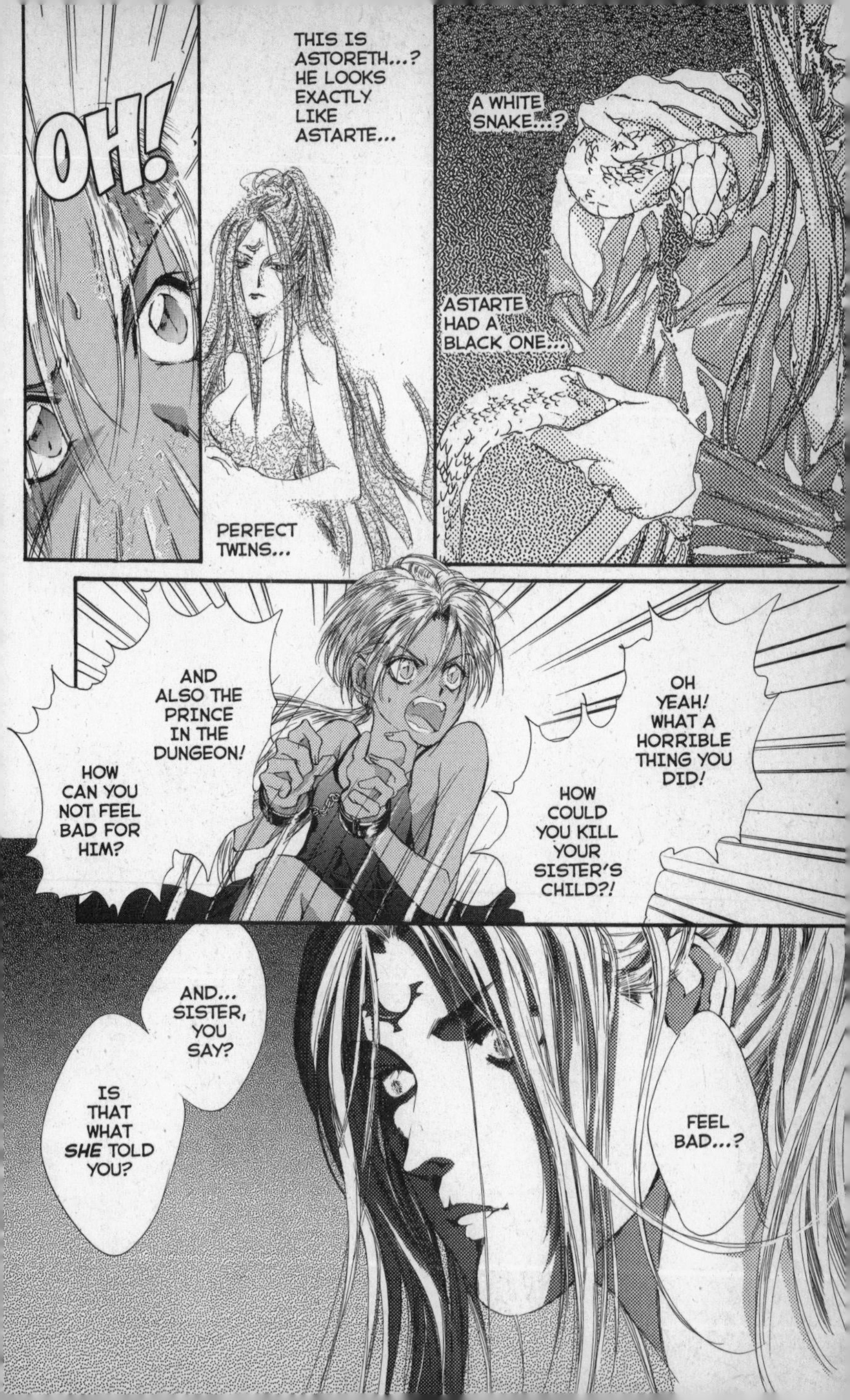
A WHITE SNAKE...?
ASTARTE HAD A BLACK ONE...
THIS IS ASTORETH...? HE LOOKS EXACTLY LIKE ASTARTE...
PERFECT TWINS...
OH!
OH YEAH! WHAT A HORRIBLE THING YOU DID!
HOW COULD YOU KILL YOUR SISTER'S CHILD?!
AND ALSO THE PRINCE IN THE DUNGEON!
HOW CAN YOU NOT FEEL BAD FOR HIM?
FEEL BAD...?
AND... SISTER, YOU SAY?
IS THAT WHAT SHE TOLD YOU?

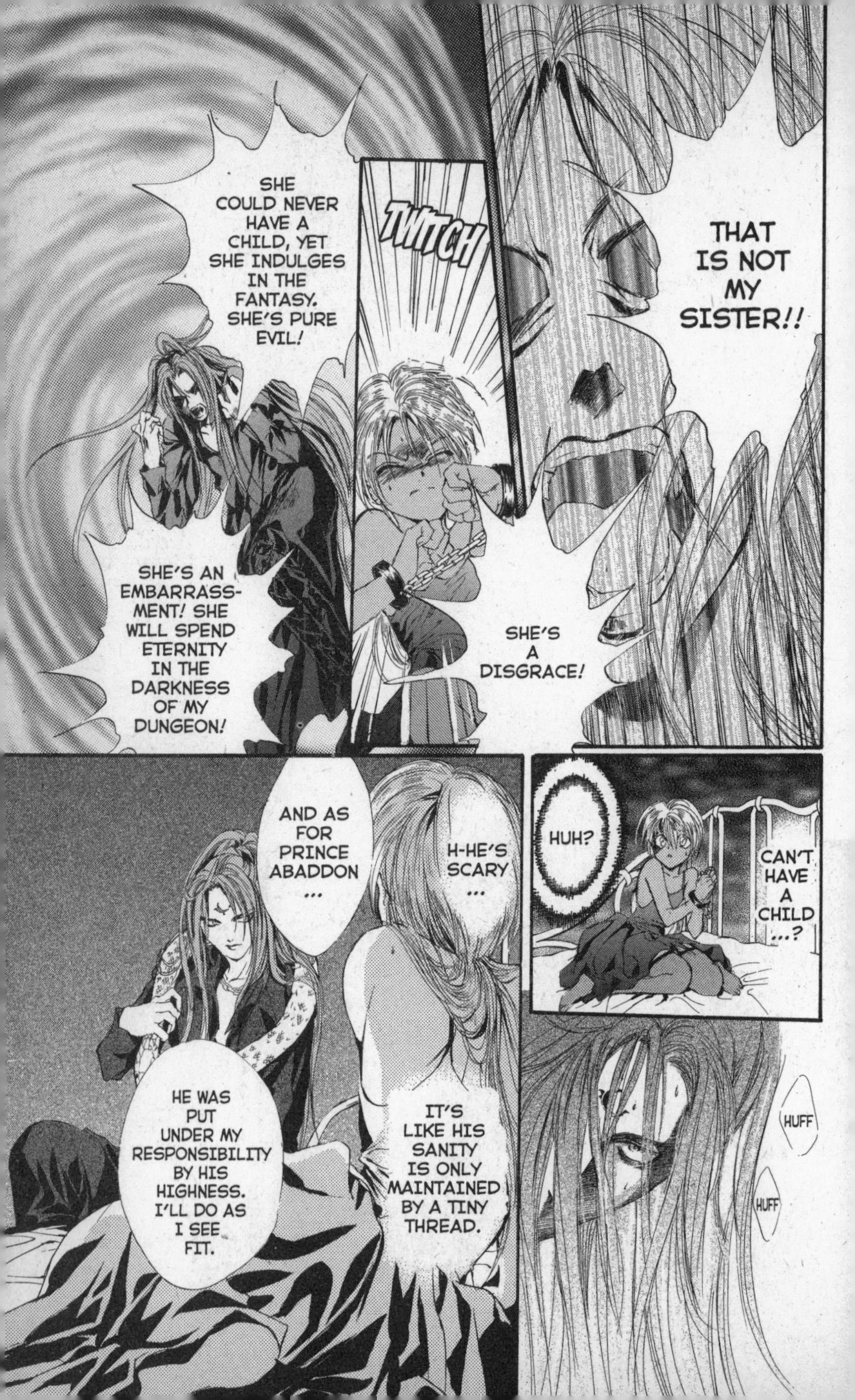
THAT IS NOT MY SISTER!!
TWITCH
SHE'S A DISGRACE!
SHE COULD NEVER HAVE A CHILD, YET SHE INDULGES IN THE FANTASY. SHE'S PURE EVIL!
SHE'S AN EMBARRASS-MENT! SHE WILL SPEND ETERNITY IN THE DARKNESS OF MY DUNGEON!
HUH?
CAN'T HAVE A CHILD ...?
HUFF
HUFF
AND AS FOR PRINCE ABADDON ...
H-HE'S SCARY ...
HE WAS PUT UNDER MY RESPONSIBILITY BY HIS HIGHNESS. I'LL DO AS I SEE FIT.
IT'S LIKE HIS SANITY IS ONLY MAINTAINED BY A TINY THREAD.

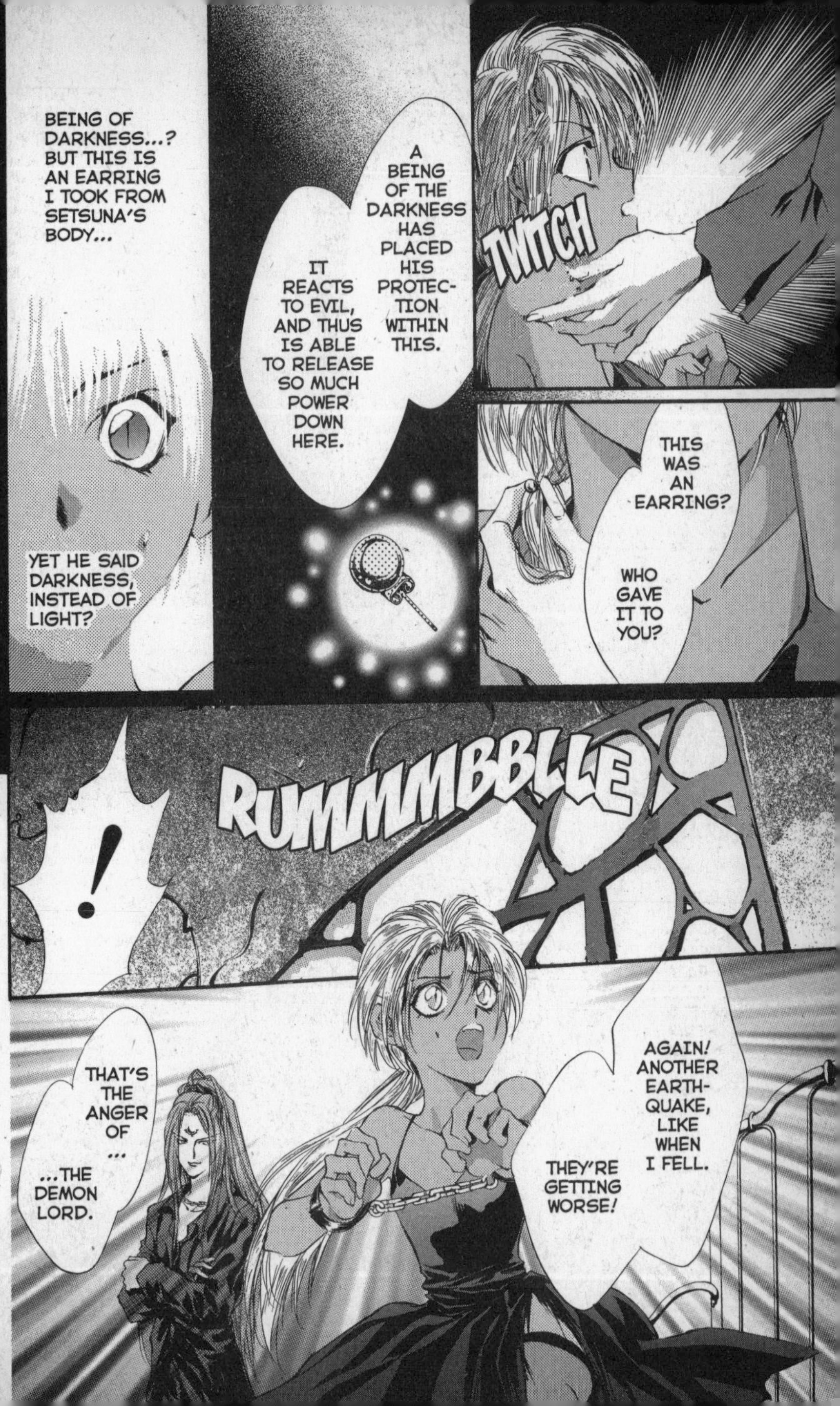
TWITCH
THIS WAS AN EARRING?
WHO GAVE IT TO YOU?
A BEING OF THE DARKNESS HAS PLACED HIS PROTECTION WITHIN THIS.
IT REACTS TO EVIL, AND THUS IS ABLE TO RELEASE SO MUCH POWER DOWN HERE.
BEING OF DARKNESS...? BUT THIS IS AN EARRING I TOOK FROM SETSUNA'S BODY...
YET HE SAID DARKNESS, INSTEAD OF LIGHT?
RUMMMBBLLE
!
AGAIN! ANOTHER EARTHQUAKE, LIKE WHEN I FELL.
THEY'RE GETTING WORSE!
THAT'S THE ANGER OF ...
...THE DEMON LORD.

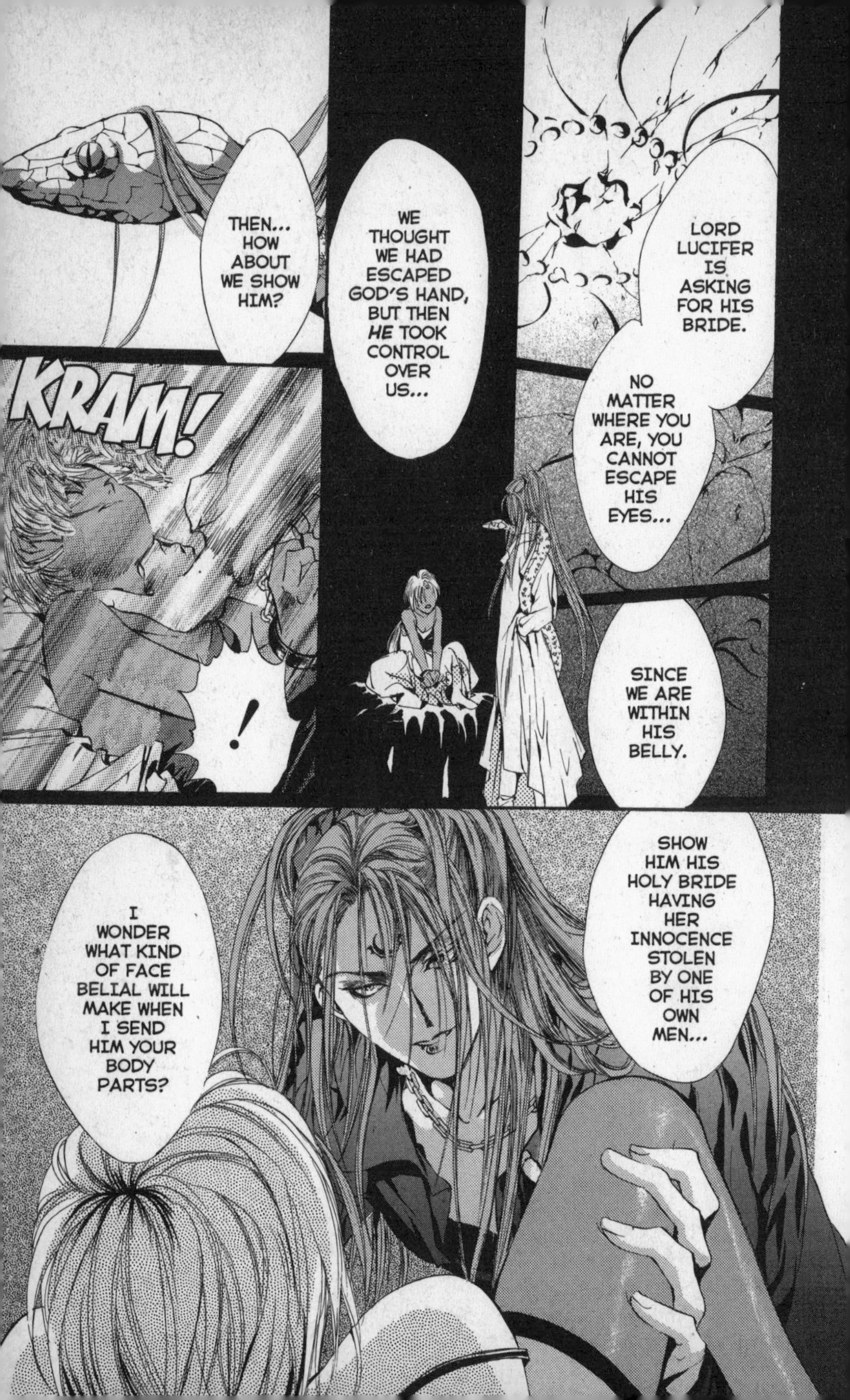
LORD LUCIFER IS ASKING FOR HIS BRIDE.
NO MATTER WHERE YOU ARE, YOU CANNOT ESCAPE HIS EYES...
SINCE WE ARE WITHIN HIS BELLY.
WE THOUGHT WE HAD ESCAPED GOD'S HAND, BUT THEN *HE* TOOK CONTROL OVER US...
THEN... HOW ABOUT WE SHOW HIM?
KRAM!
!
SHOW HIM HIS HOLY BRIDE HAVING HER INNOCENCE STOLEN BY ONE OF HIS OWN MEN...
I WONDER WHAT KIND OF FACE BELIAL WILL MAKE WHEN I SEND HIM YOUR BODY PARTS?

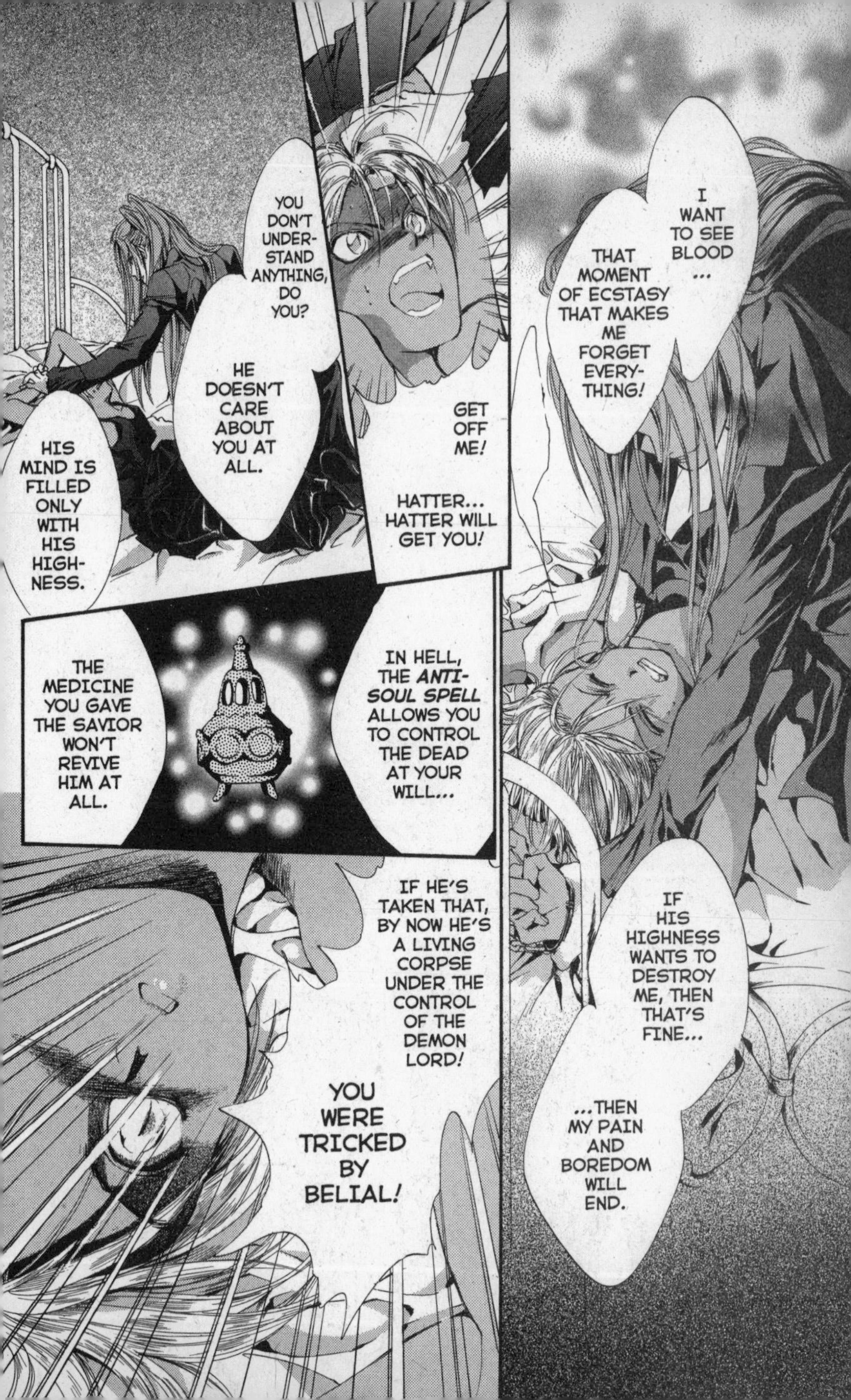
I WANT TO SEE BLOOD ...
THAT MOMENT OF ECSTASY THAT MAKES ME FORGET EVERY-THING!
IF HIS HIGHNESS WANTS TO DESTROY ME, THEN THAT'S FINE...
...THEN MY PAIN AND BOREDOM WILL END.
GET OFF ME!
HATTER... HATTER WILL GET YOU!
YOU DON'T UNDER-STAND ANYTHING, DO YOU?
HE DOESN'T CARE ABOUT YOU AT ALL.
HIS MIND IS FILLED ONLY WITH HIS HIGH-NESS.
IN HELL, THE *ANTI-SOUL SPELL* ALLOWS YOU TO CONTROL THE DEAD AT YOUR WILL...
THE MEDICINE YOU GAVE THE SAVIOR WON'T REVIVE HIM AT ALL.
IF HE'S TAKEN THAT, BY NOW HE'S A LIVING CORPSE UNDER THE CONTROL OF THE DEMON LORD!
YOU WERE TRICKED BY BELIAL!

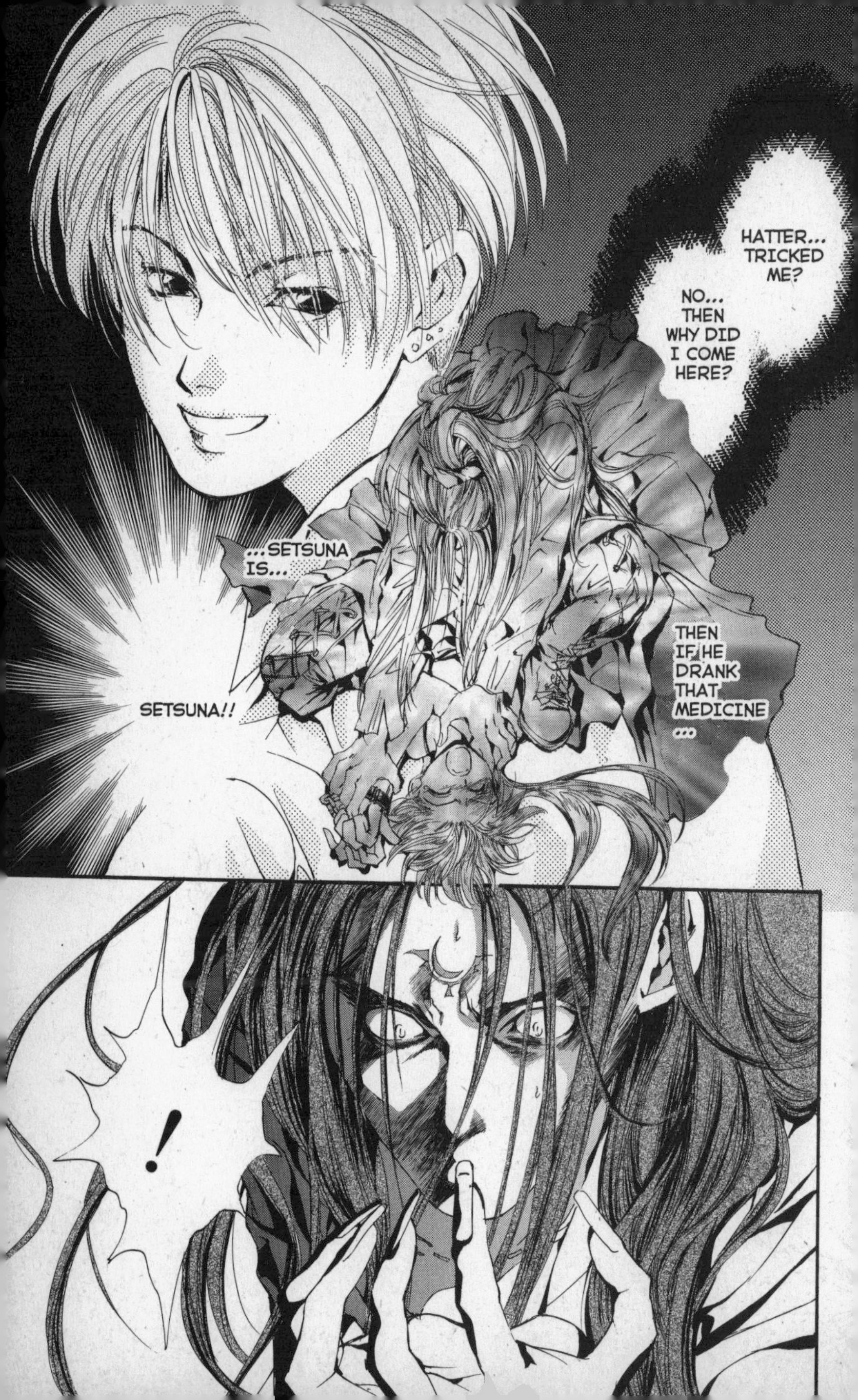
HATTER... TRICKED ME?
NO... THEN WHY DID I COME HERE?
THEN IF HE DRANK THAT MEDICINE ...
...SETSUNA IS...
SETSUNA!!
!

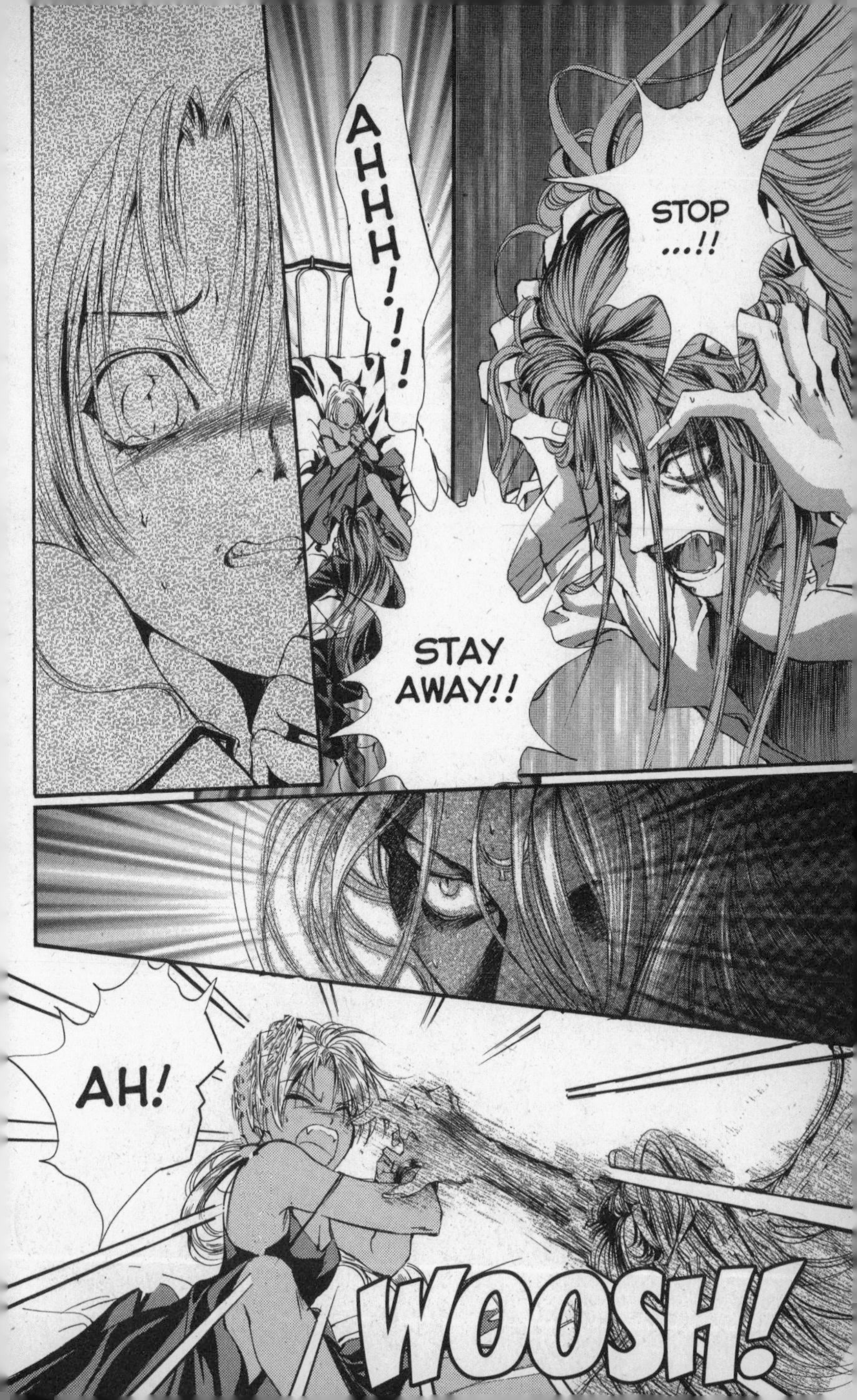
STOP ...!!
STAY AWAY!!
AHHH!!!
AH!
WOOSH!

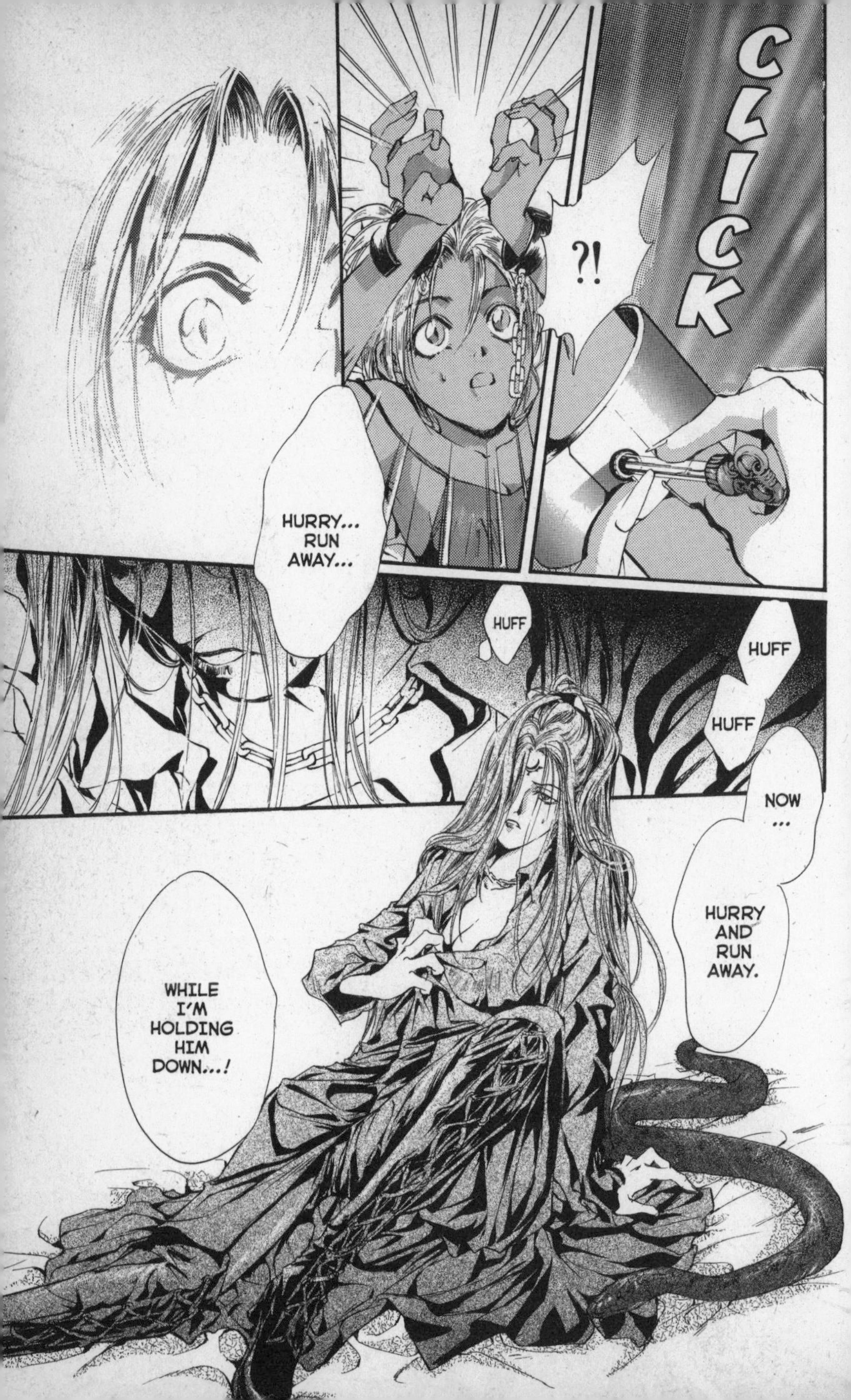
CLICK
?!
HURRY... RUN AWAY...
HUFF
HUFF
HUFF
NOW ...
HURRY AND RUN AWAY.
WHILE I'M HOLDING HIM DOWN...!

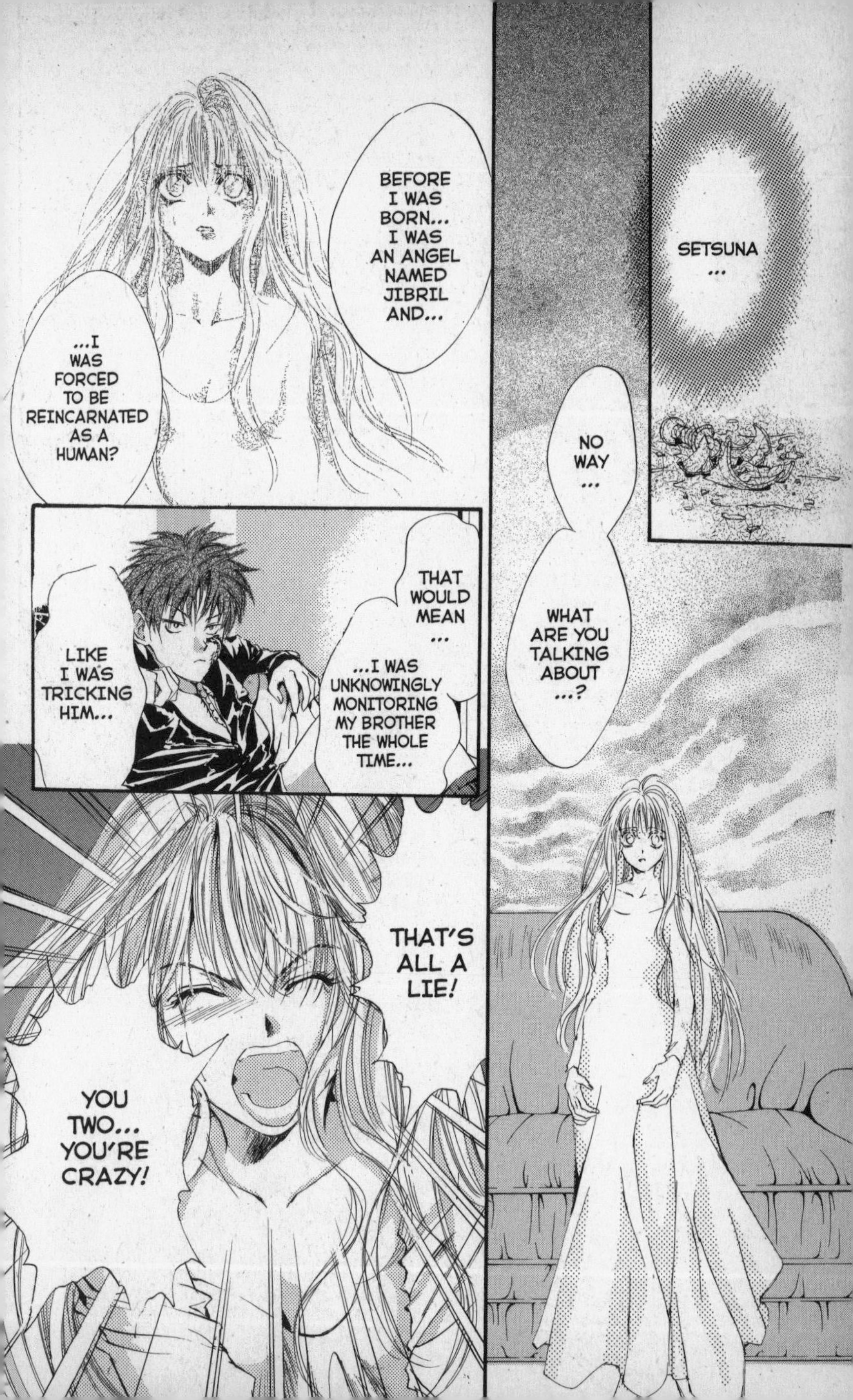
SETSUNA ...
NO WAY ...
WHAT ARE YOU TALKING ABOUT ...?
BEFORE I WAS BORN... I WAS AN ANGEL NAMED JIBRIL AND...
...I WAS FORCED TO BE REINCARNATED AS A HUMAN?
THAT WOULD MEAN ...
...I WAS UNKNOWINGLY MONITORING MY BROTHER THE WHOLE TIME...
LIKE I WAS TRICKING HIM...
THAT'S ALL A LIE!
YOU TWO... YOU'RE CRAZY!

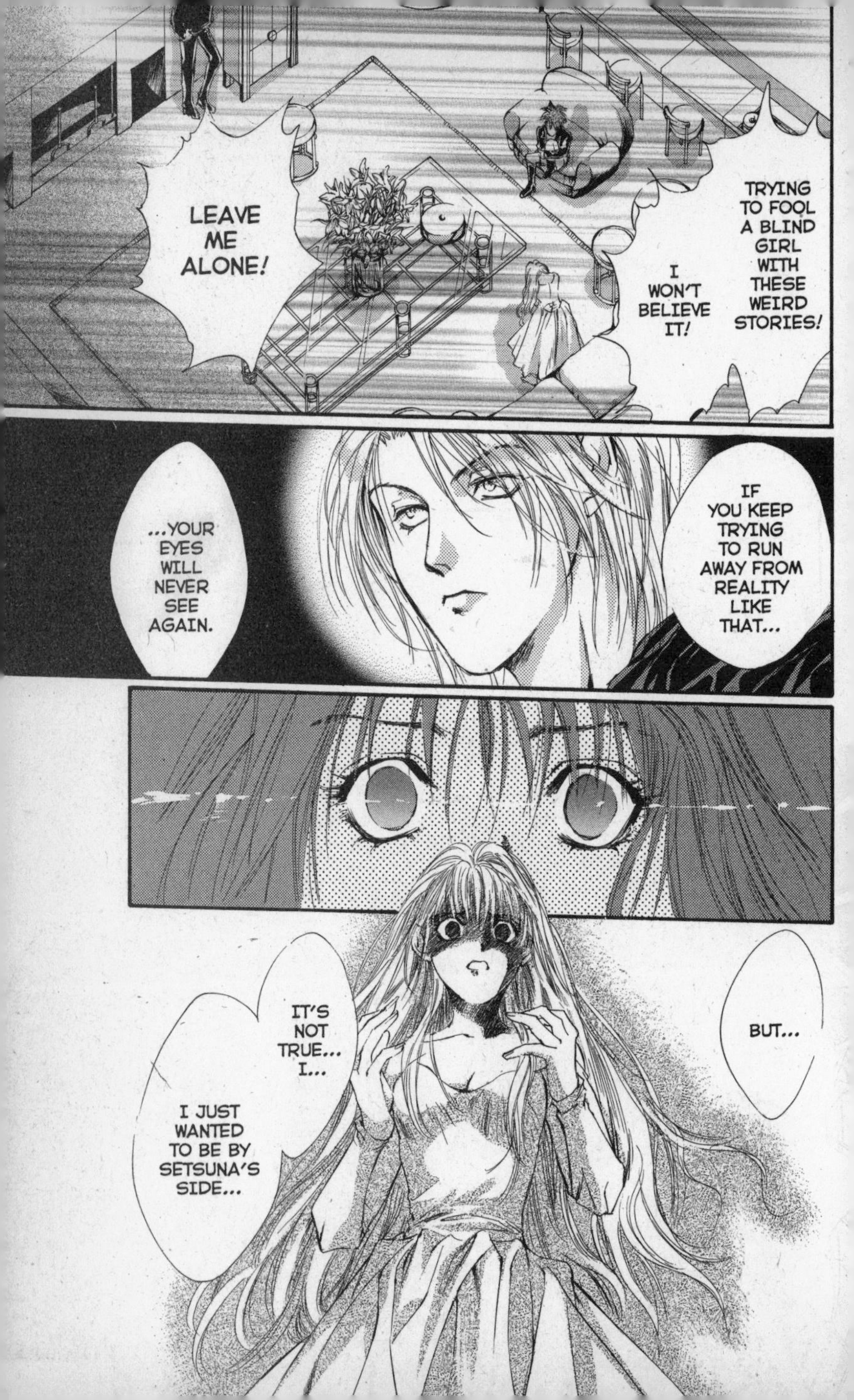
TRYING TO FOOL A BLIND GIRL WITH THESE WEIRD STORIES!
I WON'T BELIEVE IT!
LEAVE ME ALONE!
IF YOU KEEP TRYING TO RUN AWAY FROM REALITY LIKE THAT...
...YOUR EYES WILL NEVER SEE AGAIN.
BUT...
IT'S NOT TRUE... I...
I JUST WANTED TO BE BY SETSUNA'S SIDE...

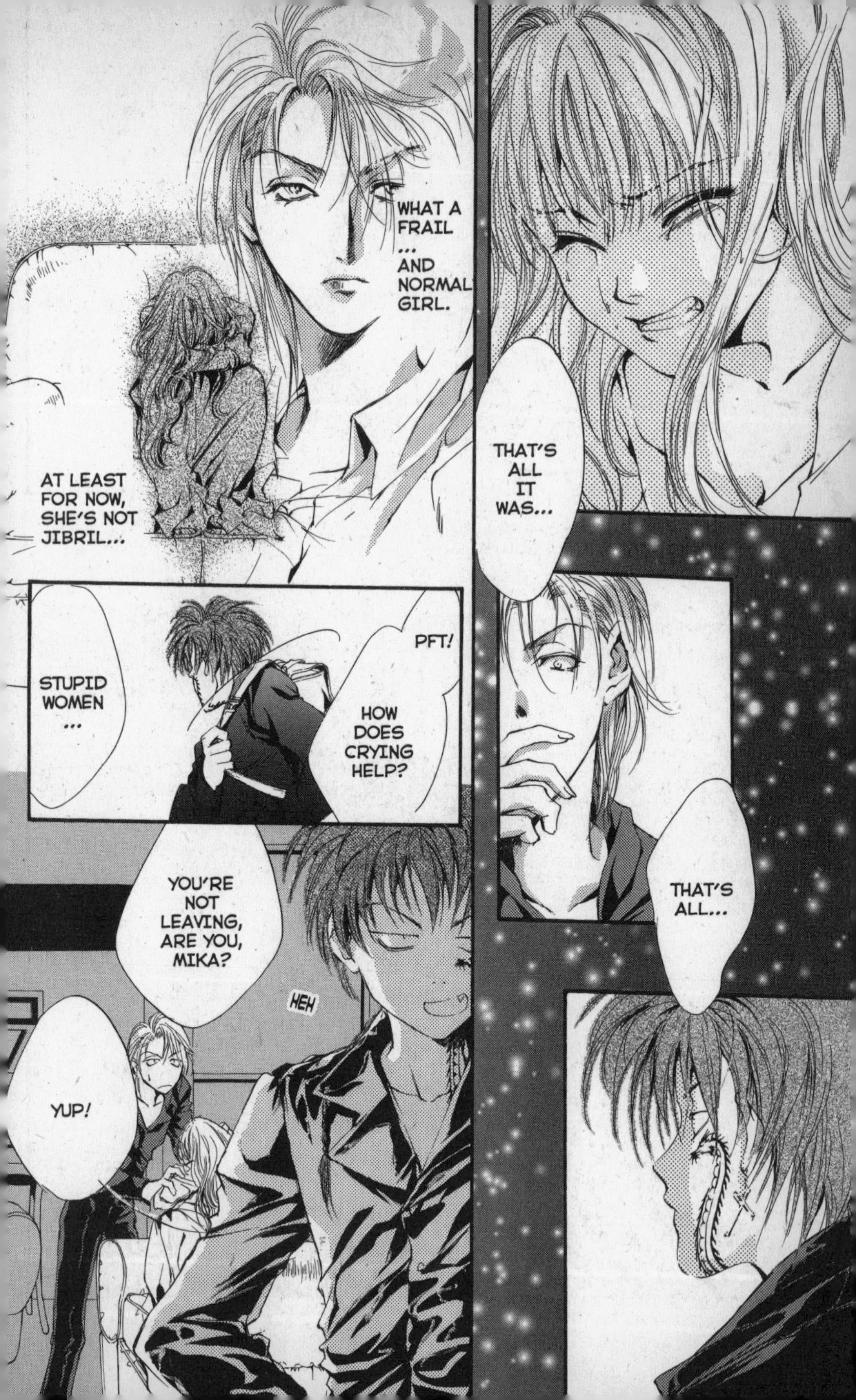
THAT'S ALL IT WAS...
THAT'S ALL...
WHAT A FRAIL ... AND NORMAL GIRL.
AT LEAST FOR NOW, SHE'S NOT JIBRIL...
PFT!
HOW DOES CRYING HELP?
STUPID WOMEN ...
YOU'RE NOT LEAVING, ARE YOU, MIKA?
HEH
YUP!

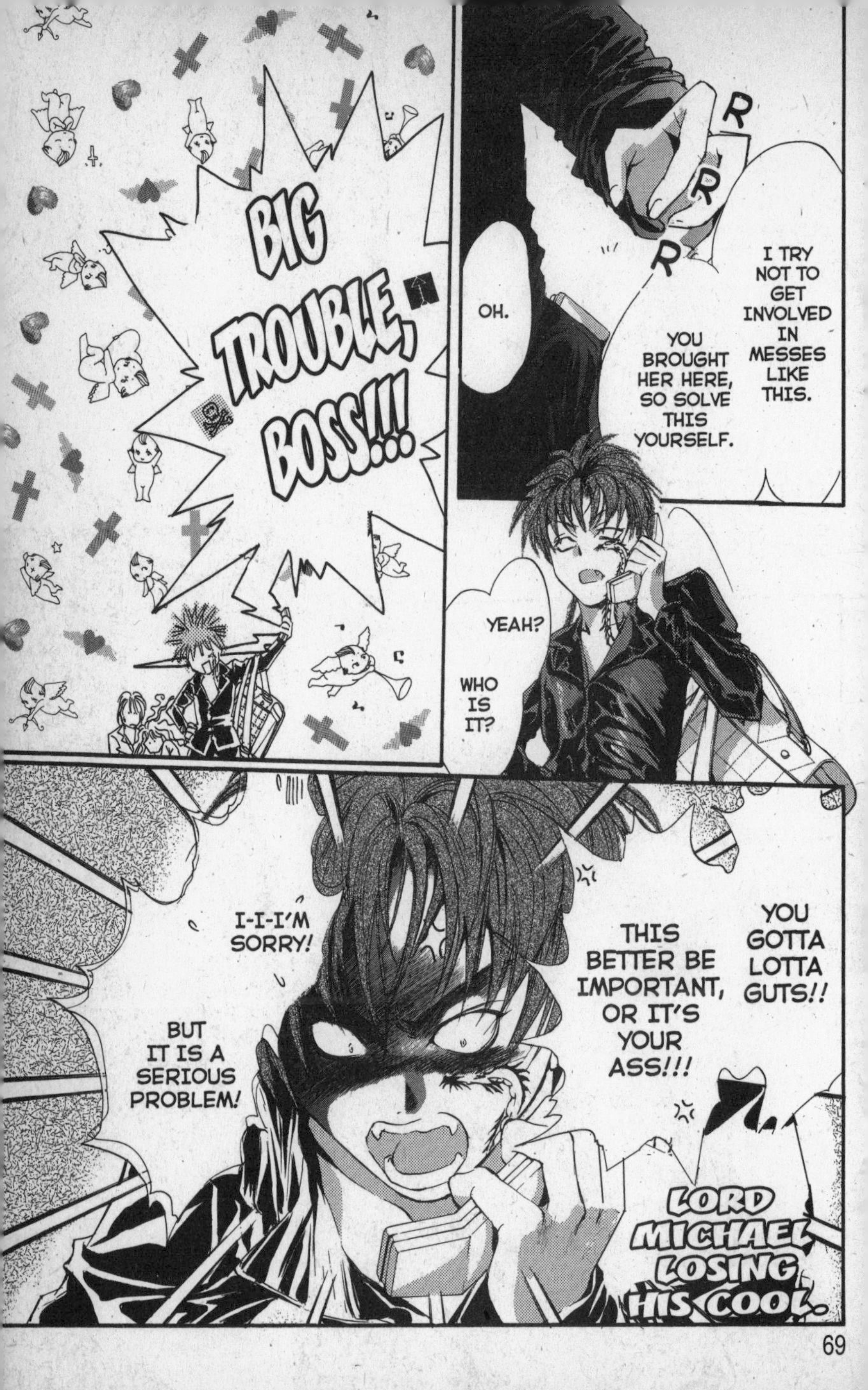
R
R
R
I TRY NOT TO GET INVOLVED IN MESSES LIKE THIS.
YOU BROUGHT HER HERE, SO SOLVE THIS YOURSELF.
OH.
BIG TROUBLE, BOSS!!!
YEAH?
WHO IS IT?
YOU GOTTA LOTTA GUTS!!
THIS BETTER BE IMPORTANT, OR IT'S YOUR ASS!!!
I-I-I'M SORRY!
BUT IT IS A SERIOUS PROBLEM!
LORD MICHAEL LOSING HIS COOL.

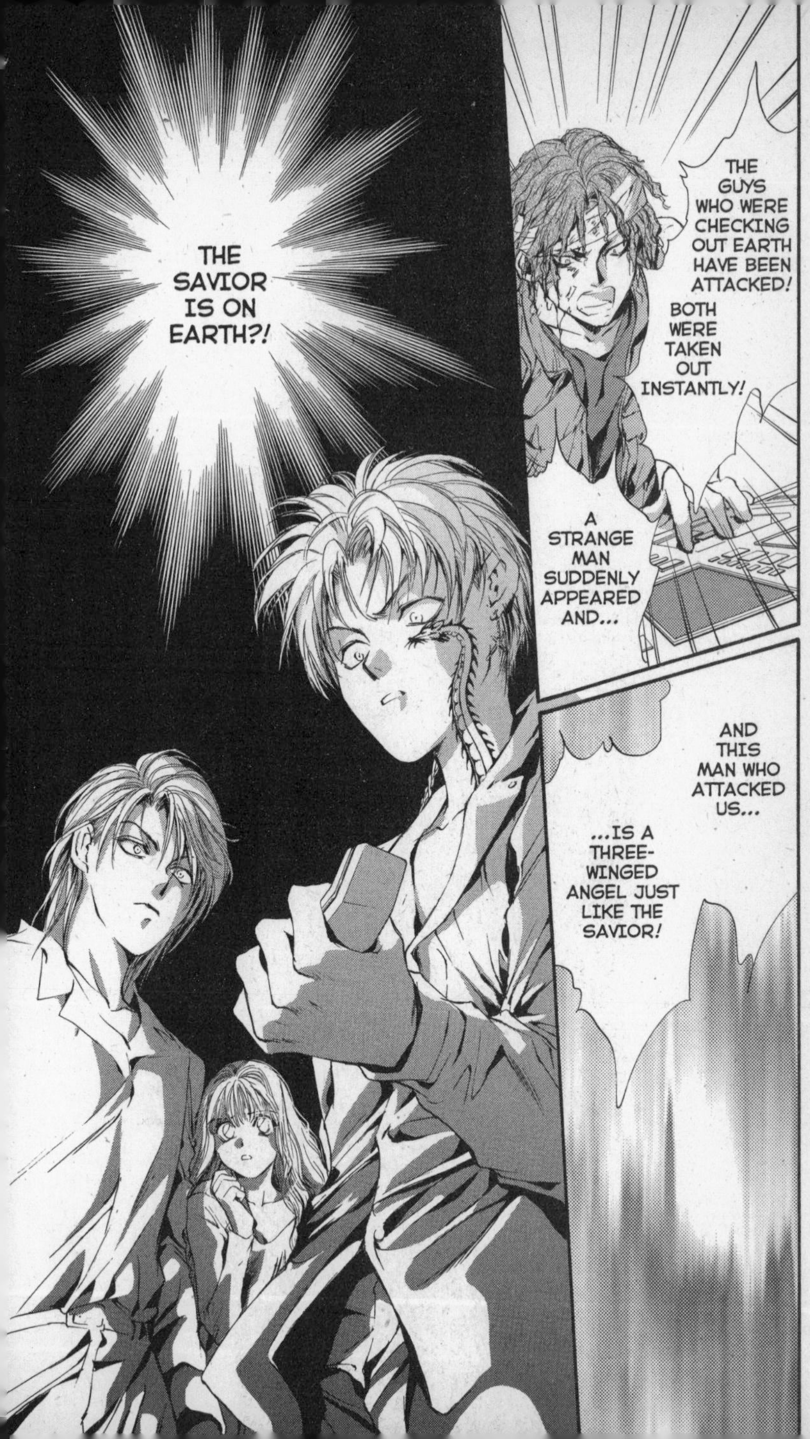
THE GUYS WHO WERE CHECKING OUT EARTH HAVE BEEN ATTACKED!
BOTH WERE TAKEN OUT INSTANTLY!
A STRANGE MAN SUDDENLY APPEARED AND...
AND THIS MAN WHO ATTACKED US...
...IS A THREE-WINGED ANGEL JUST LIKE THE SAVIOR!
THE SAVIOR IS ON EARTH?!

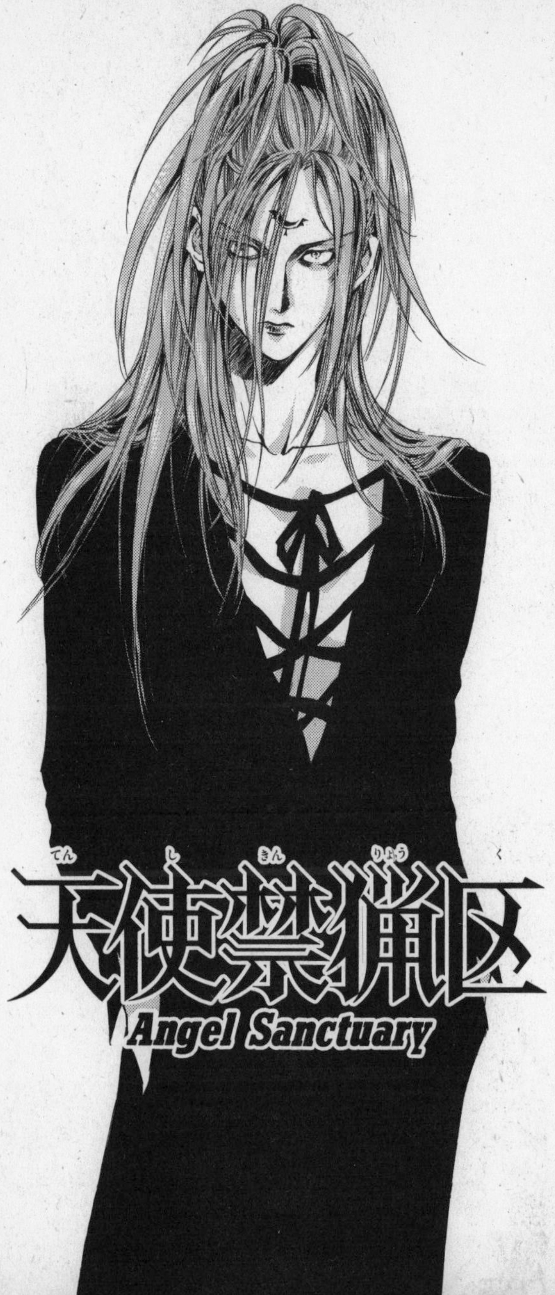
天使禁猟区
Angel Sanctuary

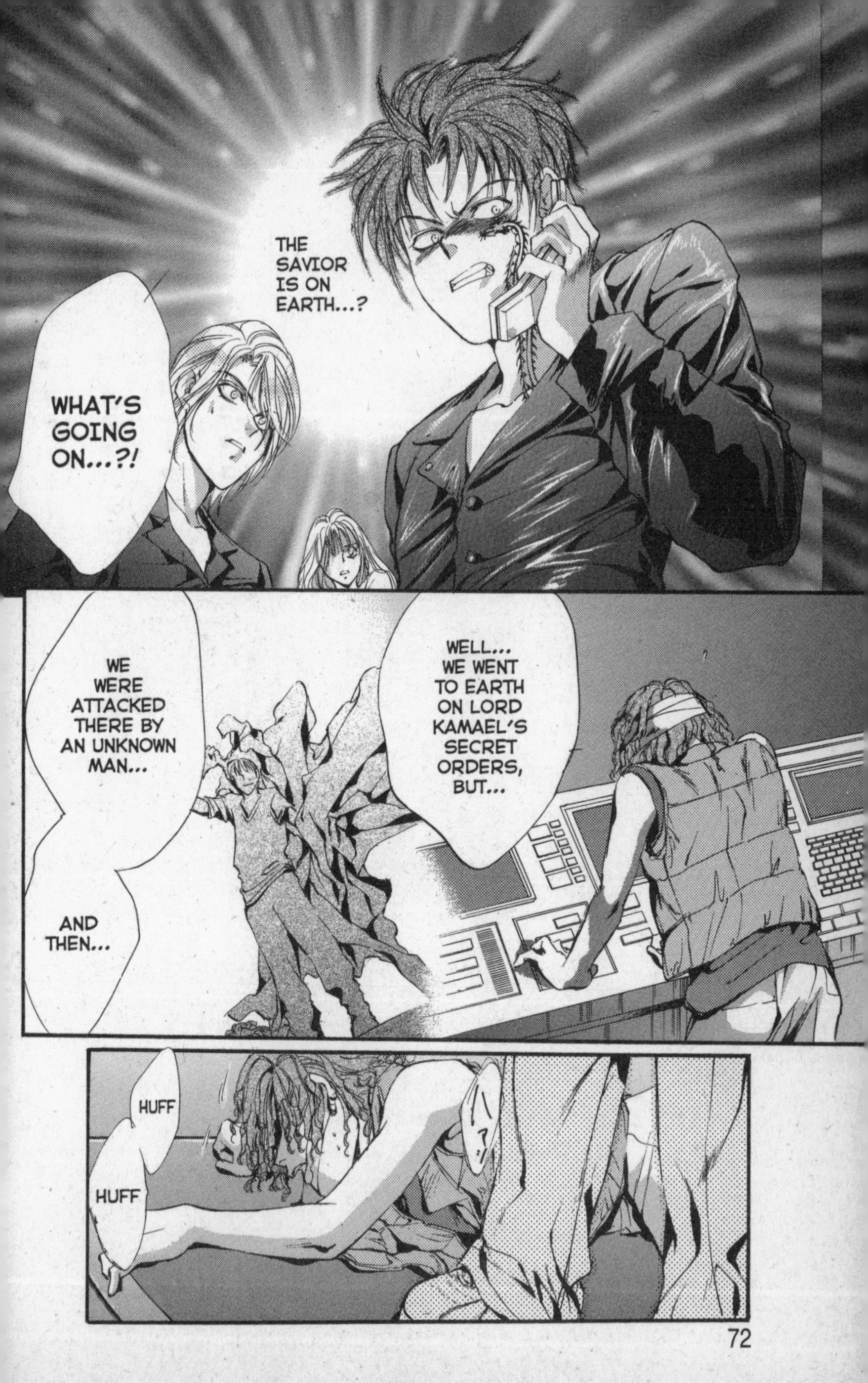
THE SAVIOR IS ON EARTH...?
WHAT'S GOING ON...?!
WELL... WE WENT TO EARTH ON LORD KAMAEL'S SECRET ORDERS, BUT...
WE WERE ATTACKED THERE BY AN UNKNOWN MAN...
AND THEN...
HUFF
HUFF

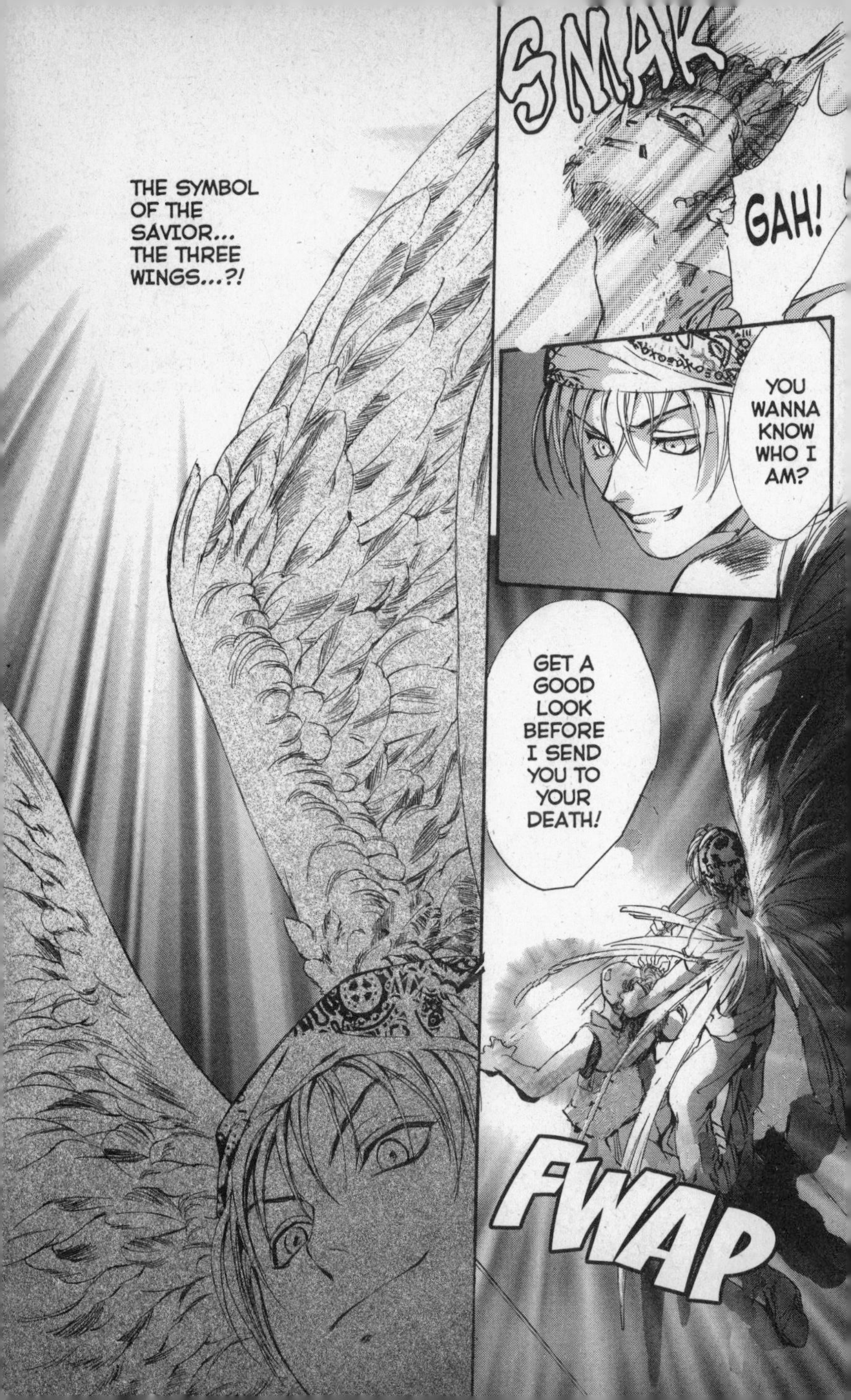
SMAK
GAH!
YOU WANNA KNOW WHO I AM?
GET A GOOD LOOK BEFORE I SEND YOU TO YOUR DEATH!
FWAP
THE SYMBOL OF THE SAVIOR... THE THREE WINGS...?!

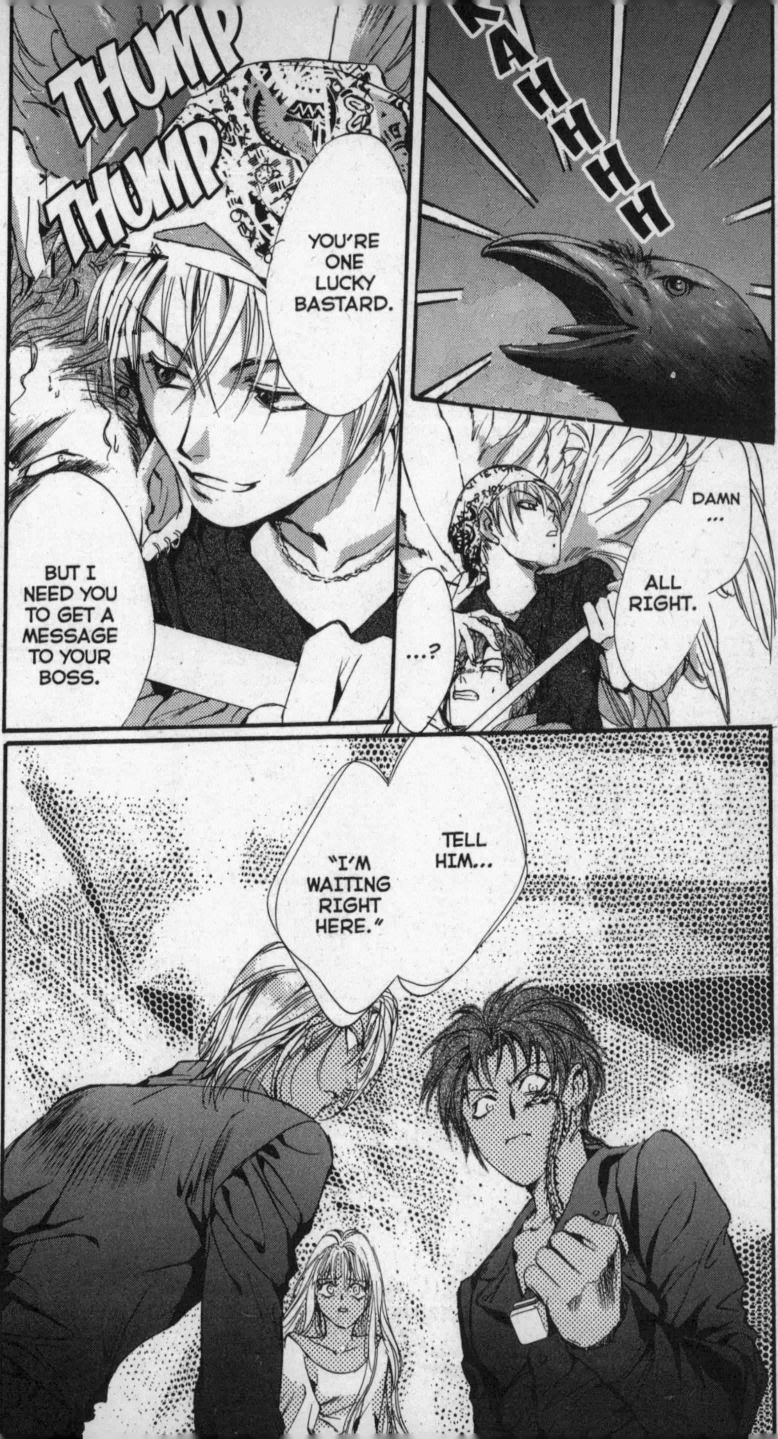
AHHHHHH
DAMN ...
ALL RIGHT.
...?
THUMP
THUMP
YOU'RE ONE LUCKY BASTARD.
BUT I NEED YOU TO GET A MESSAGE TO YOUR BOSS.
TELL HIM...
"I'M WAITING RIGHT HERE."

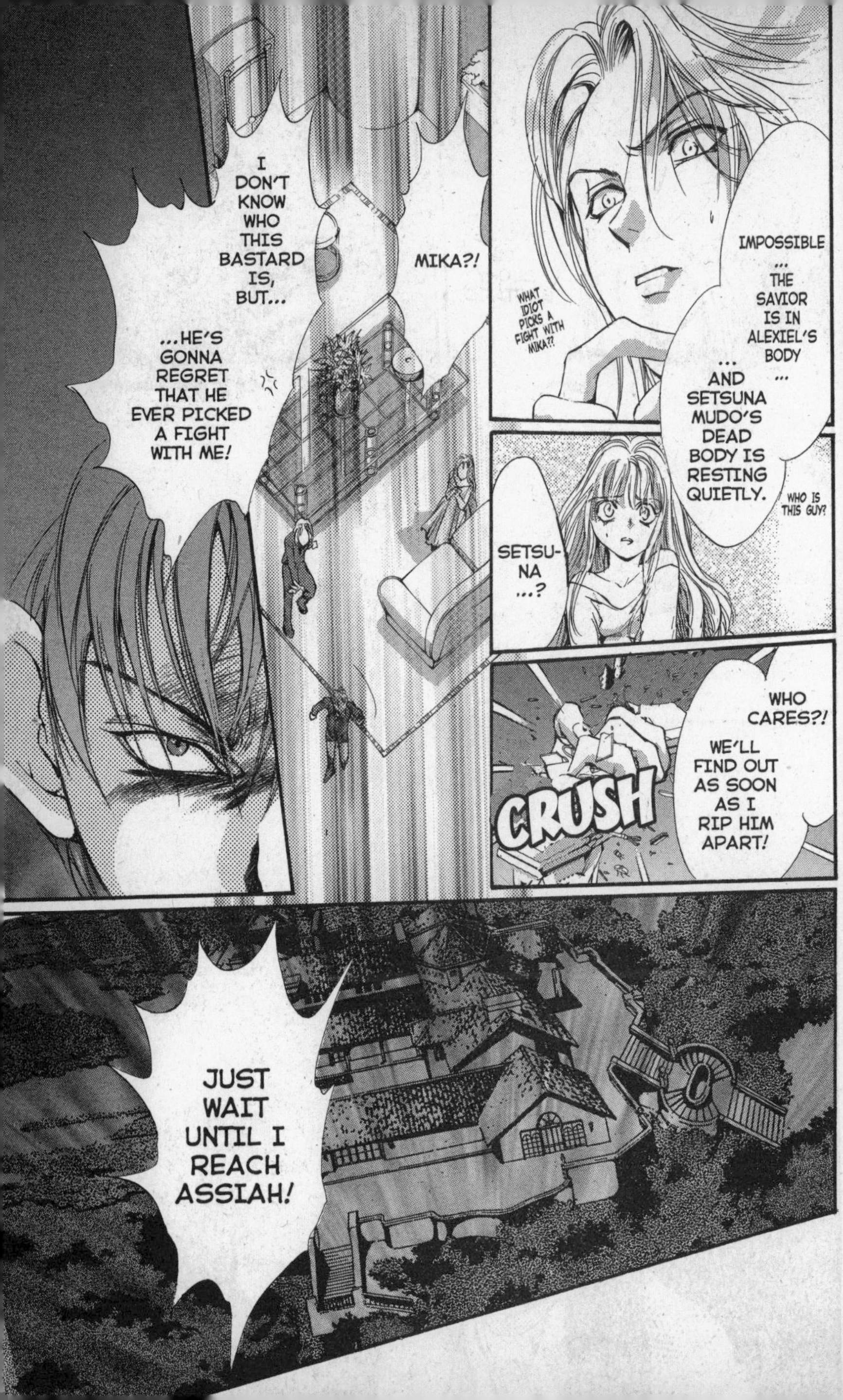
IMPOSSIBLE ... THE SAVIOR IS IN ALEXIEL'S BODY ...
... AND SETSUNA MUDO'S DEAD BODY IS RESTING QUIETLY.
WHAT IDIOT PICKS A FIGHT WITH MIKA??
WHO IS THIS GUY?
SETSU-NA ...?
WHO CARES?!
WE'LL FIND OUT AS SOON AS I RIP HIM APART!
CRUSH
MIKA?!
I DON'T KNOW WHO THIS BASTARD IS, BUT...
...HE'S GONNA REGRET THAT HE EVER PICKED A FIGHT WITH ME!
JUST WAIT UNTIL I REACH ASSIAH!

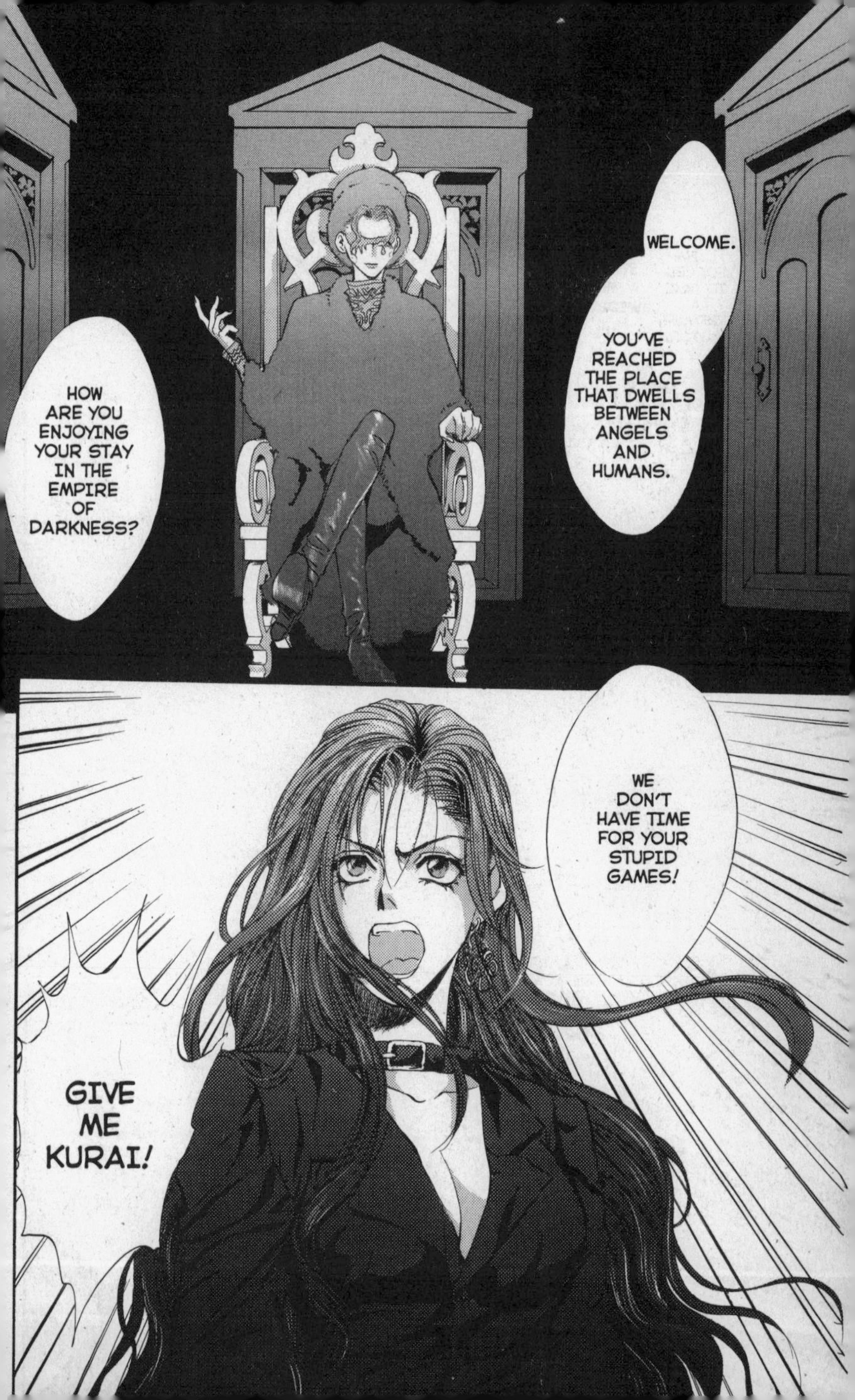
WELCOME.
YOU'VE REACHED THE PLACE THAT DWELLS BETWEEN ANGELS AND HUMANS.
HOW ARE YOU ENJOYING YOUR STAY IN THE EMPIRE OF DARKNESS?
WE DON'T HAVE TIME FOR YOUR STUPID GAMES!
GIVE ME KURAI!

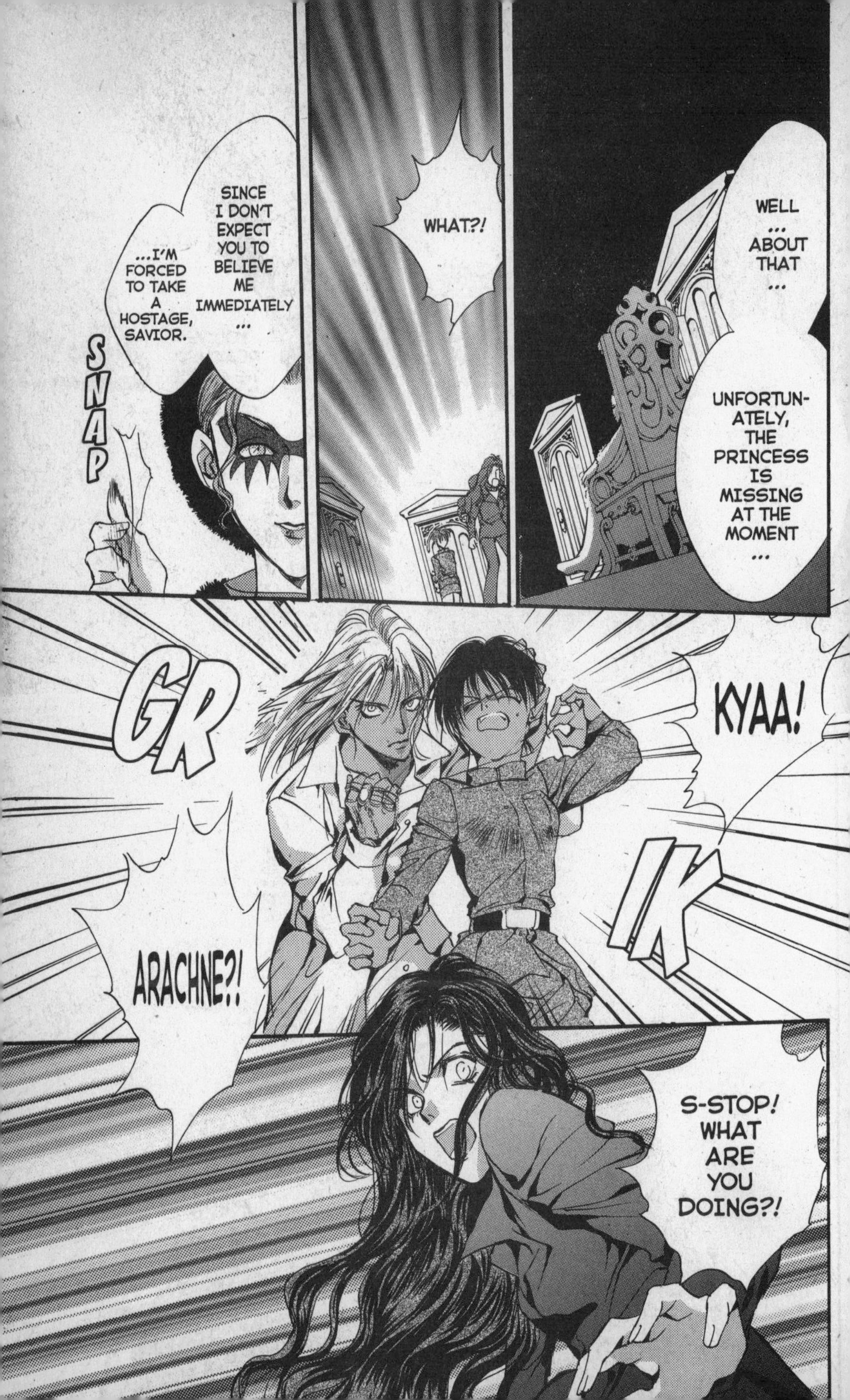
WELL ... ABOUT THAT ...
UNFORTUN-ATELY, THE PRINCESS IS MISSING AT THE MOMENT ...
WHAT?!
SINCE I DON'T EXPECT YOU TO BELIEVE ME IMMEDIATELY ...
...I'M FORCED TO TAKE A HOSTAGE, SAVIOR.
SNAP
KYAA!
GR
IK
ARACHNE?!
S-STOP! WHAT ARE YOU DOING?!

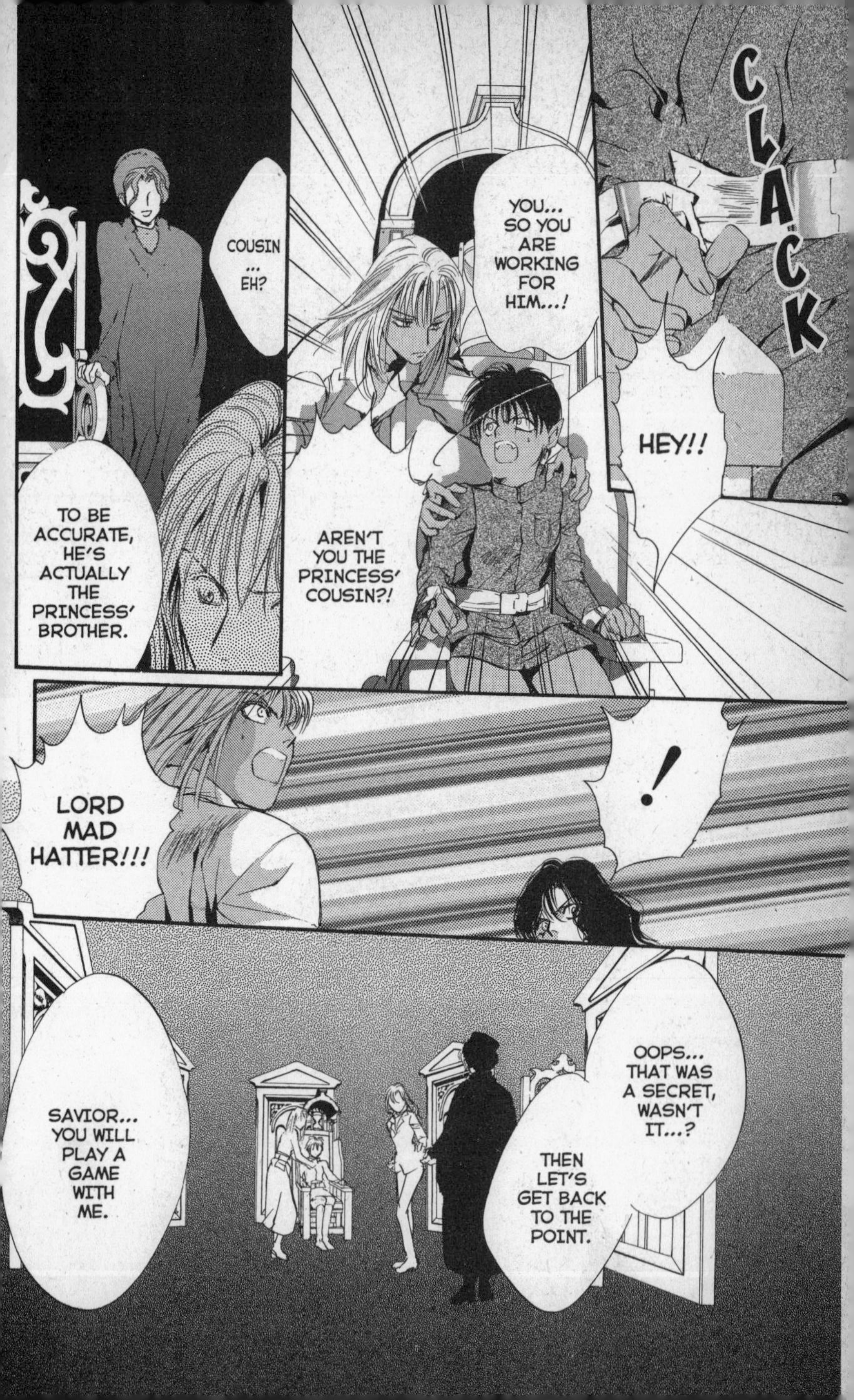
CLACK
HEY!!
YOU... SO YOU ARE WORKING FOR HIM...!
AREN'T YOU THE PRINCESS' COUSIN?!
COUSIN ... EH?
TO BE ACCURATE, HE'S ACTUALLY THE PRINCESS' BROTHER.
!
LORD MAD HATTER!!!
OOPS... THAT WAS A SECRET, WASN'T IT...?
THEN LET'S GET BACK TO THE POINT.
SAVIOR... YOU WILL PLAY A GAME WITH ME.

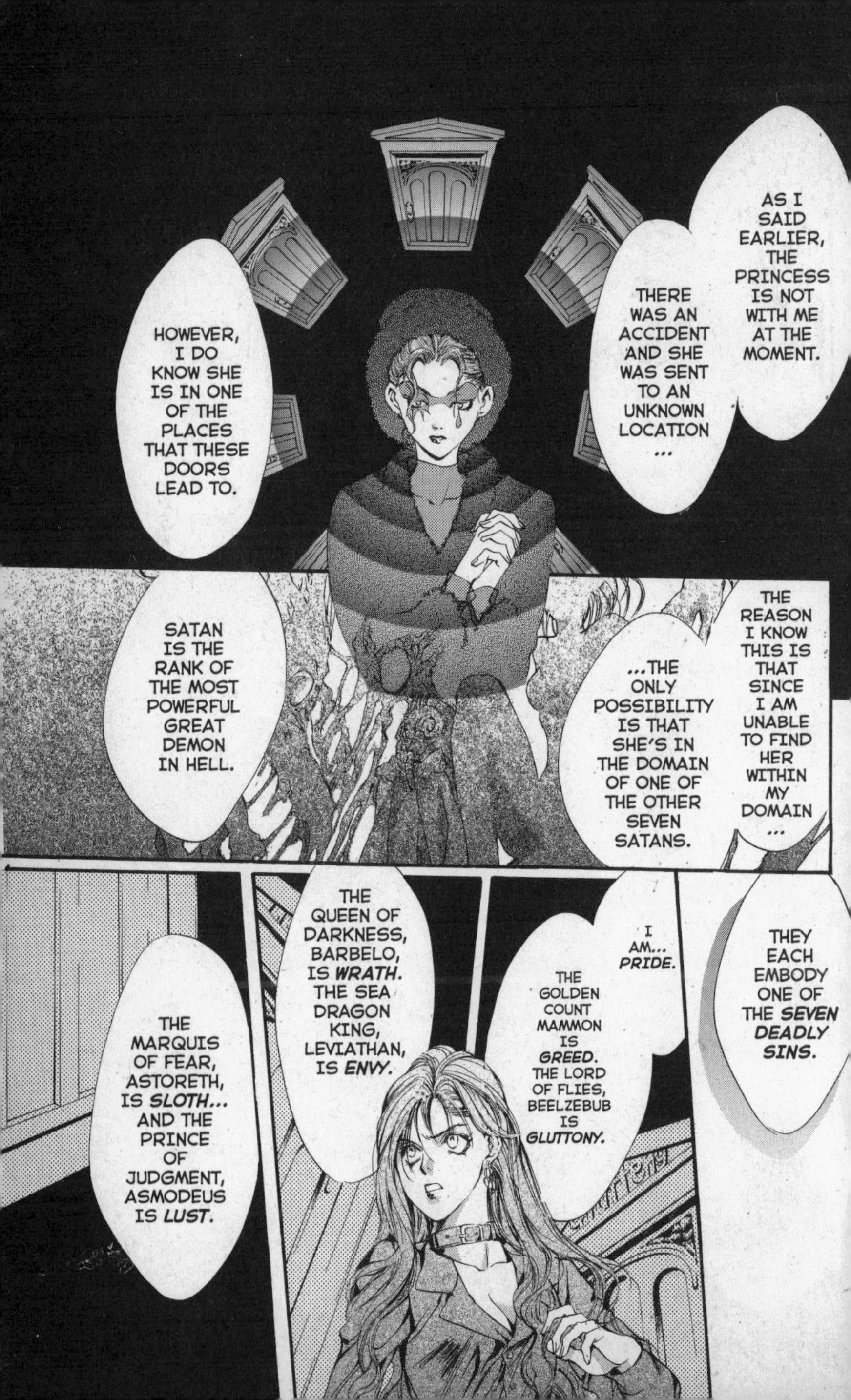
AS I SAID EARLIER, THE PRINCESS IS NOT WITH ME AT THE MOMENT.
THERE WAS AN ACCIDENT AND SHE WAS SENT TO AN UNKNOWN LOCATION ...
HOWEVER, I DO KNOW SHE IS IN ONE OF THE PLACES THAT THESE DOORS LEAD TO.
THE REASON I KNOW THIS IS THAT SINCE I AM UNABLE TO FIND HER WITHIN MY DOMAIN ...
...THE ONLY POSSIBILITY IS THAT SHE'S IN THE DOMAIN OF ONE OF THE OTHER SEVEN SATANS.
SATAN IS THE RANK OF THE MOST POWERFUL GREAT DEMON IN HELL.
THEY EACH EMBODY ONE OF THE *SEVEN DEADLY SINS*.
I AM... *PRIDE*.
THE GOLDEN COUNT MAMMON IS *GREED*. THE LORD OF FLIES, BEELZEBUB IS *GLUTTONY*.
THE QUEEN OF DARKNESS, BARBELO, IS *WRATH*. THE SEA DRAGON KING, LEVIATHAN, IS *ENVY*.
THE MARQUIS OF FEAR, ASTORETH, IS *SLOTH*... AND THE PRINCE OF JUDGMENT, ASMODEUS IS *LUST*.

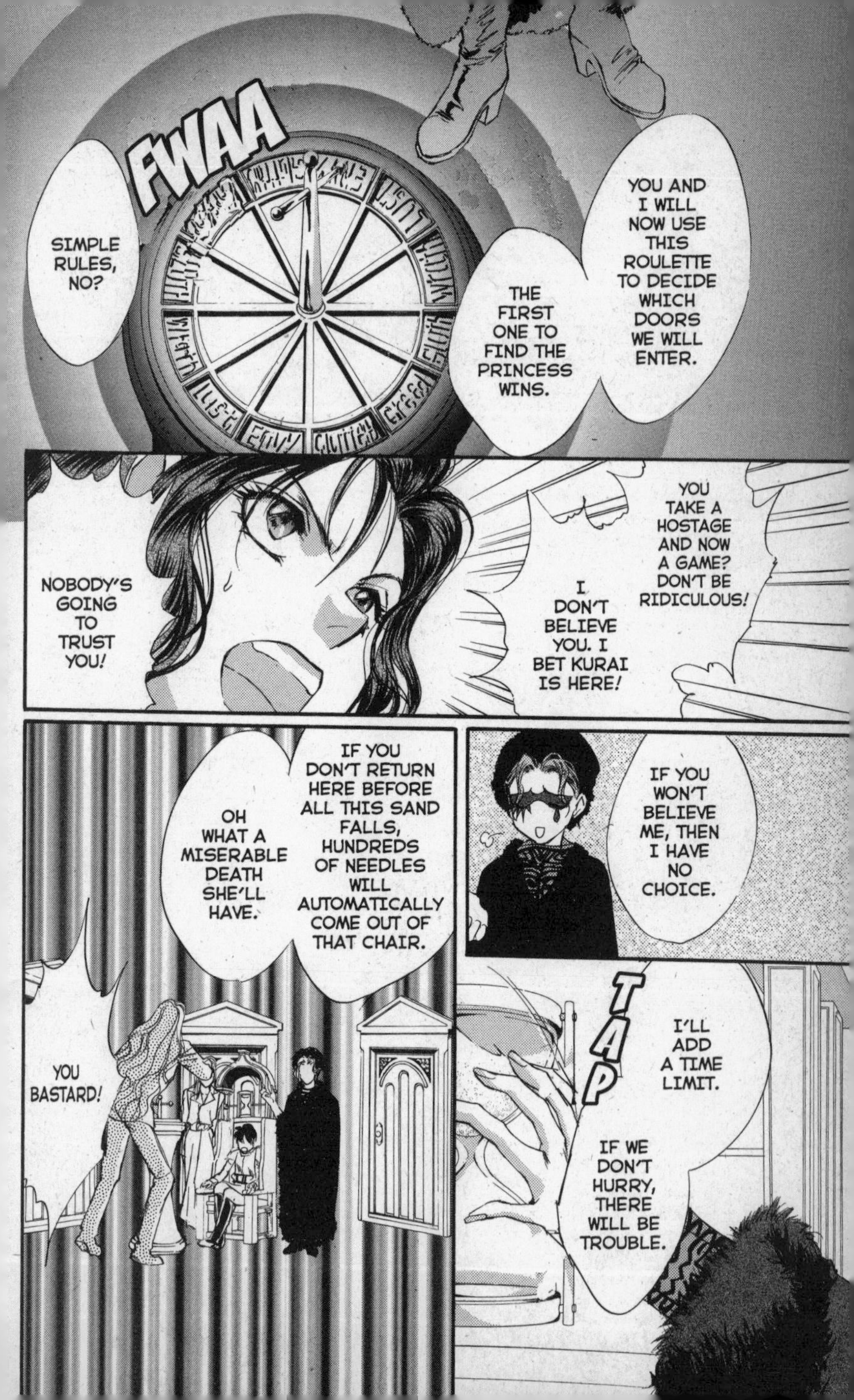
YOU AND I WILL NOW USE THIS ROULETTE TO DECIDE WHICH DOORS WE WILL ENTER.
THE FIRST ONE TO FIND THE PRINCESS WINS.
FWAA
SIMPLE RULES, NO?
YOU TAKE A HOSTAGE AND NOW A GAME? DON'T BE RIDICULOUS!
I DON'T BELIEVE YOU. I BET KURAI IS HERE!
NOBODY'S GOING TO TRUST YOU!
IF YOU WON'T BELIEVE ME, THEN I HAVE NO CHOICE.
I'LL ADD A TIME LIMIT.
TAP
IF WE DON'T HURRY, THERE WILL BE TROUBLE.
IF YOU DON'T RETURN HERE BEFORE ALL THIS SAND FALLS, HUNDREDS OF NEEDLES WILL AUTOMATICALLY COME OUT OF THAT CHAIR.
OH WHAT A MISERABLE DEATH SHE'LL HAVE.
YOU BASTARD!

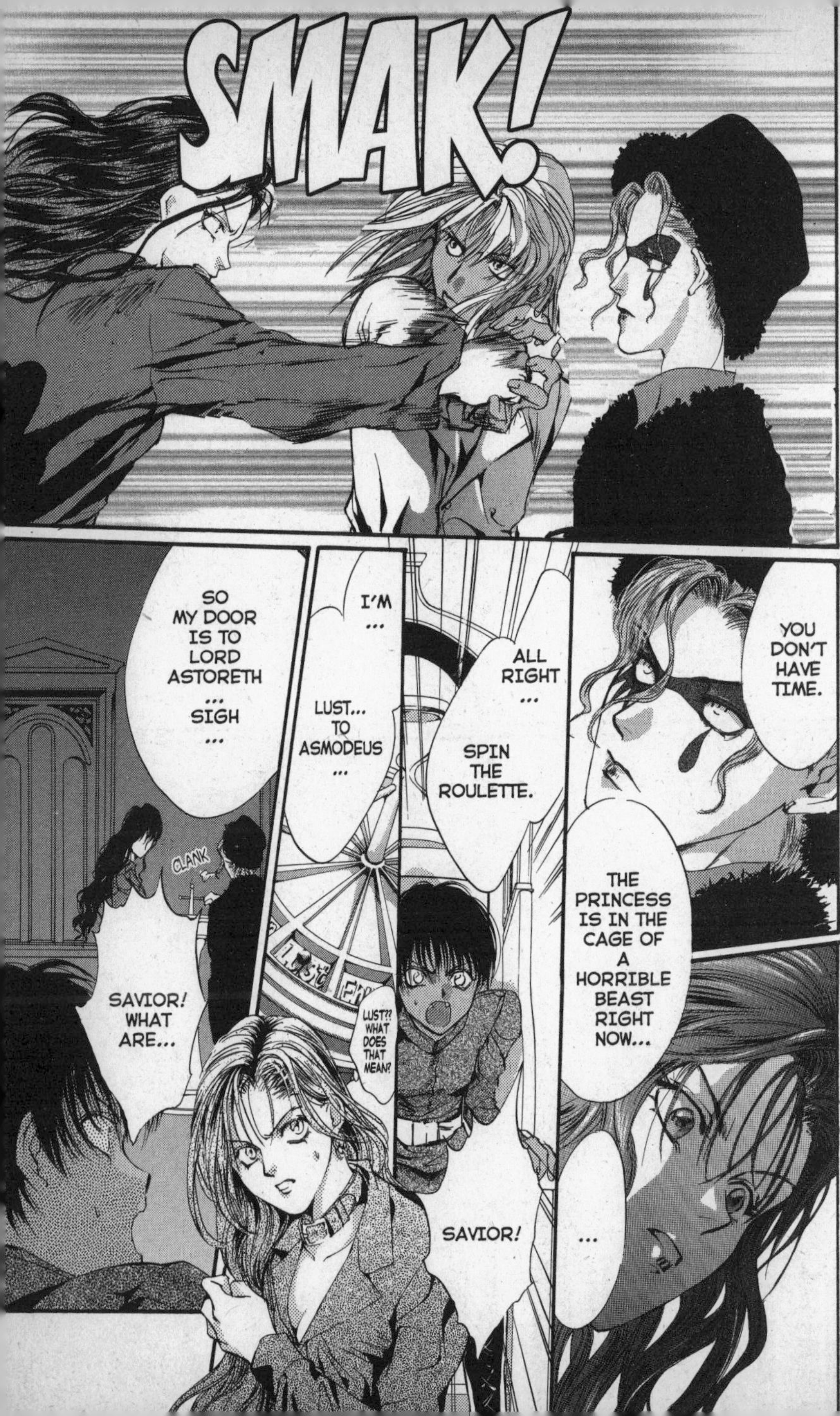
SMAK!
YOU DON'T HAVE TIME.
THE PRINCESS IS IN THE CAGE OF A HORRIBLE BEAST RIGHT NOW...
...
ALL RIGHT ...
SPIN THE ROULETTE.
I'M ...
LUST... TO ASMODEUS ...
LUST?? WHAT DOES THAT MEAN?
SAVIOR!
SO MY DOOR IS TO LORD ASTORETH ... SIGH ...
CLANK
SAVIOR! WHAT ARE...

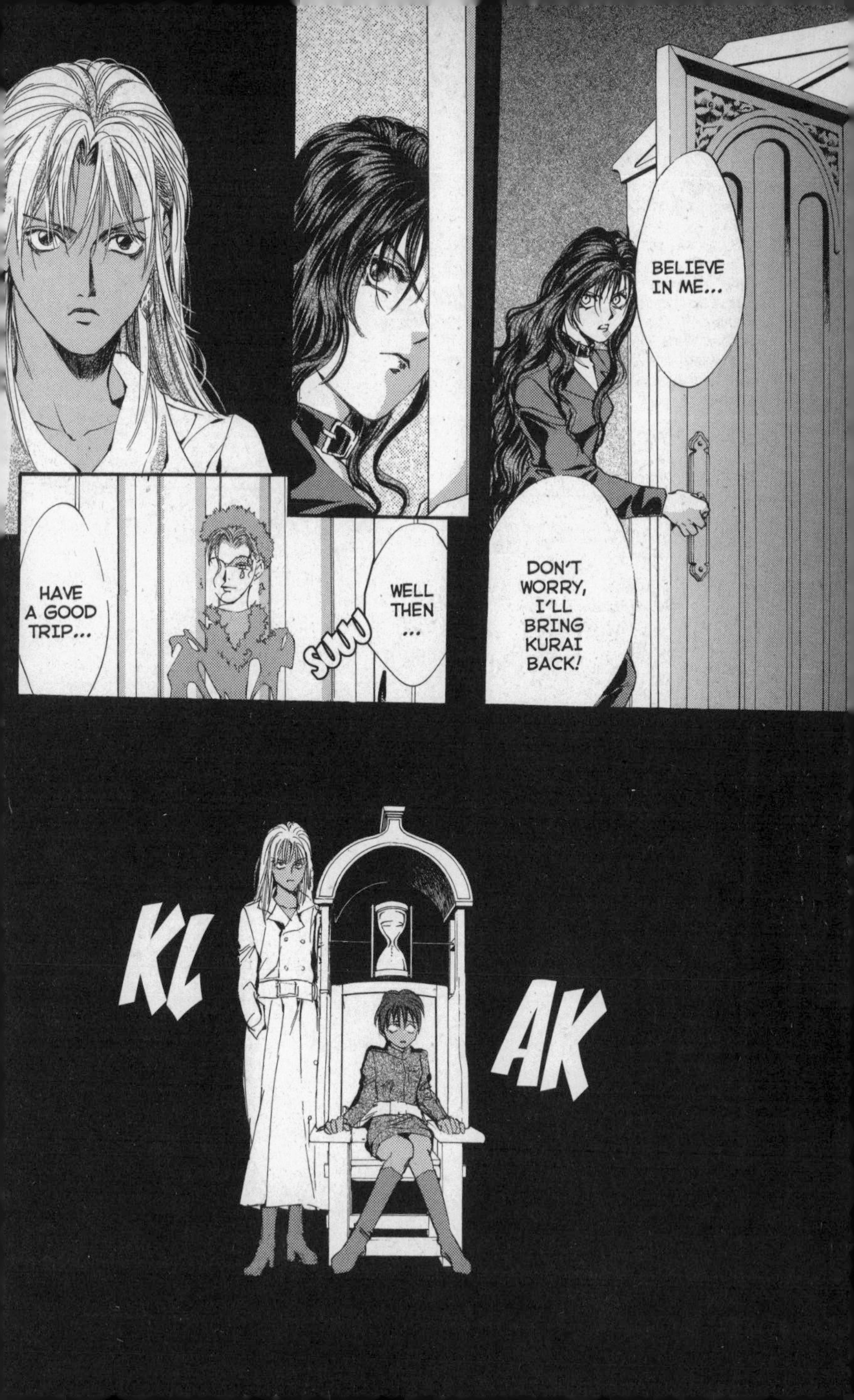
BELIEVE IN ME...
DON'T WORRY, I'LL BRING KURAI BACK!
WELL THEN ...
SUUU
HAVE A GOOD TRIP...
KLAK

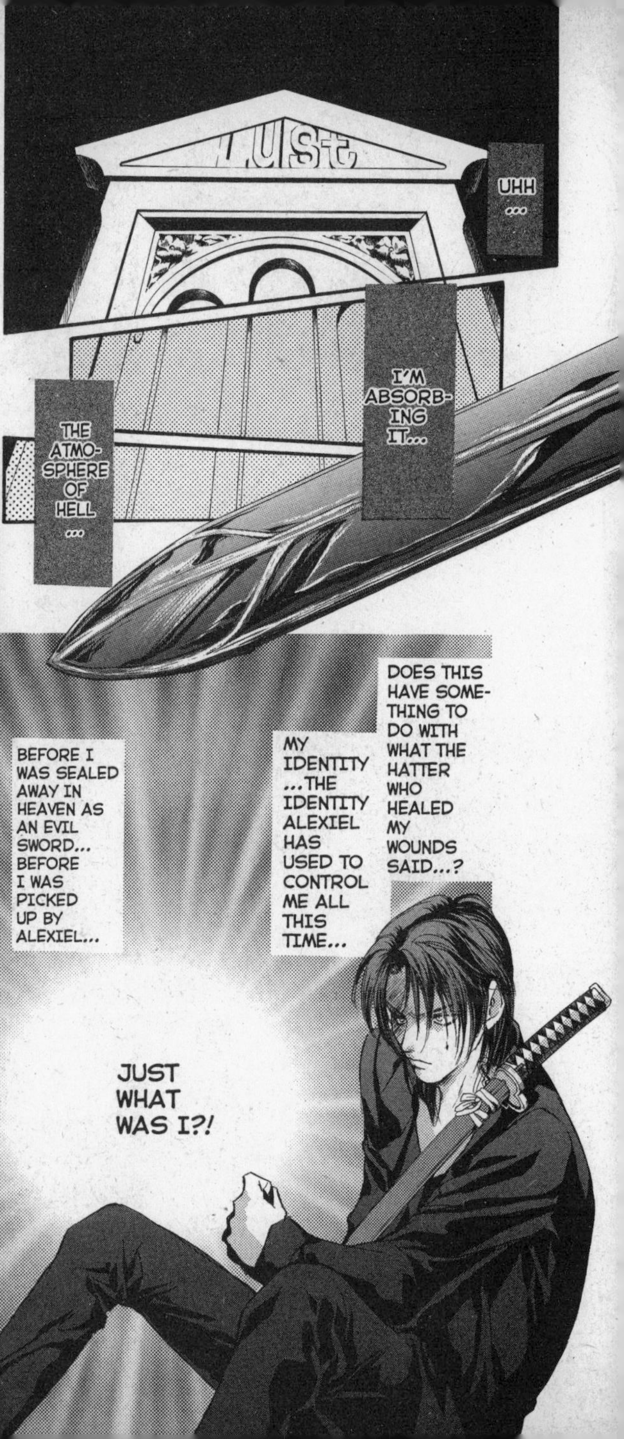
LUST
UHH...
I'M ABSORB-ING IT...
THE ATMO-SPHERE OF HELL...
DOES THIS HAVE SOME-THING TO DO WITH WHAT THE HATTER WHO HEALED MY WOUNDS SAID...?
MY IDENTITY ...THE IDENTITY ALEXIEL HAS USED TO CONTROL ME ALL THIS TIME...
BEFORE I WAS SEALED AWAY IN HEAVEN AS AN EVIL SWORD... BEFORE I WAS PICKED UP BY ALEXIEL...
JUST WHAT WAS I?!

Astaroth
Former member of the thrones and now known as the Marquis of fear. Deadly sin is "sloth." Modeled after a Goddess, so gender is unknown. Wets lips in blood and carries around a poisonous black snake.

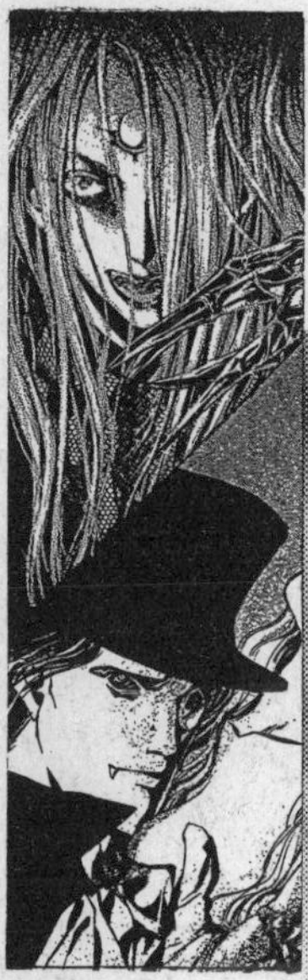

Asmodeus
Former member of the Cherubim, and now the Prince of Judgment. Deadly sin is "lust." It seems long ago he possessed a girl named Sara and fought Raphael. A womanizer who has the heads of a human, a bull and a lamb. He has a snake tail and likes alcohol and gambling. Very decadent...

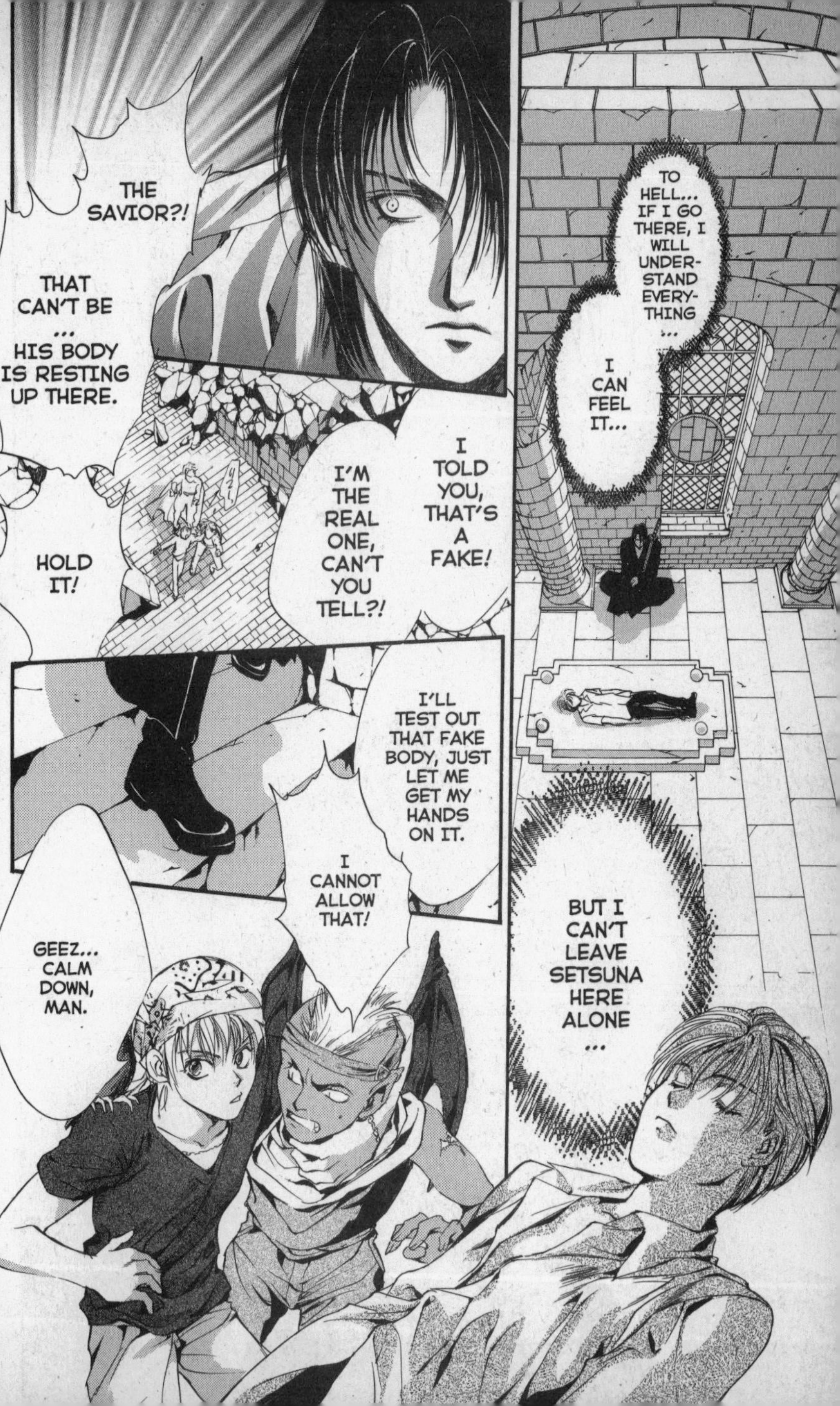
TO HELL... IF I GO THERE, I WILL UNDER-STAND EVERY-THING...
I CAN FEEL IT...
BUT I CAN'T LEAVE SETSUNA HERE ALONE...
THE SAVIOR?!
THAT CAN'T BE... HIS BODY IS RESTING UP THERE.
I TOLD YOU, THAT'S A FAKE!
I'M THE REAL ONE, CAN'T YOU TELL?!
HOLD IT!
I'LL TEST OUT THAT FAKE BODY, JUST LET ME GET MY HANDS ON IT.
I CANNOT ALLOW THAT!
GEEZ... CALM DOWN, MAN.

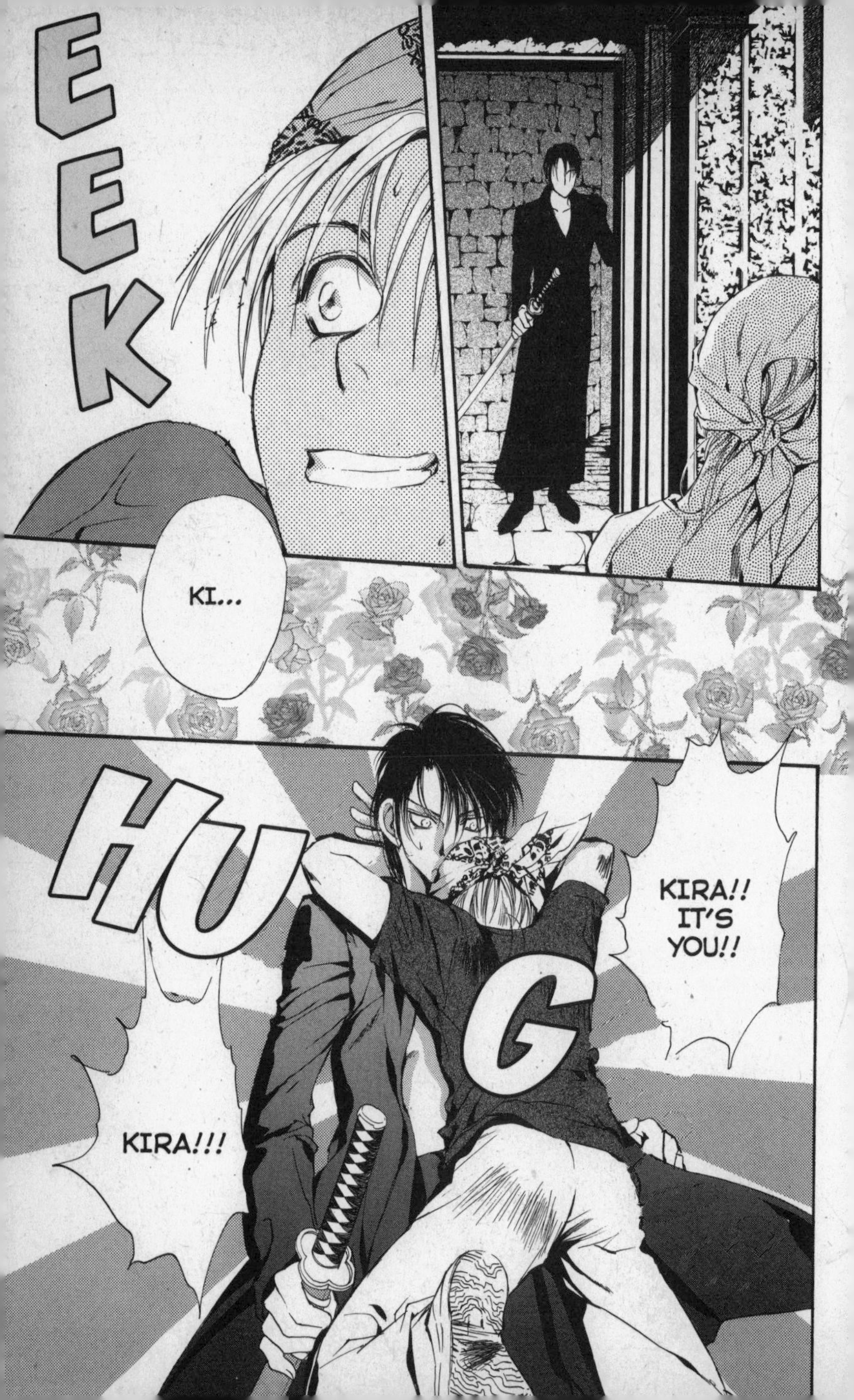
EEK
KI...
HUG
KIRA!! IT'S YOU!!
KIRA!!!

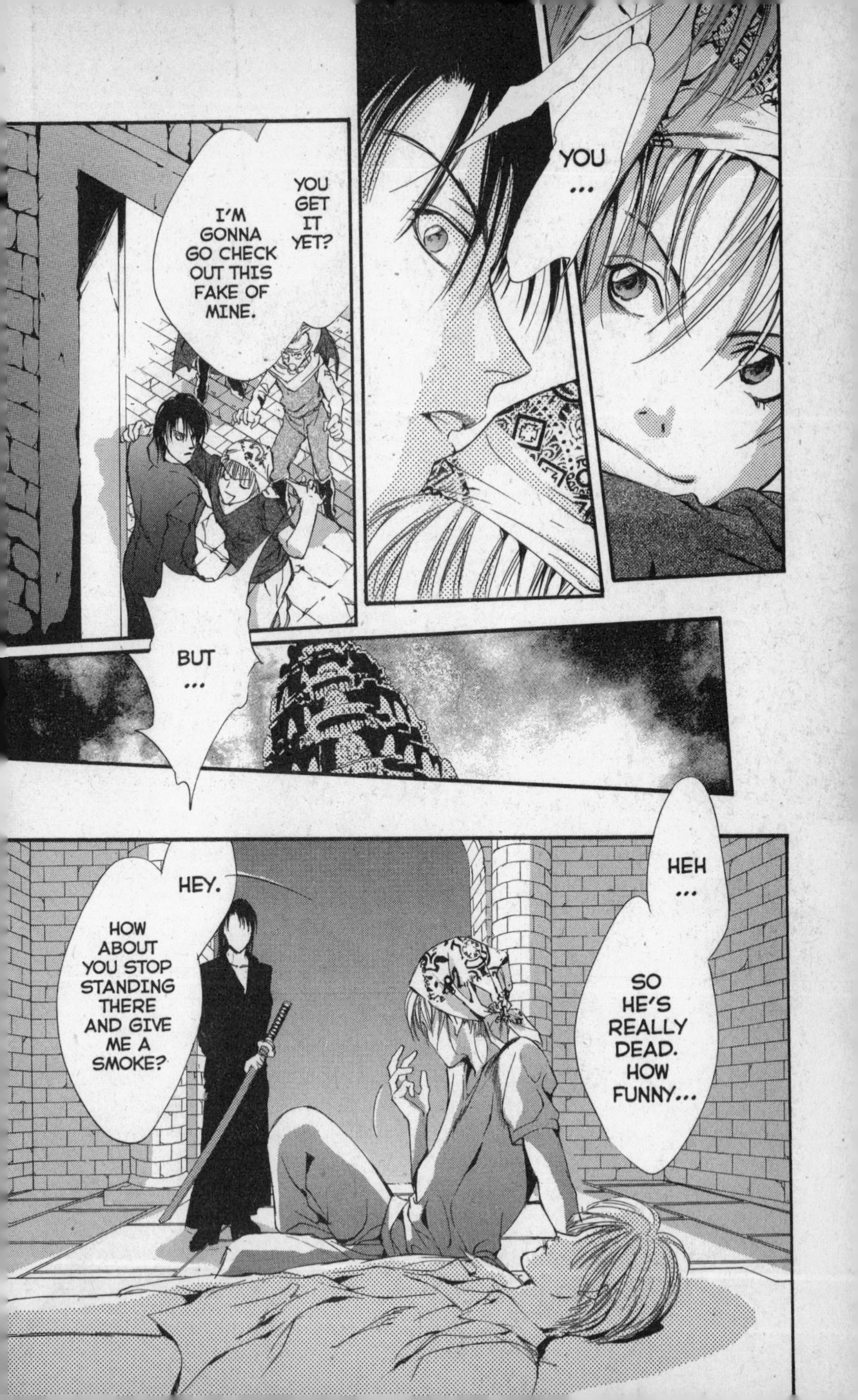
YOU ...
YOU GET IT YET?
I'M GONNA GO CHECK OUT THIS FAKE OF MINE.
BUT ...
HEH ...
SO HE'S REALLY DEAD. HOW FUNNY...
HEY.
HOW ABOUT YOU STOP STANDING THERE AND GIVE ME A SMOKE?

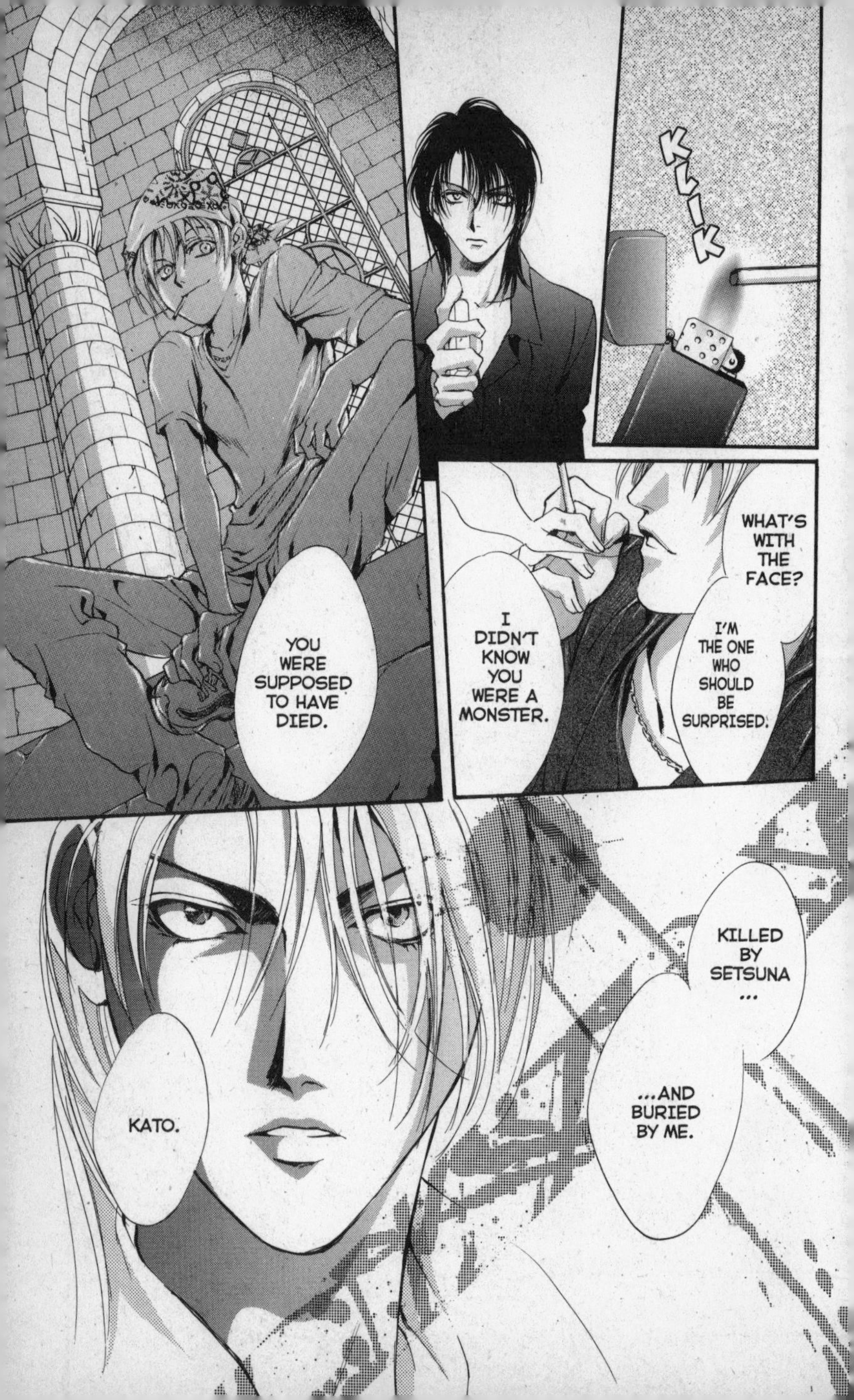
KLIK
WHAT'S WITH THE FACE?
I'M THE ONE WHO SHOULD BE SURPRISED.
I DIDN'T KNOW YOU WERE A MONSTER.
YOU WERE SUPPOSED TO HAVE DIED.
KILLED BY SETSUNA ...
...AND BURIED BY ME.
KATO.

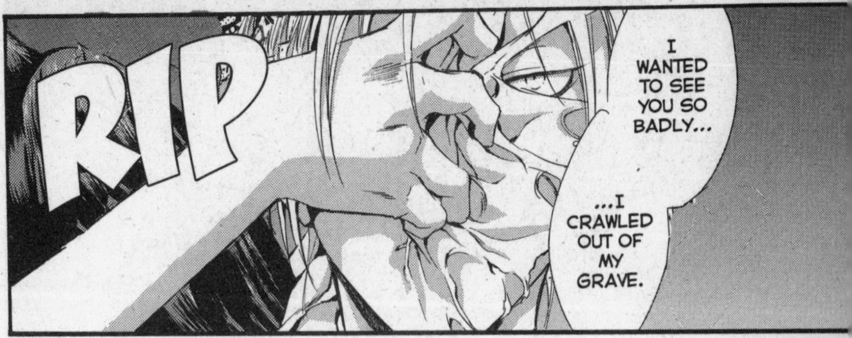
I WANTED TO SEE YOU SO BADLY...
...I CRAWLED OUT OF MY GRAVE.
RIP
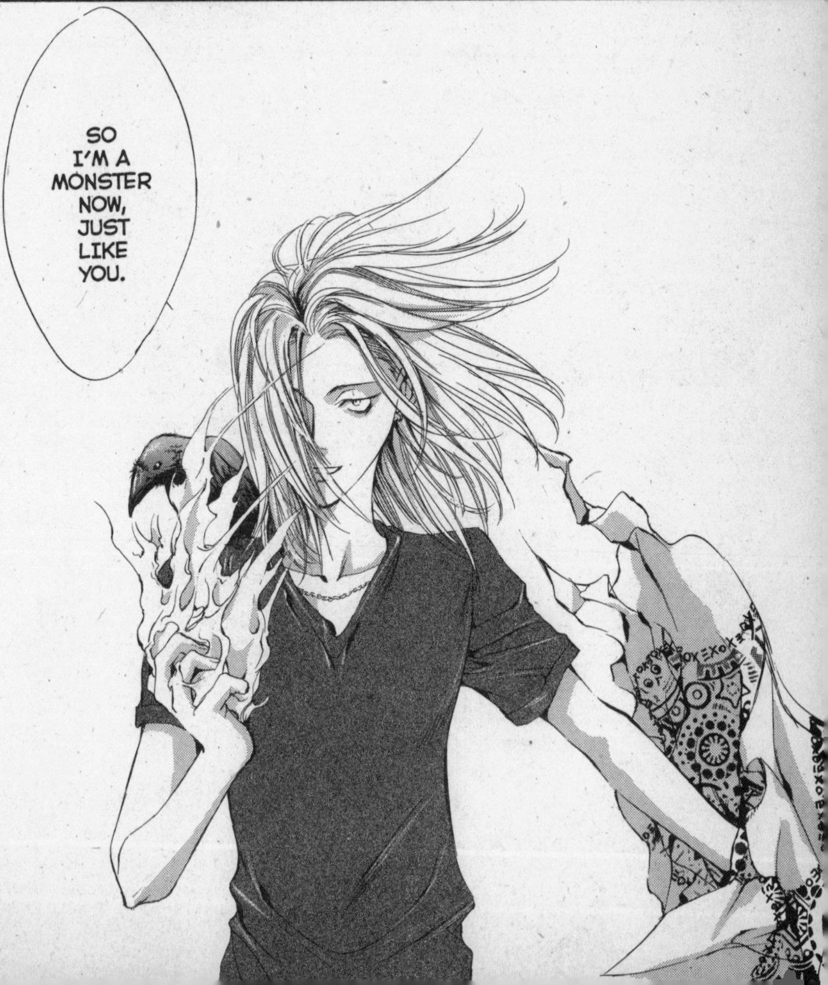
SO I'M A MONSTER NOW, JUST LIKE YOU.

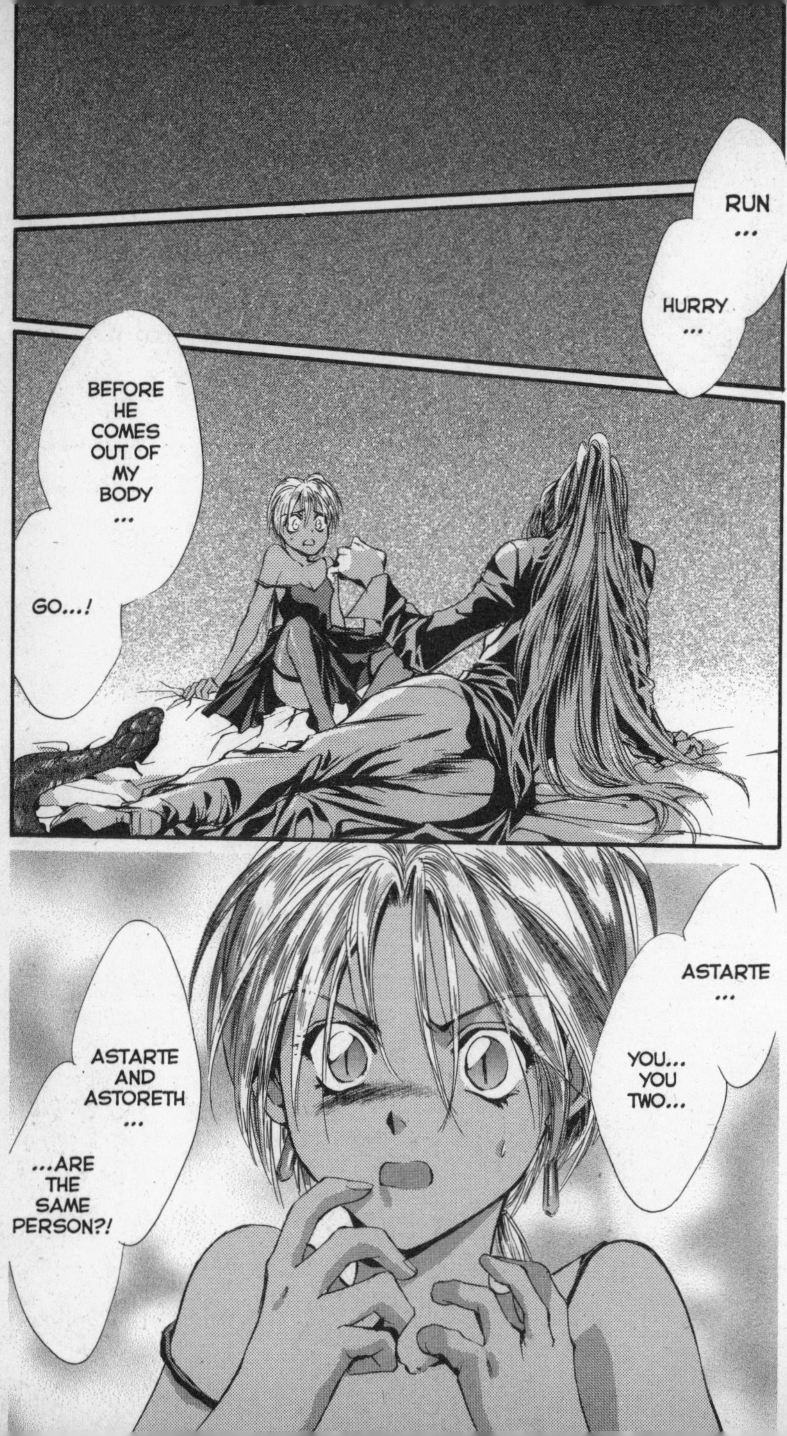
RUN ...
HURRY ...
BEFORE HE COMES OUT OF MY BODY ...
GO...!
ASTARTE ...
YOU... YOU TWO...
ASTARTE AND ASTORETH ...
...ARE THE SAME PERSON?!

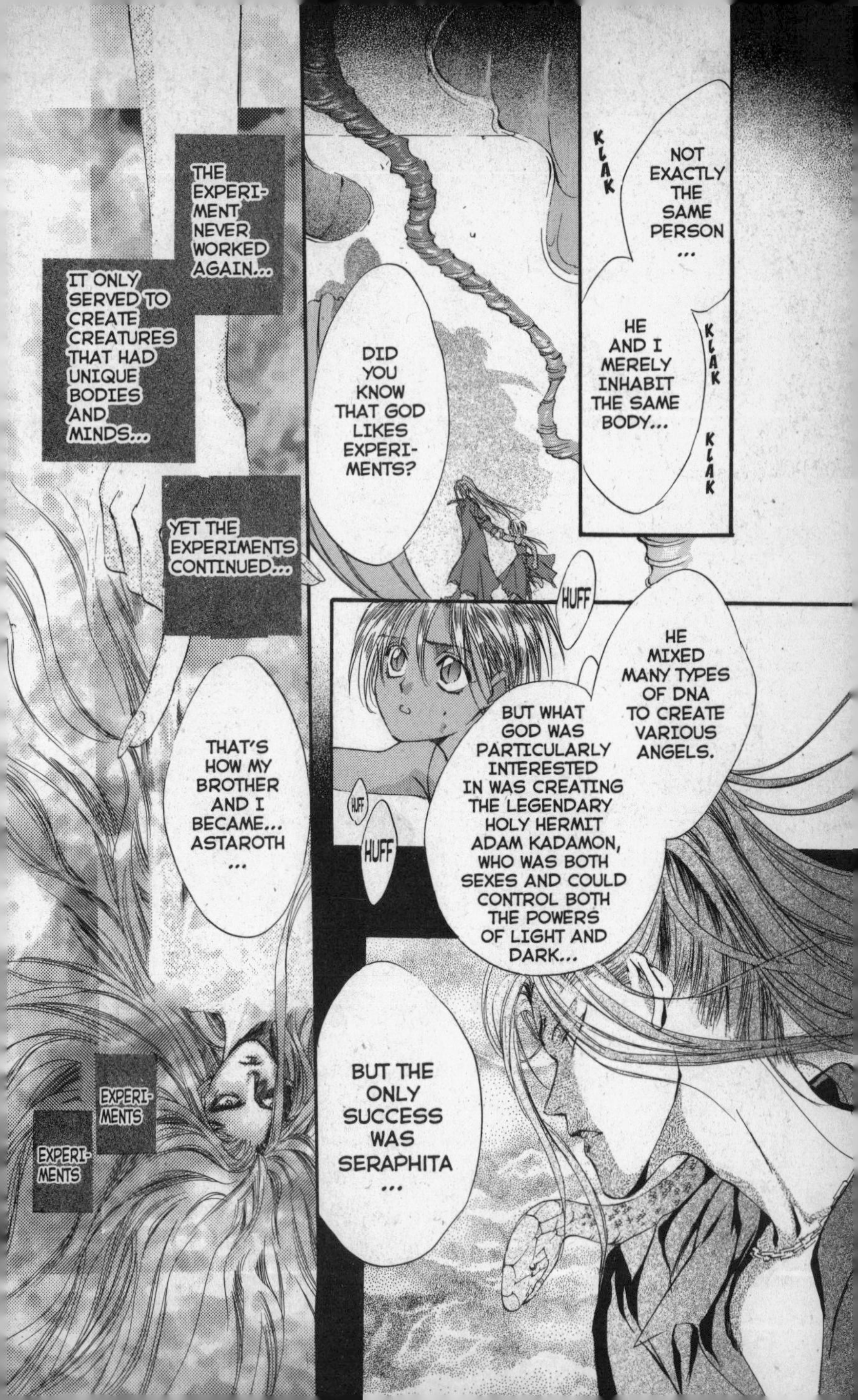
NOT EXACTLY THE SAME PERSON ...
KLAK
HE AND I MERELY INHABIT THE SAME BODY...
KLAK KLAK
DID YOU KNOW THAT GOD LIKES EXPERI-MENTS?
HUFF
HE MIXED MANY TYPES OF DNA TO CREATE VARIOUS ANGELS.
BUT WHAT GOD WAS PARTICULARLY INTERESTED IN WAS CREATING THE LEGENDARY HOLY HERMIT ADAM KADAMON, WHO WAS BOTH SEXES AND COULD CONTROL BOTH THE POWERS OF LIGHT AND DARK...
HUFF
HUFF
BUT THE ONLY SUCCESS WAS SERAPHITA ...
THE EXPERI-MENT NEVER WORKED AGAIN...
IT ONLY SERVED TO CREATE CREATURES THAT HAD UNIQUE BODIES AND MINDS...
YET THE EXPERIMENTS CONTINUED...
THAT'S HOW MY BROTHER AND I BECAME... ASTAROTH ...
EXPERI-MENTS
EXPERI-MENTS

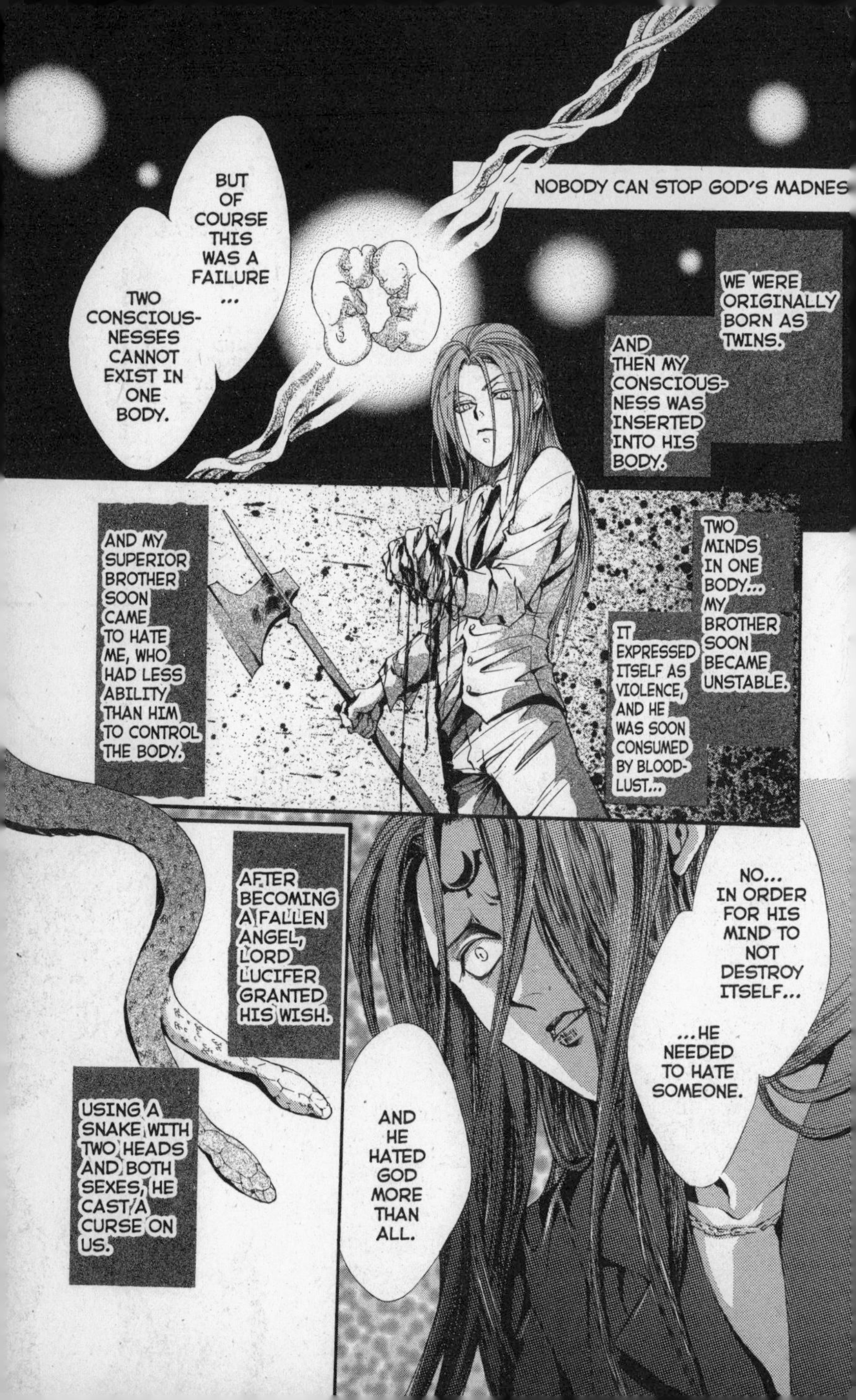
NOBODY CAN STOP GOD'S MADNES
WE WERE ORIGINALLY BORN AS TWINS.
AND THEN MY CONSCIOUSNESS WAS INSERTED INTO HIS BODY.
BUT OF COURSE THIS WAS A FAILURE ...
TWO CONSCIOUSNESSES CANNOT EXIST IN ONE BODY.
TWO MINDS IN ONE BODY... MY BROTHER SOON BECAME UNSTABLE.
IT EXPRESSED ITSELF AS VIOLENCE, AND HE WAS SOON CONSUMED BY BLOOD-LUST...
AND MY SUPERIOR BROTHER SOON CAME TO HATE ME, WHO HAD LESS ABILITY THAN HIM TO CONTROL THE BODY.
NO... IN ORDER FOR HIS MIND TO NOT DESTROY ITSELF...
...HE NEEDED TO HATE SOMEONE.
AND HE HATED GOD MORE THAN ALL.
AFTER BECOMING A FALLEN ANGEL, LORD LUCIFER GRANTED HIS WISH.
USING A SNAKE WITH TWO HEADS AND BOTH SEXES, HE CAST A CURSE ON US.

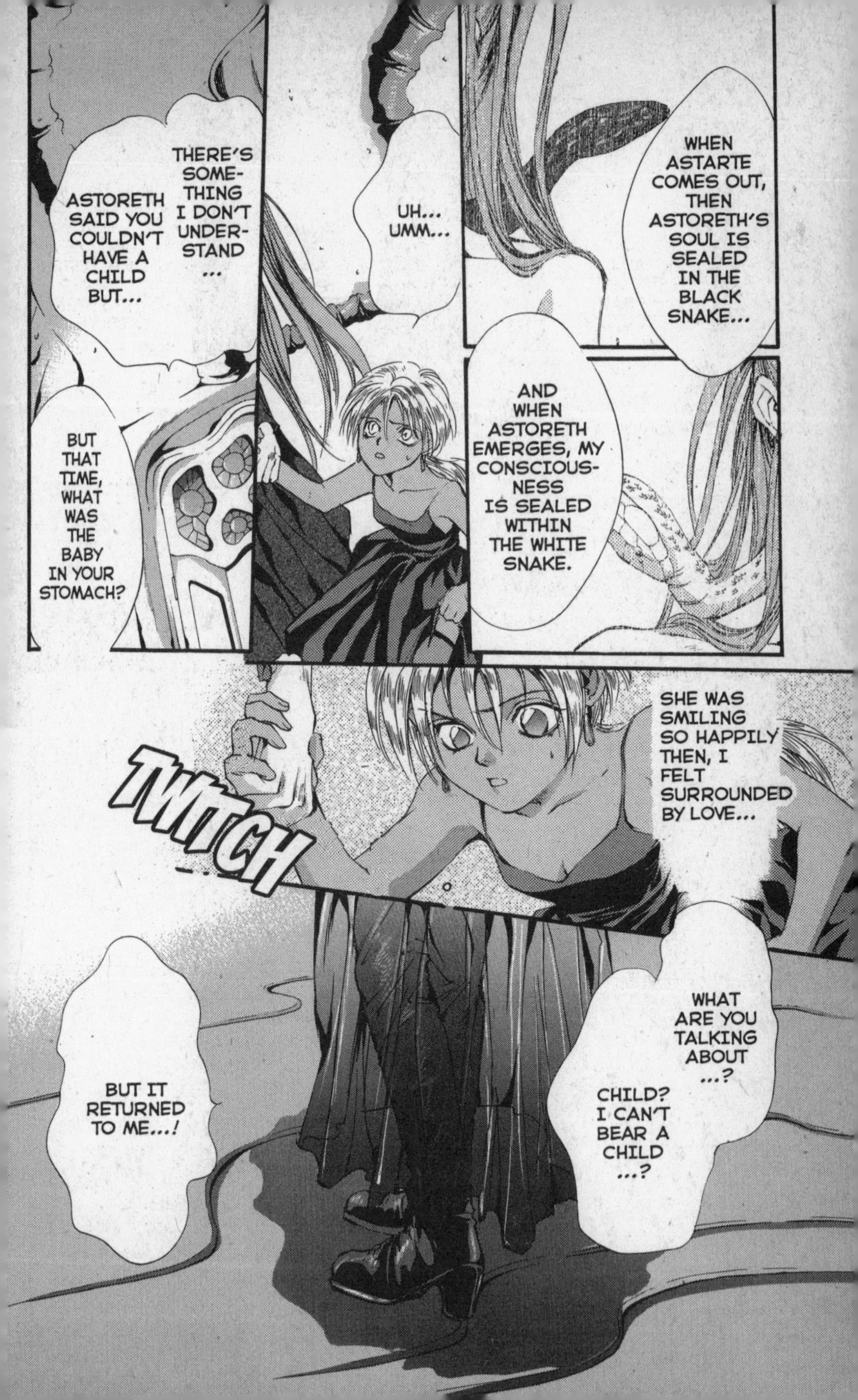
WHEN ASTARTE COMES OUT, THEN ASTORETH'S SOUL IS SEALED IN THE BLACK SNAKE...
AND WHEN ASTORETH EMERGES, MY CONSCIOUSNESS IS SEALED WITHIN THE WHITE SNAKE.
UH... UMM...
THERE'S SOMETHING I DON'T UNDERSTAND...
ASTORETH SAID YOU COULDN'T HAVE A CHILD BUT...
BUT THAT TIME, WHAT WAS THE BABY IN YOUR STOMACH?
SHE WAS SMILING SO HAPPILY THEN, I FELT SURROUNDED BY LOVE...
TWITCH
WHAT ARE YOU TALKING ABOUT...?
CHILD? I CAN'T BEAR A CHILD...?
BUT IT RETURNED TO ME...!

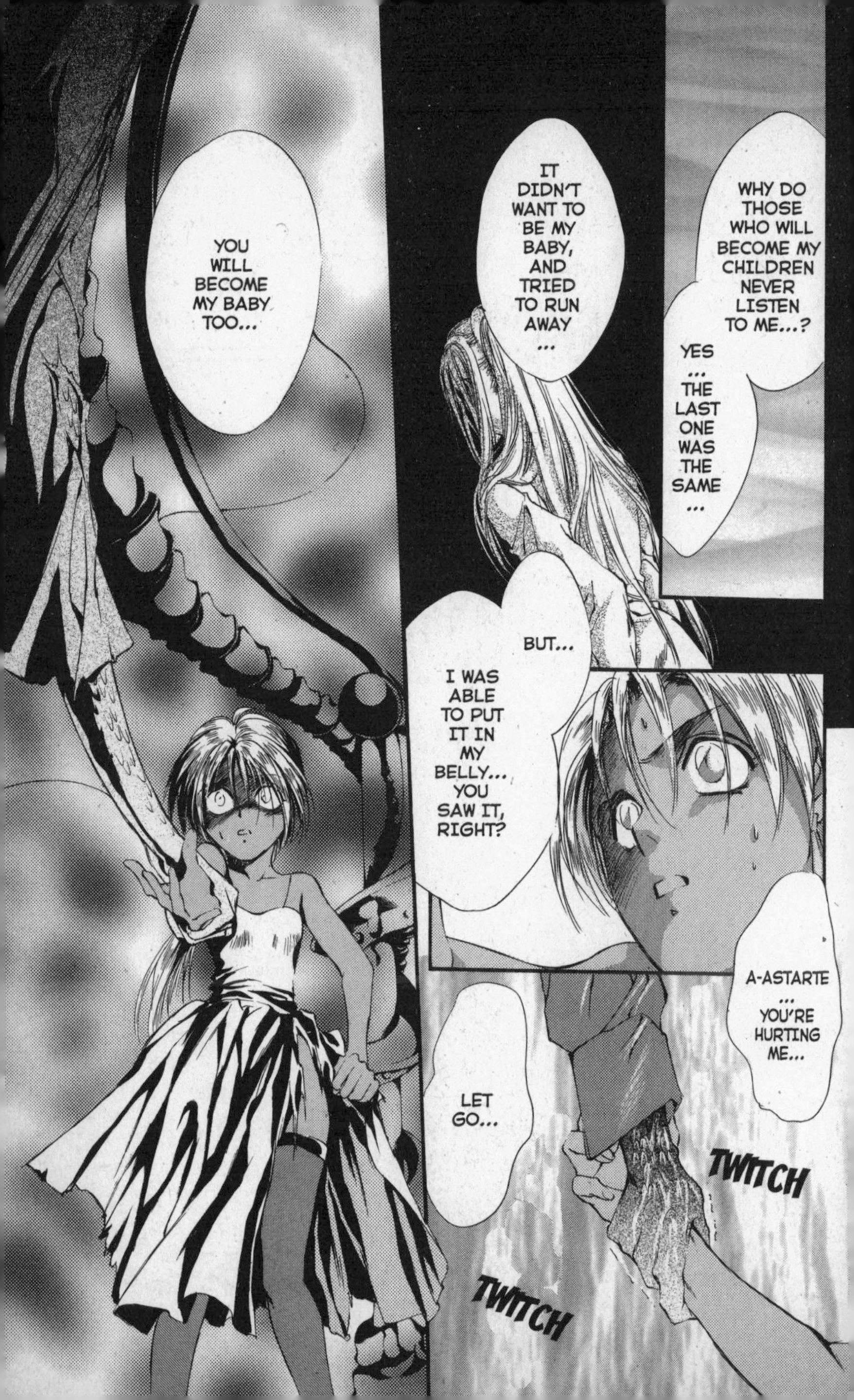
WHY DO THOSE WHO WILL BECOME MY CHILDREN NEVER LISTEN TO ME...?
YES ... THE LAST ONE WAS THE SAME ...
IT DIDN'T WANT TO BE MY BABY, AND TRIED TO RUN AWAY ...
BUT...
I WAS ABLE TO PUT IT IN MY BELLY... YOU SAW IT, RIGHT?
A-ASTARTE ... YOU'RE HURTING ME...
LET GO...
TWITCH
TWITCH
YOU WILL BECOME MY BABY TOO...

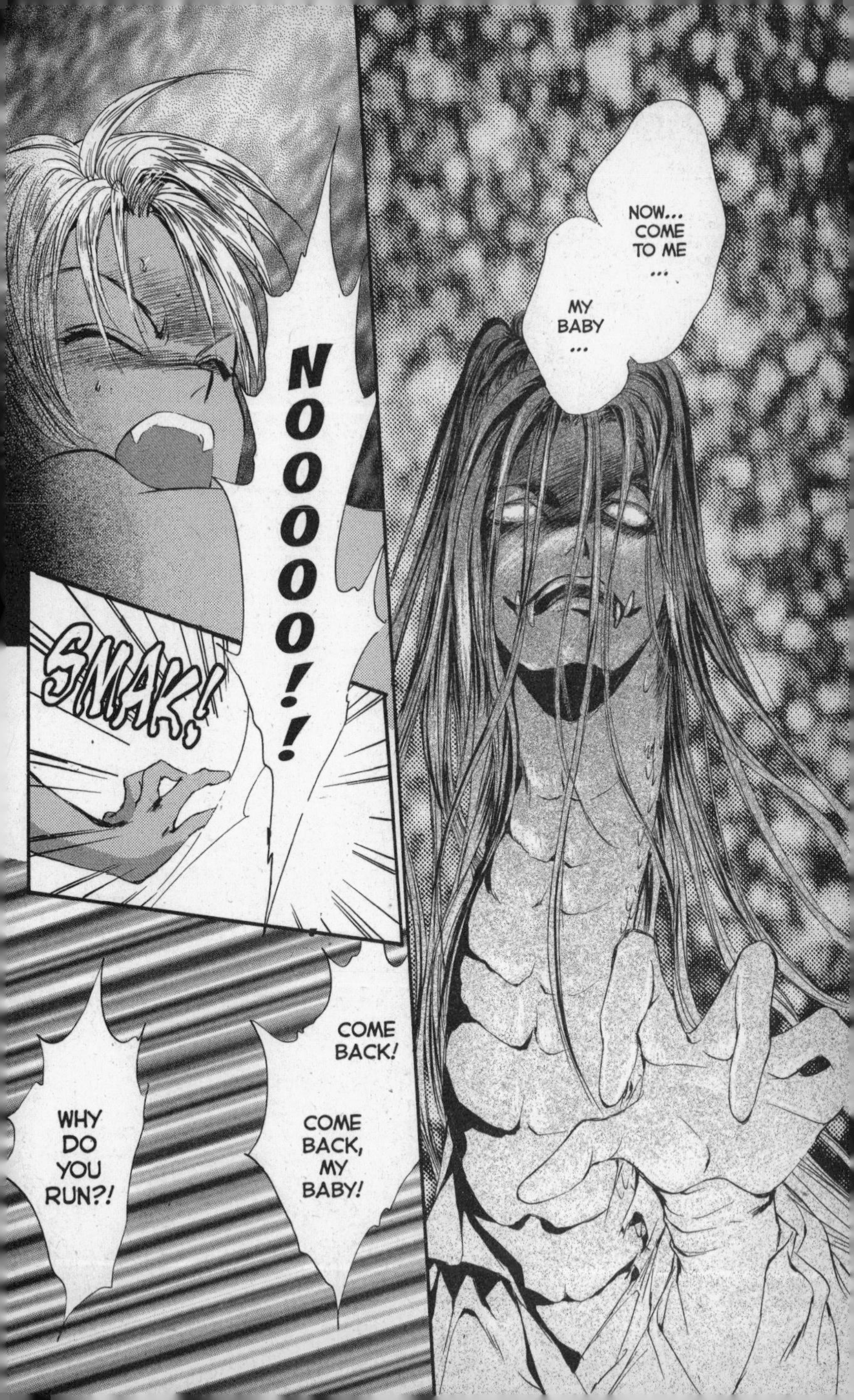
NOW... COME TO ME ...
MY BABY ...
NOOOOOO!!
SMAK!
COME BACK!
COME BACK, MY BABY!
WHY DO YOU RUN?!

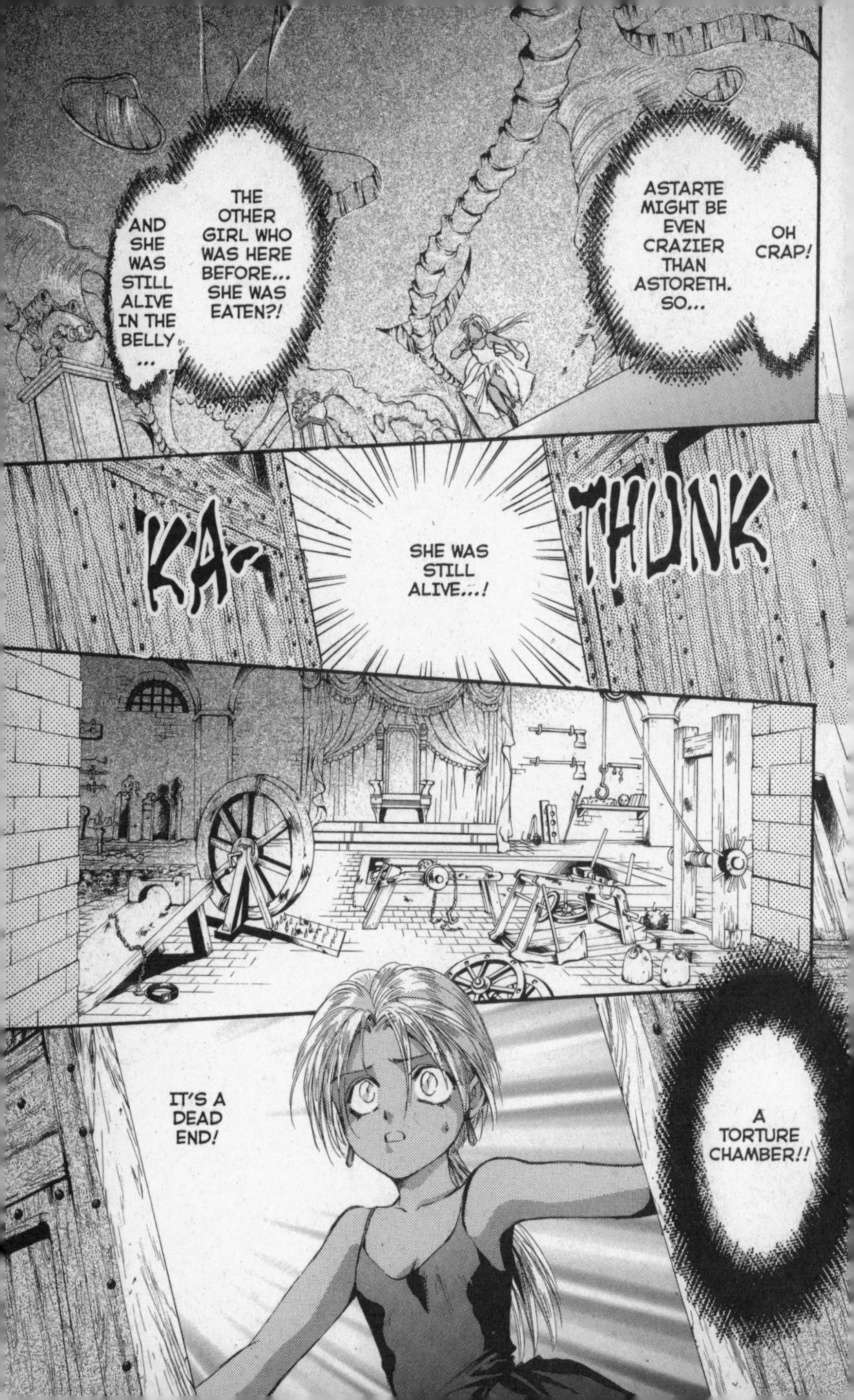
OH CRAP!
ASTARTE MIGHT BE EVEN CRAZIER THAN ASTORETH. SO...
THE OTHER GIRL WHO WAS HERE BEFORE... SHE WAS EATEN?!
AND SHE WAS STILL ALIVE IN THE BELLY...
KA-
THUNK
SHE WAS STILL ALIVE...!
A TORTURE CHAMBER!!
IT'S A DEAD END!

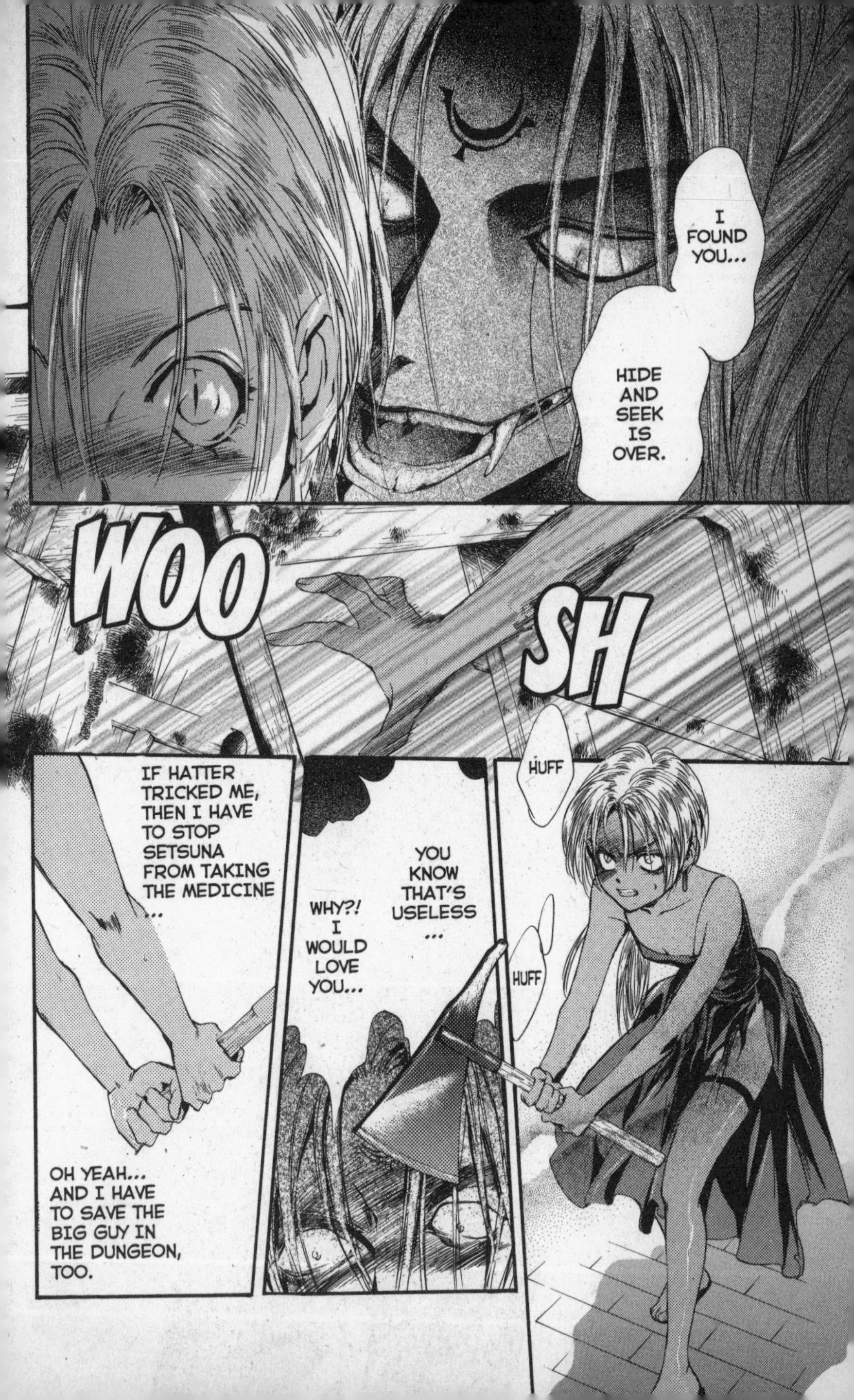
I FOUND YOU...
HIDE AND SEEK IS OVER.
WOOSH
HUFF
HUFF
YOU KNOW THAT'S USELESS...
WHY?! I WOULD LOVE YOU...
IF HATTER TRICKED ME, THEN I HAVE TO STOP SETSUNA FROM TAKING THE MEDICINE...
OH YEAH... AND I HAVE TO SAVE THE BIG GUY IN THE DUNGEON, TOO.

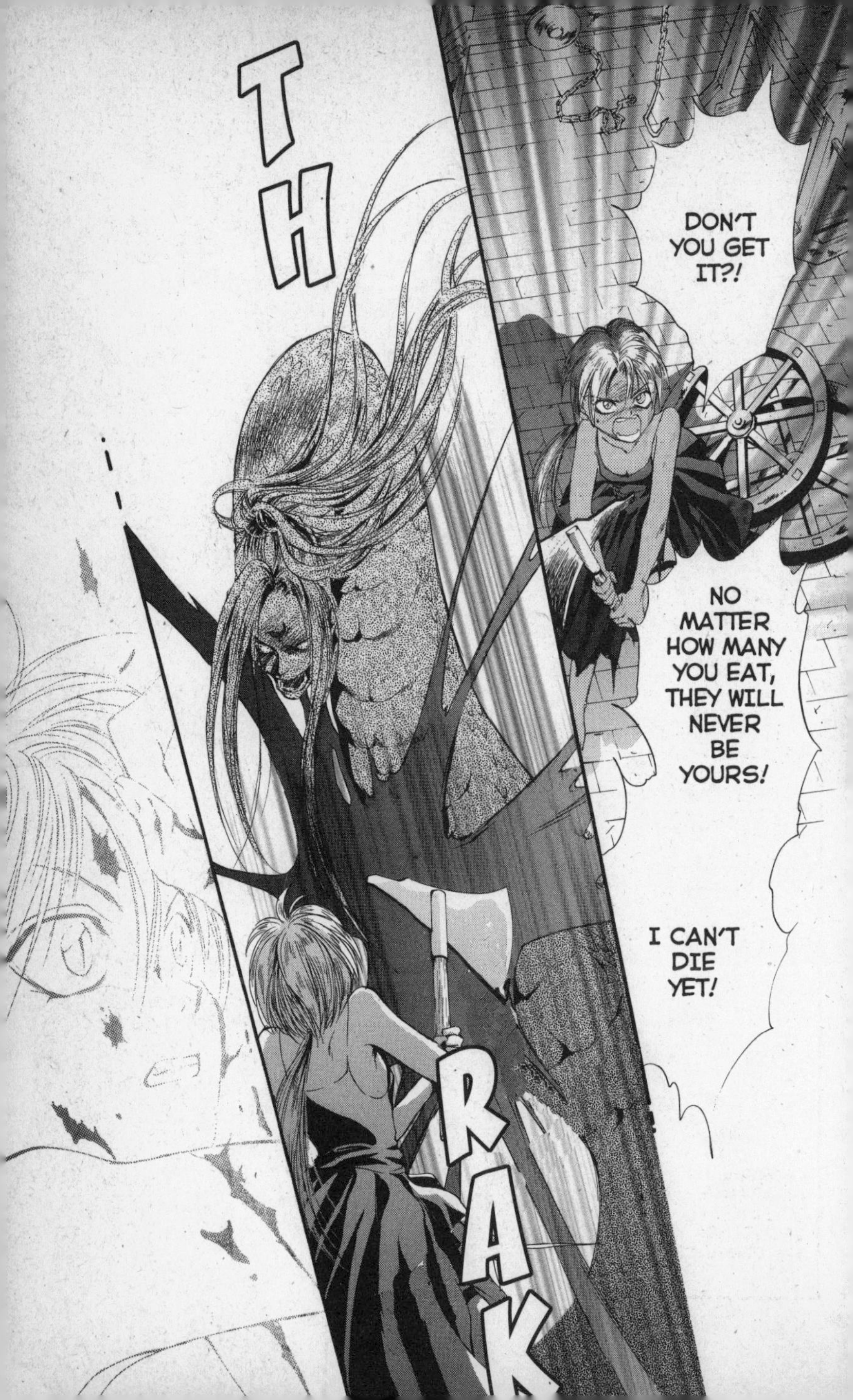
DON'T YOU GET IT?!
NO MATTER HOW MANY YOU EAT, THEY WILL NEVER BE YOURS!
I CAN'T DIE YET!
THRAK
...

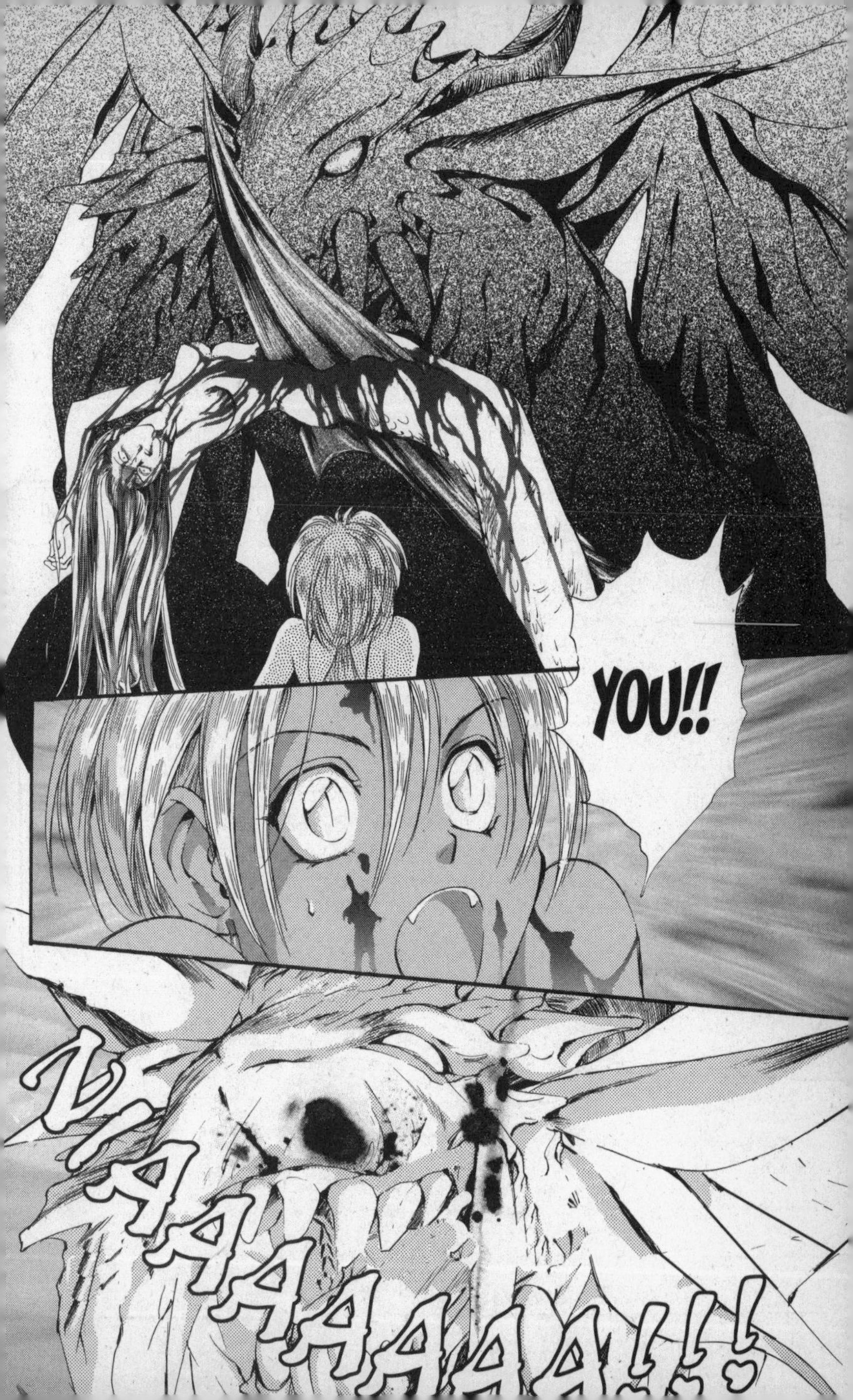
YOU!!
VAAAAAAA!!!

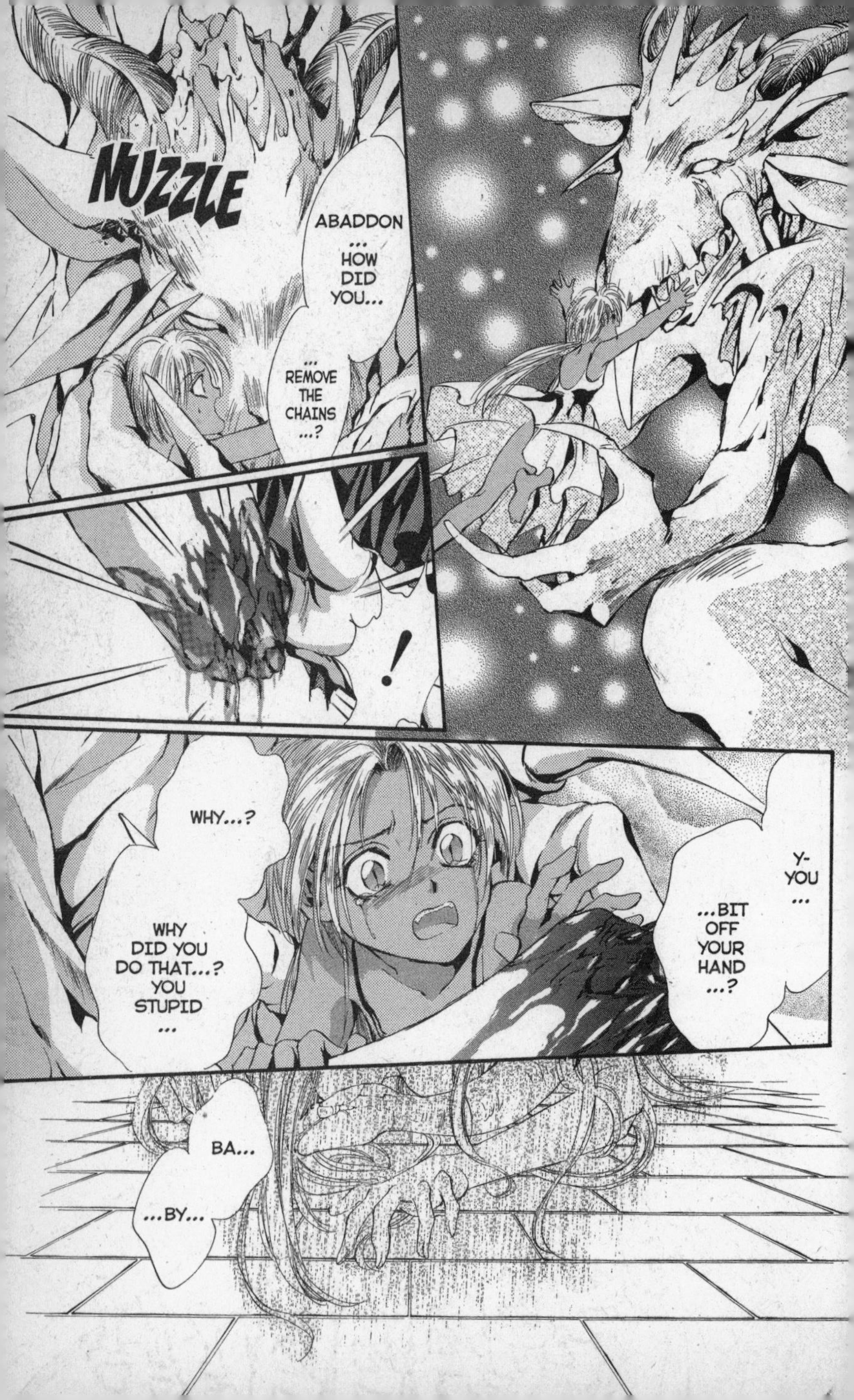
NUZZLE
ABADDON ... HOW DID YOU...
... REMOVE THE CHAINS ...?
!
Y- YOU ...
...BIT OFF YOUR HAND ...?
WHY...?
WHY DID YOU DO THAT...? YOU STUPID ...
BA...
...BY...

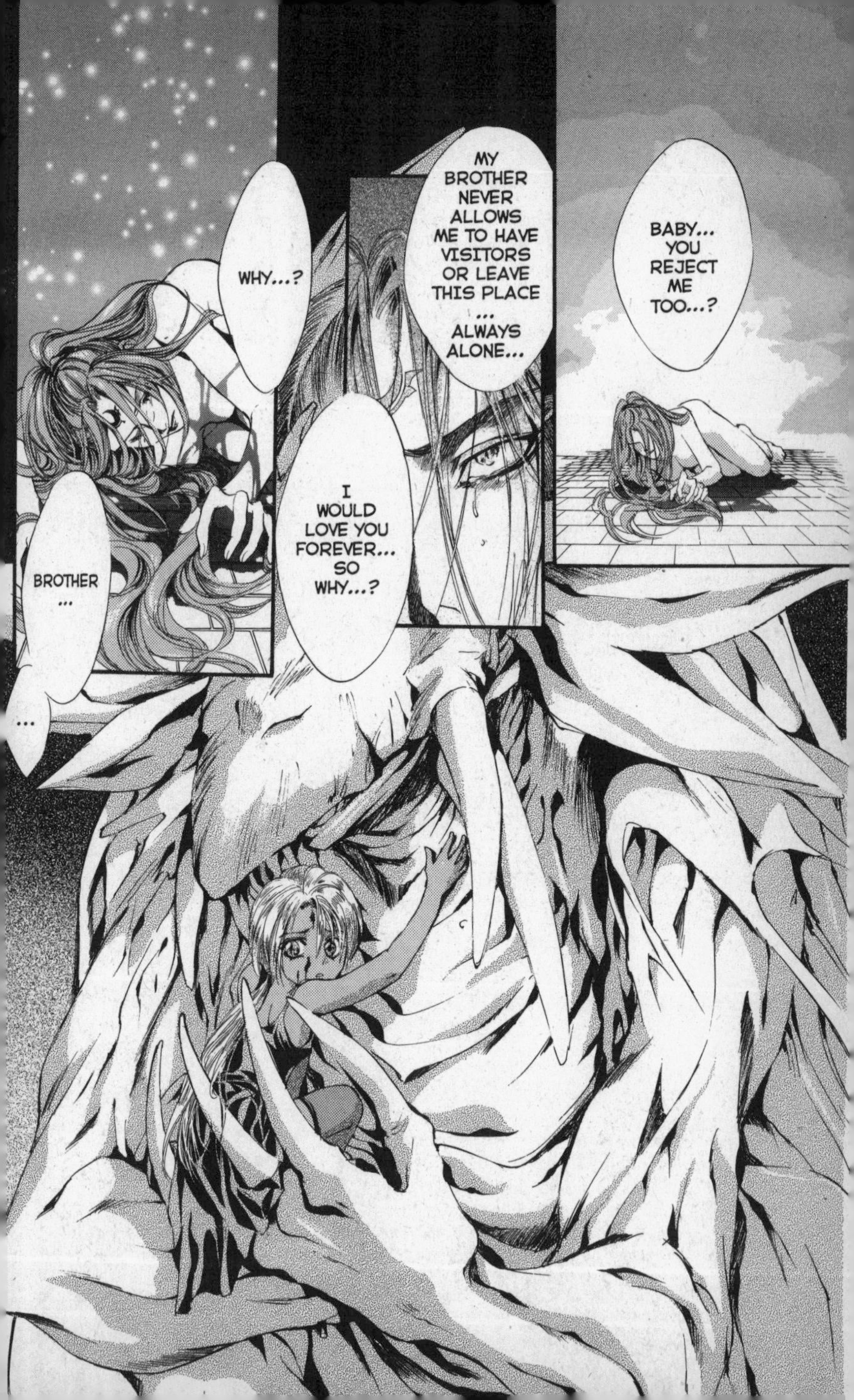
BABY... YOU REJECT ME TOO...?
MY BROTHER NEVER ALLOWS ME TO HAVE VISITORS OR LEAVE THIS PLACE ... ALWAYS ALONE...
I WOULD LOVE YOU FOREVER... SO WHY...?
WHY...?
BROTHER ...
...

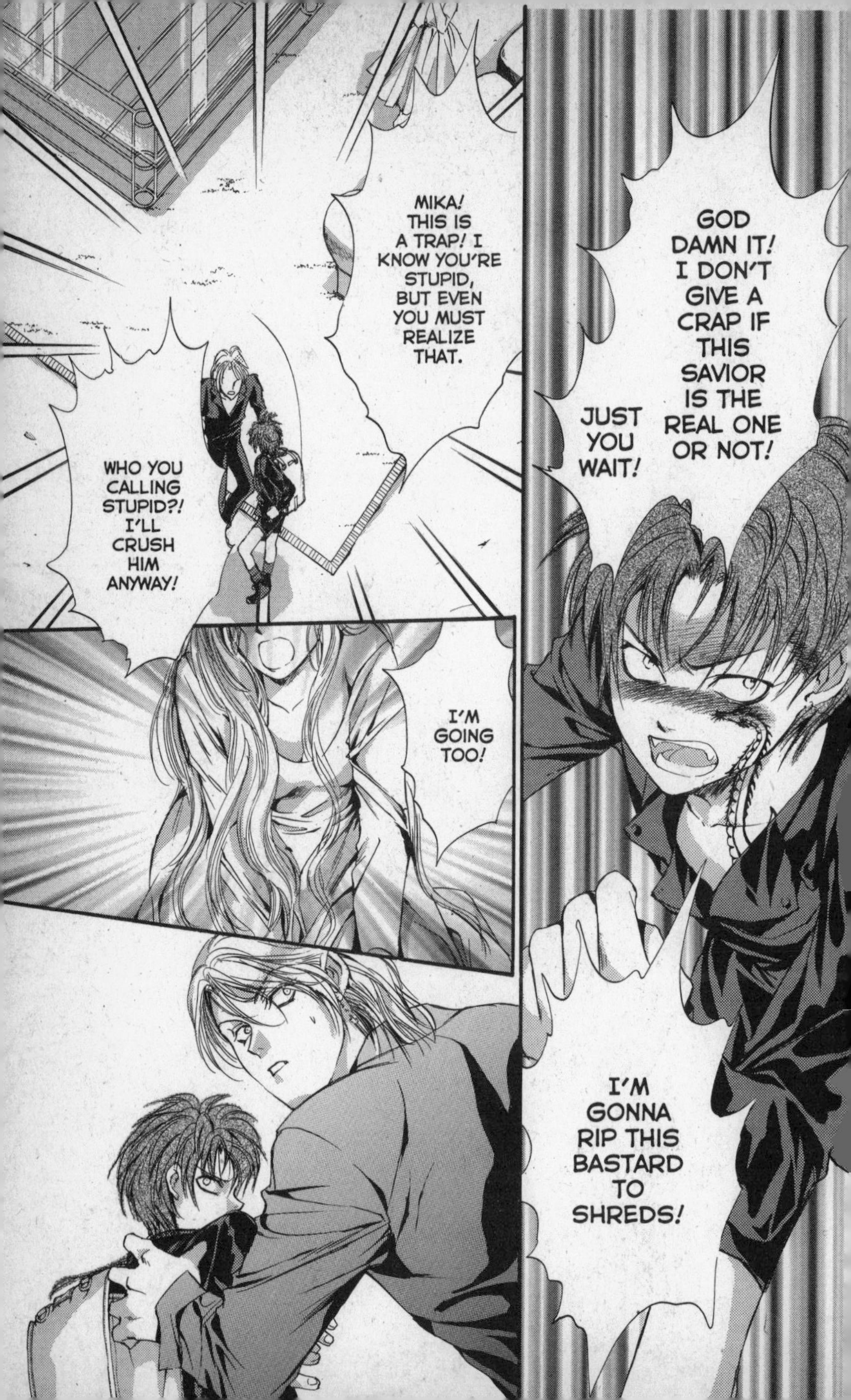
GOD DAMN IT! I DON'T GIVE A CRAP IF THIS SAVIOR IS THE REAL ONE OR NOT!
JUST YOU WAIT!
I'M GONNA RIP THIS BASTARD TO SHREDS!
MIKA! THIS IS A TRAP! I KNOW YOU'RE STUPID, BUT EVEN YOU MUST REALIZE THAT.
WHO YOU CALLING STUPID?! I'LL CRUSH HIM ANYWAY!
I'M GOING TOO!

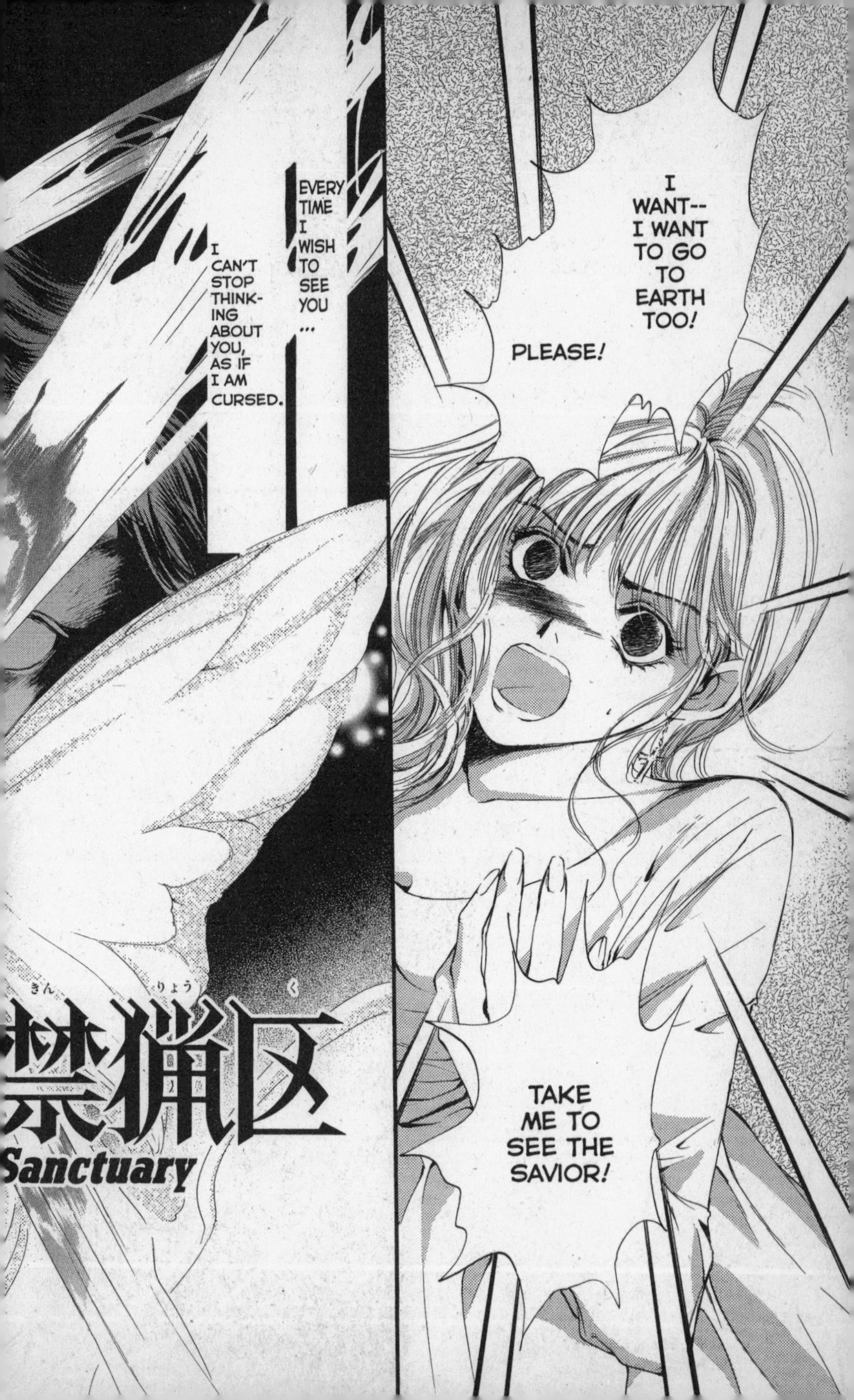
I WANT-- I WANT TO GO TO EARTH TOO!
PLEASE!
TAKE ME TO SEE THE SAVIOR!
EVERY TIME I WISH TO SEE YOU ...
I CAN'T STOP THINKING ABOUT YOU, AS IF I AM CURSED.
禁猟区
Sanctuary

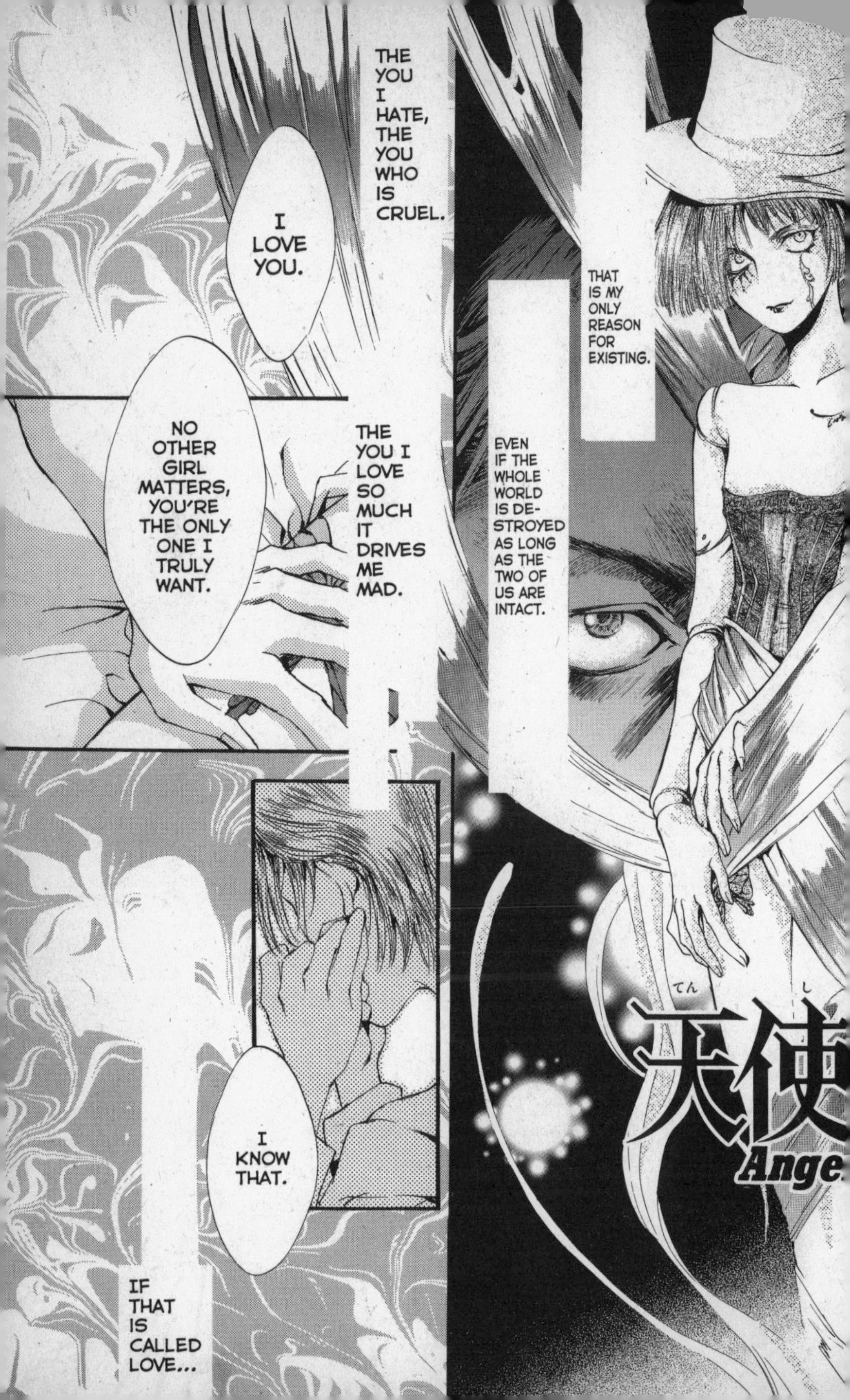
THAT IS MY ONLY REASON FOR EXISTING.
EVEN IF THE WHOLE WORLD IS DE-STROYED AS LONG AS THE TWO OF US ARE INTACT.
天使
Ange
THE YOU I HATE, THE YOU WHO IS CRUEL.
I LOVE YOU.
THE YOU I LOVE SO MUCH IT DRIVES ME MAD.
NO OTHER GIRL MATTERS, YOU'RE THE ONLY ONE I TRULY WANT.
I KNOW THAT.
IF THAT IS CALLED LOVE...

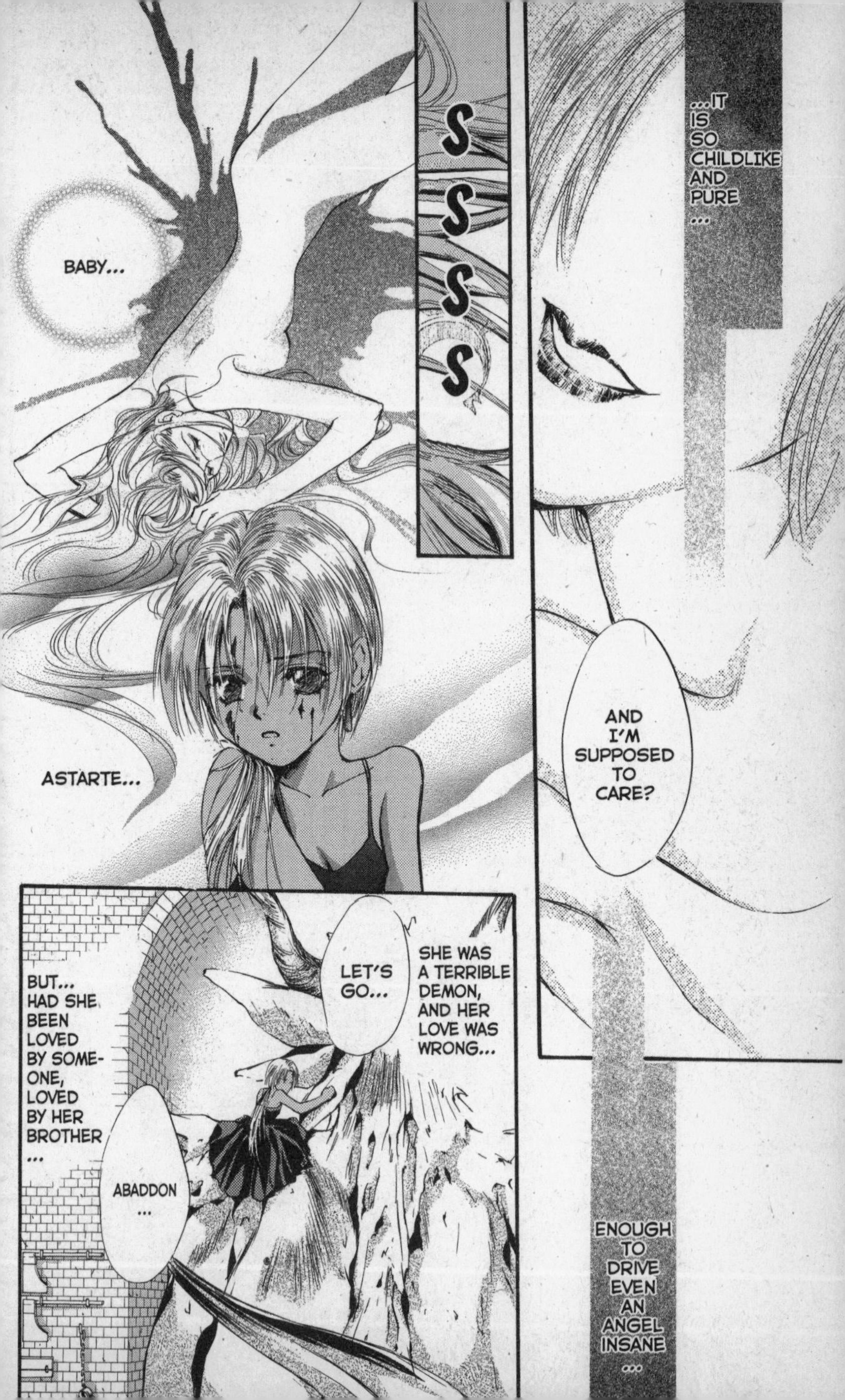
...IT IS SO CHILDLIKE AND PURE ...
AND I'M SUPPOSED TO CARE?
SSSS
BABY...
ASTARTE...
ENOUGH TO DRIVE EVEN AN ANGEL INSANE ...
SHE WAS A TERRIBLE DEMON, AND HER LOVE WAS WRONG...
LET'S GO...
BUT... HAD SHE BEEN LOVED BY SOME-ONE, LOVED BY HER BROTHER ...
ABADDON ...

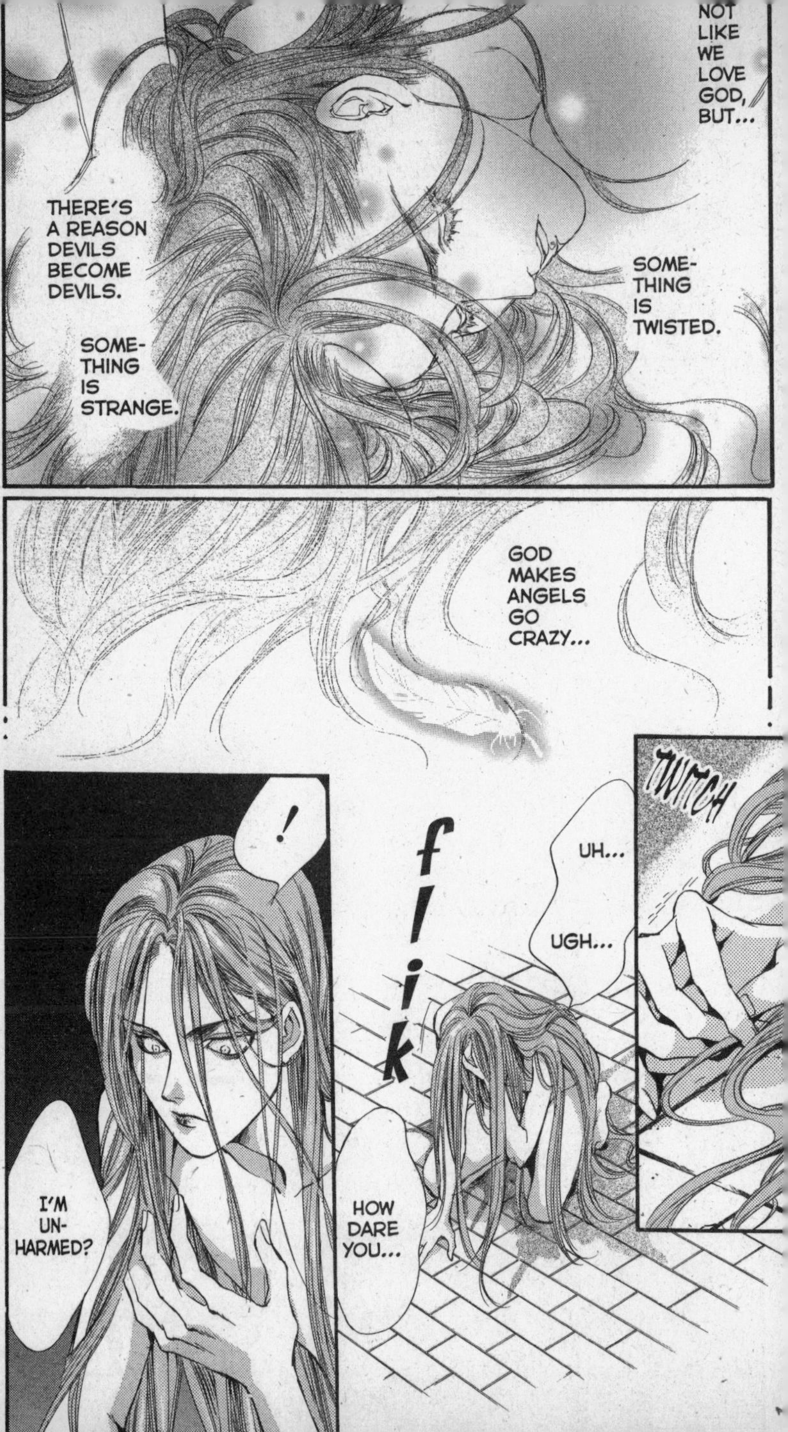
NOT LIKE WE LOVE GOD, BUT...
SOME-THING IS TWISTED.
THERE'S A REASON DEVILS BECOME DEVILS.
SOME-THING IS STRANGE.
GOD MAKES ANGELS GO CRAZY...
TWITCH
UH...
UGH...
flik
HOW DARE YOU...
!
I'M UN-HARMED?

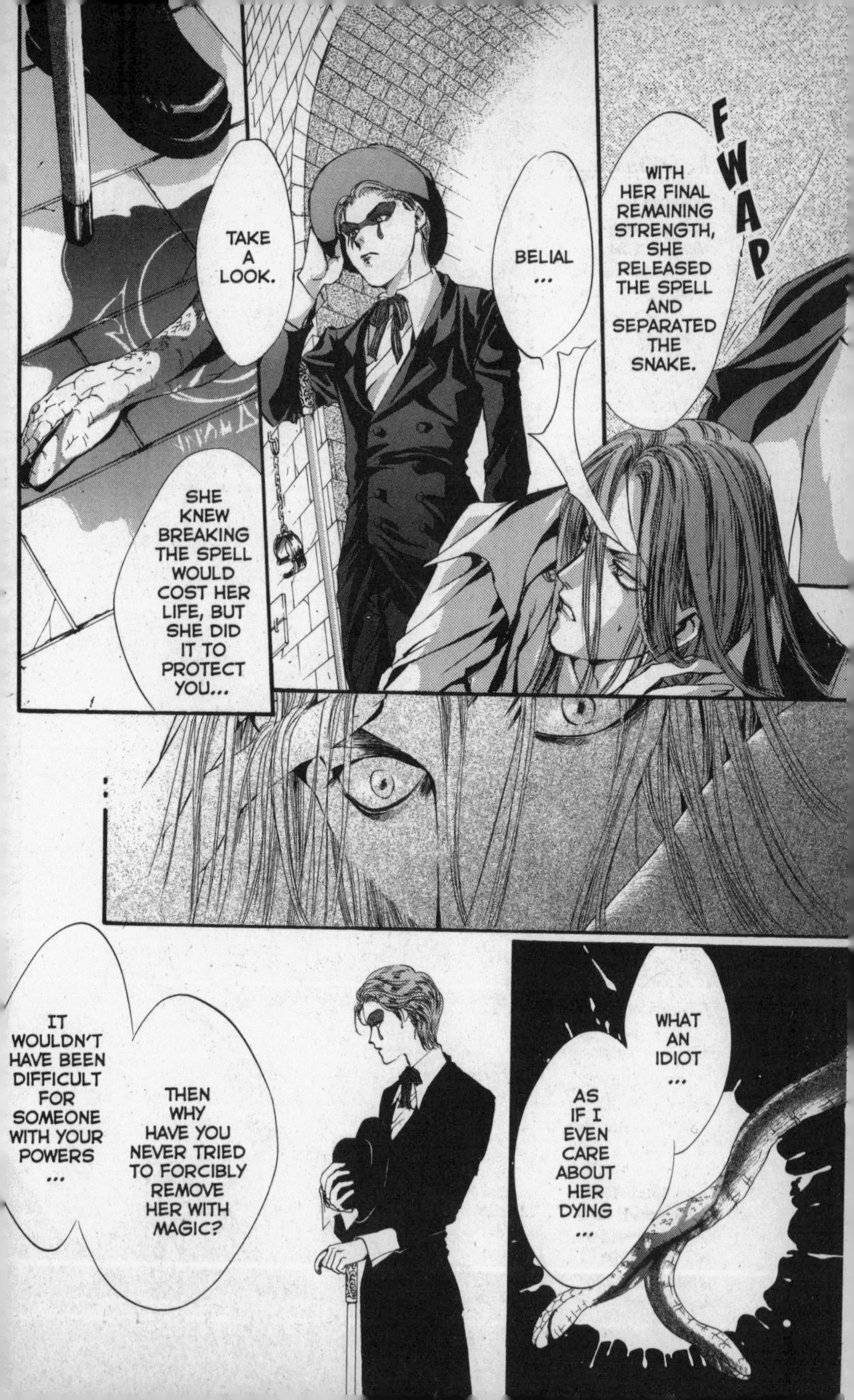
FWAP
WITH HER FINAL REMAINING STRENGTH, SHE RELEASED THE SPELL AND SEPARATED THE SNAKE.
BELIAL ...
TAKE A LOOK.
SHE KNEW BREAKING THE SPELL WOULD COST HER LIFE, BUT SHE DID IT TO PROTECT YOU...
...
WHAT AN IDIOT ...
AS IF I EVEN CARE ABOUT HER DYING ...
THEN WHY HAVE YOU NEVER TRIED TO FORCIBLY REMOVE HER WITH MAGIC?
IT WOULDN'T HAVE BEEN DIFFICULT FOR SOMEONE WITH YOUR POWERS ...

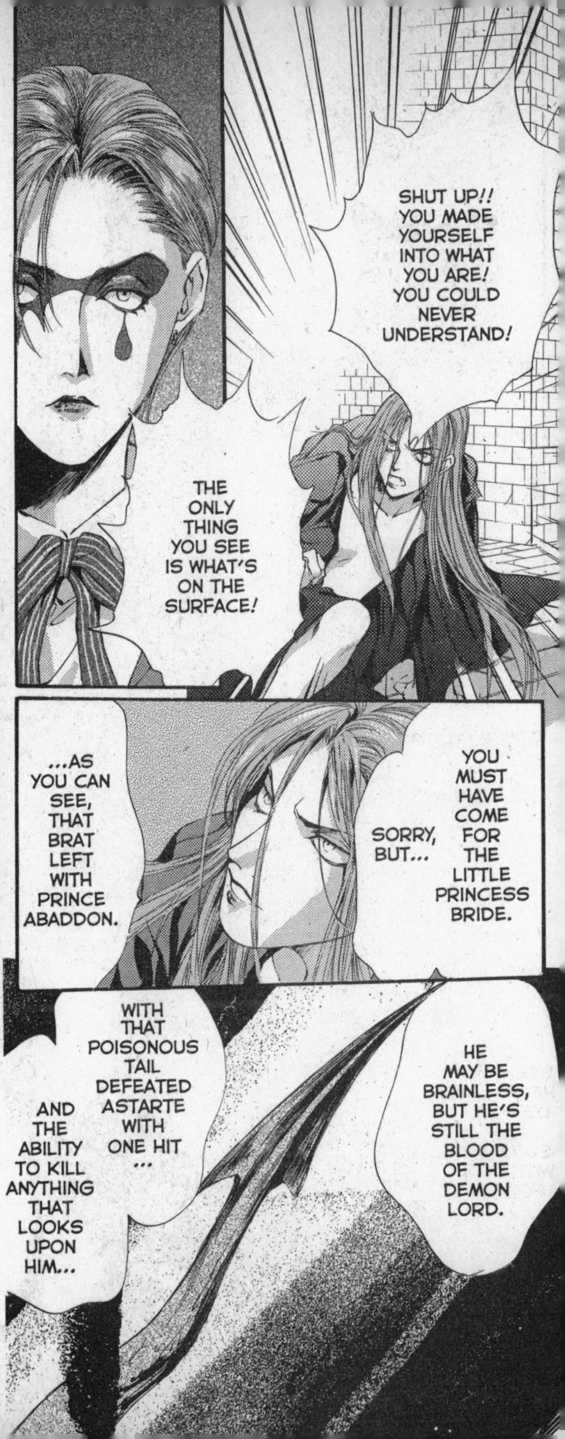
SHUT UP!! YOU MADE YOURSELF INTO WHAT YOU ARE! YOU COULD NEVER UNDERSTAND!
THE ONLY THING YOU SEE IS WHAT'S ON THE SURFACE!
YOU MUST HAVE COME FOR THE LITTLE PRINCESS BRIDE.
SORRY, BUT...
...AS YOU CAN SEE, THAT BRAT LEFT WITH PRINCE ABADDON.
HE MAY BE BRAINLESS, BUT HE'S STILL THE BLOOD OF THE DEMON LORD.
WITH THAT POISONOUS TAIL DEFEATED ASTARTE WITH ONE HIT...
AND THE ABILITY TO KILL ANYTHING THAT LOOKS UPON HIM...

Mammon
Former angel. The Golden Count, "Avarice" of the seven sins. Two bird heads and clawed hands and feet. The Palace of Hell is covered in gold thanks to him.

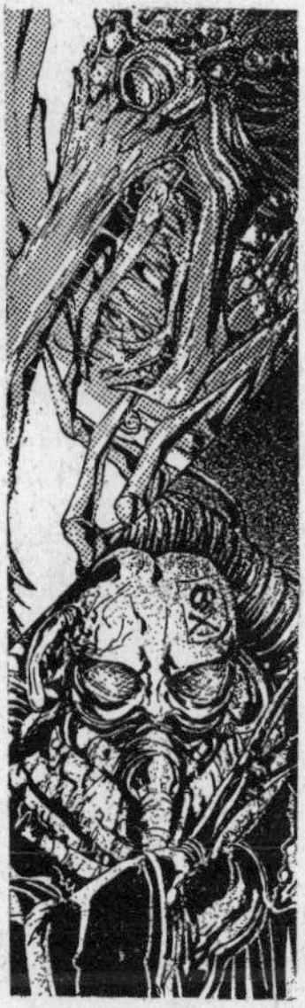

Beelzebub
Former Seraphim. The Lord of Flies, "Gluttony" of the seven sins. A powerful bug in hell. Surprisingly, they say he was in the *Choir* when he was a Seraphim. He's hard to draw, so he's not in the series... Well, not exactly, but...

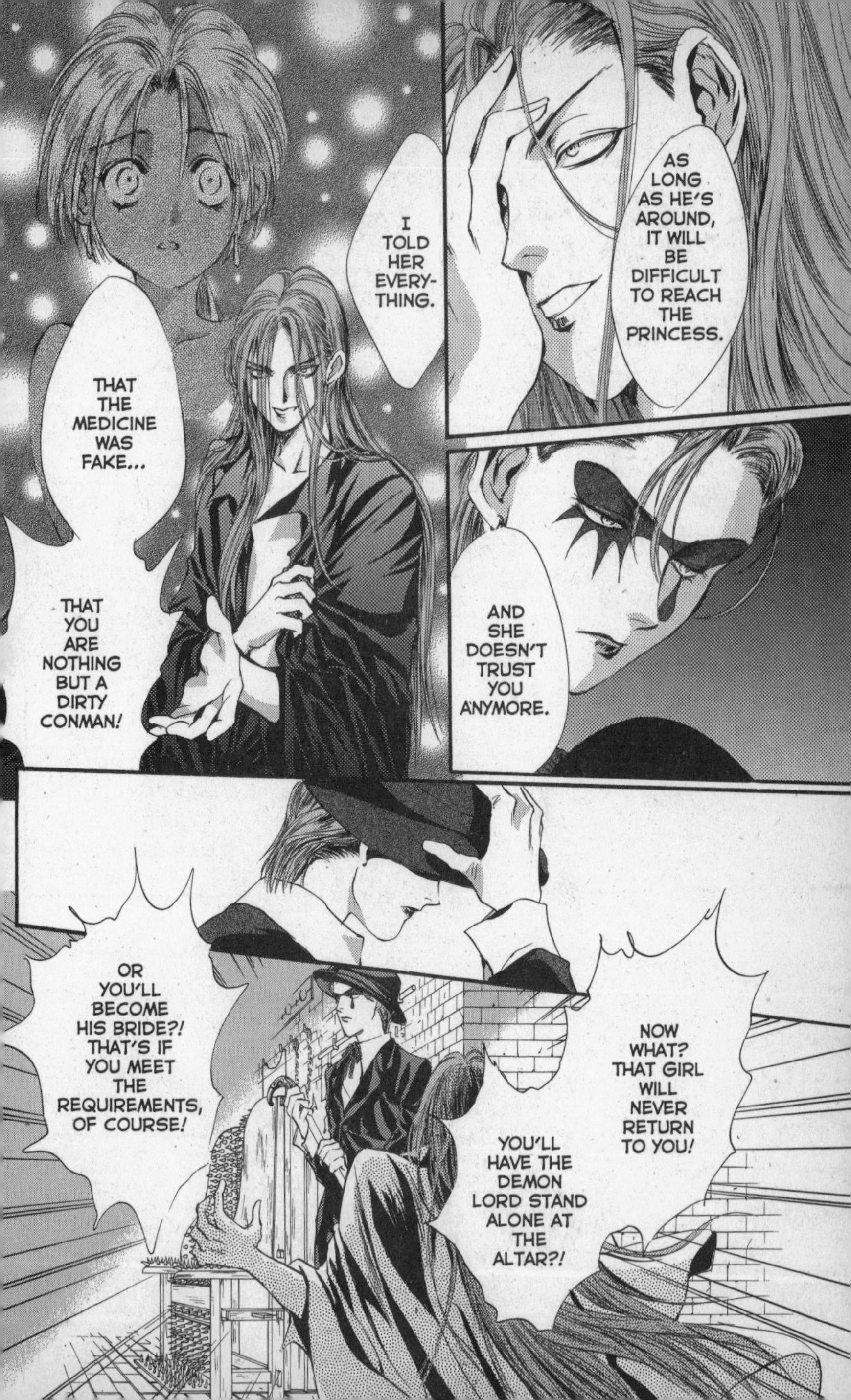
AS LONG AS HE'S AROUND, IT WILL BE DIFFICULT TO REACH THE PRINCESS.
AND SHE DOESN'T TRUST YOU ANYMORE.
I TOLD HER EVERY-THING.
THAT THE MEDICINE WAS FAKE...
THAT YOU ARE NOTHING BUT A DIRTY CONMAN!
NOW WHAT? THAT GIRL WILL NEVER RETURN TO YOU!
YOU'LL HAVE THE DEMON LORD STAND ALONE AT THE ALTAR?!
OR YOU'LL BECOME HIS BRIDE?! THAT'S IF YOU MEET THE REQUIREMENTS, OF COURSE!

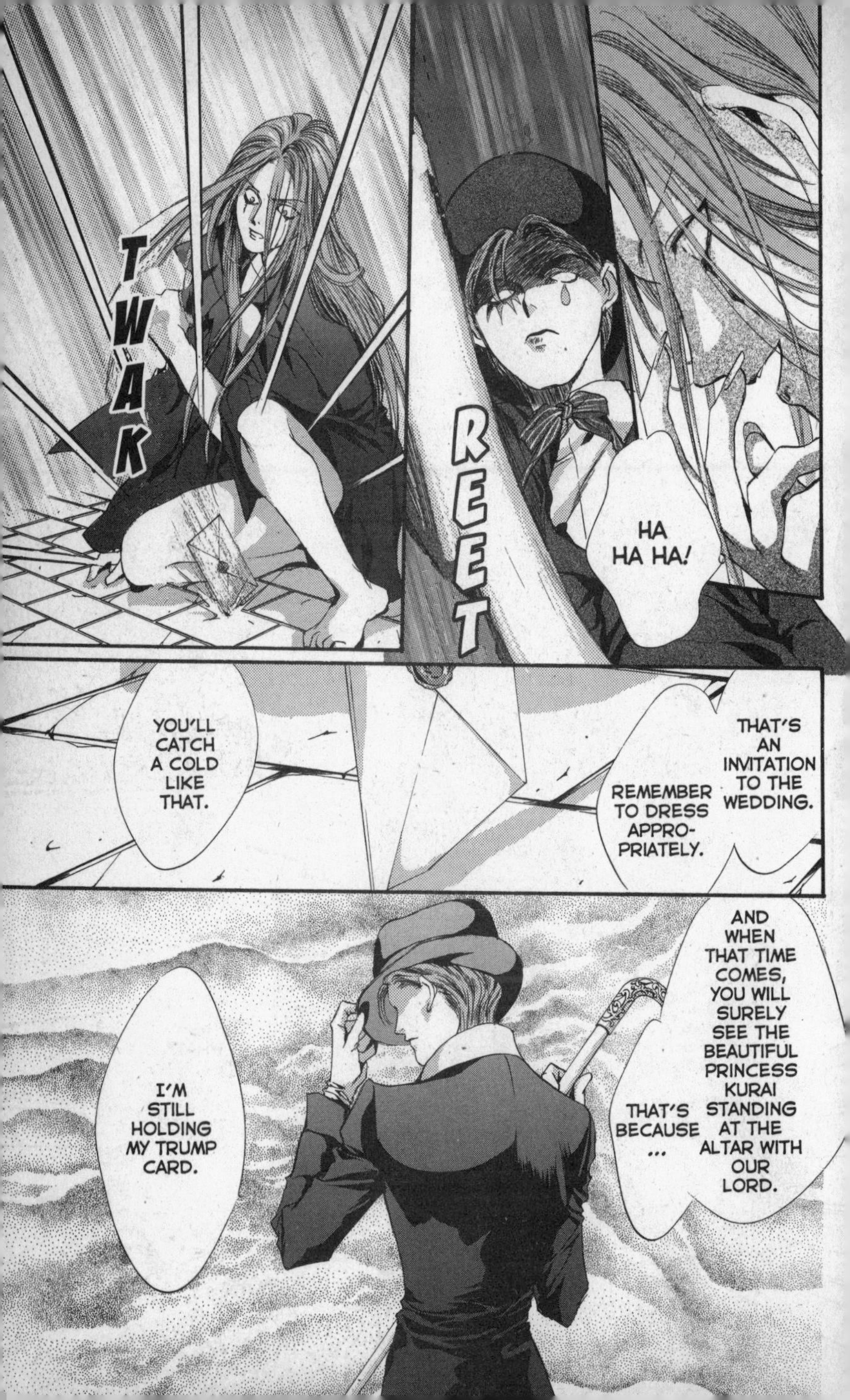
HA HA HA!
REEET
TWAK
THAT'S AN INVITATION TO THE WEDDING.
REMEMBER TO DRESS APPROPRIATELY.
YOU'LL CATCH A COLD LIKE THAT.
AND WHEN THAT TIME COMES, YOU WILL SURELY SEE THE BEAUTIFUL PRINCESS KURAI STANDING AT THE ALTAR WITH OUR LORD.
THAT'S BECAUSE ...
I'M STILL HOLDING MY TRUMP CARD.

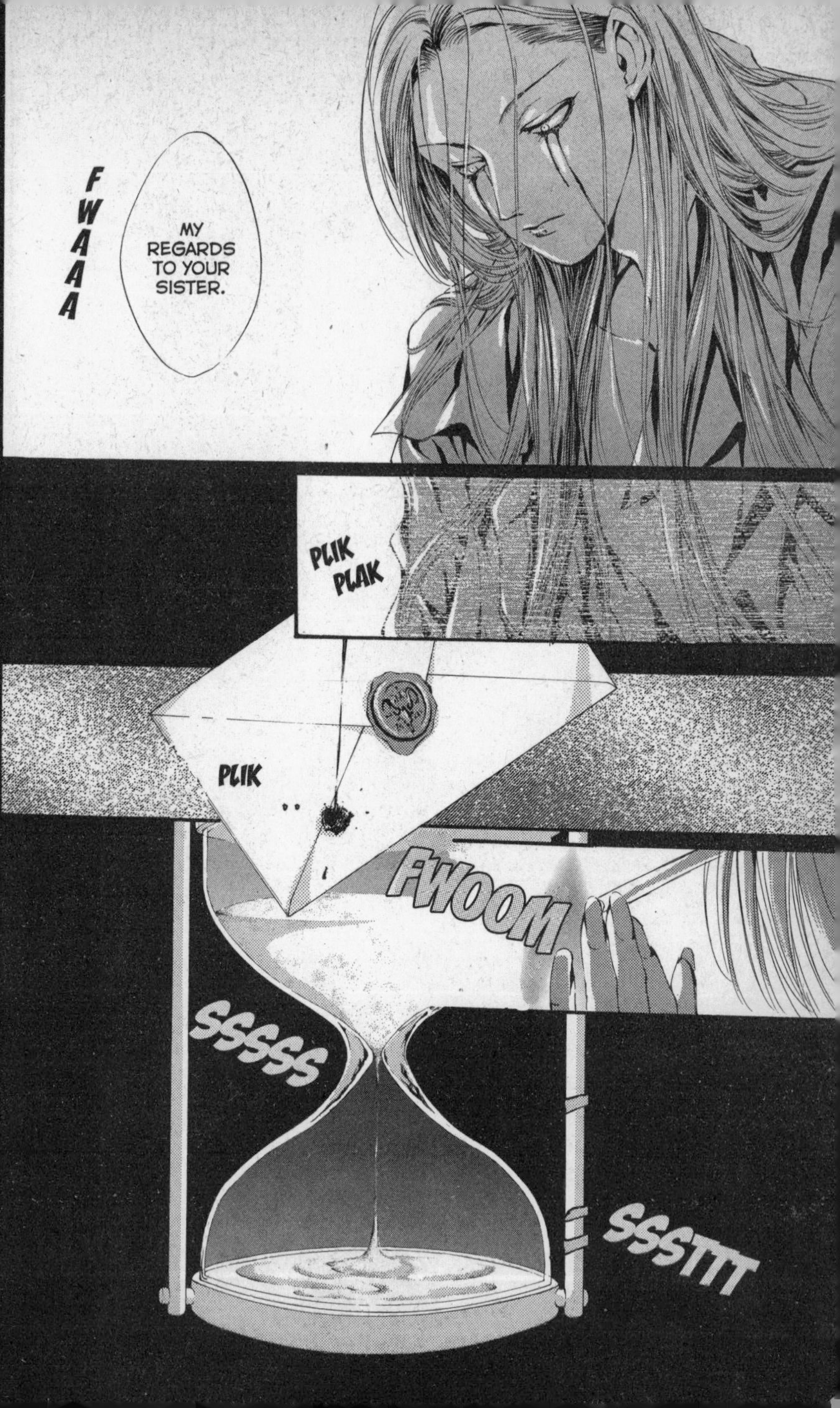
MY REGARDS TO YOUR SISTER.
FWAAA
PLIK PLAK
PLIK
FWOOM
SSSSS
SSSTTT

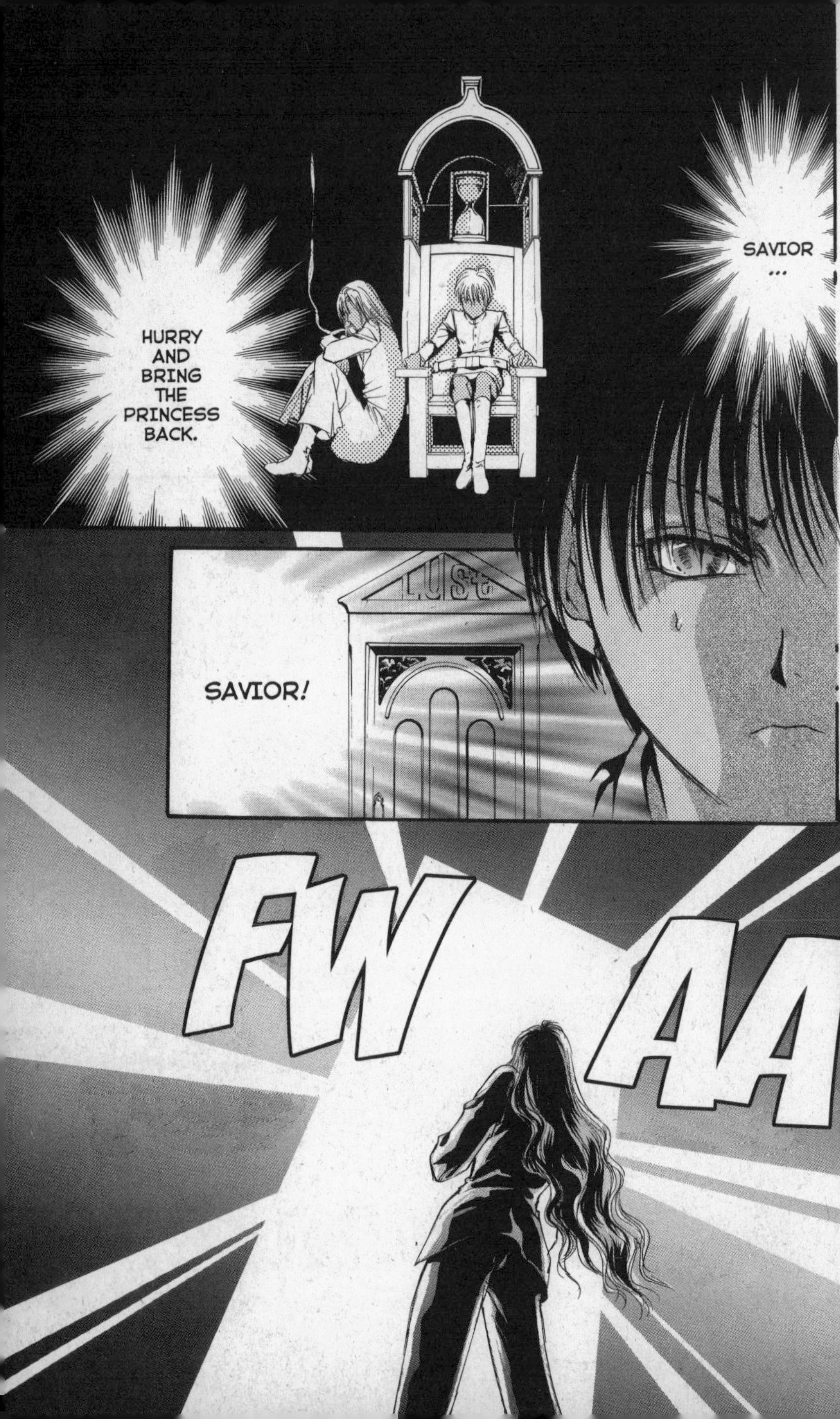
SAVIOR ...
HURRY AND BRING THE PRINCESS BACK.
SAVIOR!
FWAA

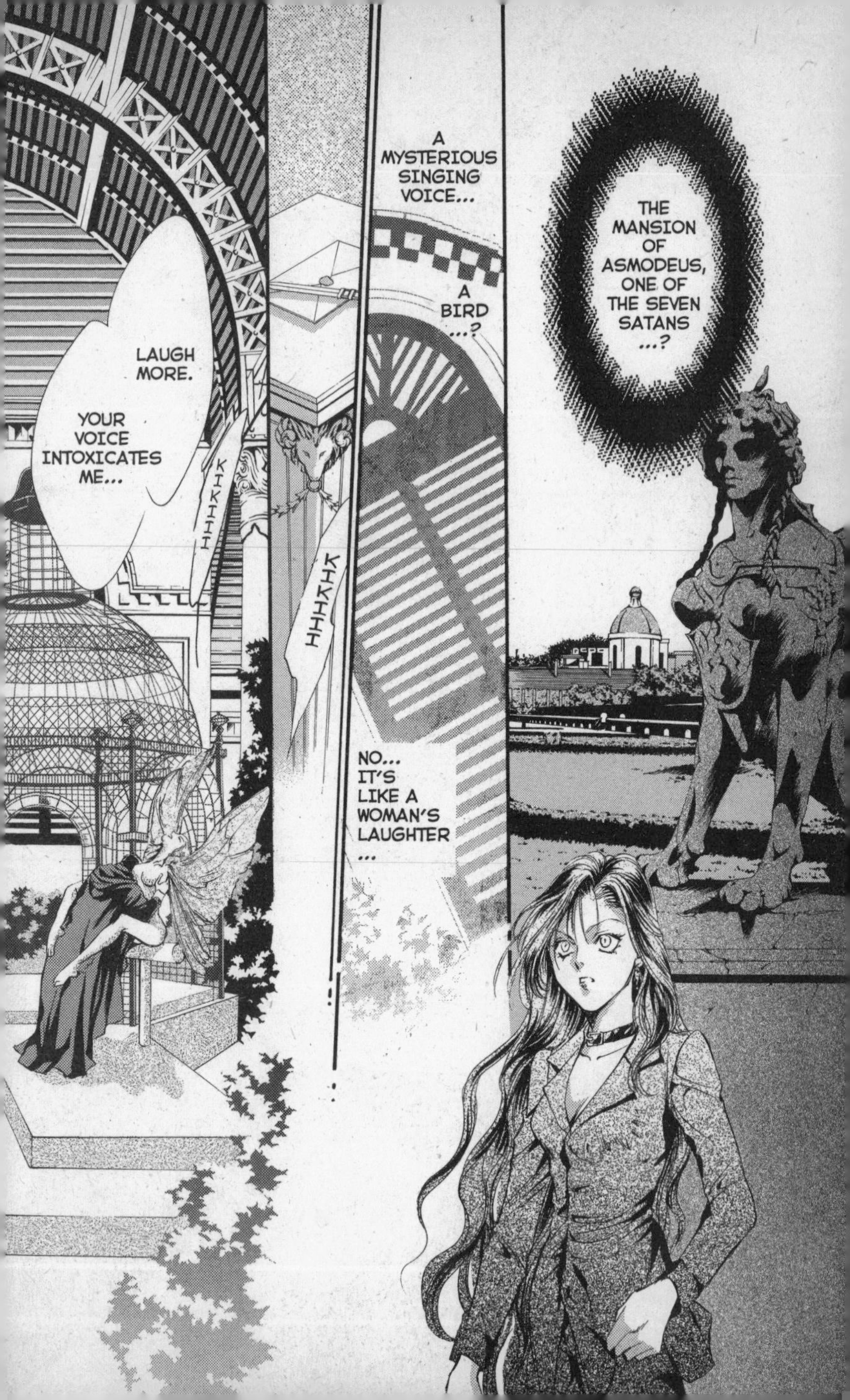
THE MANSION OF ASMODEUS, ONE OF THE SEVEN SATANS ...?
A MYSTERIOUS SINGING VOICE...
A BIRD ...?
NO... IT'S LIKE A WOMAN'S LAUGHTER ...
KHKHHH
KIKIIII
LAUGH MORE.
YOUR VOICE INTOXICATES ME...

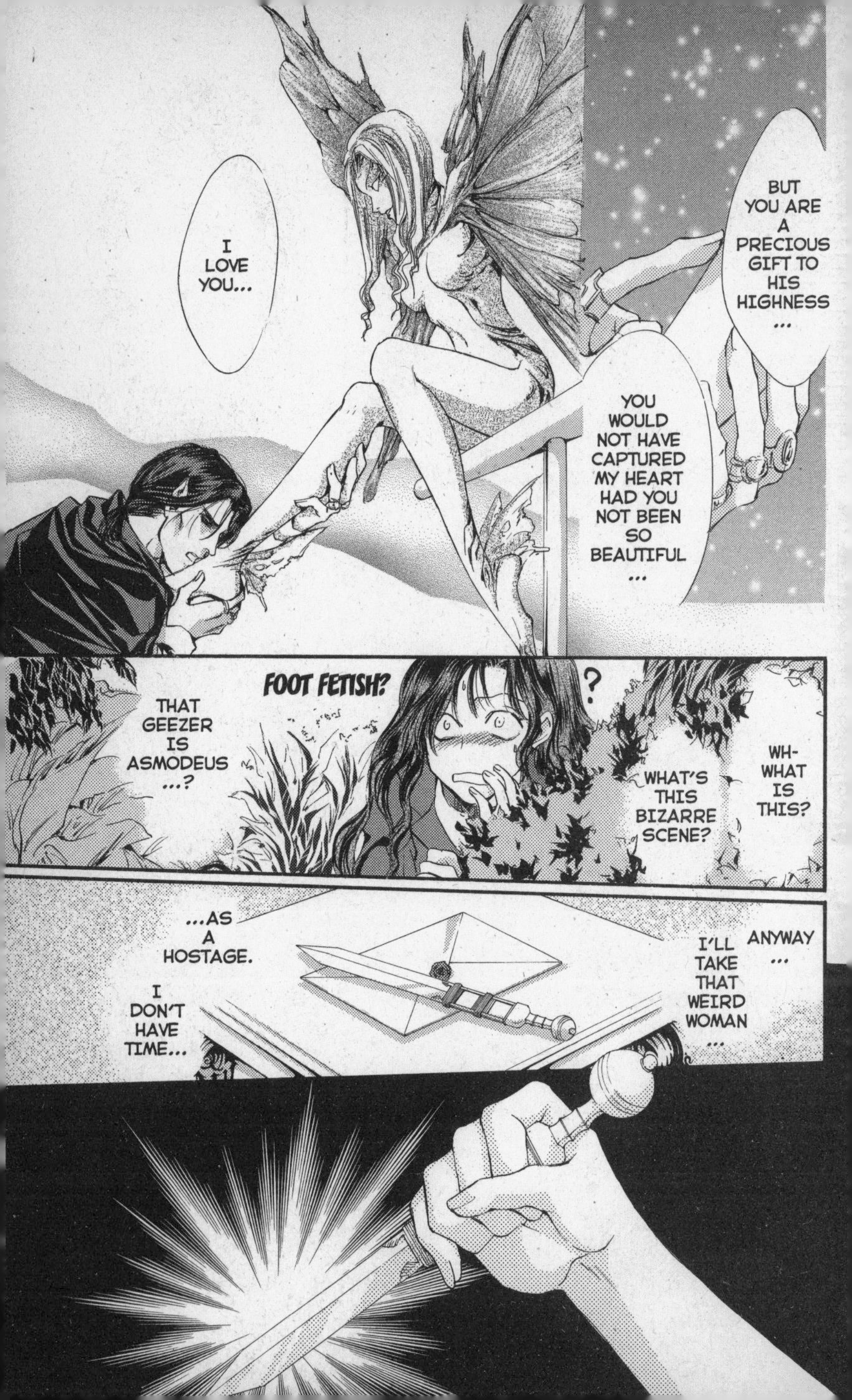
BUT YOU ARE A PRECIOUS GIFT TO HIS HIGHNESS ...
YOU WOULD NOT HAVE CAPTURED MY HEART HAD YOU NOT BEEN SO BEAUTIFUL ...
I LOVE YOU...
WH- WHAT IS THIS?
WHAT'S THIS BIZARRE SCENE?
?
FOOT FETISH?
THAT GEEZER IS ASMODEUS ...?
ANYWAY ...
I'LL TAKE THAT WEIRD WOMAN ...
...AS A HOSTAGE.
I DON'T HAVE TIME...

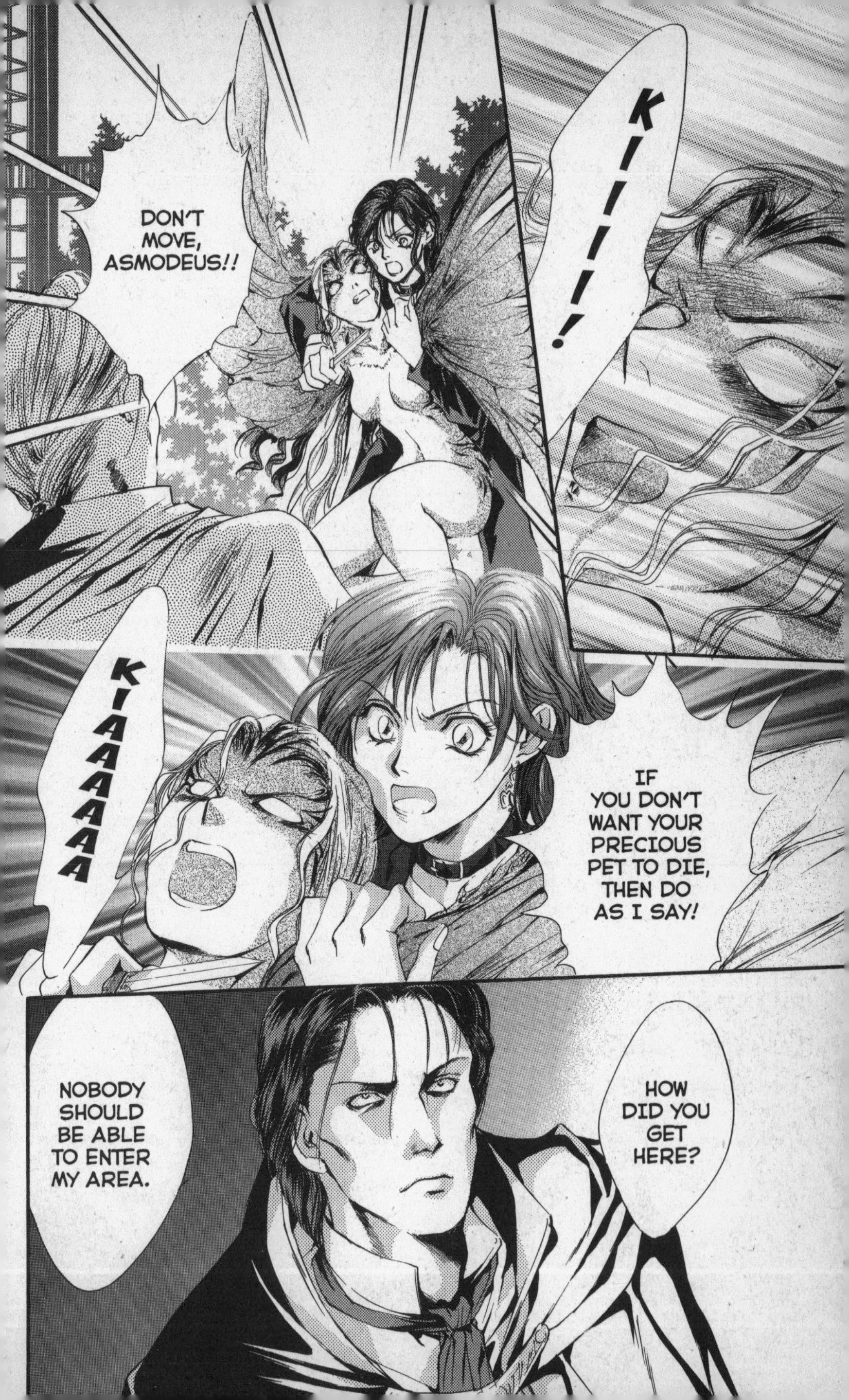
KIIII!
DON'T MOVE, ASMODEUS!!
IF YOU DON'T WANT YOUR PRECIOUS PET TO DIE, THEN DO AS I SAY!
KIAAAAAA
HOW DID YOU GET HERE?
NOBODY SHOULD BE ABLE TO ENTER MY AREA.

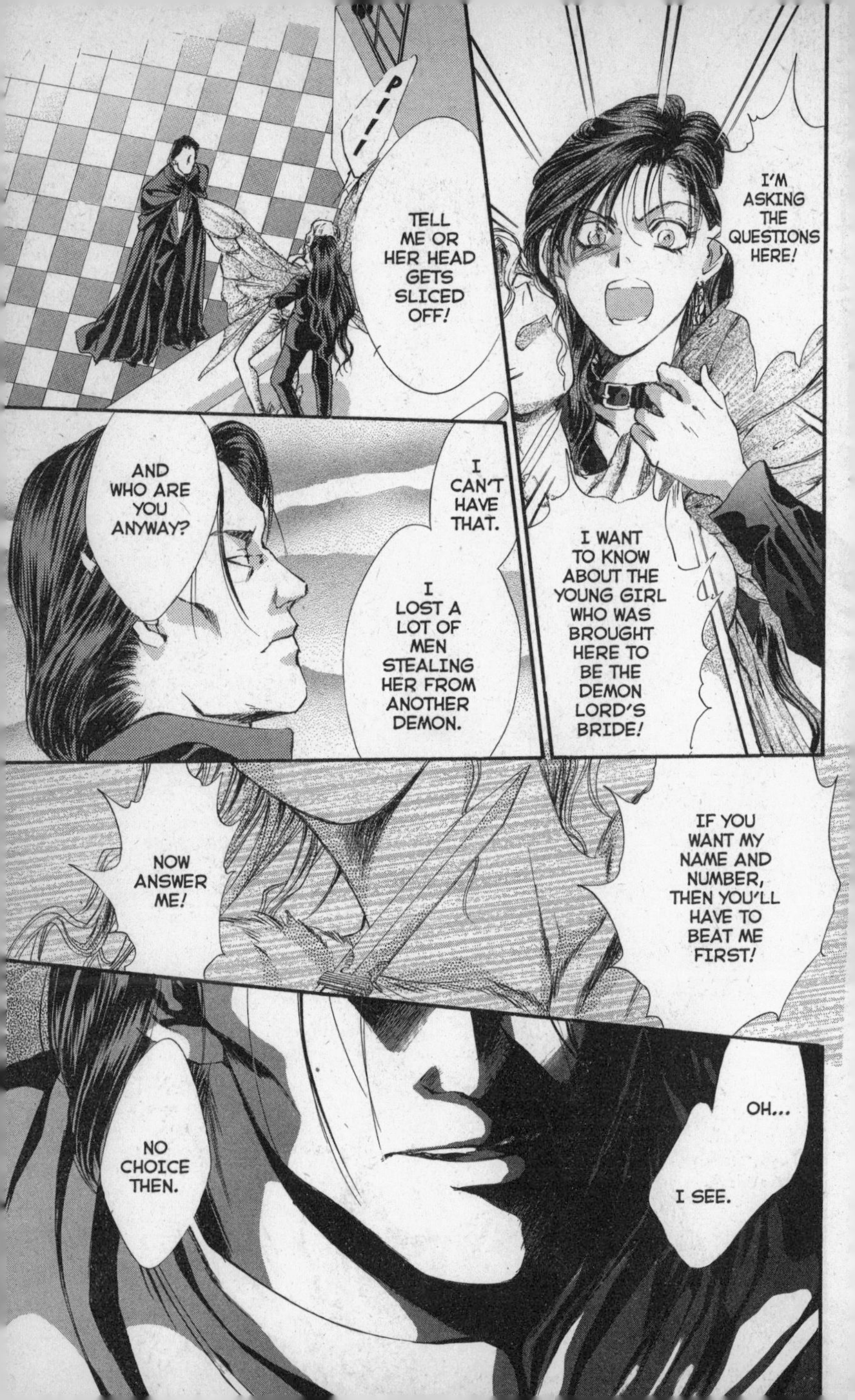
I'M ASKING THE QUESTIONS HERE!
I WANT TO KNOW ABOUT THE YOUNG GIRL WHO WAS BROUGHT HERE TO BE THE DEMON LORD'S BRIDE!
P I I I
TELL ME OR HER HEAD GETS SLICED OFF!
I CAN'T HAVE THAT.
I LOST A LOT OF MEN STEALING HER FROM ANOTHER DEMON.
AND WHO ARE YOU ANYWAY?
IF YOU WANT MY NAME AND NUMBER, THEN YOU'LL HAVE TO BEAT ME FIRST!
NOW ANSWER ME!
OH...
I SEE.
NO CHOICE THEN.

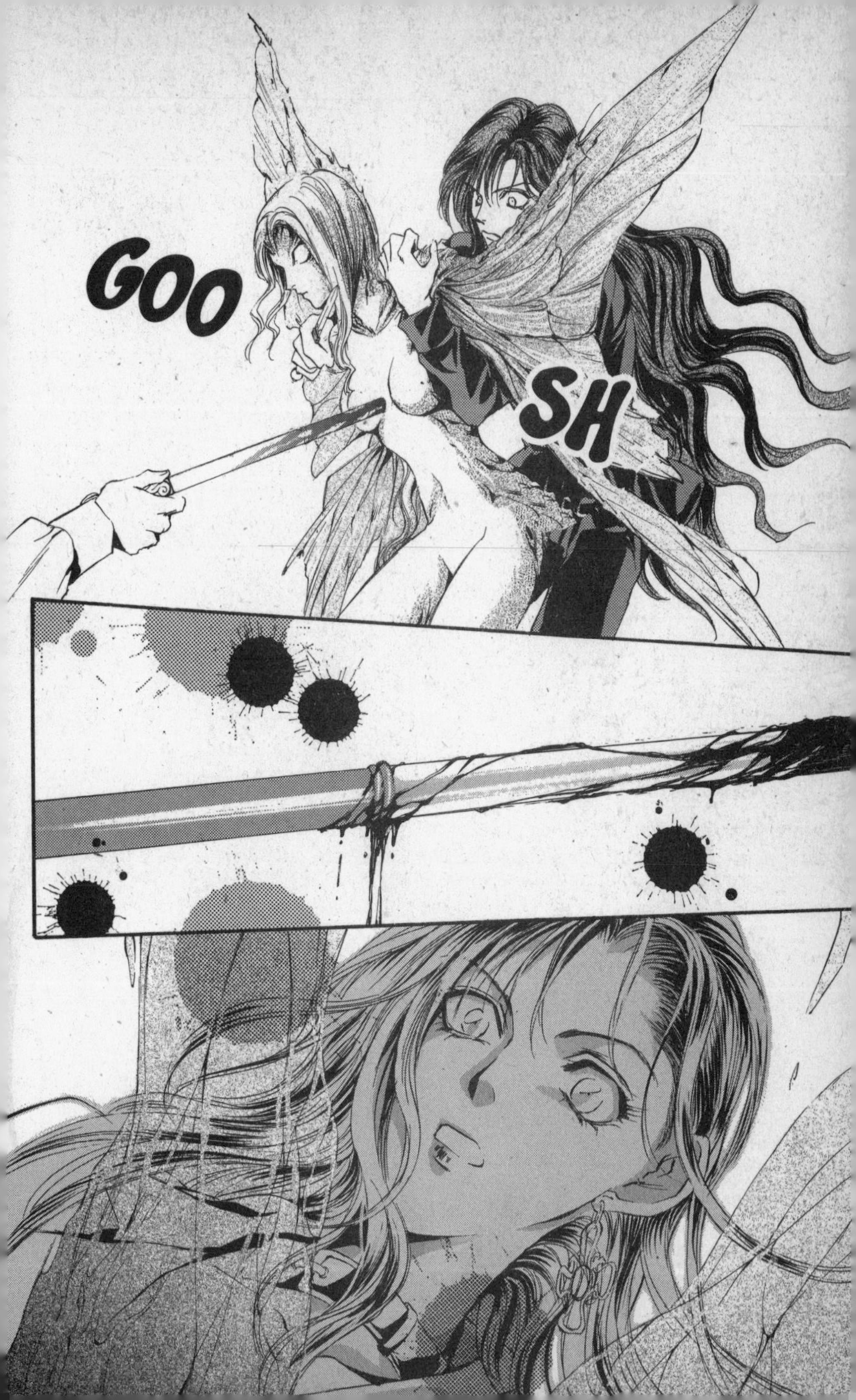
GOO
SH

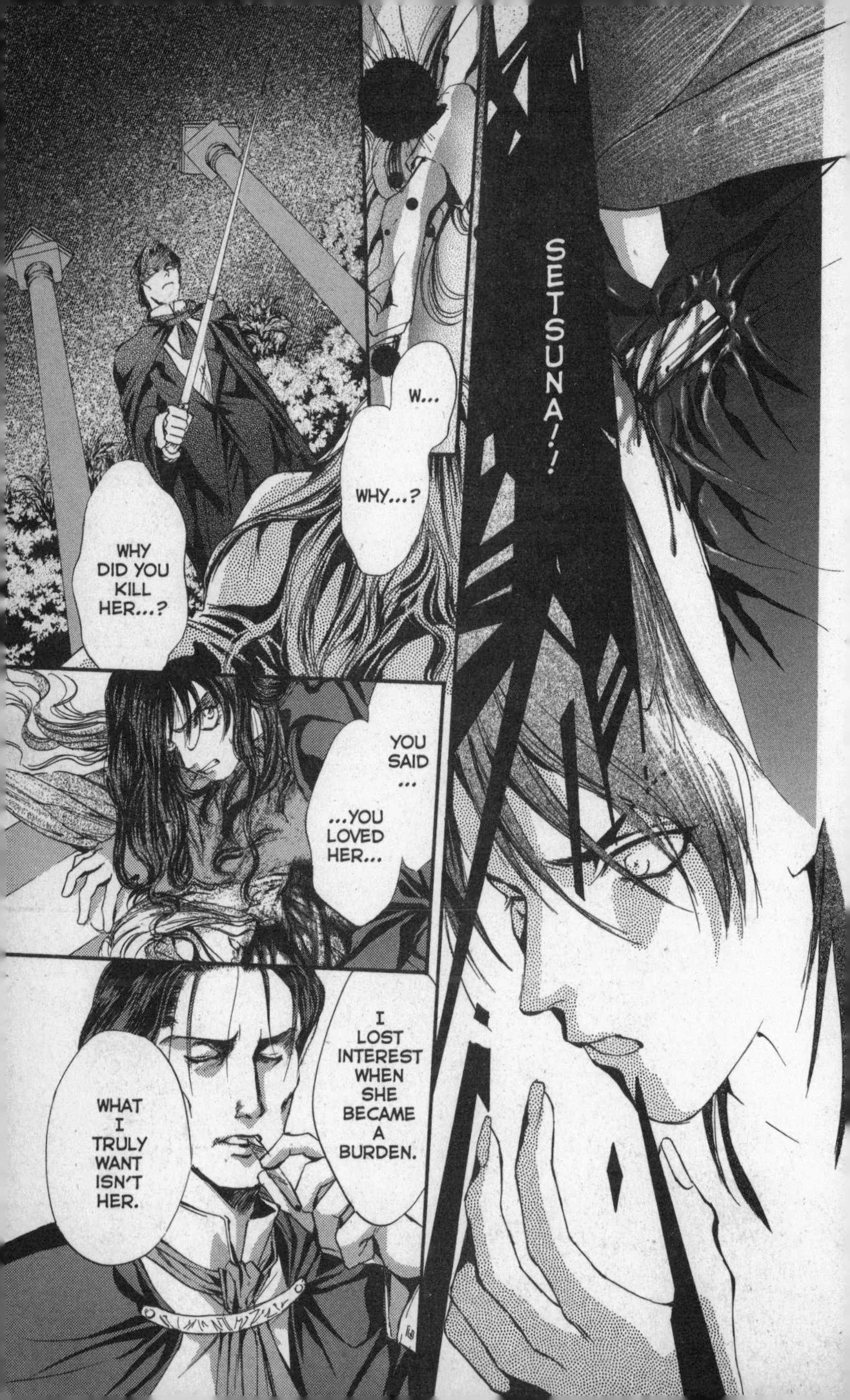
SETSUNA!!
W...
WHY...?
WHY DID YOU KILL HER...?
YOU SAID ...
...YOU LOVED HER...
I LOST INTEREST WHEN SHE BECAME A BURDEN.
WHAT I TRULY WANT ISN'T HER.

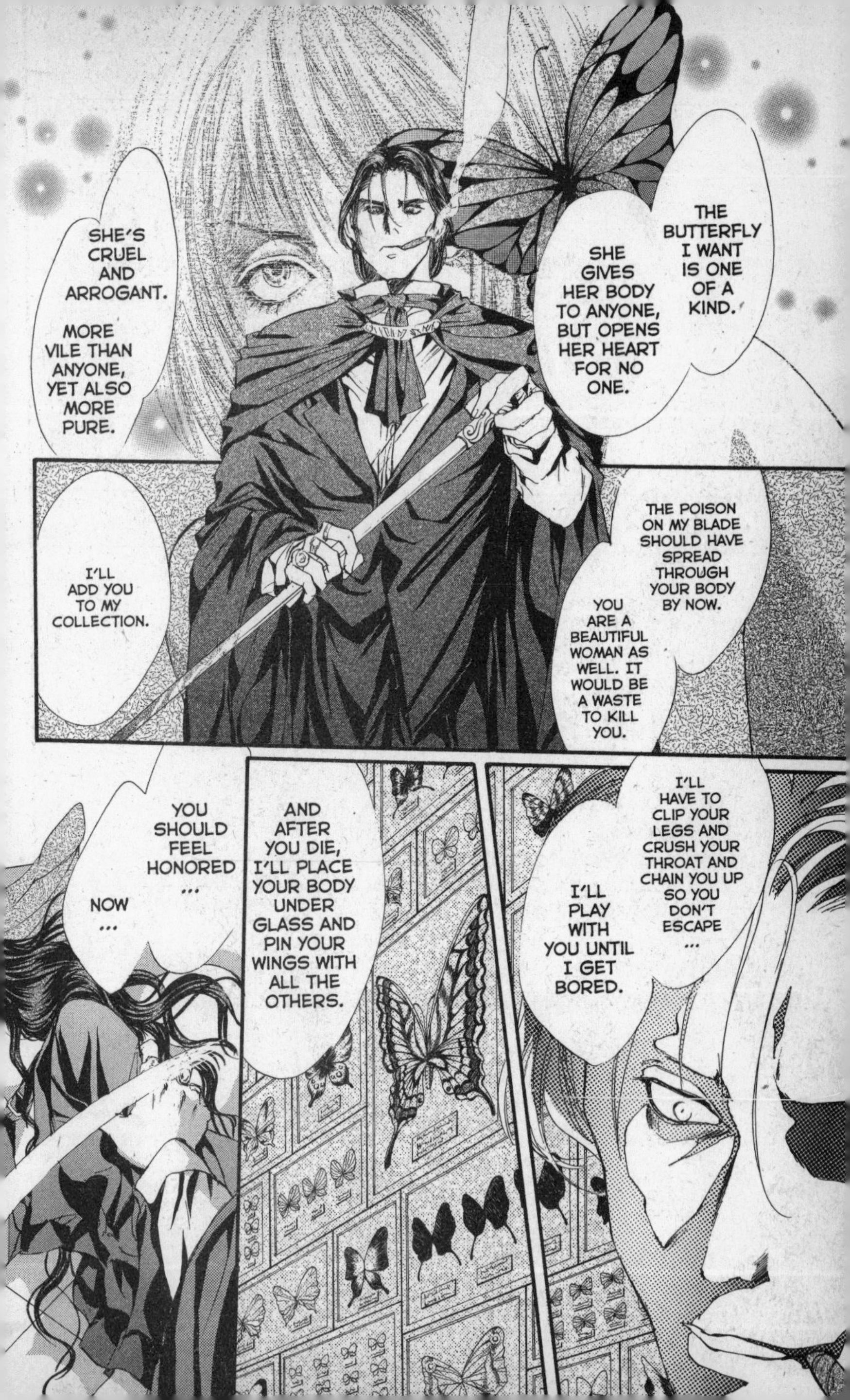
THE BUTTERFLY I WANT IS ONE OF A KIND.
SHE GIVES HER BODY TO ANYONE, BUT OPENS HER HEART FOR NO ONE.
SHE'S CRUEL AND ARROGANT.
MORE VILE THAN ANYONE, YET ALSO MORE PURE.
THE POISON ON MY BLADE SHOULD HAVE SPREAD THROUGH YOUR BODY BY NOW.
YOU ARE A BEAUTIFUL WOMAN AS WELL. IT WOULD BE A WASTE TO KILL YOU.
I'LL ADD YOU TO MY COLLECTION.
I'LL HAVE TO CLIP YOUR LEGS AND CRUSH YOUR THROAT AND CHAIN YOU UP SO YOU DON'T ESCAPE ...
I'LL PLAY WITH YOU UNTIL I GET BORED.
AND AFTER YOU DIE, I'LL PLACE YOUR BODY UNDER GLASS AND PIN YOUR WINGS WITH ALL THE OTHERS.
YOU SHOULD FEEL HONORED ...
NOW ...

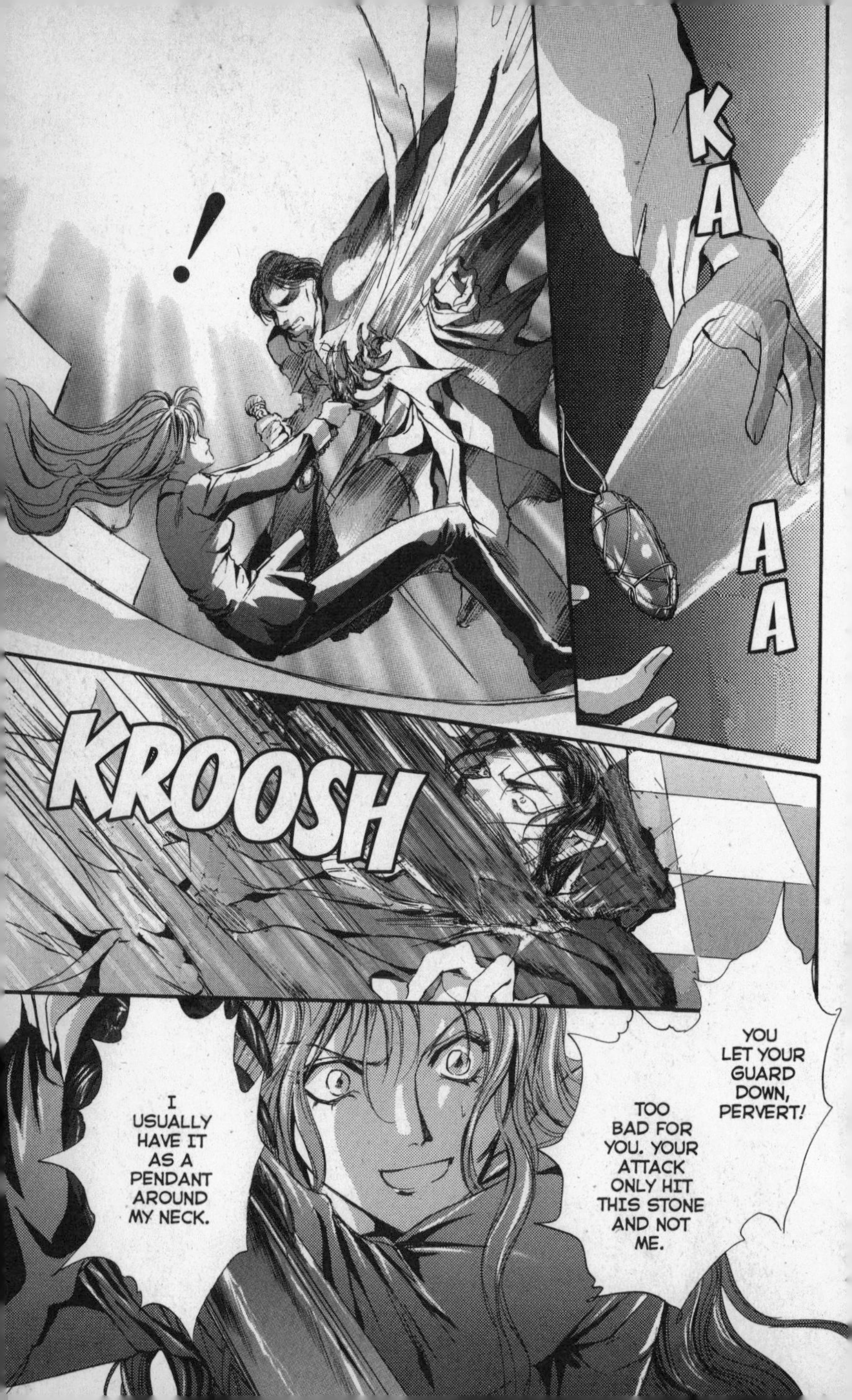
KAAAA
!
KROOSH
YOU LET YOUR GUARD DOWN, PERVERT!
TOO BAD FOR YOU. YOUR ATTACK ONLY HIT THIS STONE AND NOT ME.
I USUALLY HAVE IT AS A PENDANT AROUND MY NECK.

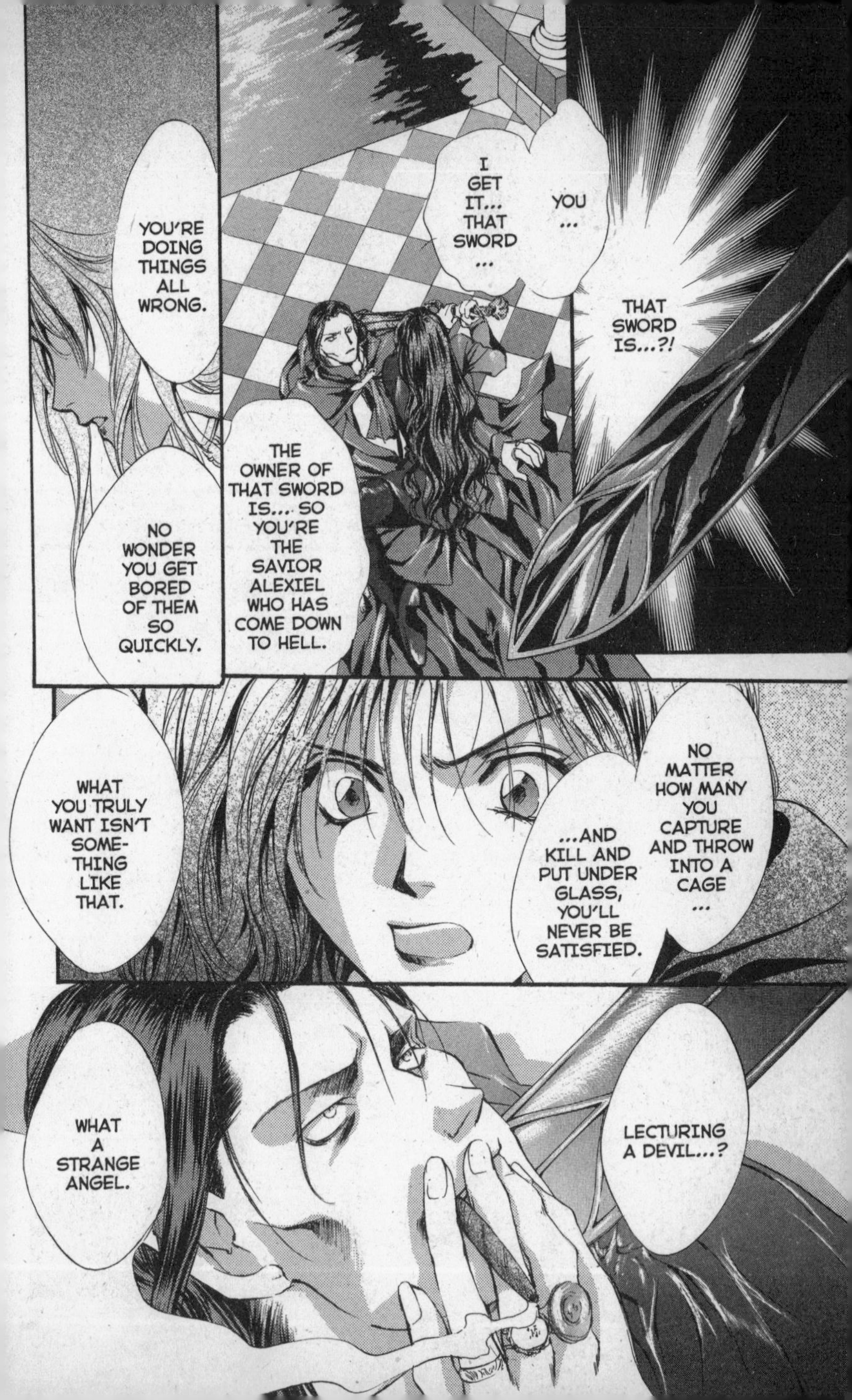
THAT SWORD IS...?!
I GET IT... THAT SWORD ...
YOU ...
THE OWNER OF THAT SWORD IS... SO YOU'RE THE SAVIOR ALEXIEL WHO HAS COME DOWN TO HELL.
YOU'RE DOING THINGS ALL WRONG.
NO WONDER YOU GET BORED OF THEM SO QUICKLY.
NO MATTER HOW MANY YOU CAPTURE AND THROW INTO A CAGE ...
...AND KILL AND PUT UNDER GLASS, YOU'LL NEVER BE SATISFIED.
WHAT YOU TRULY WANT ISN'T SOME-THING LIKE THAT.
LECTURING A DEVIL...?
WHAT A STRANGE ANGEL.

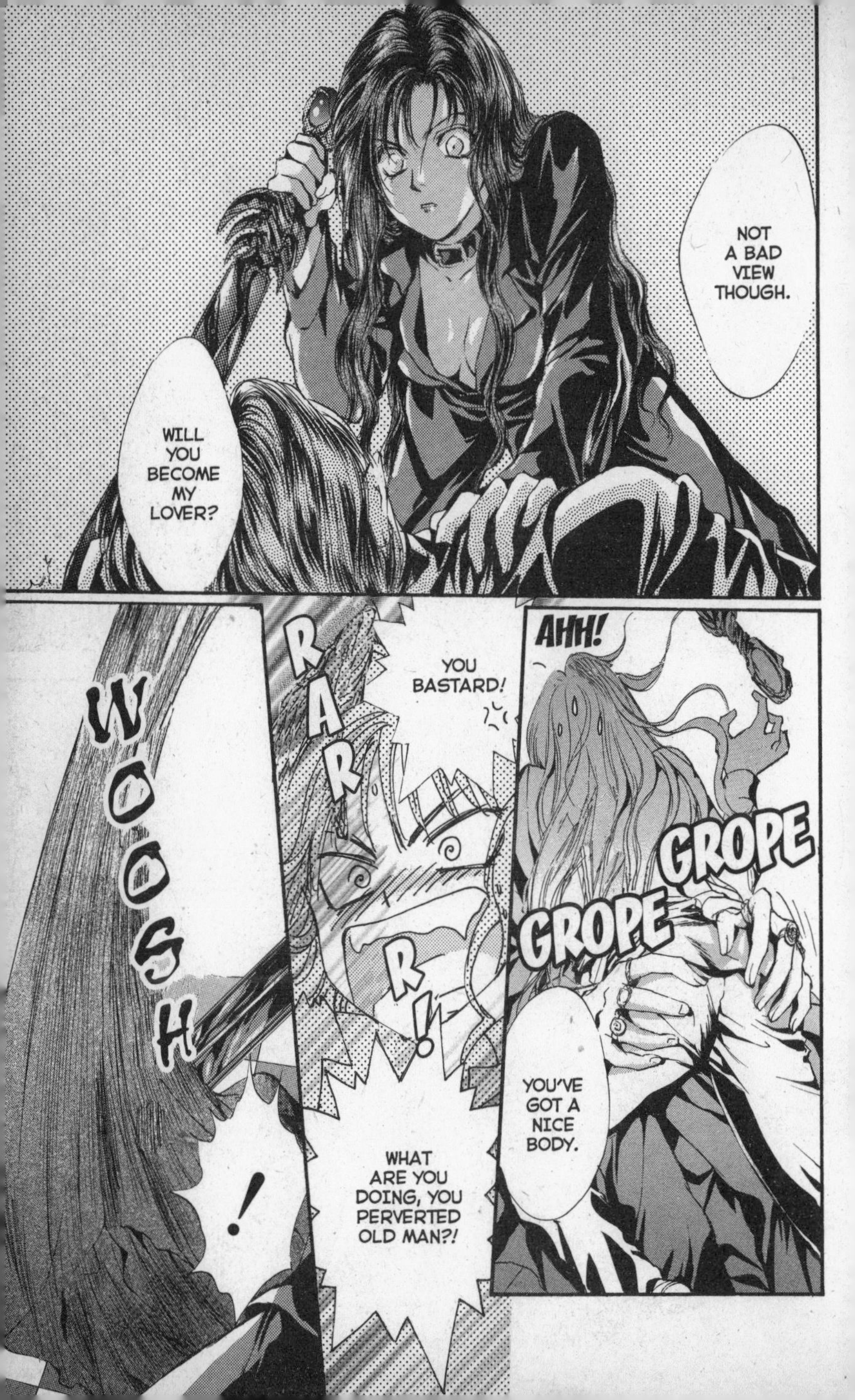
NOT A BAD VIEW THOUGH.
WILL YOU BECOME MY LOVER?
AHH!
GROPE GROPE
YOU'VE GOT A NICE BODY.
YOU BASTARD!
RARR!
WHAT ARE YOU DOING, YOU PERVERTED OLD MAN?!
WOOSH
!

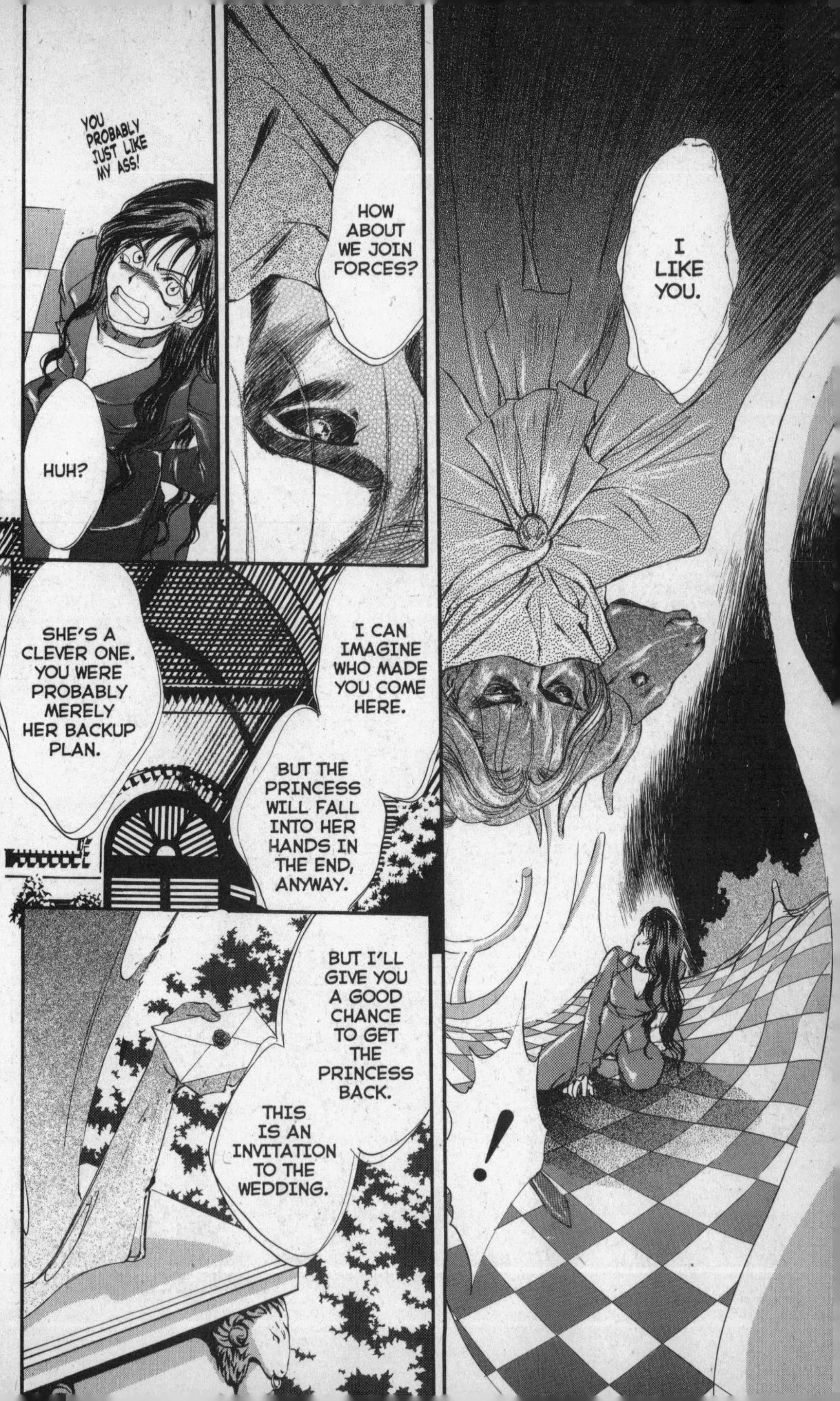
I LIKE YOU.
!
HOW ABOUT WE JOIN FORCES?
HUH?
YOU PROBABLY JUST LIKE MY ASS!
I CAN IMAGINE WHO MADE YOU COME HERE.
BUT THE PRINCESS WILL FALL INTO HER HANDS IN THE END, ANYWAY.
SHE'S A CLEVER ONE. YOU WERE PROBABLY MERELY HER BACKUP PLAN.
BUT I'LL GIVE YOU A GOOD CHANCE TO GET THE PRINCESS BACK.
THIS IS AN INVITATION TO THE WEDDING.

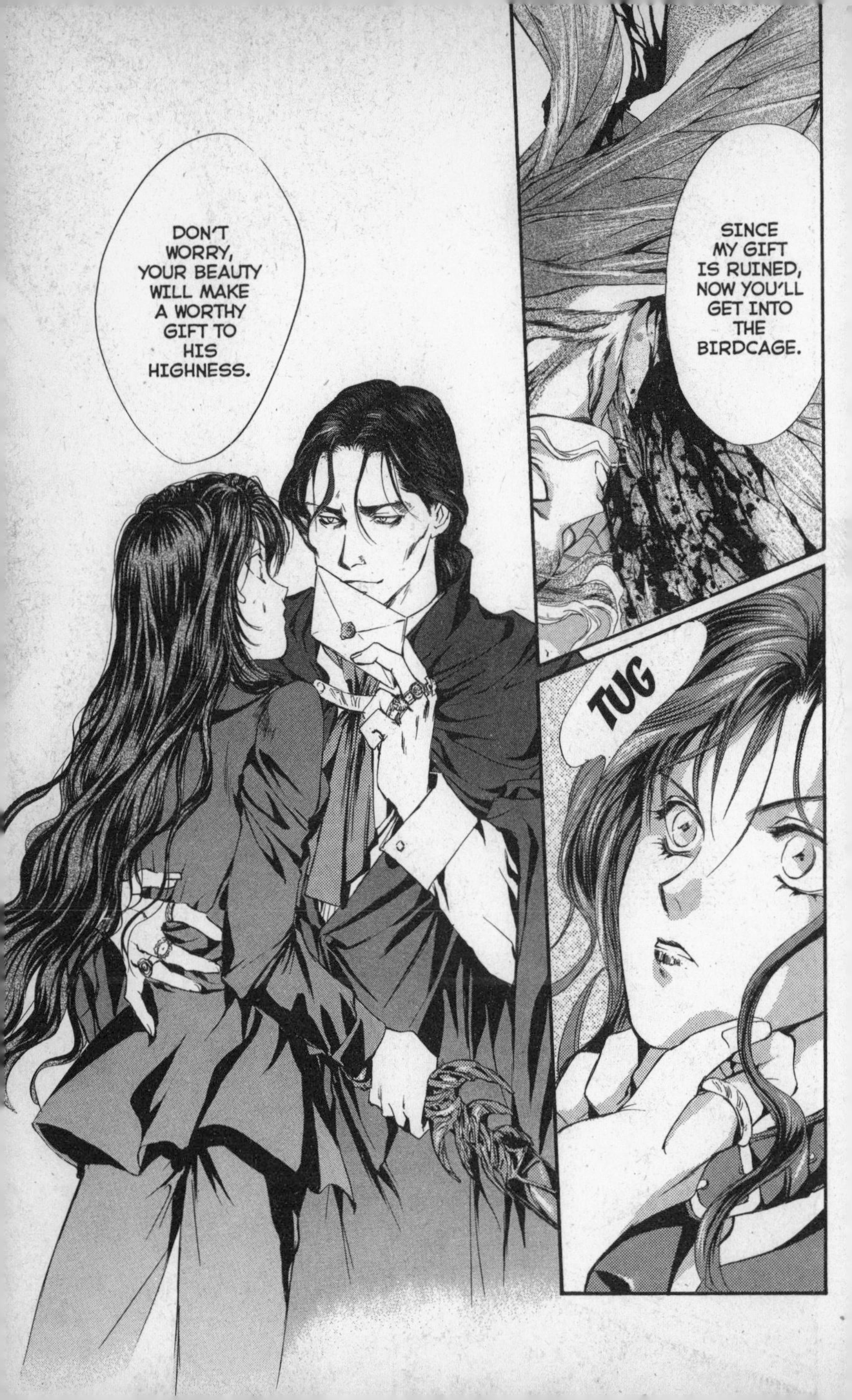
SINCE MY GIFT IS RUINED, NOW YOU'LL GET INTO THE BIRDCAGE.
TUG
DON'T WORRY, YOUR BEAUTY WILL MAKE A WORTHY GIFT TO HIS HIGHNESS.

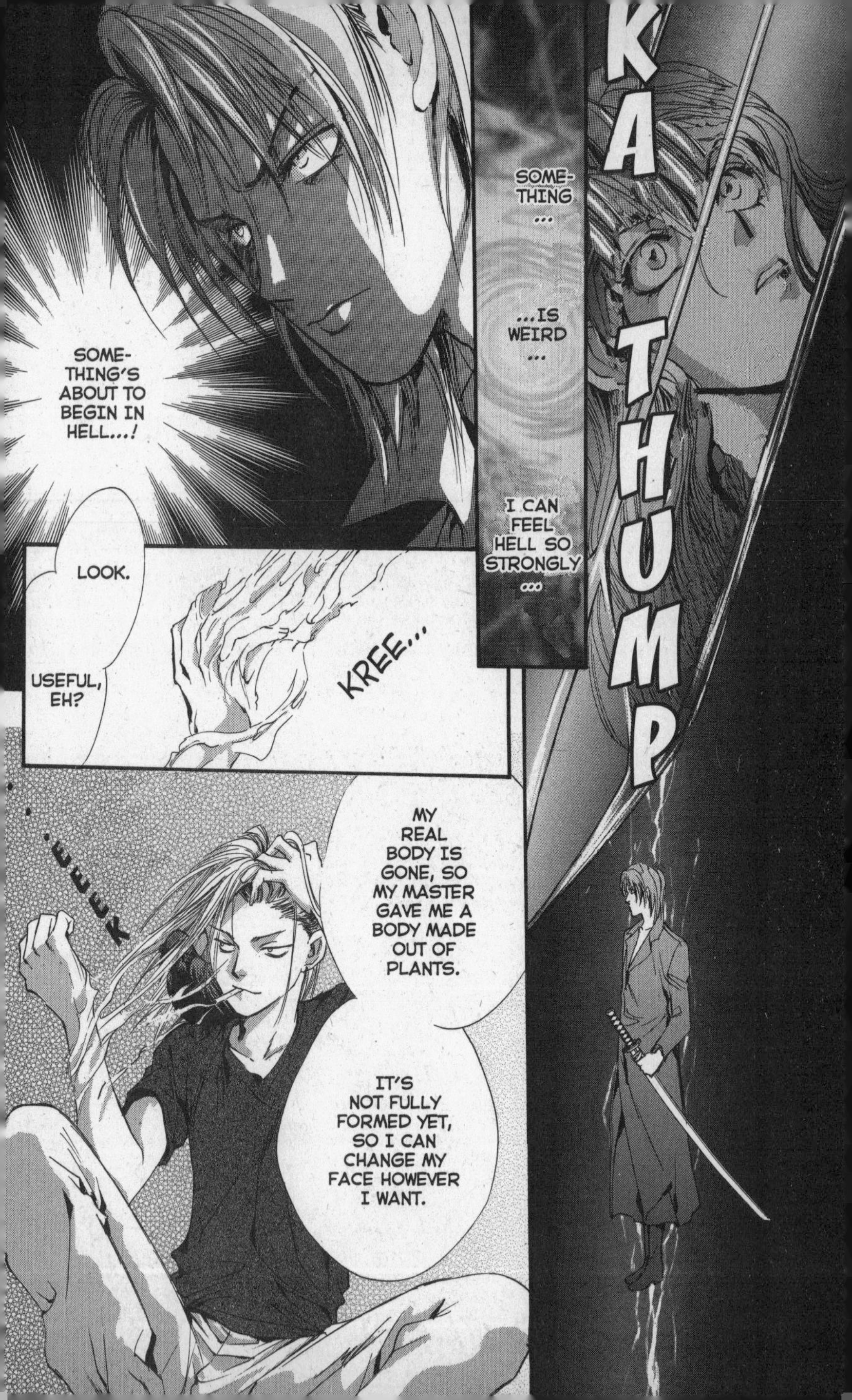
KATHUMP
SOMETHING...
...IS WEIRD...
I CAN FEEL HELL SO STRONGLY...
SOMETHING'S ABOUT TO BEGIN IN HELL...!
LOOK.
USEFUL, EH?
KREE...
EEEK...
MY REAL BODY IS GONE, SO MY MASTER GAVE ME A BODY MADE OUT OF PLANTS.
IT'S NOT FULLY FORMED YET, SO I CAN CHANGE MY FACE HOWEVER I WANT.

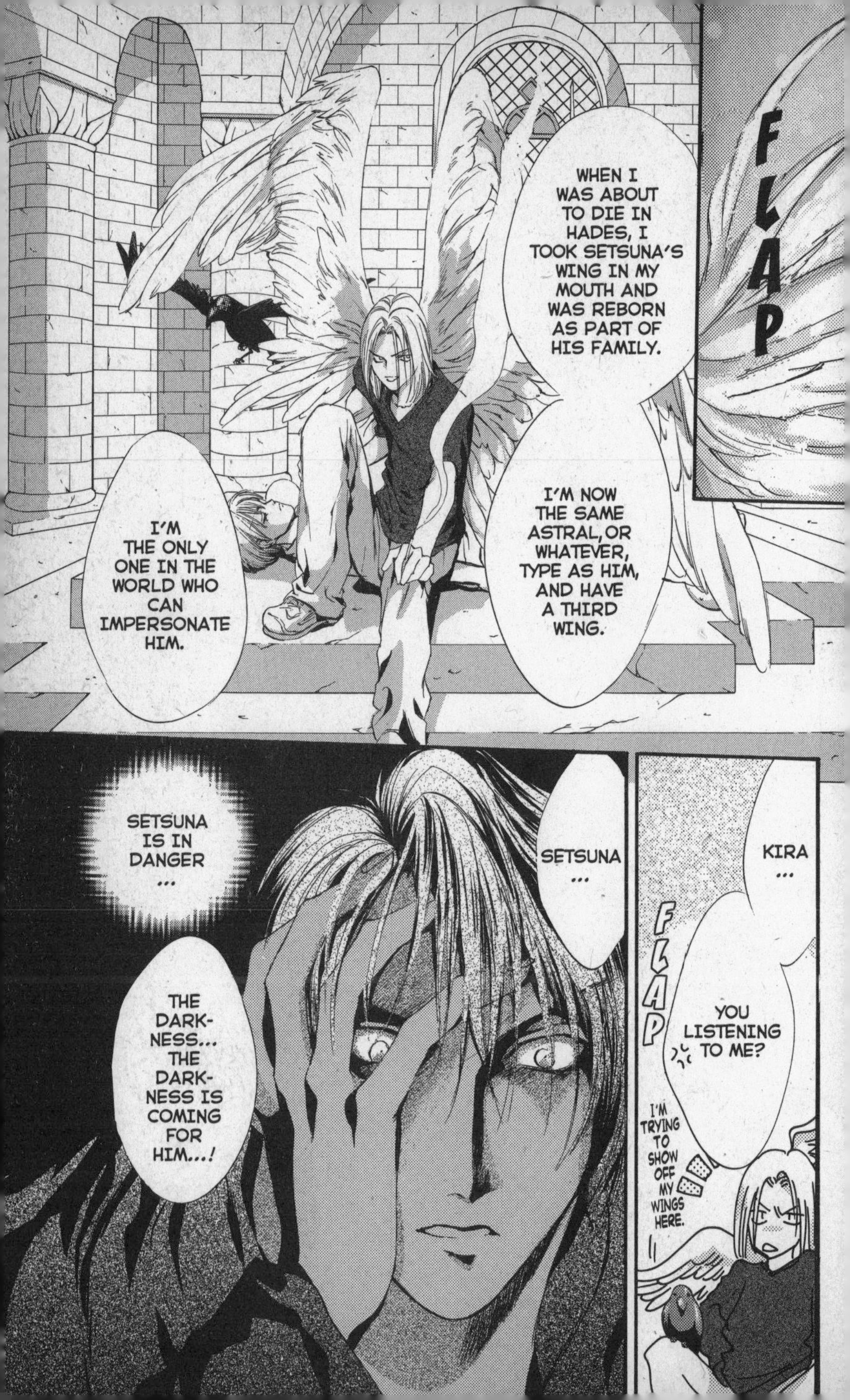
FLAP
WHEN I WAS ABOUT TO DIE IN HADES, I TOOK SETSUNA'S WING IN MY MOUTH AND WAS REBORN AS PART OF HIS FAMILY.
I'M NOW THE SAME ASTRAL, OR WHATEVER, TYPE AS HIM, AND HAVE A THIRD WING.
I'M THE ONLY ONE IN THE WORLD WHO CAN IMPERSONATE HIM.
KIRA ...
FLAP
YOU LISTENING TO ME?
I'M TRYING TO SHOW OFF MY WINGS HERE.
SETSUNA ...
SETSUNA IS IN DANGER ...
THE DARKNESS... THE DARKNESS IS COMING FOR HIM...!

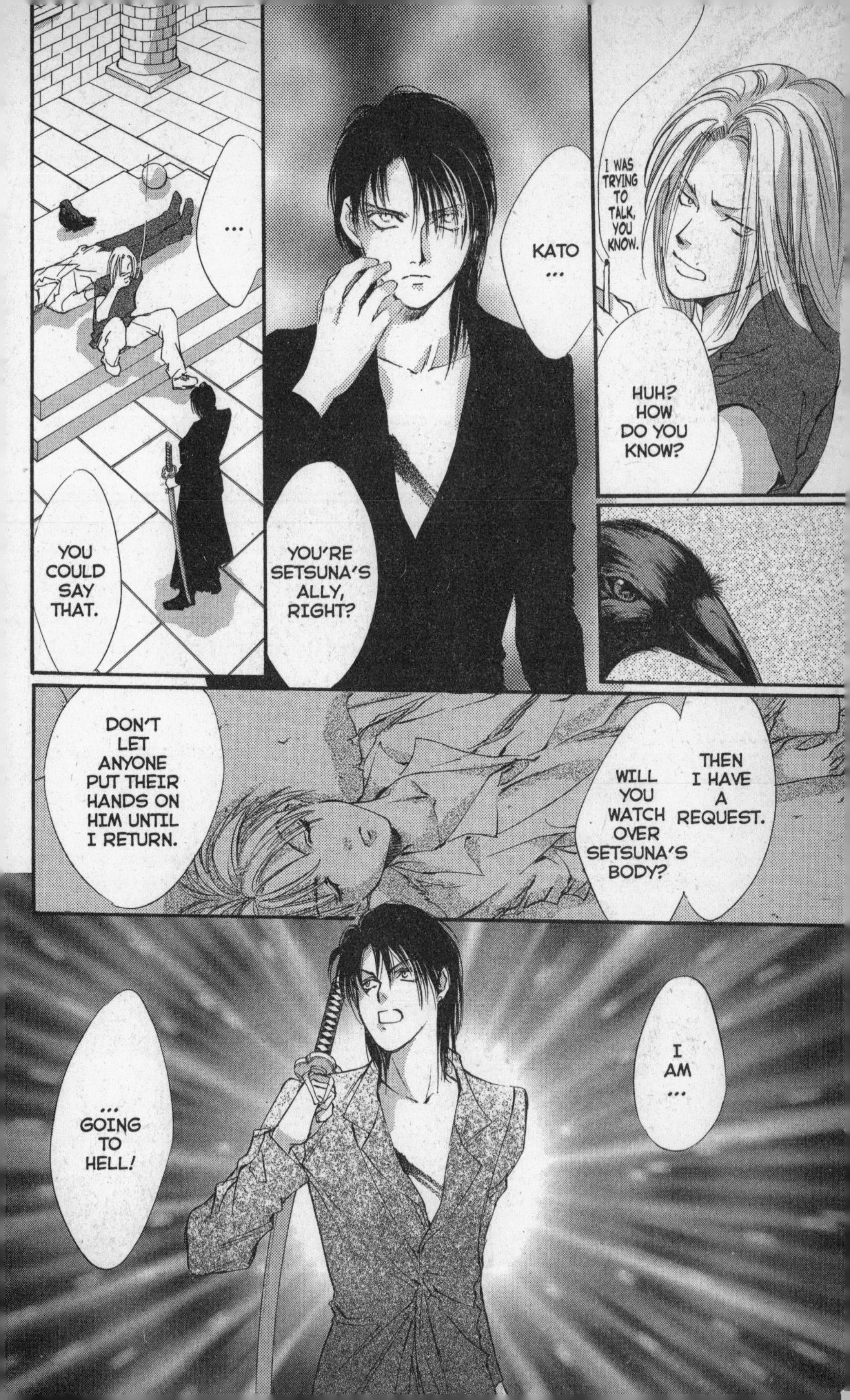
I WAS TRYING TO TALK, YOU KNOW.
HUH? HOW DO YOU KNOW?
KATO ...
YOU'RE SETSUNA'S ALLY, RIGHT?
...
YOU COULD SAY THAT.
THEN I HAVE A REQUEST.
WILL YOU WATCH OVER SETSUNA'S BODY?
DON'T LET ANYONE PUT THEIR HANDS ON HIM UNTIL I RETURN.
I AM ...
... GOING TO HELL!

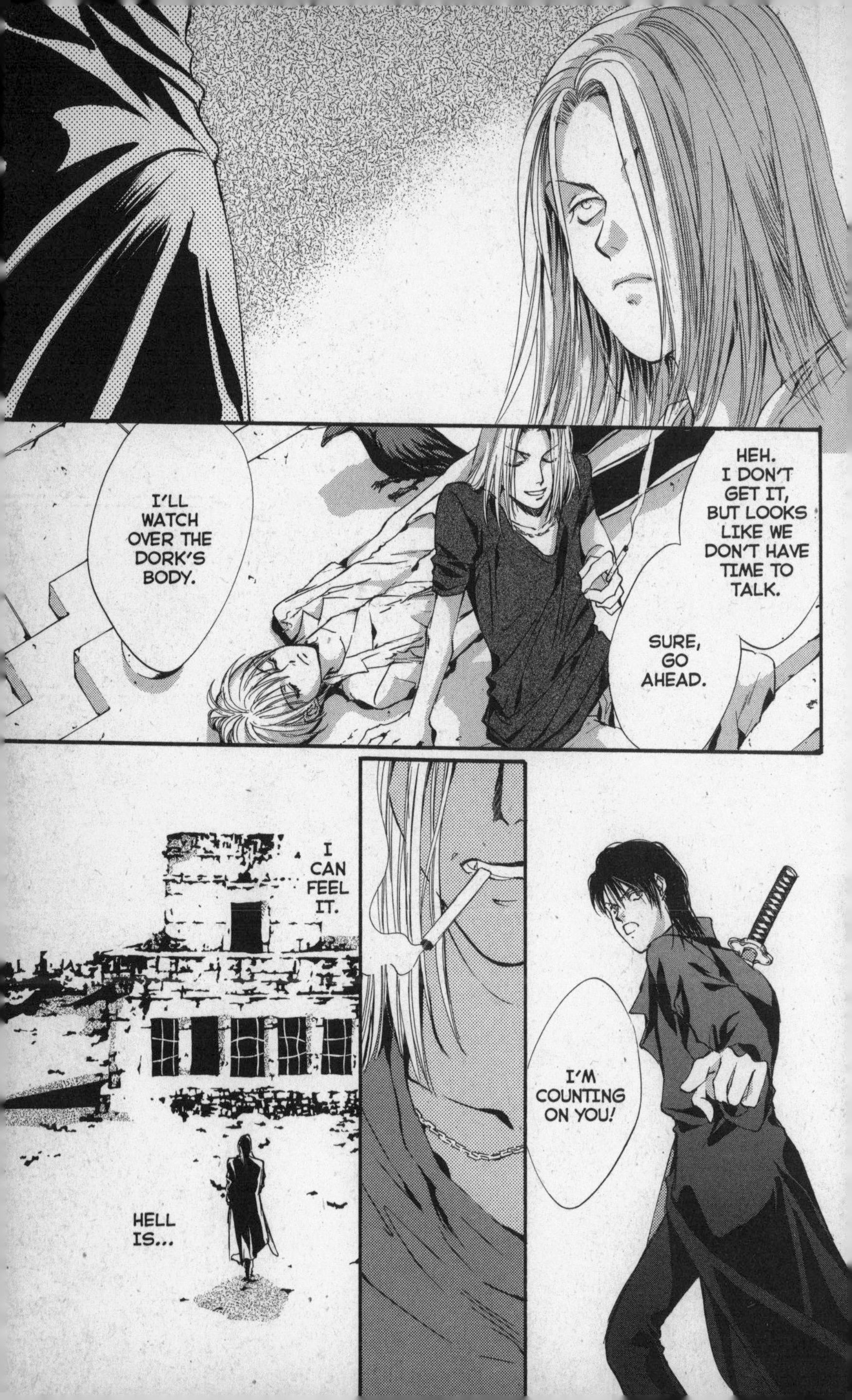
HEH. I DON'T GET IT, BUT LOOKS LIKE WE DON'T HAVE TIME TO TALK.
SURE, GO AHEAD.
I'LL WATCH OVER THE DORK'S BODY.
I'M COUNTING ON YOU!
I CAN FEEL IT.
HELL IS...

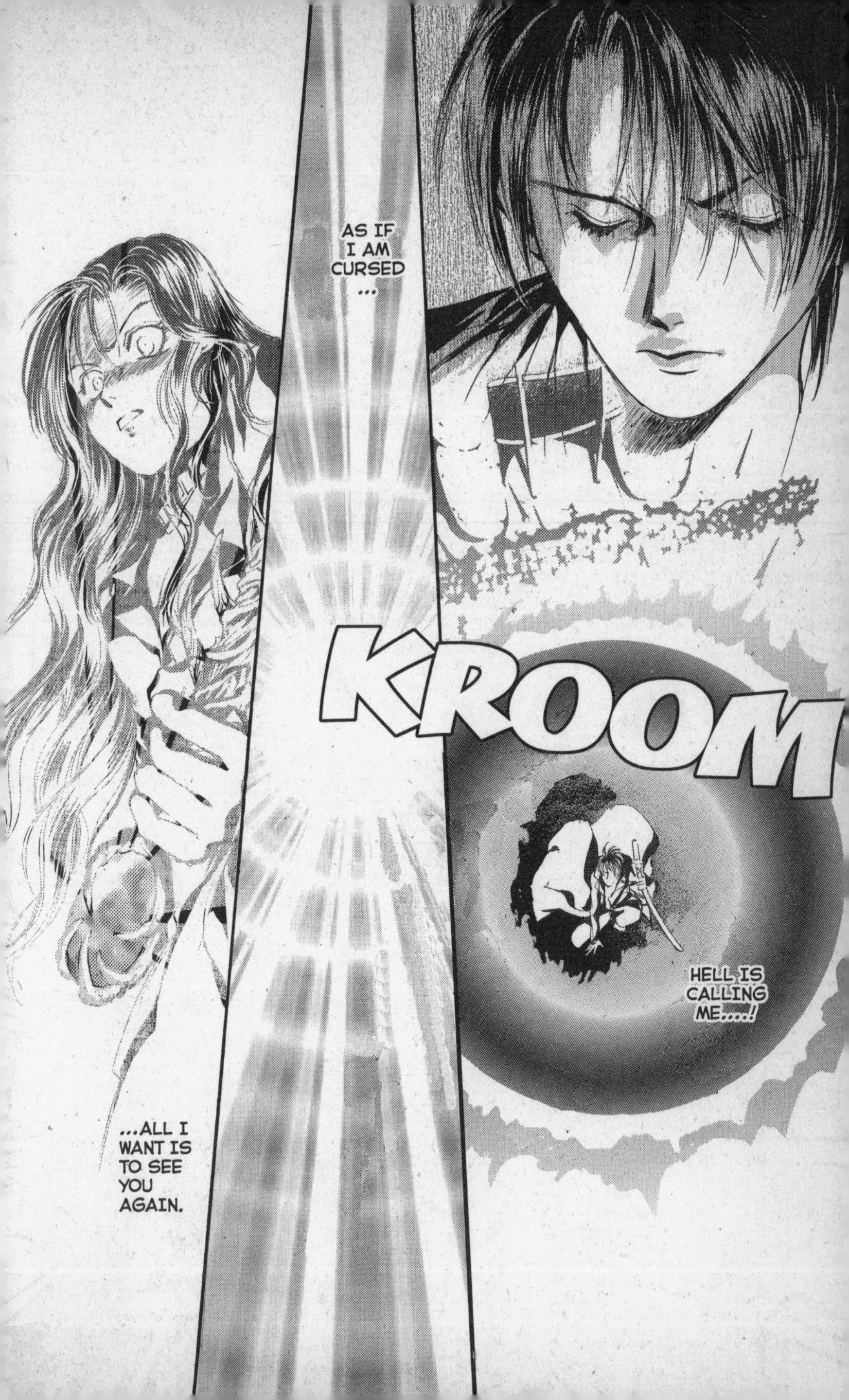
KROOM
HELL IS CALLING ME.....!
AS IF I AM CURSED ...
...ALL I WANT IS TO SEE YOU AGAIN.

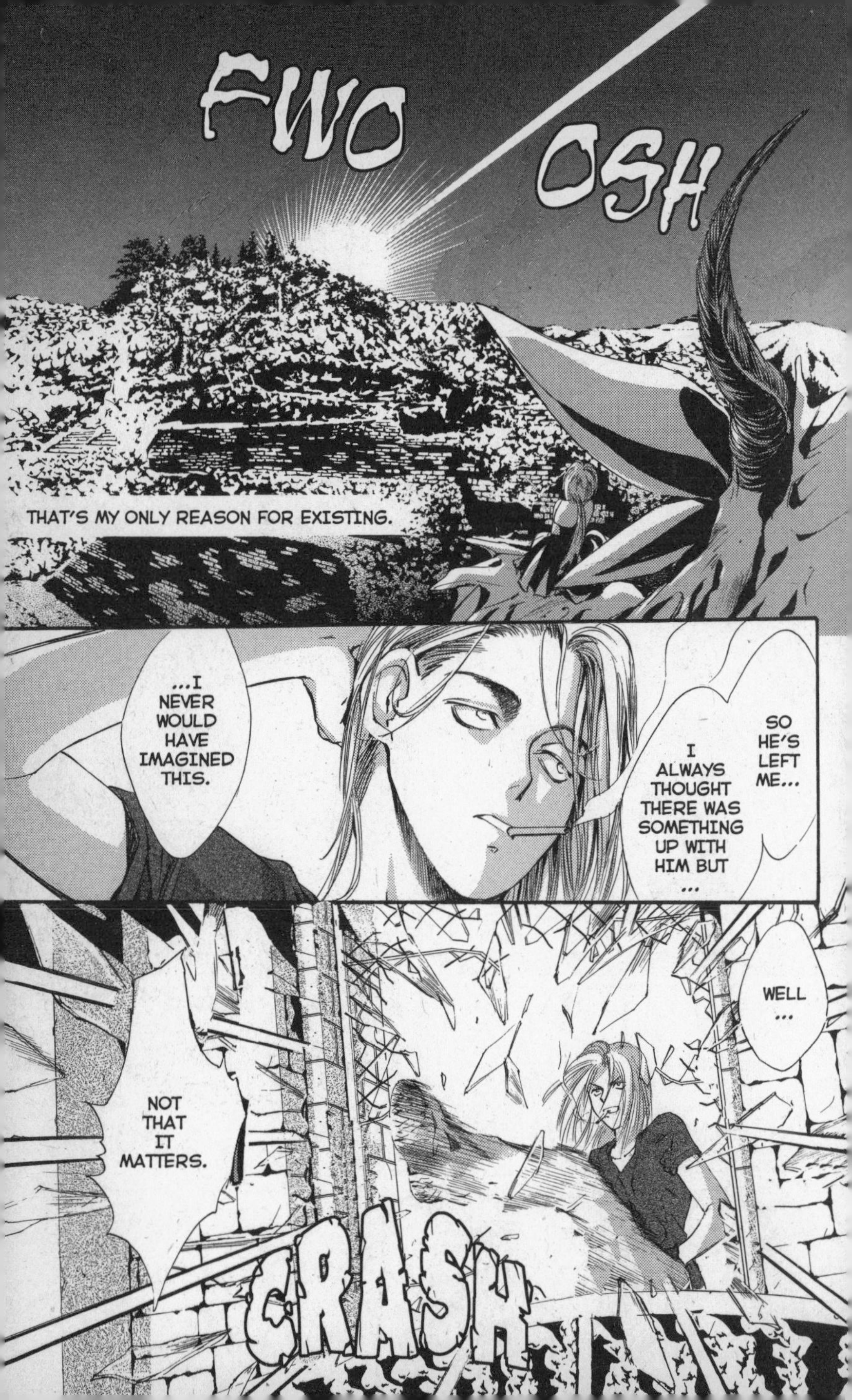
FWOOSH
THAT'S MY ONLY REASON FOR EXISTING.
SO HE'S LEFT ME...
I ALWAYS THOUGHT THERE WAS SOMETHING UP WITH HIM BUT ...
...I NEVER WOULD HAVE IMAGINED THIS.
WELL ...
NOT THAT IT MATTERS.
CRASH

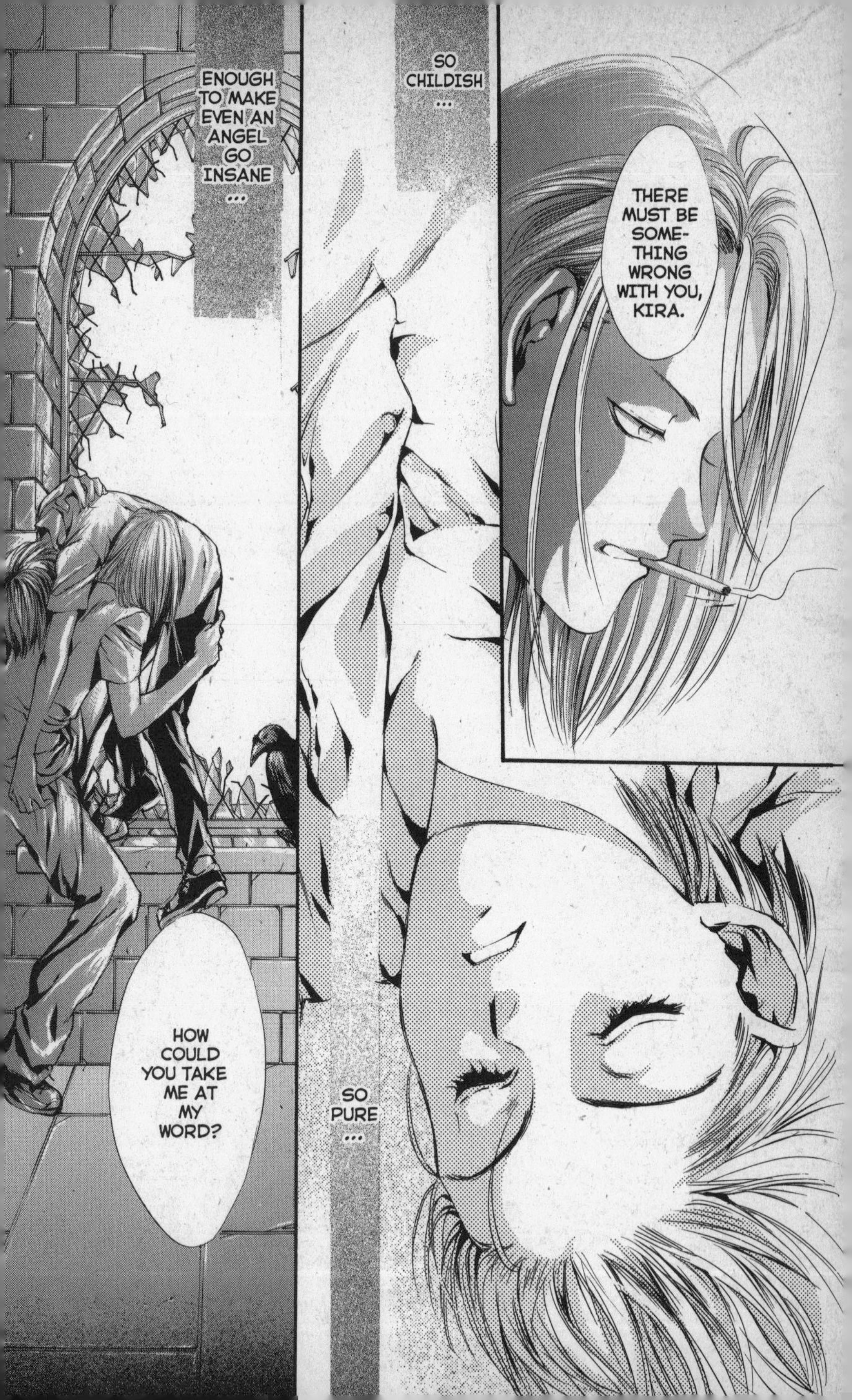
THERE MUST BE SOME-THING WRONG WITH YOU, KIRA.
SO CHILDISH ...
SO PURE ...
ENOUGH TO MAKE EVEN AN ANGEL GO INSANE ...
HOW COULD YOU TAKE ME AT MY WORD?

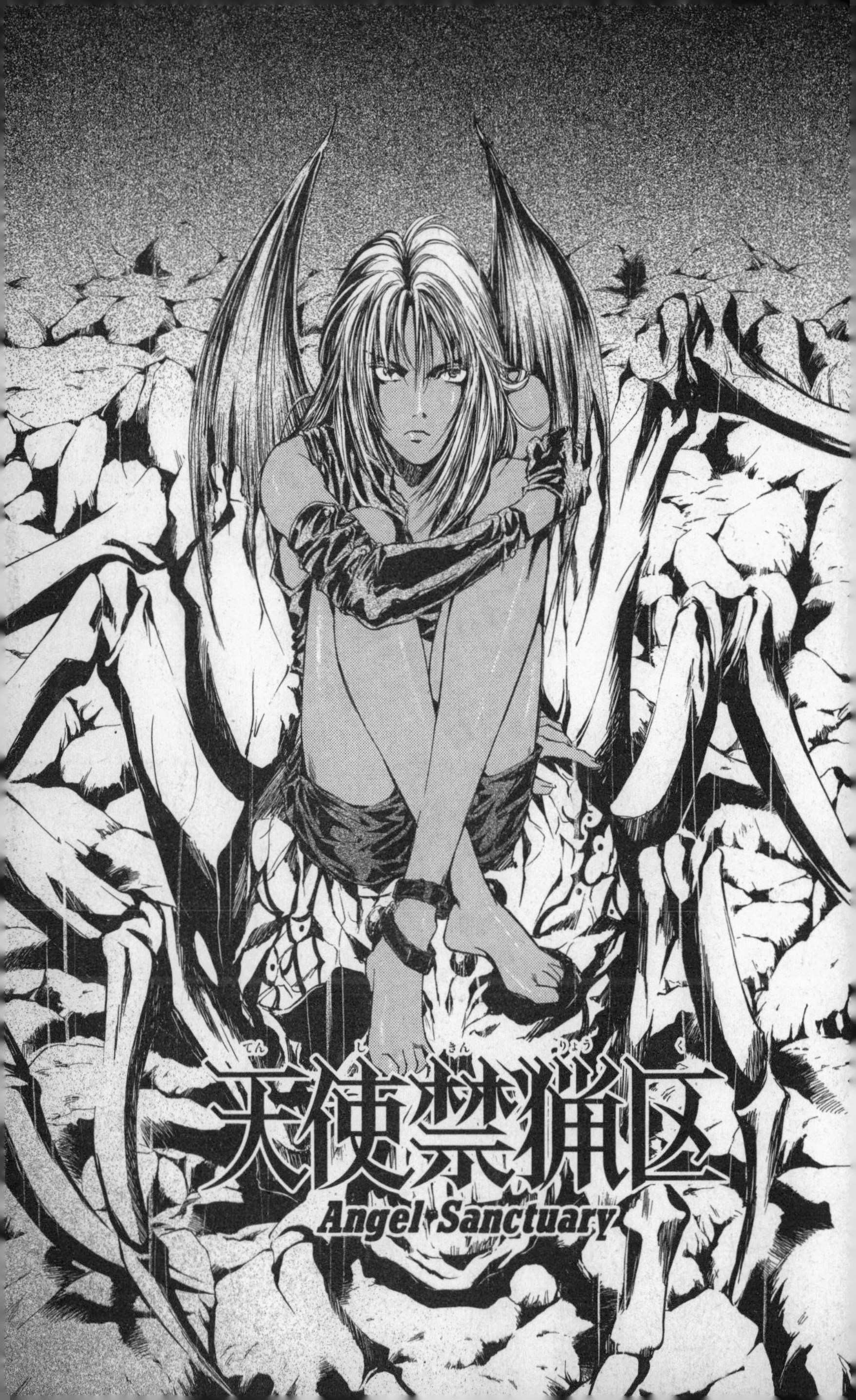
天使禁猟区
Angel Sanctuary

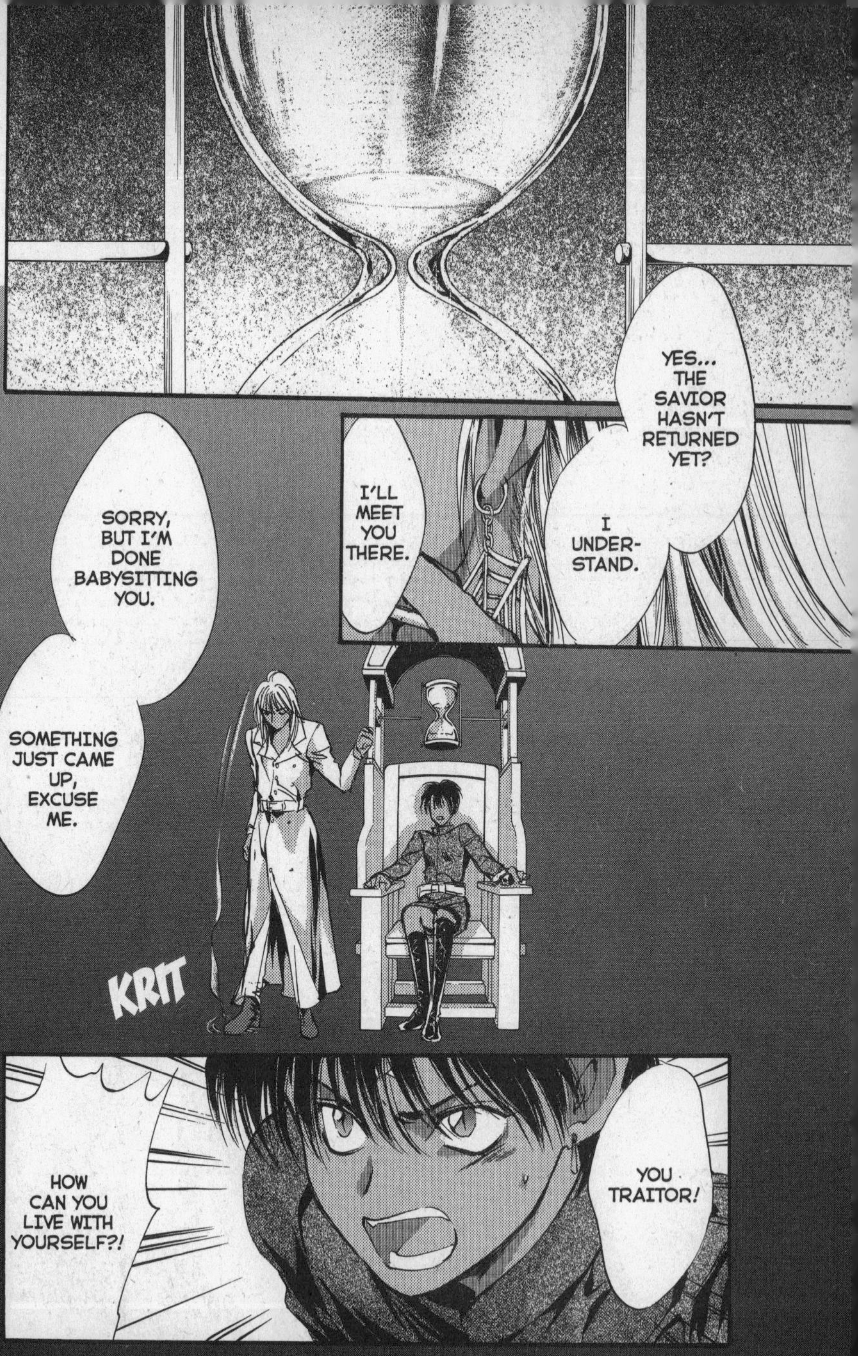
YES... THE SAVIOR HASN'T RETURNED YET?
I UNDER-STAND.
I'LL MEET YOU THERE.
SORRY, BUT I'M DONE BABYSITTING YOU.
SOMETHING JUST CAME UP, EXCUSE ME.
KRIT
YOU TRAITOR!
HOW CAN YOU LIVE WITH YOURSELF?!

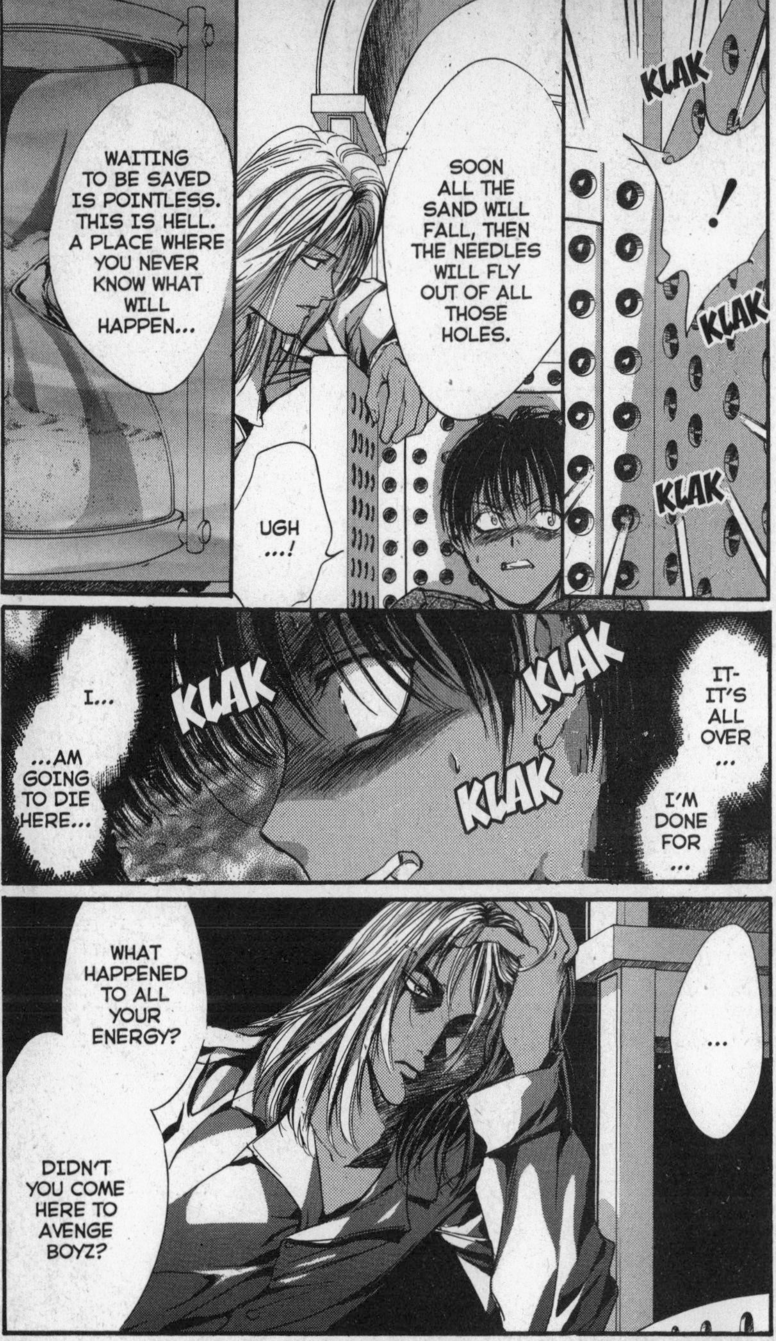
KLAK
!
KLAK
KLAK
SOON ALL THE SAND WILL FALL, THEN THE NEEDLES WILL FLY OUT OF ALL THOSE HOLES.
UGH ...!
WAITING TO BE SAVED IS POINTLESS. THIS IS HELL. A PLACE WHERE YOU NEVER KNOW WHAT WILL HAPPEN...
IT-IT'S ALL OVER ...
I'M DONE FOR ...
KLAK
KLAK
KLAK
I...
...AM GOING TO DIE HERE...
...
WHAT HAPPENED TO ALL YOUR ENERGY?
DIDN'T YOU COME HERE TO AVENGE BOYZ?

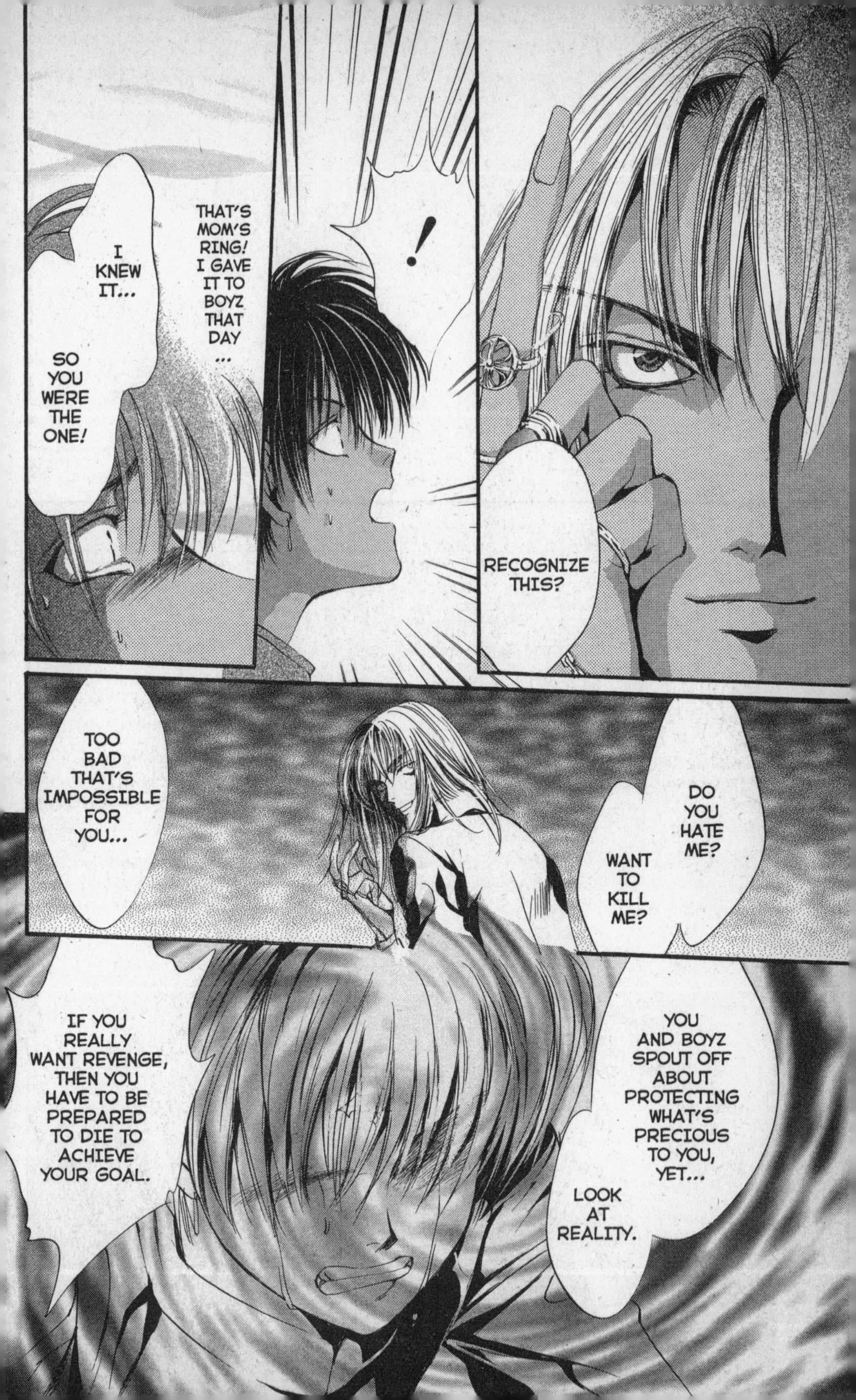
RECOGNIZE THIS?
!
THAT'S MOM'S RING! I GAVE IT TO BOYZ THAT DAY ...
I KNEW IT...
SO YOU WERE THE ONE!
DO YOU HATE ME?
WANT TO KILL ME?
TOO BAD THAT'S IMPOSSIBLE FOR YOU...
YOU AND BOYZ SPOUT OFF ABOUT PROTECTING WHAT'S PRECIOUS TO YOU, YET...
LOOK AT REALITY.
IF YOU REALLY WANT REVENGE, THEN YOU HAVE TO BE PREPARED TO DIE TO ACHIEVE YOUR GOAL.

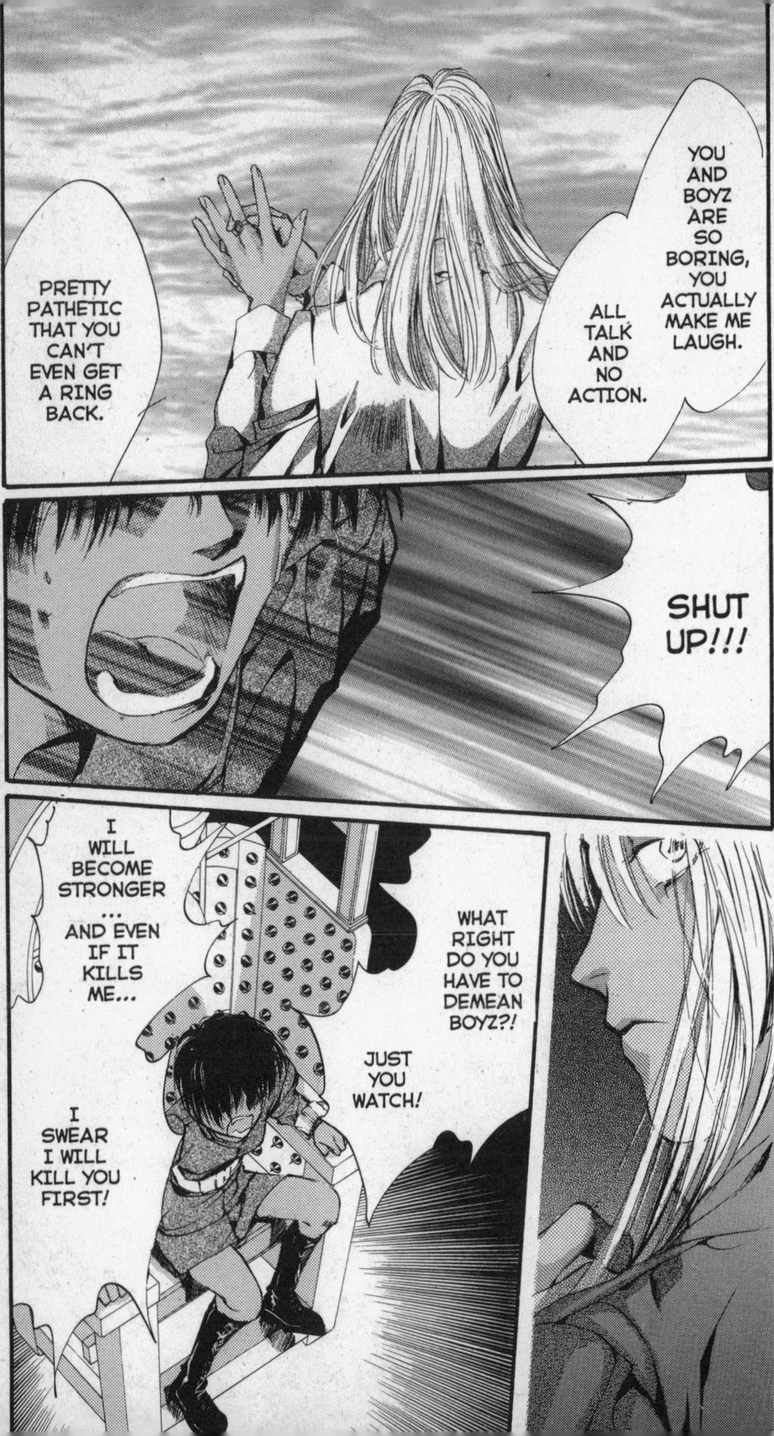
YOU AND BOYZ ARE SO BORING, YOU ACTUALLY MAKE ME LAUGH.
ALL TALK AND NO ACTION.
PRETTY PATHETIC THAT YOU CAN'T EVEN GET A RING BACK.
SHUT UP!!!
WHAT RIGHT DO YOU HAVE TO DEMEAN BOYZ?!
JUST YOU WATCH!
I WILL BECOME STRONGER ... AND EVEN IF IT KILLS ME...
I SWEAR I WILL KILL YOU FIRST!

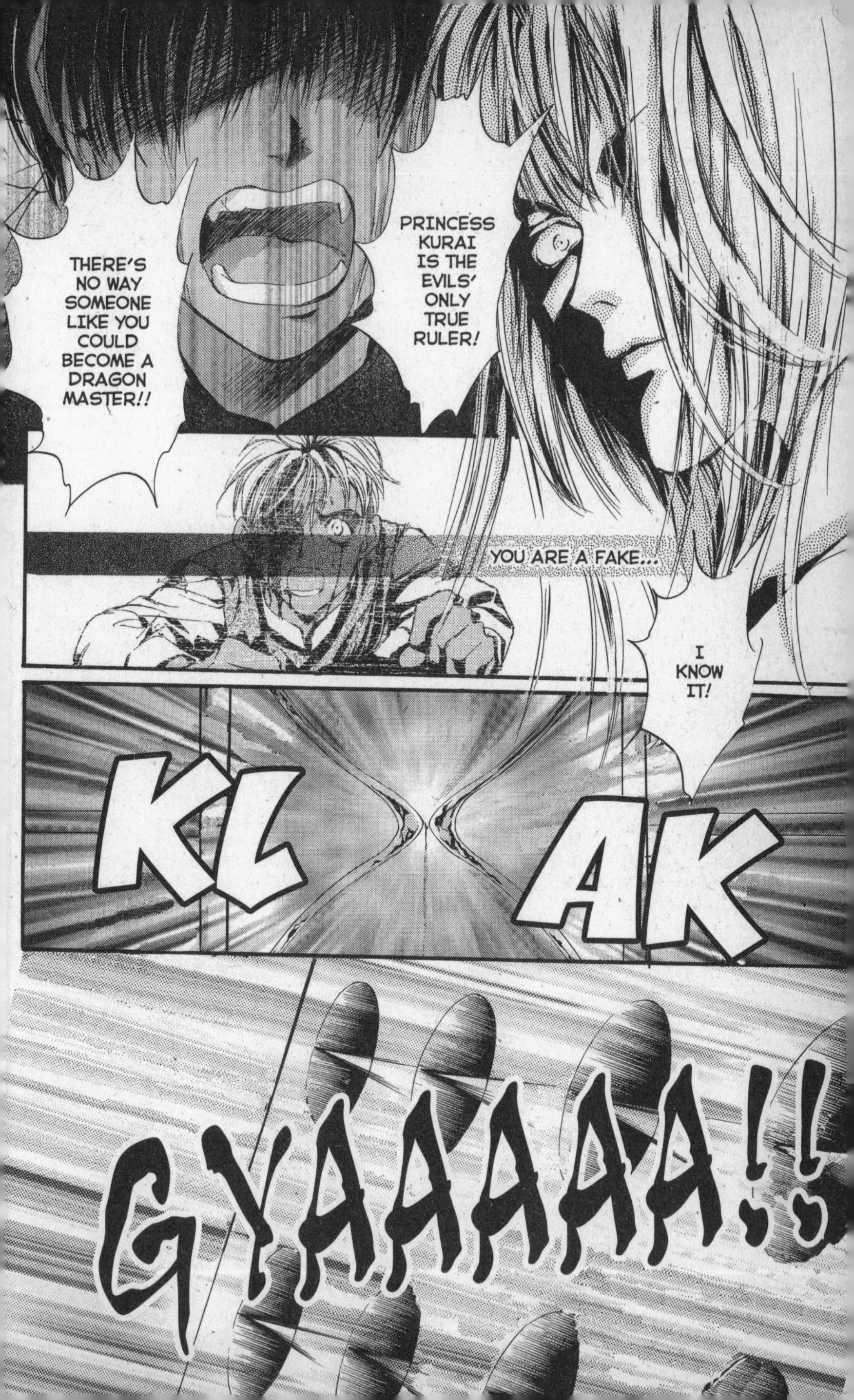
PRINCESS KURAI IS THE EVILS' ONLY TRUE RULER!
THERE'S NO WAY SOMEONE LIKE YOU COULD BECOME A DRAGON MASTER!!
YOU ARE A FAKE...
I KNOW IT!
KL
AK
GYAAAAA!!

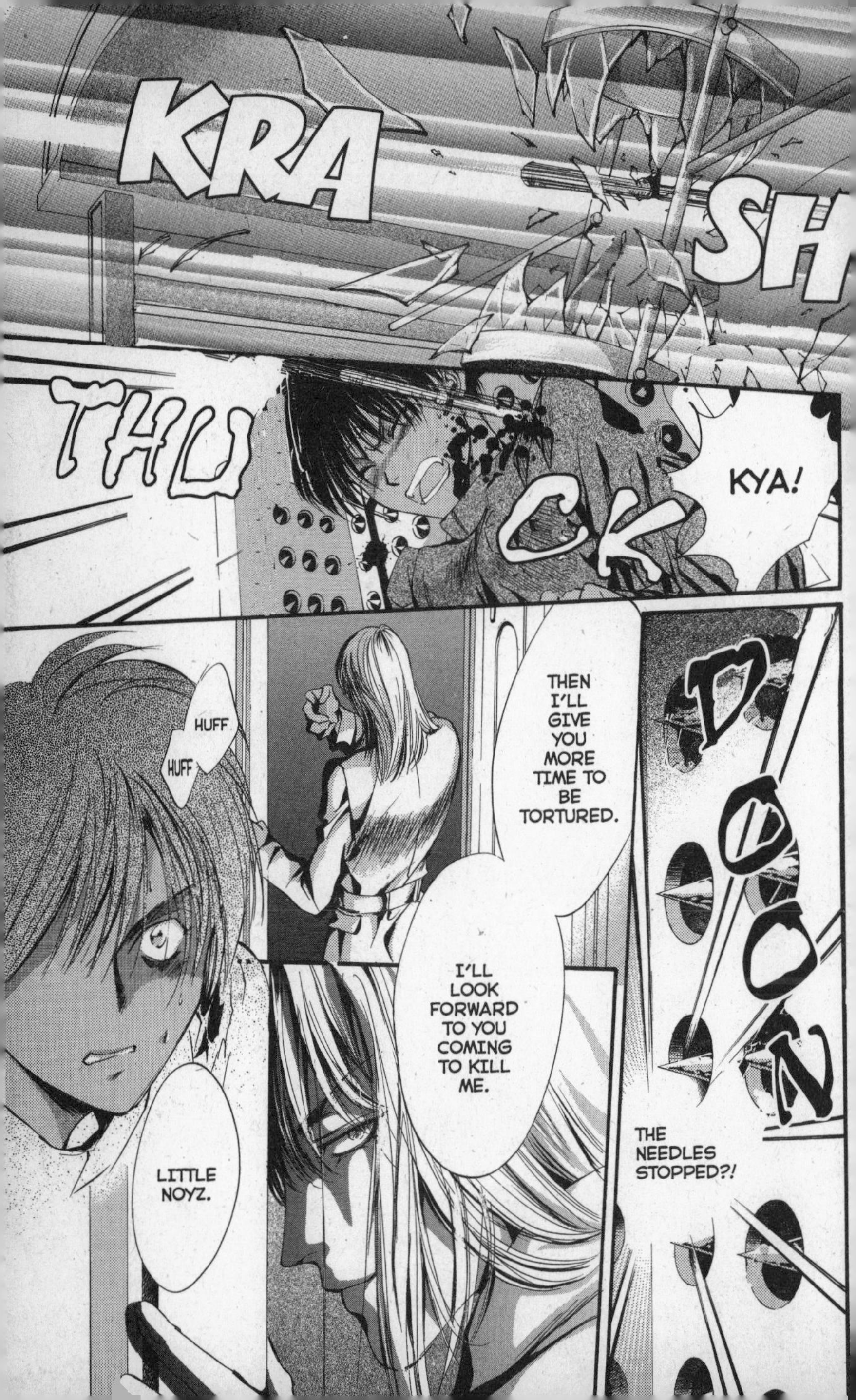
KRASH
KYA!
THUCK
DOON
THE NEEDLES STOPPED?!
THEN I'LL GIVE YOU MORE TIME TO BE TORTURED.
I'LL LOOK FORWARD TO YOU COMING TO KILL ME.
HUFF
HUFF
LITTLE NOYZ.

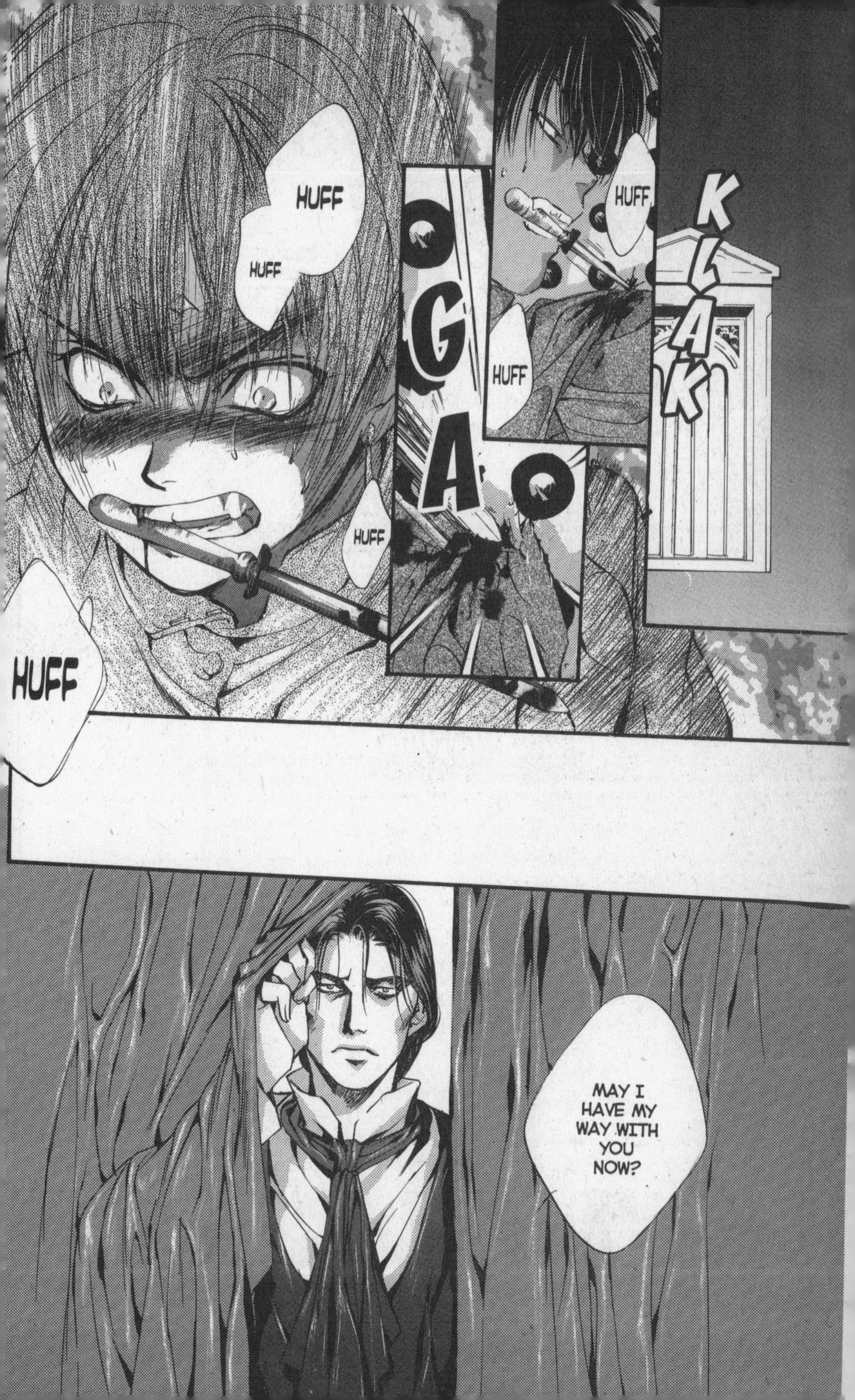
KLAK
HUFF
HUFF
OGAO
HUFF
HUFF
HUFF
HUFF
MAY I HAVE MY WAY WITH YOU NOW?

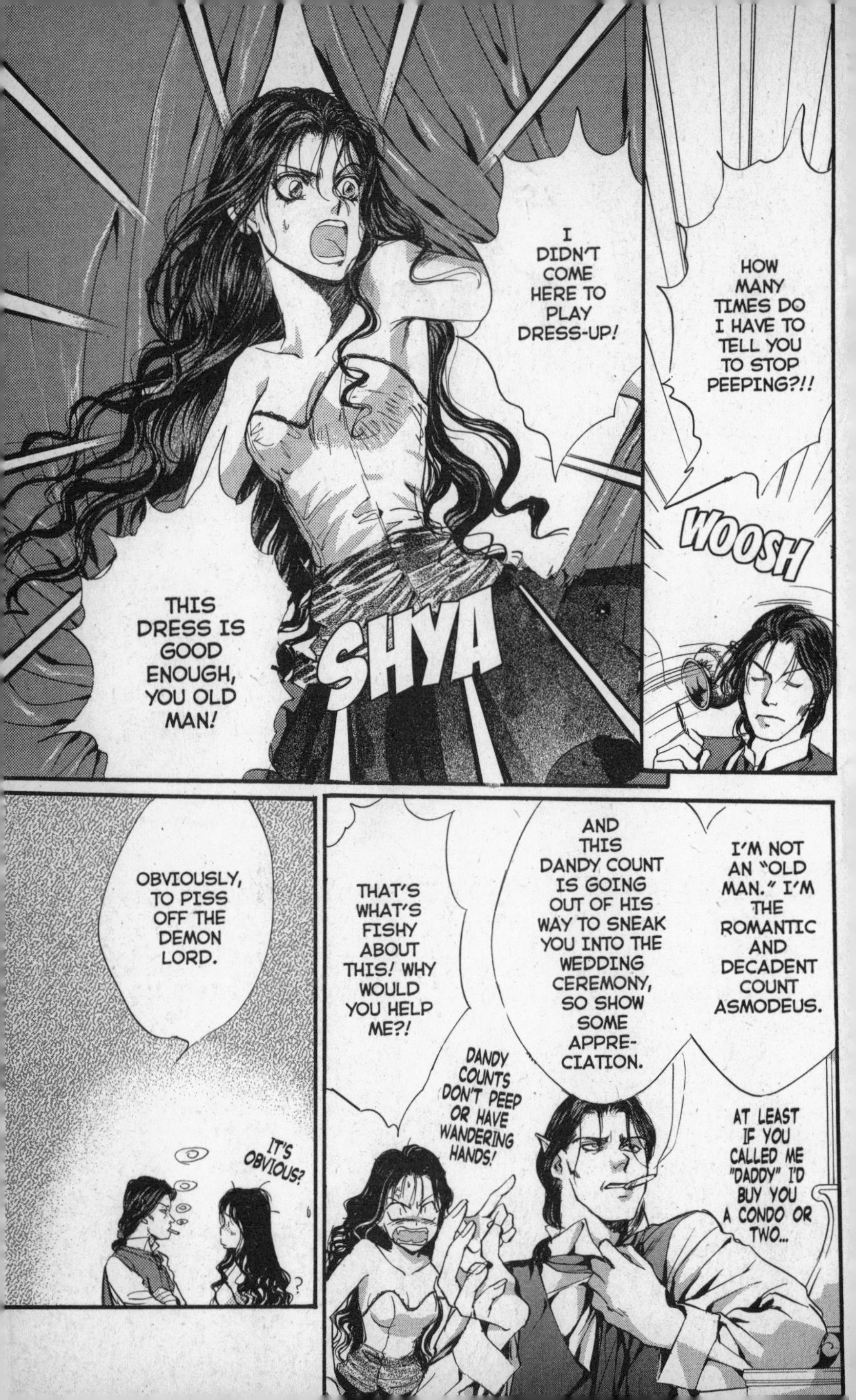
HOW MANY TIMES DO I HAVE TO TELL YOU TO STOP PEEPING?!!
WOOSH
I DIDN'T COME HERE TO PLAY DRESS-UP!
THIS DRESS IS GOOD ENOUGH, YOU OLD MAN!
SHYA
I'M NOT AN "OLD MAN." I'M THE ROMANTIC AND DECADENT COUNT ASMODEUS.
AND THIS DANDY COUNT IS GOING OUT OF HIS WAY TO SNEAK YOU INTO THE WEDDING CEREMONY, SO SHOW SOME APPRE-CIATION.
THAT'S WHAT'S FISHY ABOUT THIS! WHY WOULD YOU HELP ME?!
AT LEAST IF YOU CALLED ME "DADDY" I'D BUY YOU A CONDO OR TWO...
DANDY COUNTS DON'T PEEP OR HAVE WANDERING HANDS!
OBVIOUSLY, TO PISS OFF THE DEMON LORD.
IT'S OBVIOUS?
?

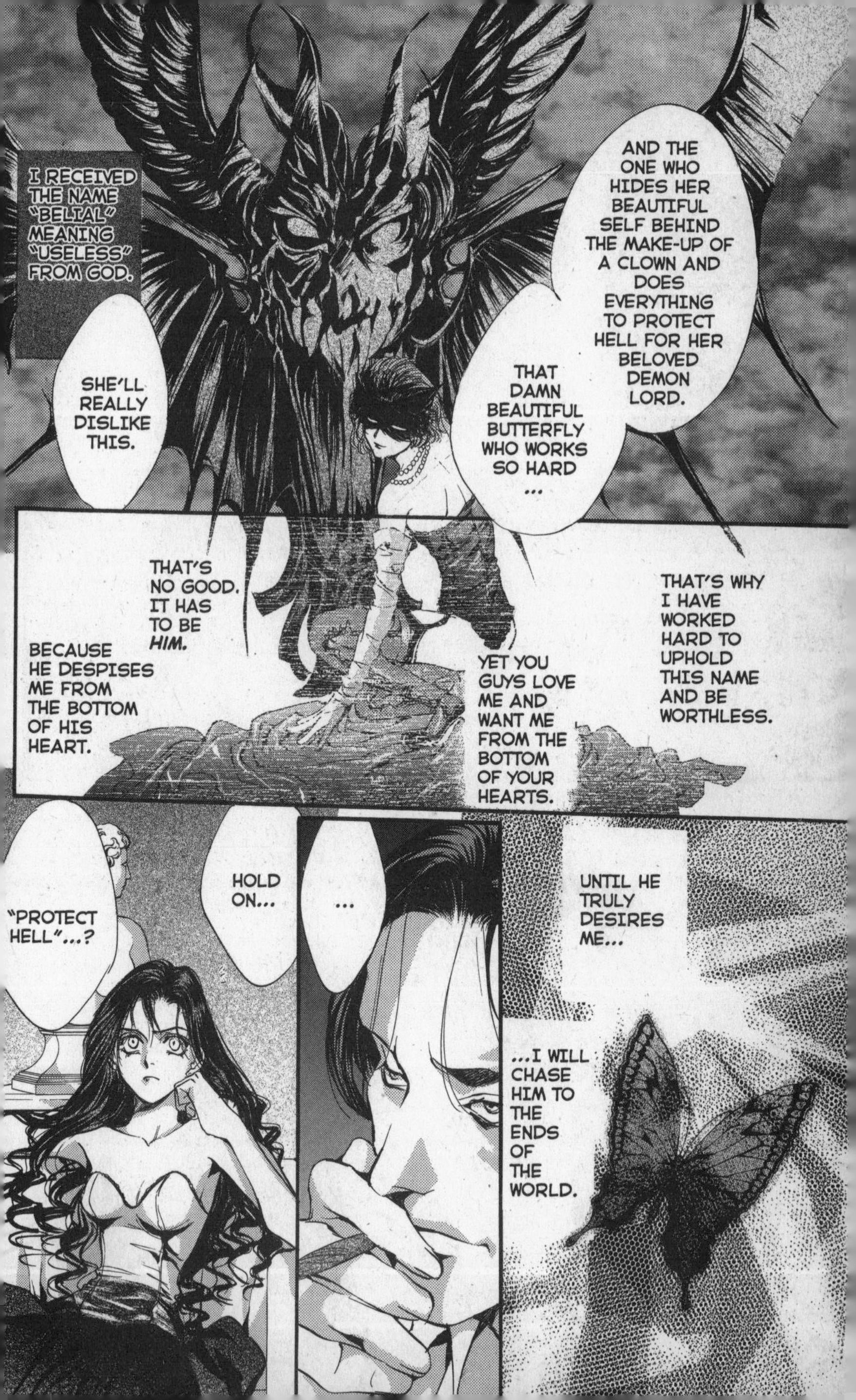
AND THE ONE WHO HIDES HER BEAUTIFUL SELF BEHIND THE MAKE-UP OF A CLOWN AND DOES EVERYTHING TO PROTECT HELL FOR HER BELOVED DEMON LORD.
THAT DAMN BEAUTIFUL BUTTERFLY WHO WORKS SO HARD ...
SHE'LL REALLY DISLIKE THIS.
I RECEIVED THE NAME "BELIAL" MEANING "USELESS" FROM GOD.
THAT'S WHY I HAVE WORKED HARD TO UPHOLD THIS NAME AND BE WORTHLESS.
YET YOU GUYS LOVE ME AND WANT ME FROM THE BOTTOM OF YOUR HEARTS.
THAT'S NO GOOD. IT HAS TO BE *HIM*.
BECAUSE HE DESPISES ME FROM THE BOTTOM OF HIS HEART.
UNTIL HE TRULY DESIRES ME...
...I WILL CHASE HIM TO THE ENDS OF THE WORLD.
...
HOLD ON...
"PROTECT HELL"...?

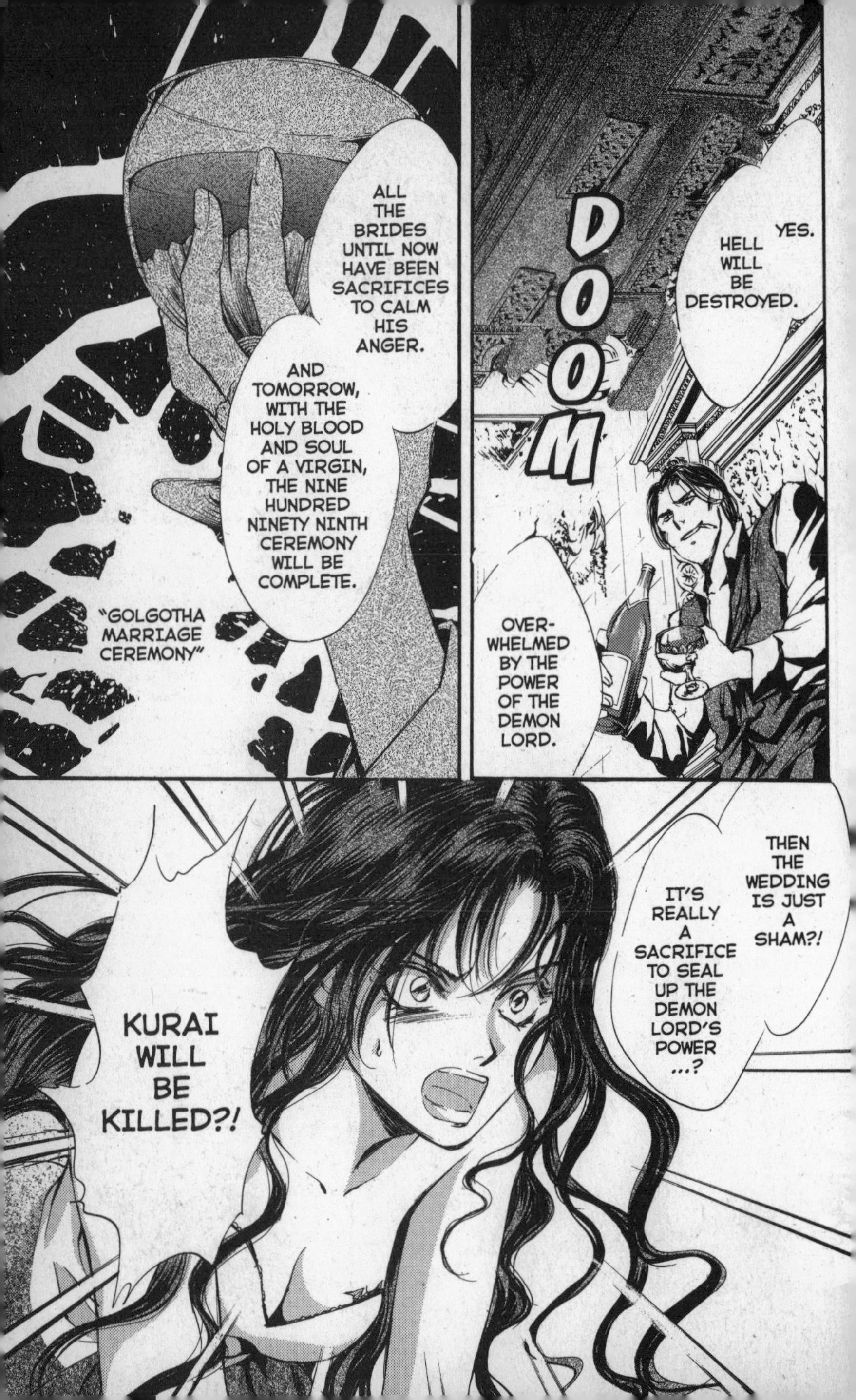
YES. HELL WILL BE DESTROYED.
DOOOM
OVER-WHELMED BY THE POWER OF THE DEMON LORD.
ALL THE BRIDES UNTIL NOW HAVE BEEN SACRIFICES TO CALM HIS ANGER.
AND TOMORROW, WITH THE HOLY BLOOD AND SOUL OF A VIRGIN, THE NINE HUNDRED NINETY NINTH CEREMONY WILL BE COMPLETE.
"GOLGOTHA MARRIAGE CEREMONY"
THEN THE WEDDING IS JUST A SHAM?!
IT'S REALLY A SACRIFICE TO SEAL UP THE DEMON LORD'S POWER ...?
KURAI WILL BE KILLED?!

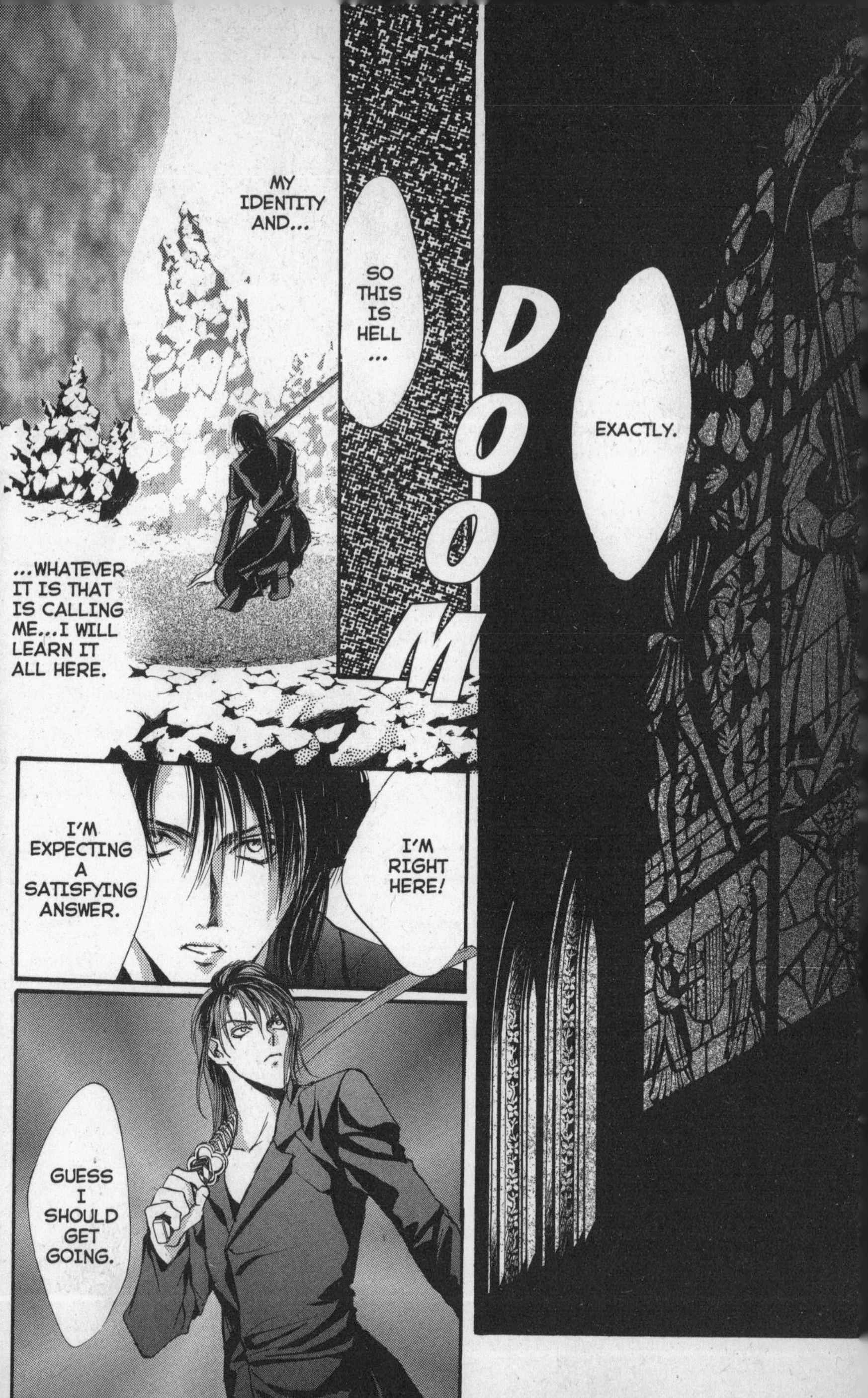
EXACTLY.
DOOOM
MY IDENTITY AND...
SO THIS IS HELL...
...WHATEVER IT IS THAT IS CALLING ME...I WILL LEARN IT ALL HERE.
I'M RIGHT HERE!
I'M EXPECTING A SATISFYING ANSWER.
GUESS I SHOULD GET GOING.

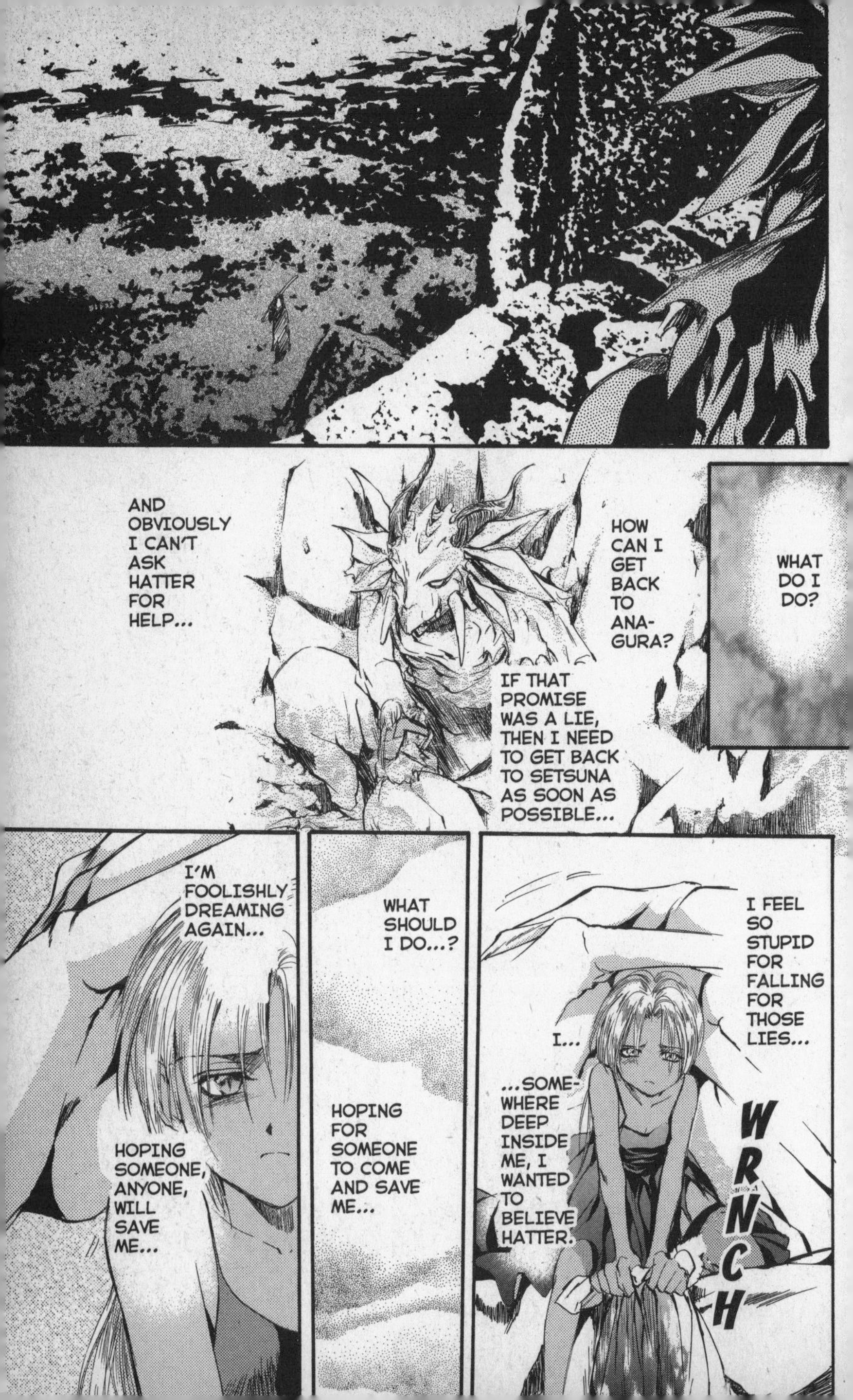
WHAT DO I DO?
HOW CAN I GET BACK TO ANA-GURA?
IF THAT PROMISE WAS A LIE, THEN I NEED TO GET BACK TO SETSUNA AS SOON AS POSSIBLE...
AND OBVIOUSLY I CAN'T ASK HATTER FOR HELP...
I FEEL SO STUPID FOR FALLING FOR THOSE LIES...
I...
...SOME-WHERE DEEP INSIDE ME, I WANTED TO BELIEVE HATTER.
WRNCH
WHAT SHOULD I DO...?
HOPING FOR SOMEONE TO COME AND SAVE ME...
I'M FOOLISHLY DREAMING AGAIN...
HOPING SOMEONE, ANYONE, WILL SAVE ME...

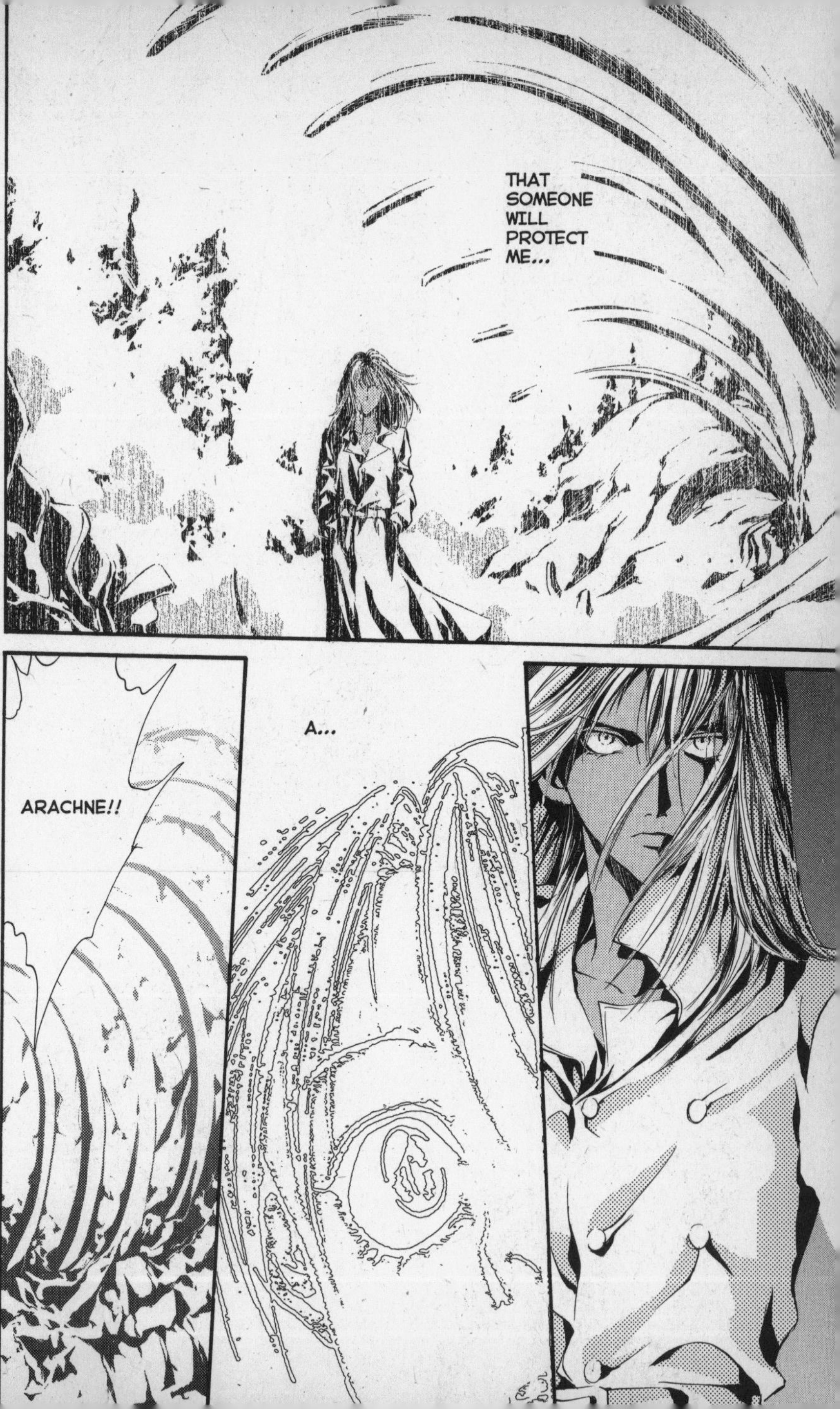
THAT SOMEONE WILL PROTECT ME...
A...
ARACHNE!!

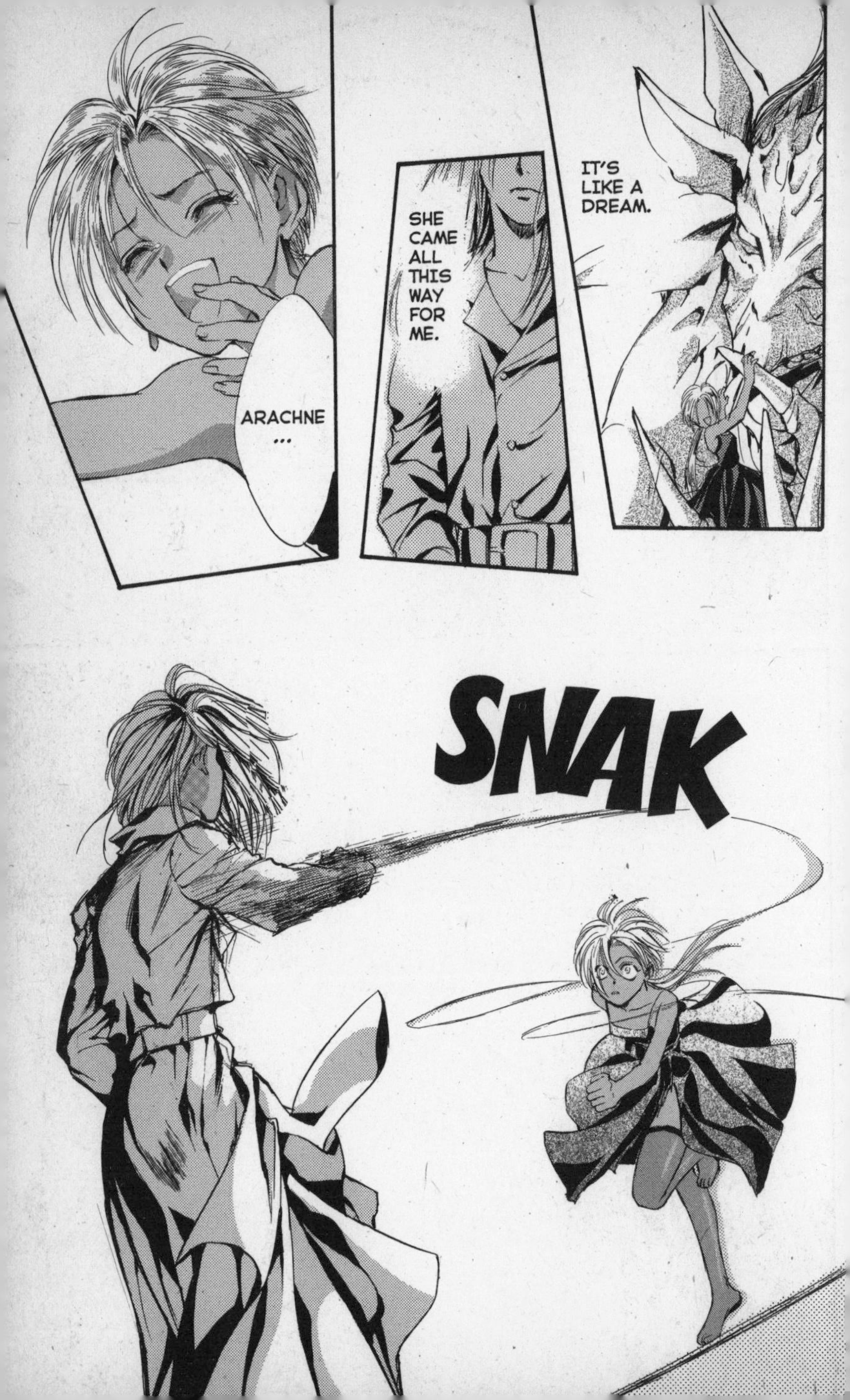
IT'S LIKE A DREAM.
SHE CAME ALL THIS WAY FOR ME.
ARACHNE ...
SNAK

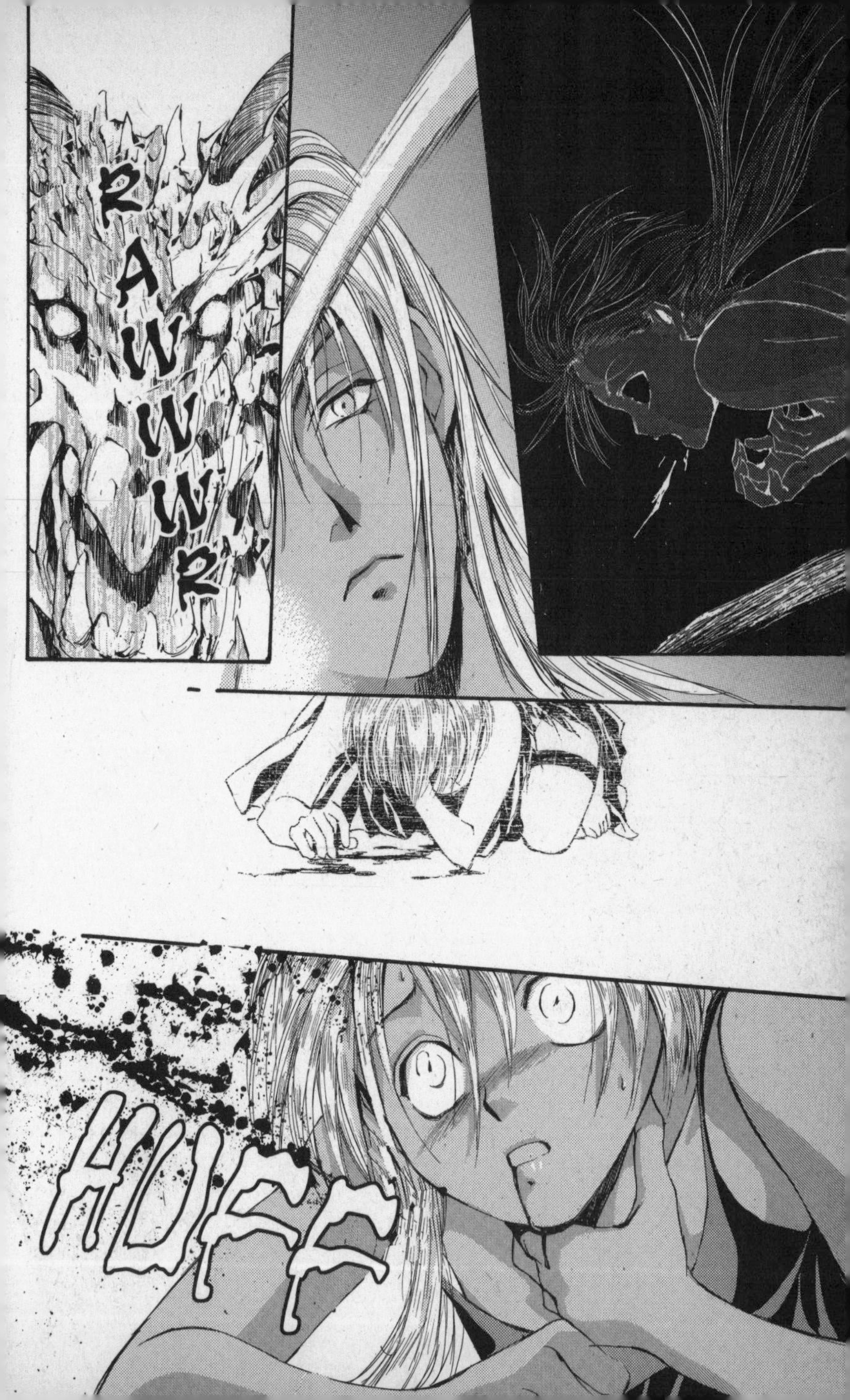
RAWWWR
HUFF

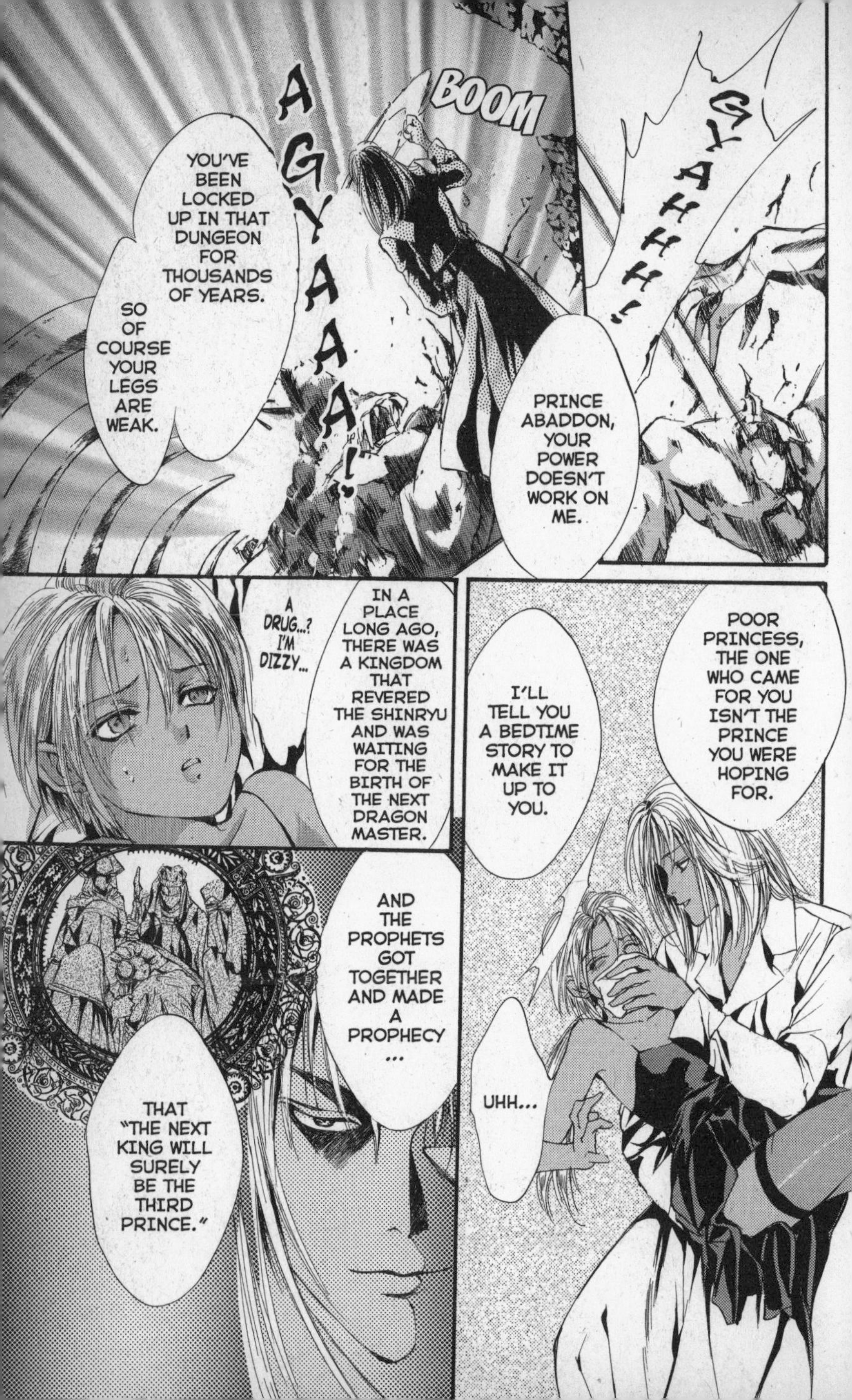
GYAHHH!
PRINCE ABADDON, YOUR POWER DOESN'T WORK ON ME.
BOOM
AGYAAA!
YOU'VE BEEN LOCKED UP IN THAT DUNGEON FOR THOUSANDS OF YEARS.
SO OF COURSE YOUR LEGS ARE WEAK.
POOR PRINCESS, THE ONE WHO CAME FOR YOU ISN'T THE PRINCE YOU WERE HOPING FOR.
I'LL TELL YOU A BEDTIME STORY TO MAKE IT UP TO YOU.
UHH...
IN A PLACE LONG AGO, THERE WAS A KINGDOM THAT REVERED THE SHINRYU AND WAS WAITING FOR THE BIRTH OF THE NEXT DRAGON MASTER.
A DRUG...? I'M DIZZY...
AND THE PROPHETS GOT TOGETHER AND MADE A PROPHECY...
THAT "THE NEXT KING WILL SURELY BE THE THIRD PRINCE."

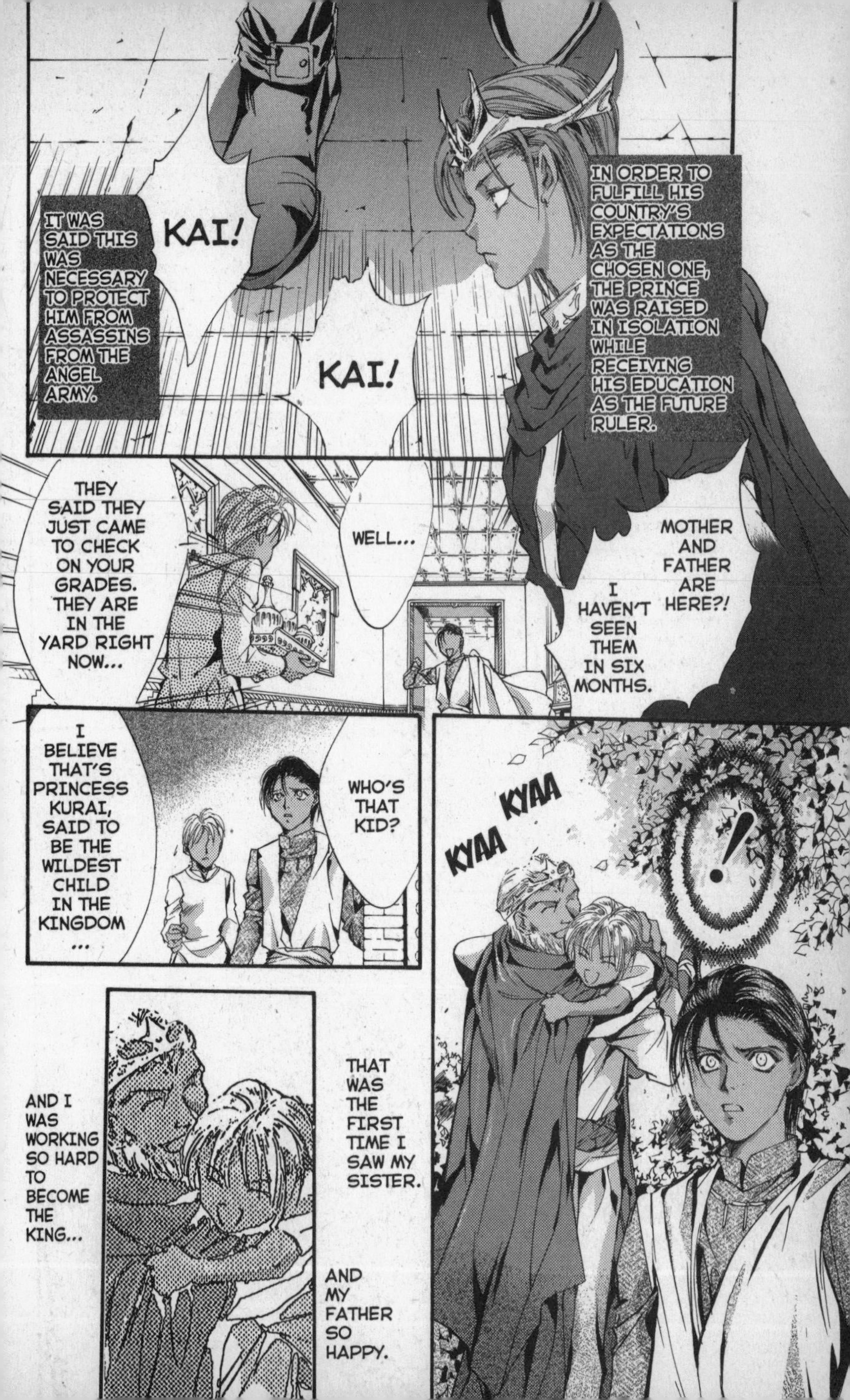
IN ORDER TO FULFILL HIS COUNTRY'S EXPECTATIONS AS THE CHOSEN ONE, THE PRINCE WAS RAISED IN ISOLATION WHILE RECEIVING HIS EDUCATION AS THE FUTURE RULER.
KAI!
KAI!
IT WAS SAID THIS WAS NECESSARY TO PROTECT HIM FROM ASSASSINS FROM THE ANGEL ARMY.
MOTHER AND FATHER ARE HERE?!
I HAVEN'T SEEN THEM IN SIX MONTHS.
WELL...
THEY SAID THEY JUST CAME TO CHECK ON YOUR GRADES. THEY ARE IN THE YARD RIGHT NOW...
KYAA
KYAA
!
WHO'S THAT KID?
I BELIEVE THAT'S PRINCESS KURAI, SAID TO BE THE WILDEST CHILD IN THE KINGDOM...
THAT WAS THE FIRST TIME I SAW MY SISTER.
AND MY FATHER SO HAPPY.
AND I WAS WORKING SO HARD TO BECOME THE KING...

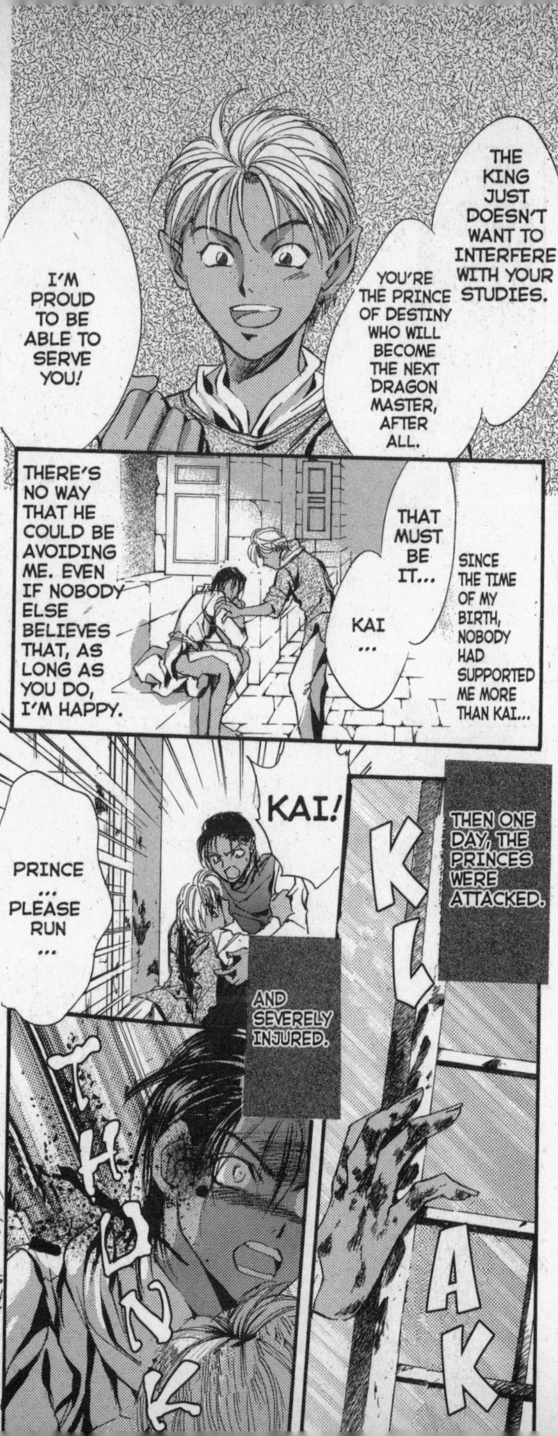
THE KING JUST DOESN'T WANT TO INTERFERE WITH YOUR STUDIES.
YOU'RE THE PRINCE OF DESTINY WHO WILL BECOME THE NEXT DRAGON MASTER, AFTER ALL.
I'M PROUD TO BE ABLE TO SERVE YOU!
SINCE THE TIME OF MY BIRTH, NOBODY HAD SUPPORTED ME MORE THAN KAI...
KAI ...
THAT MUST BE IT...
THERE'S NO WAY THAT HE COULD BE AVOIDING ME. EVEN IF NOBODY ELSE BELIEVES THAT, AS LONG AS YOU DO, I'M HAPPY.
THEN ONE DAY, THE PRINCES WERE ATTACKED.
KLAK
KAI!
PRINCE ... PLEASE RUN ...
AND SEVERELY INJURED.
THUNK

I drew Asmodeus as a cute older man and he was pretty popular. Though I did get a few rude requests asking to be clearer with Belial's body... I've put thought into it, you know? You want to know everything? She quit in the middle of the process of becoming a woman (angels are born genderless), so basically she's like a woman with no breasts... The story of Arachne's past was pretty incredible for this manga. I worried about whether I'd be able to convey everything in the amount of pages I had. Poor Arachne.

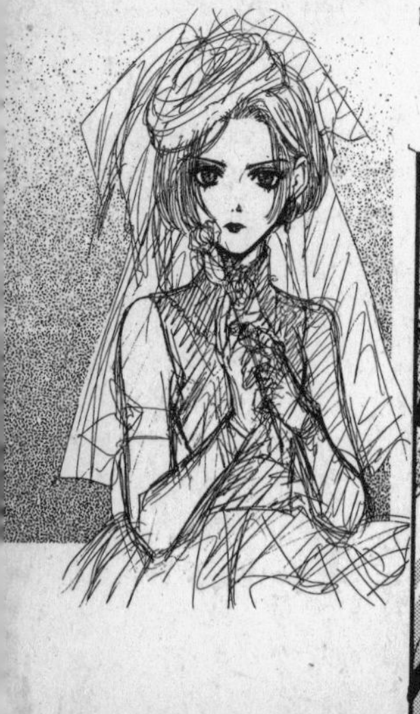

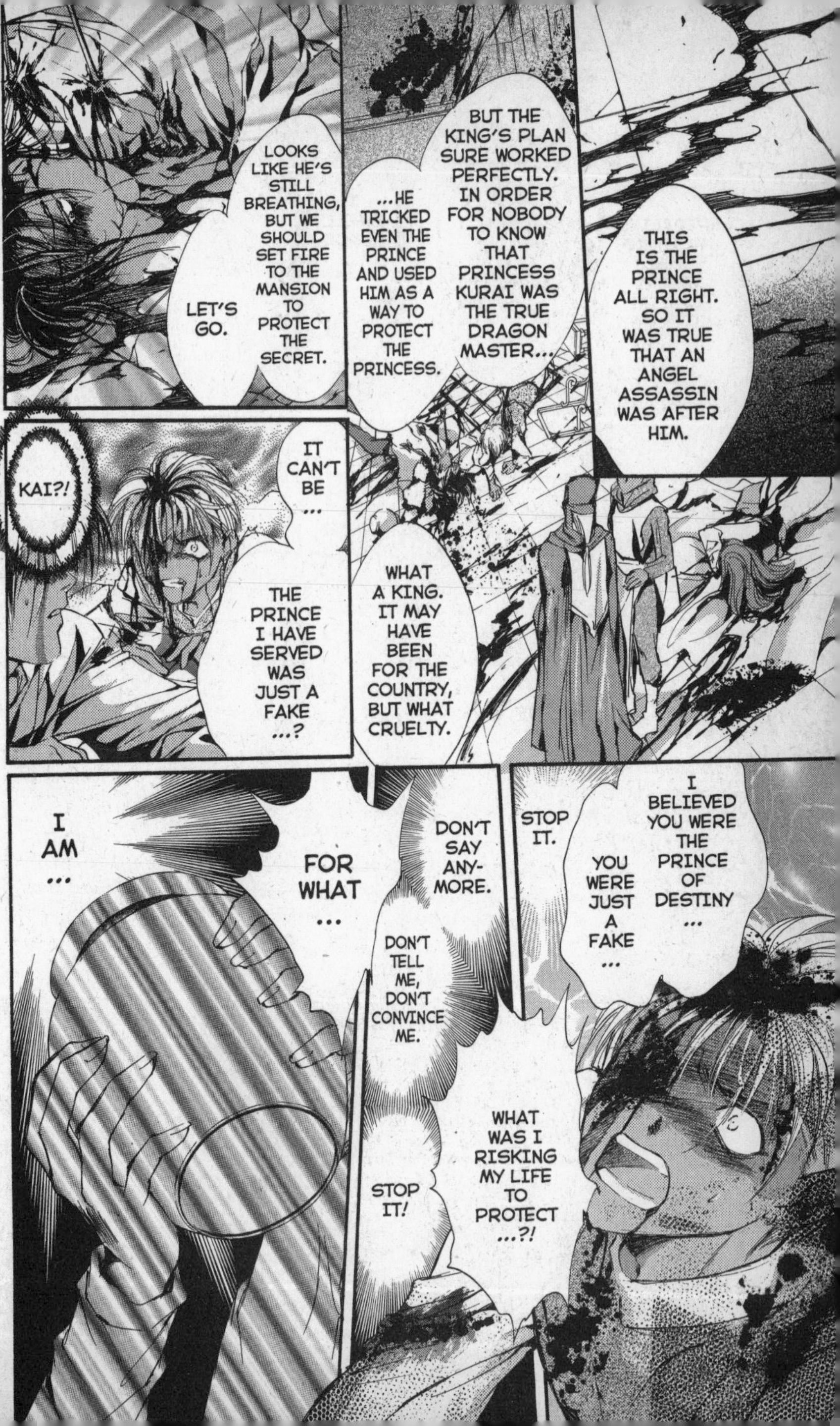
THIS IS THE PRINCE ALL RIGHT. SO IT WAS TRUE THAT AN ANGEL ASSASSIN WAS AFTER HIM.
BUT THE KING'S PLAN SURE WORKED PERFECTLY. IN ORDER FOR NOBODY TO KNOW THAT PRINCESS KURAI WAS THE TRUE DRAGON MASTER...
...HE TRICKED EVEN THE PRINCE AND USED HIM AS A WAY TO PROTECT THE PRINCESS.
LOOKS LIKE HE'S STILL BREATHING, BUT WE SHOULD SET FIRE TO THE MANSION TO PROTECT THE SECRET.
LET'S GO.
WHAT A KING. IT MAY HAVE BEEN FOR THE COUNTRY, BUT WHAT CRUELTY.
IT CAN'T BE ...
KAI?!
THE PRINCE I HAVE SERVED WAS JUST A FAKE ...?
I BELIEVED YOU WERE THE PRINCE OF DESTINY ...
YOU WERE JUST A FAKE ...
STOP IT.
DON'T SAY ANY-MORE.
DON'T TELL ME, DON'T CONVINCE ME.
WHAT WAS I RISKING MY LIFE TO PROTECT ...?!
STOP IT!
FOR WHAT ...
I AM ...

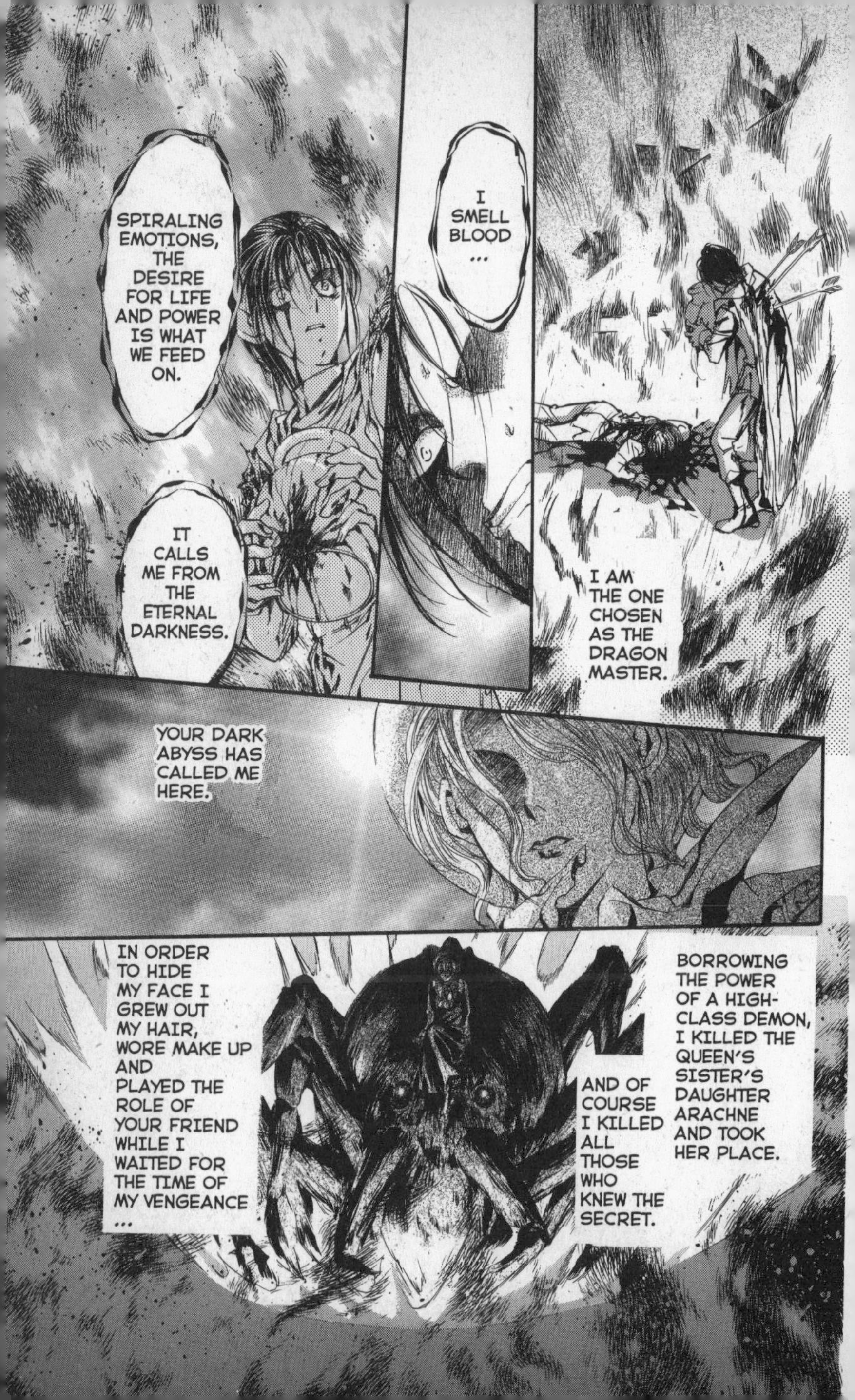
I AM THE ONE CHOSEN AS THE DRAGON MASTER.
I SMELL BLOOD...
SPIRALING EMOTIONS, THE DESIRE FOR LIFE AND POWER IS WHAT WE FEED ON.
IT CALLS ME FROM THE ETERNAL DARKNESS.
YOUR DARK ABYSS HAS CALLED ME HERE.
BORROWING THE POWER OF A HIGH-CLASS DEMON, I KILLED THE QUEEN'S SISTER'S DAUGHTER ARACHNE AND TOOK HER PLACE.
AND OF COURSE I KILLED ALL THOSE WHO KNEW THE SECRET.
IN ORDER TO HIDE MY FACE I GREW OUT MY HAIR, WORE MAKE UP AND PLAYED THE ROLE OF YOUR FRIEND WHILE I WAITED FOR THE TIME OF MY VENGEANCE...

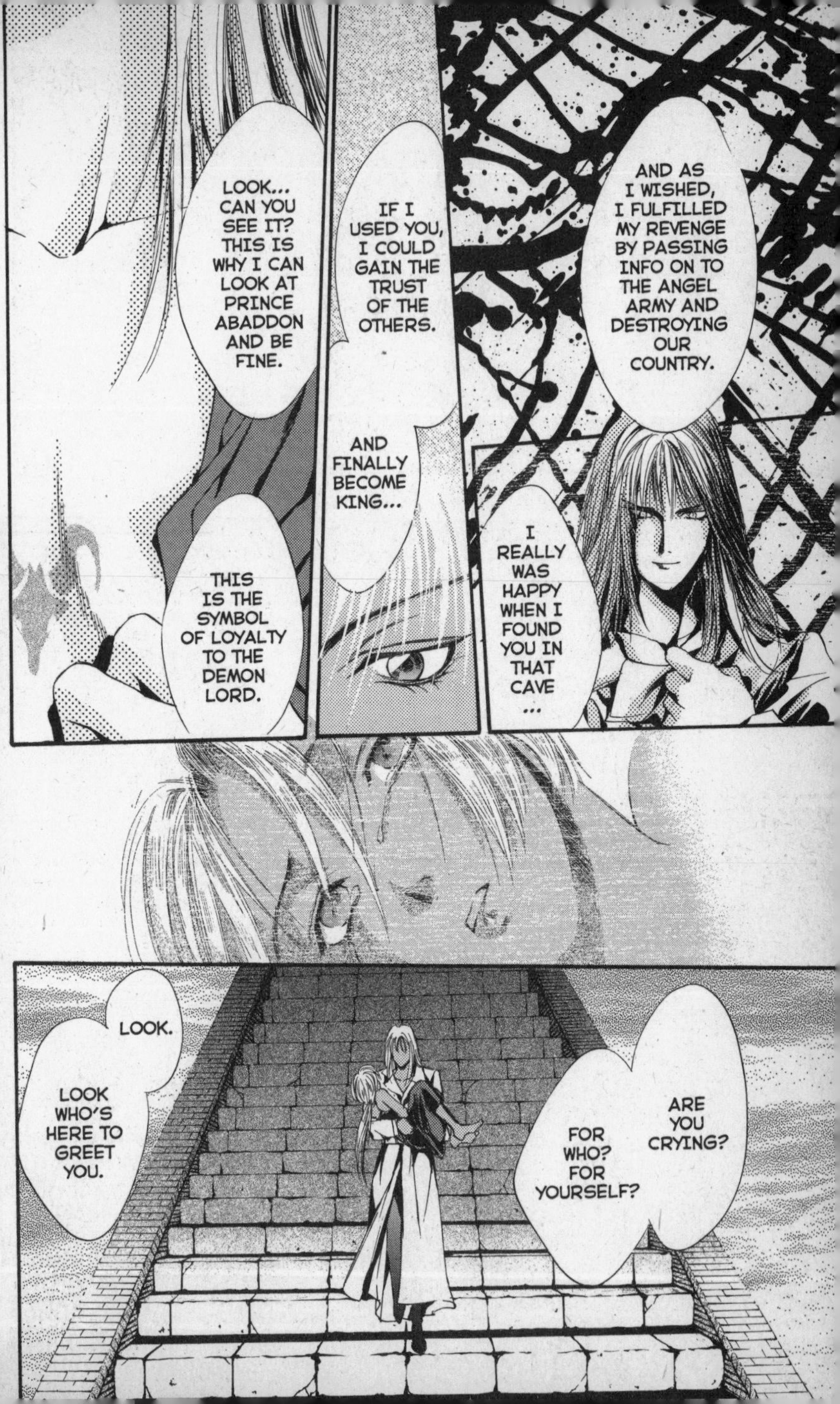
AND AS I WISHED, I FULFILLED MY REVENGE BY PASSING INFO ON TO THE ANGEL ARMY AND DESTROYING OUR COUNTRY.
I REALLY WAS HAPPY WHEN I FOUND YOU IN THAT CAVE ...
IF I USED YOU, I COULD GAIN THE TRUST OF THE OTHERS.
AND FINALLY BECOME KING...
LOOK... CAN YOU SEE IT? THIS IS WHY I CAN LOOK AT PRINCE ABADDON AND BE FINE.
THIS IS THE SYMBOL OF LOYALTY TO THE DEMON LORD.
ARE YOU CRYING?
FOR WHO? FOR YOURSELF?
LOOK.
LOOK WHO'S HERE TO GREET YOU.

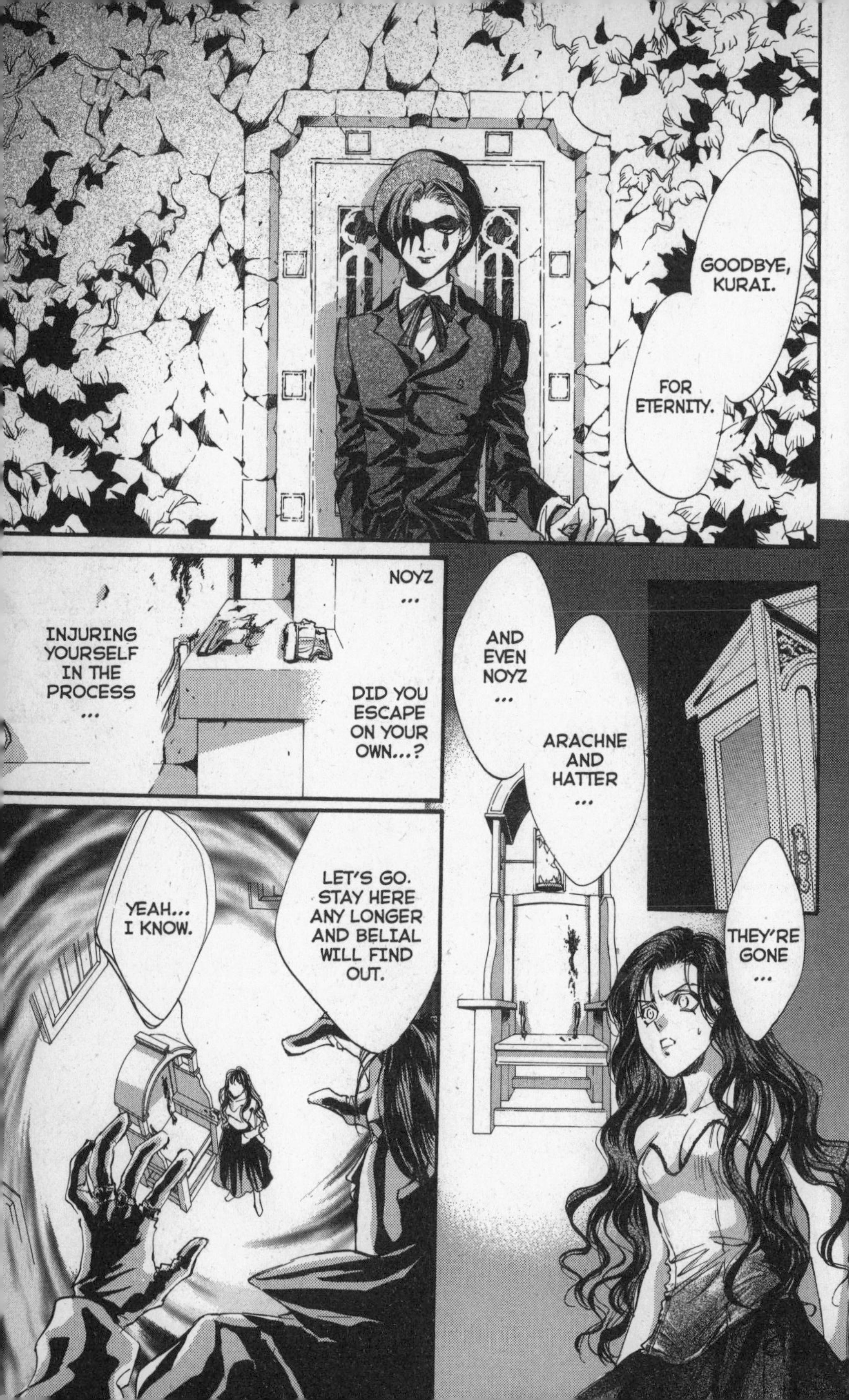
GOODBYE, KURAI.
FOR ETERNITY.
AND EVEN NOYZ ...
ARACHNE AND HATTER ...
THEY'RE GONE ...
NOYZ ...
DID YOU ESCAPE ON YOUR OWN...?
INJURING YOURSELF IN THE PROCESS ...
LET'S GO. STAY HERE ANY LONGER AND BELIAL WILL FIND OUT.
YEAH... I KNOW.

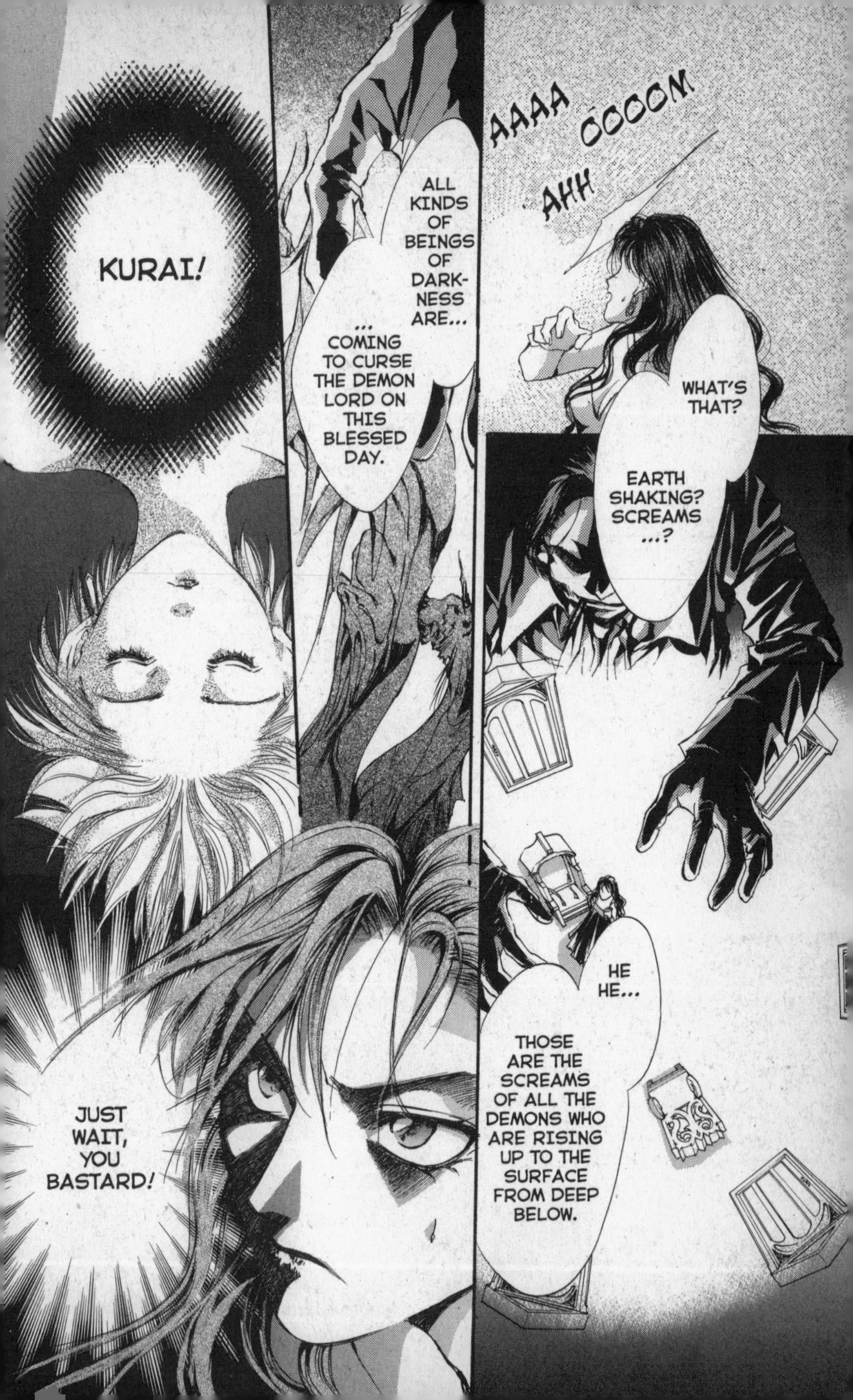
AAAA OOOOM AHH
WHAT'S THAT?
EARTH SHAKING? SCREAMS ...?
HE HE...
THOSE ARE THE SCREAMS OF ALL THE DEMONS WHO ARE RISING UP TO THE SURFACE FROM DEEP BELOW.
ALL KINDS OF BEINGS OF DARKNESS ARE...
... COMING TO CURSE THE DEMON LORD ON THIS BLESSED DAY.
KURAI!
JUST WAIT, YOU BASTARD!

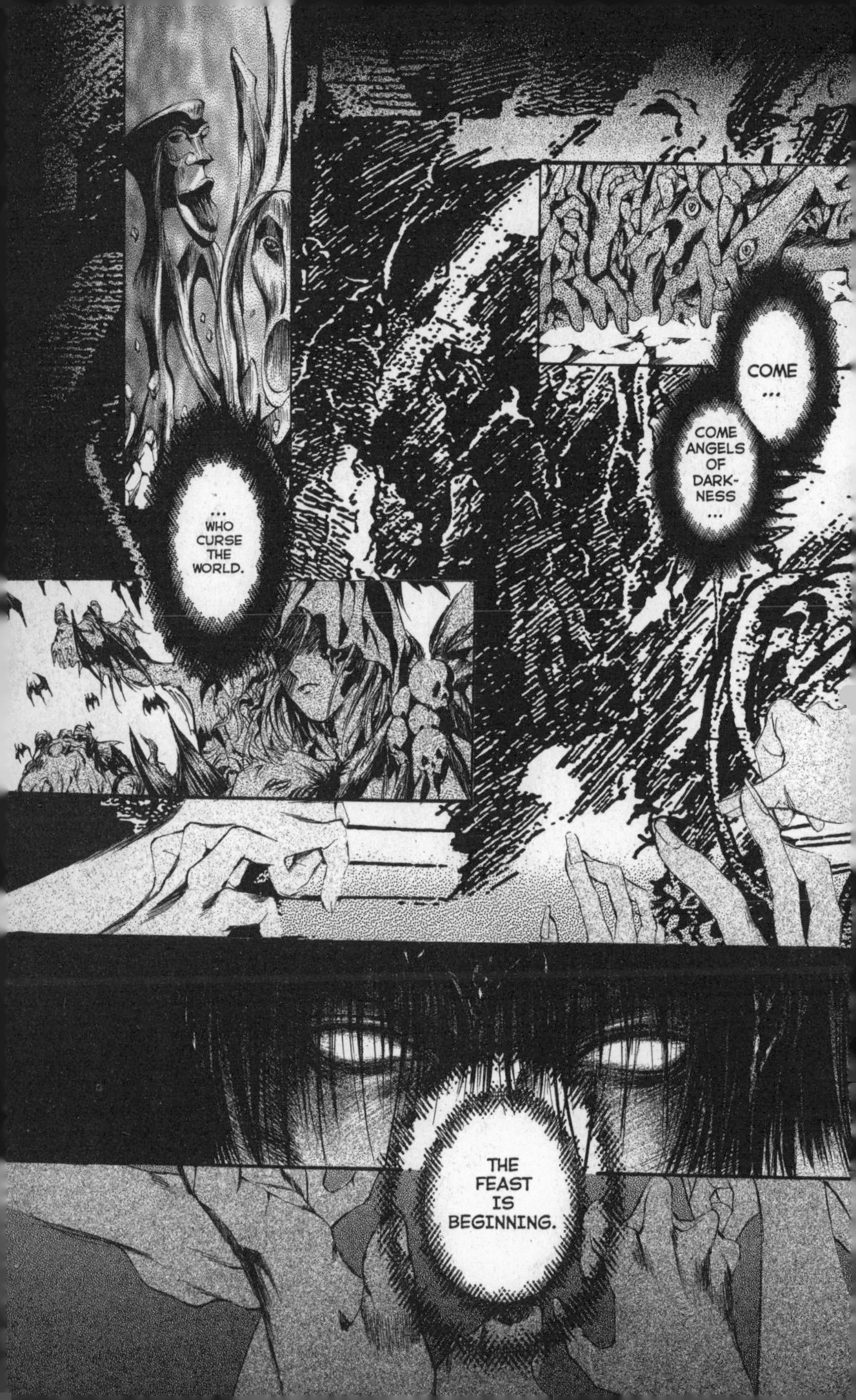
COME ...
COME ANGELS OF DARK-NESS ...
... WHO CURSE THE WORLD.
THE FEAST IS BEGINNING.

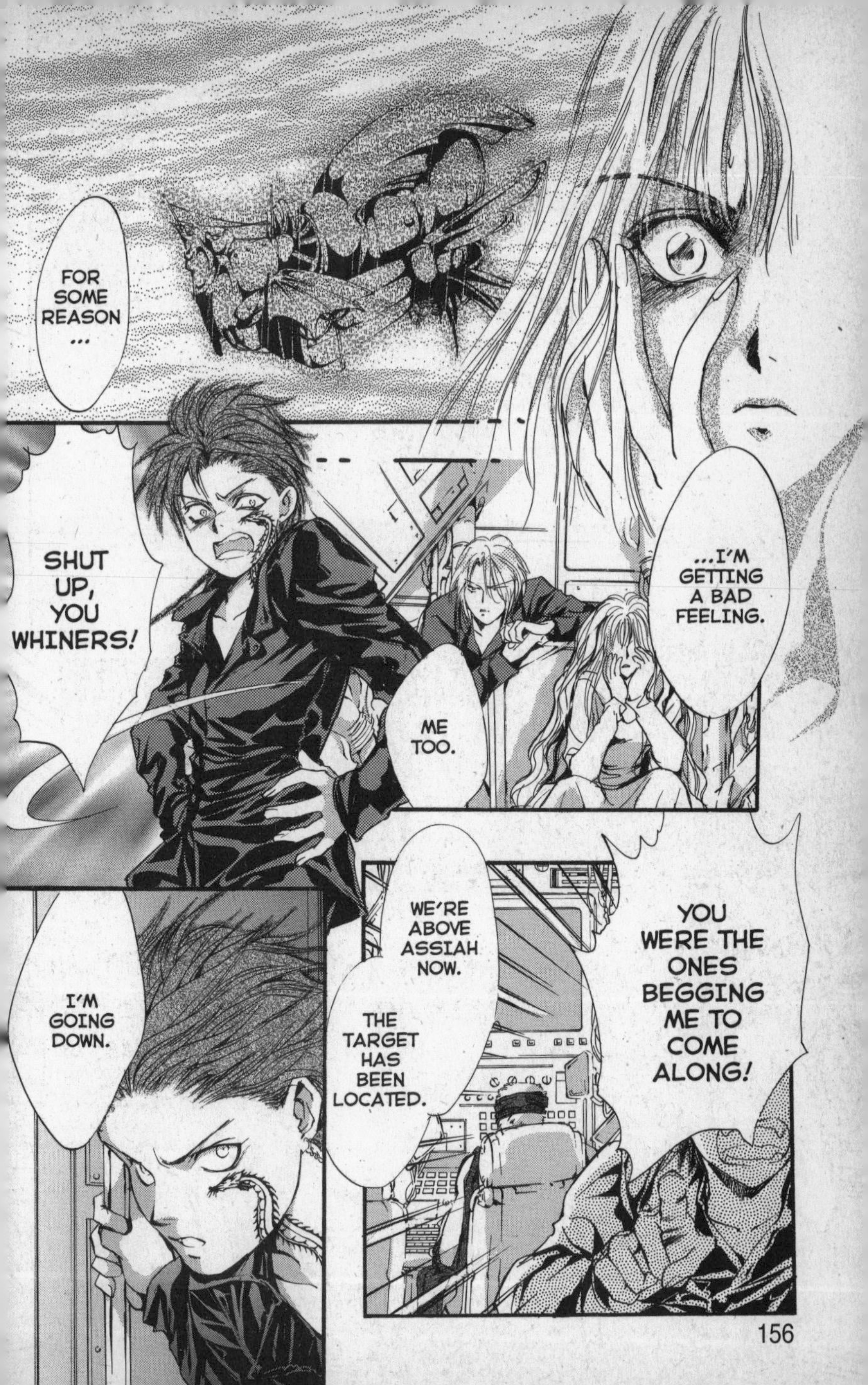
FOR SOME REASON ...
...I'M GETTING A BAD FEELING.
ME TOO.
SHUT UP, YOU WHINERS!
YOU WERE THE ONES BEGGING ME TO COME ALONG!
WE'RE ABOVE ASSIAH NOW.
THE TARGET HAS BEEN LOCATED.
I'M GOING DOWN.

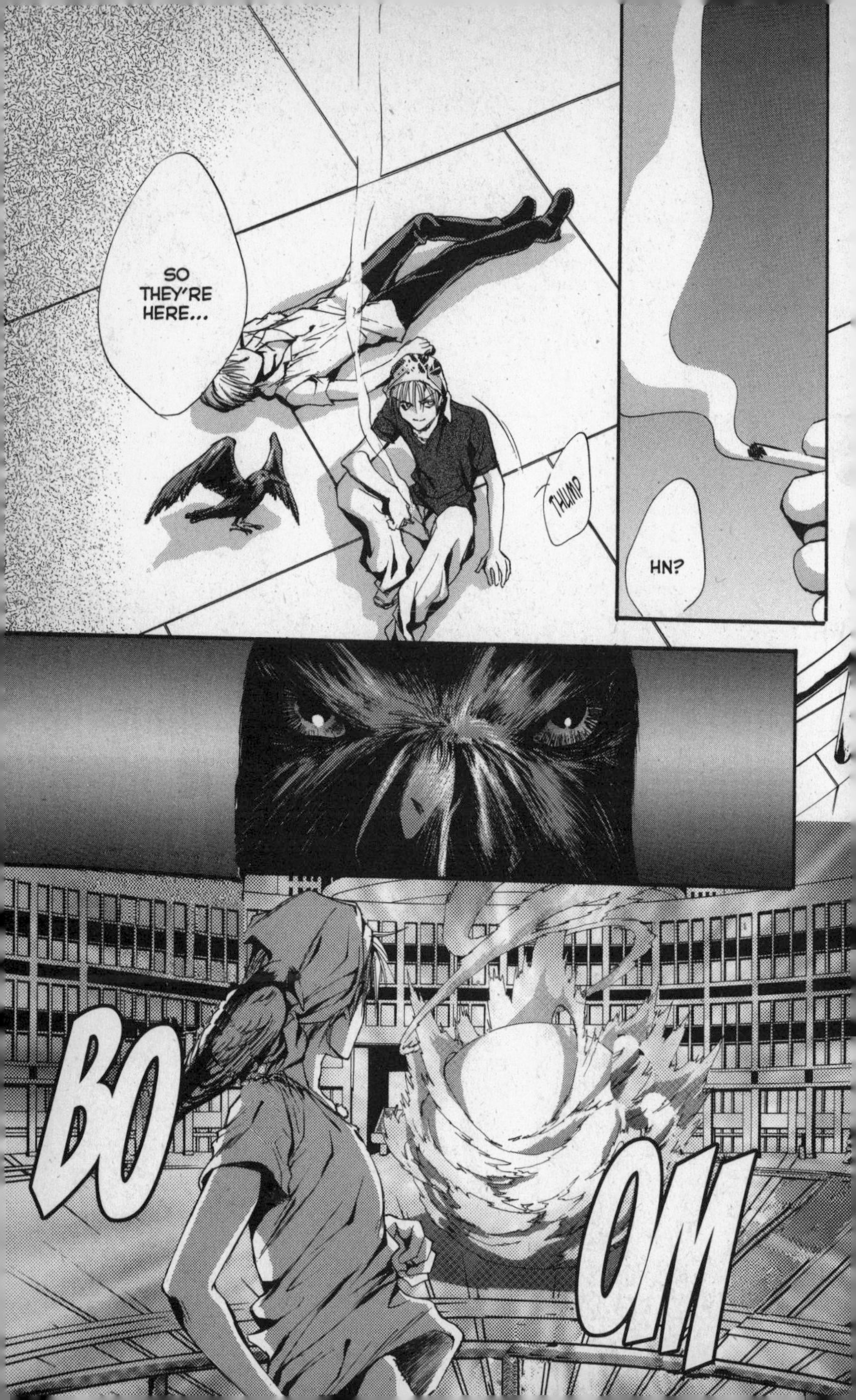
HN?
THUMP
SO THEY'RE HERE...
BOOM

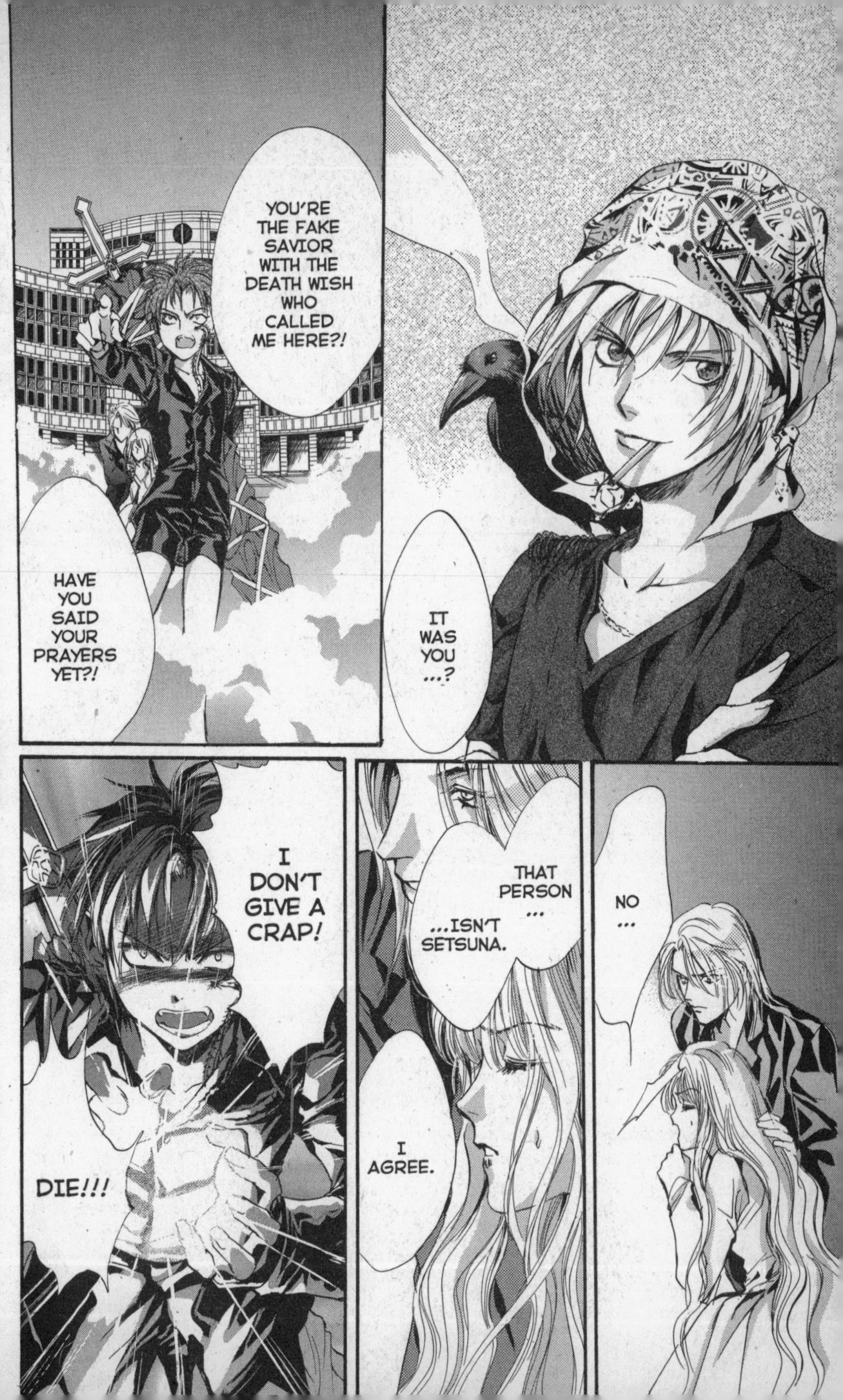
IT WAS YOU ...?
YOU'RE THE FAKE SAVIOR WITH THE DEATH WISH WHO CALLED ME HERE?!
HAVE YOU SAID YOUR PRAYERS YET?!
NO ...
THAT PERSON ...
...ISN'T SETSUNA.
I AGREE.
I DON'T GIVE A CRAP!
DIE!!!

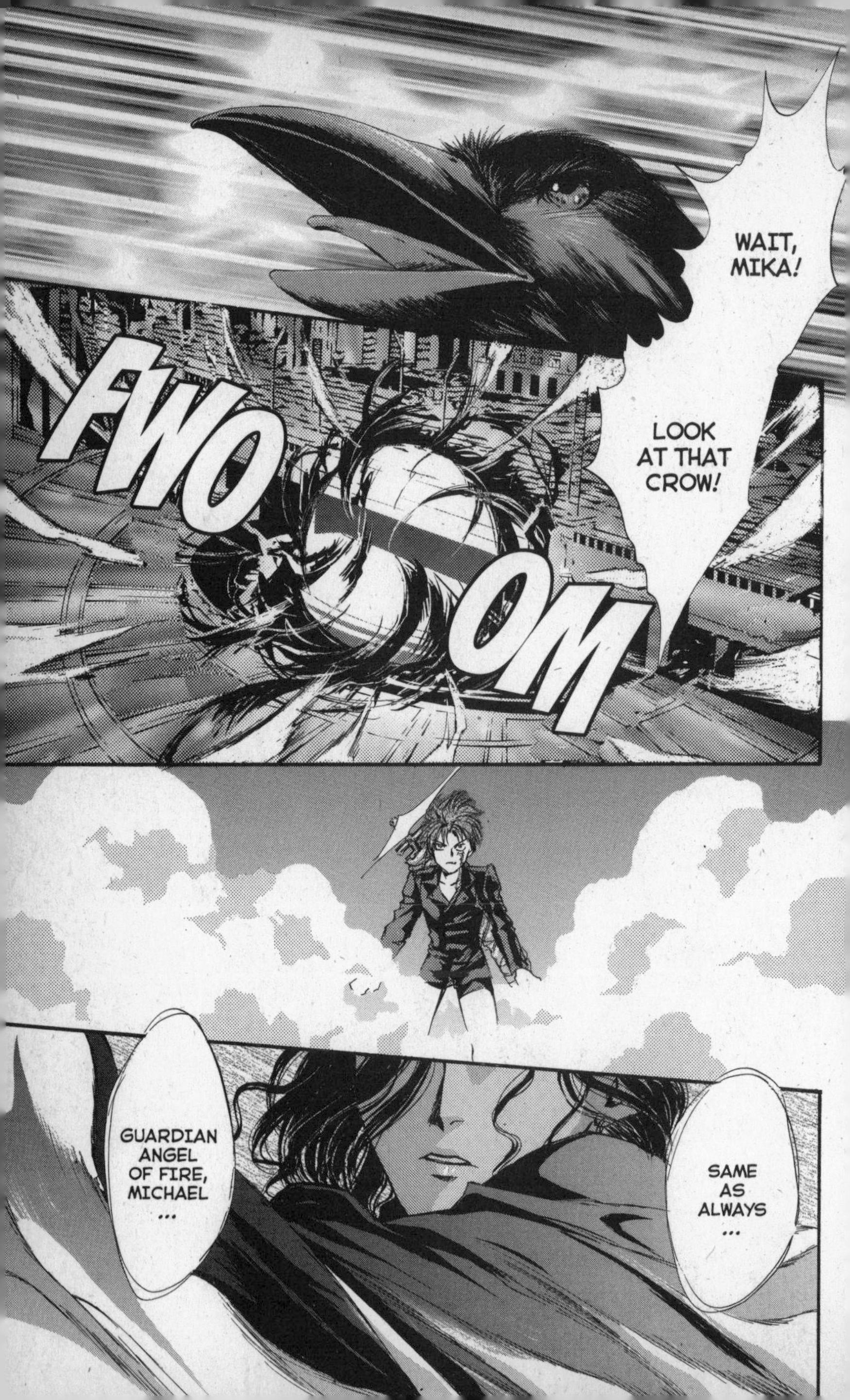
WAIT, MIKA!
LOOK AT THAT CROW!
FWOOM
SAME AS ALWAYS ...
GUARDIAN ANGEL OF FIRE, MICHAEL ...

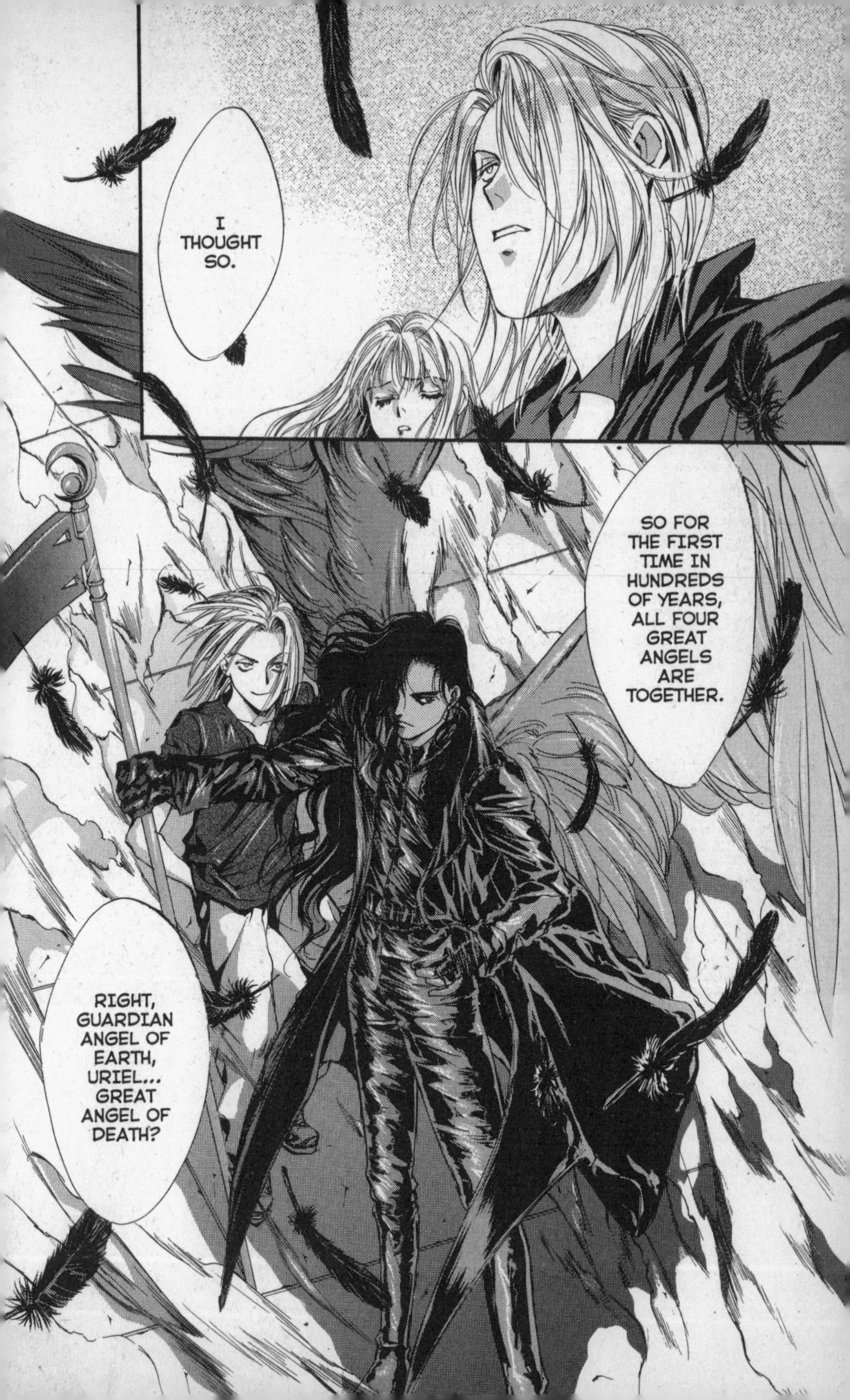
I THOUGHT SO.
SO FOR THE FIRST TIME IN HUNDREDS OF YEARS, ALL FOUR GREAT ANGELS ARE TOGETHER.
RIGHT, GUARDIAN ANGEL OF EARTH, URIEL... GREAT ANGEL OF DEATH?

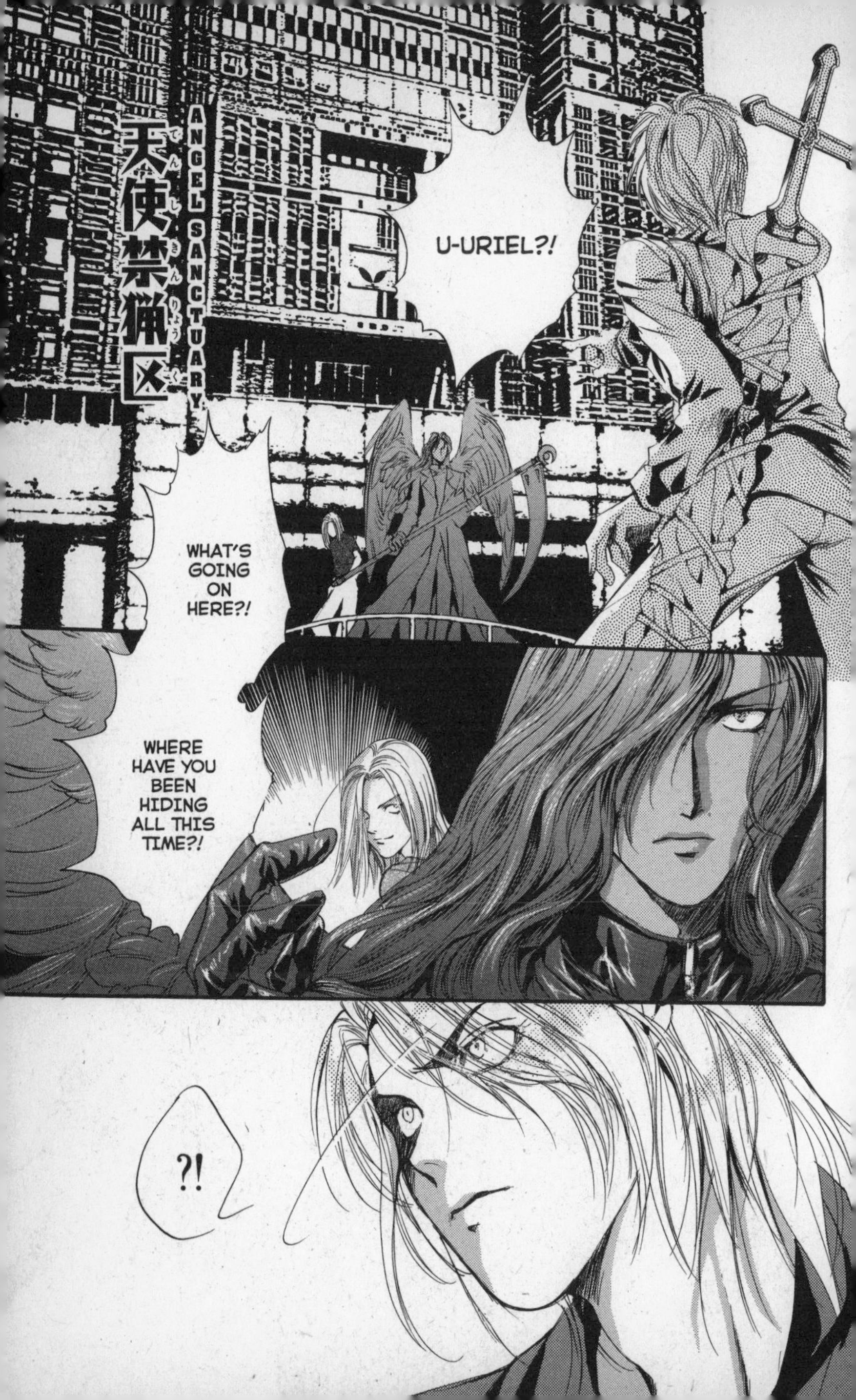
U-URIEL?!
WHAT'S GOING ON HERE?!
天使禁猟区
ANGEL SANCTUARY
WHERE HAVE YOU BEEN HIDING ALL THIS TIME?!
?!

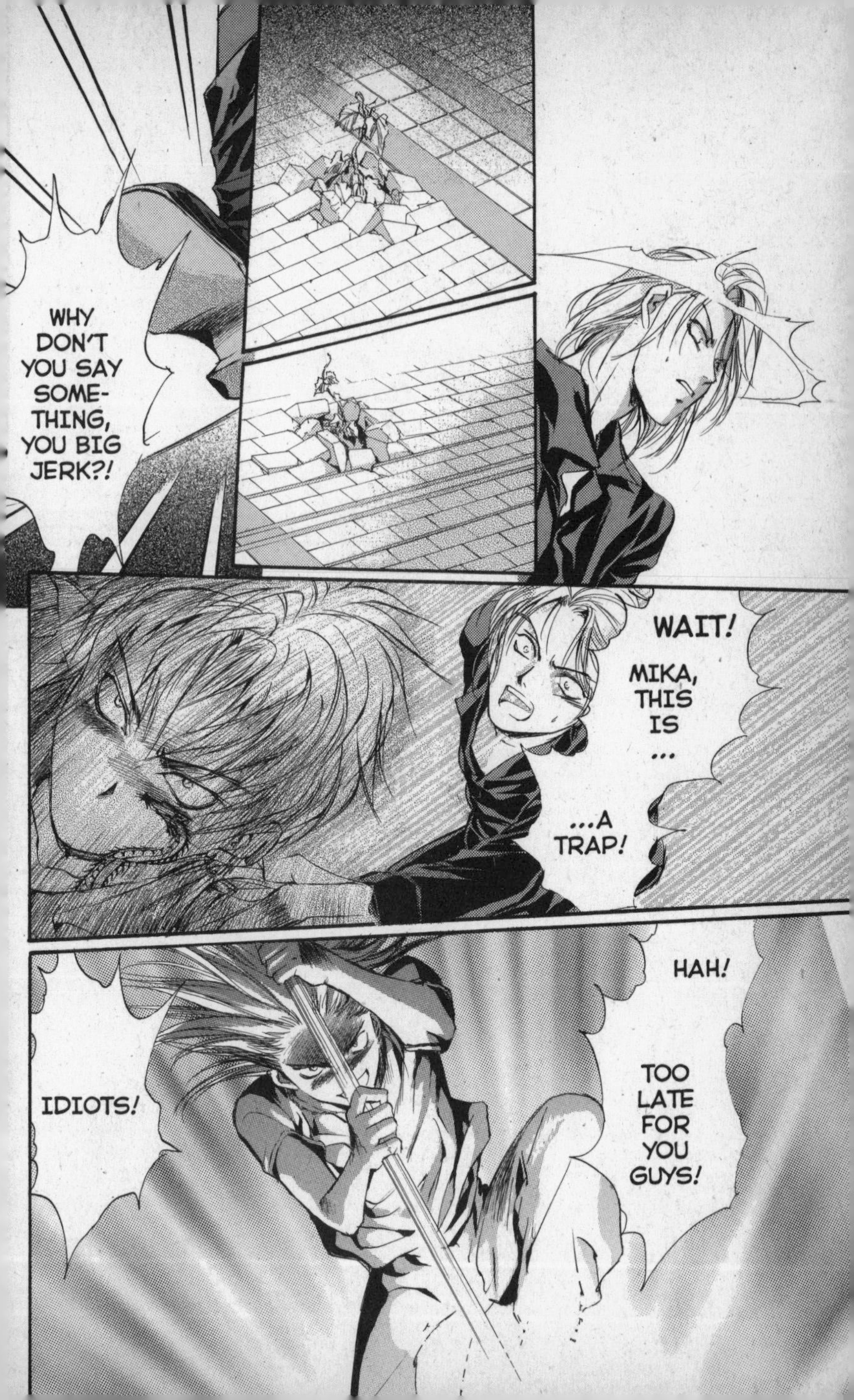
WHY DON'T YOU SAY SOME-THING, YOU BIG JERK?!
WAIT!
MIKA, THIS IS ...
...A TRAP!
HAH!
TOO LATE FOR YOU GUYS!
IDIOTS!

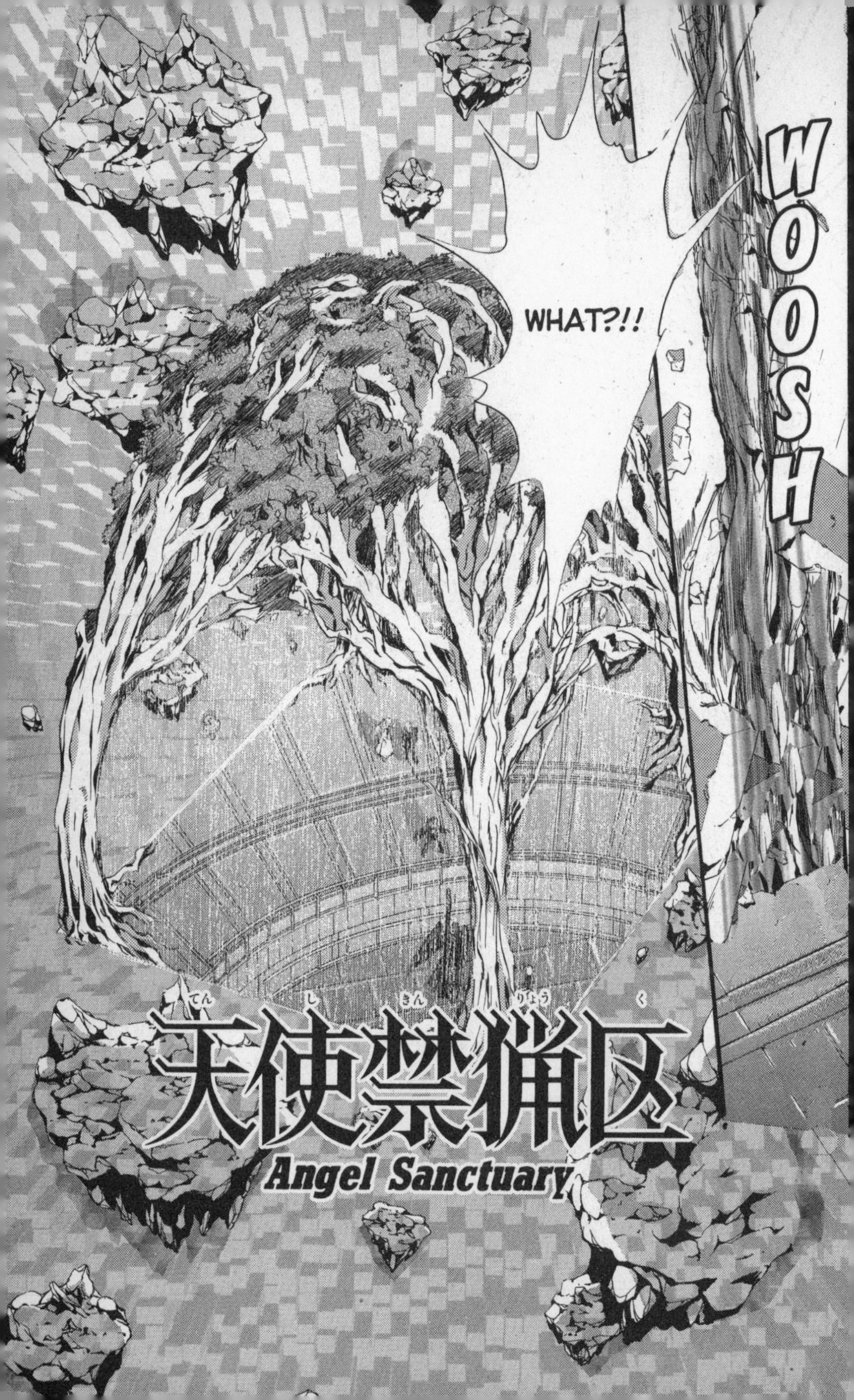
WOOSH
WHAT?!!
天使禁猟区
Angel Sanctuary

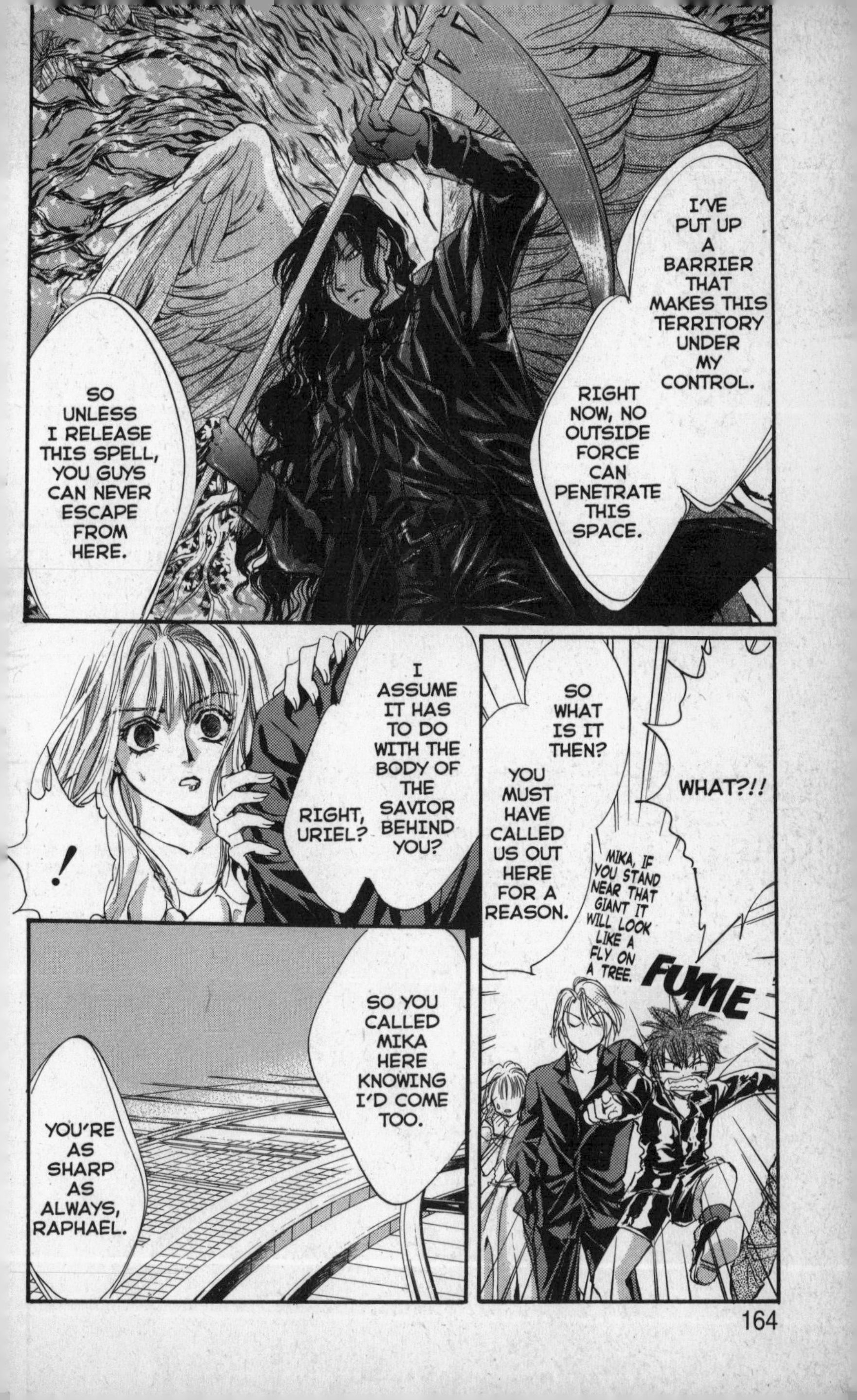
I'VE PUT UP A BARRIER THAT MAKES THIS TERRITORY UNDER MY CONTROL.
RIGHT NOW, NO OUTSIDE FORCE CAN PENETRATE THIS SPACE.
SO UNLESS I RELEASE THIS SPELL, YOU GUYS CAN NEVER ESCAPE FROM HERE.
SO WHAT IS IT THEN?
YOU MUST HAVE CALLED US OUT HERE FOR A REASON.
WHAT?!!
MIKA, IF YOU STAND NEAR THAT GIANT IT WILL LOOK LIKE A FLY ON A TREE.
FUME
!
I ASSUME IT HAS TO DO WITH THE BODY OF THE SAVIOR BEHIND YOU?
RIGHT, URIEL?
SO YOU CALLED MIKA HERE KNOWING I'D COME TOO.
YOU'RE AS SHARP AS ALWAYS, RAPHAEL.

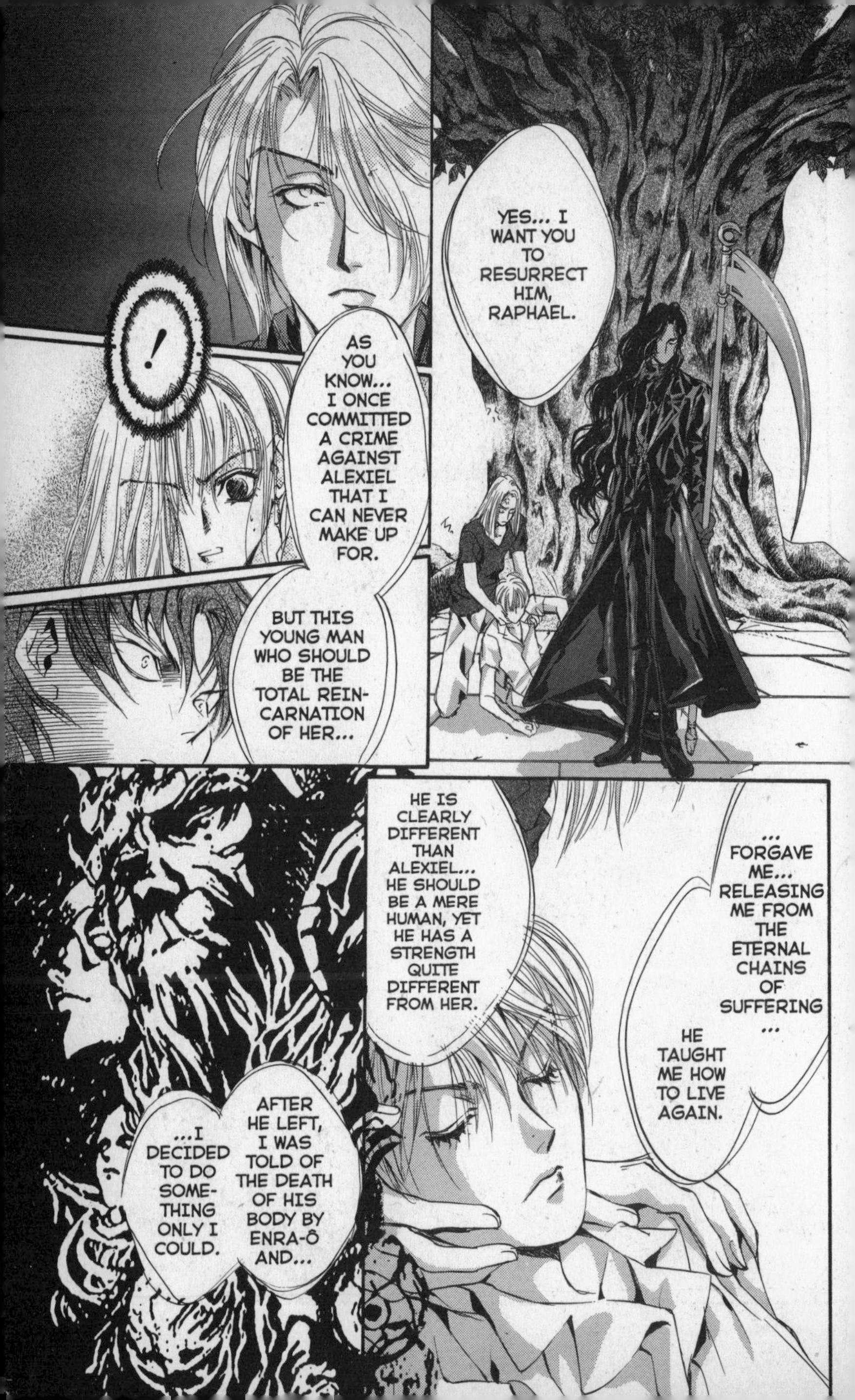
YES... I WANT YOU TO RESURRECT HIM, RAPHAEL.
!
AS YOU KNOW... I ONCE COMMITTED A CRIME AGAINST ALEXIEL THAT I CAN NEVER MAKE UP FOR.
BUT THIS YOUNG MAN WHO SHOULD BE THE TOTAL REIN-CARNATION OF HER...
...FORGAVE ME... RELEASING ME FROM THE ETERNAL CHAINS OF SUFFERING...
HE TAUGHT ME HOW TO LIVE AGAIN.
HE IS CLEARLY DIFFERENT THAN ALEXIEL... HE SHOULD BE A MERE HUMAN, YET HE HAS A STRENGTH QUITE DIFFERENT FROM HER.
AFTER HE LEFT, I WAS TOLD OF THE DEATH OF HIS BODY BY ENRA-Ô AND...
...I DECIDED TO DO SOME-THING ONLY I COULD.

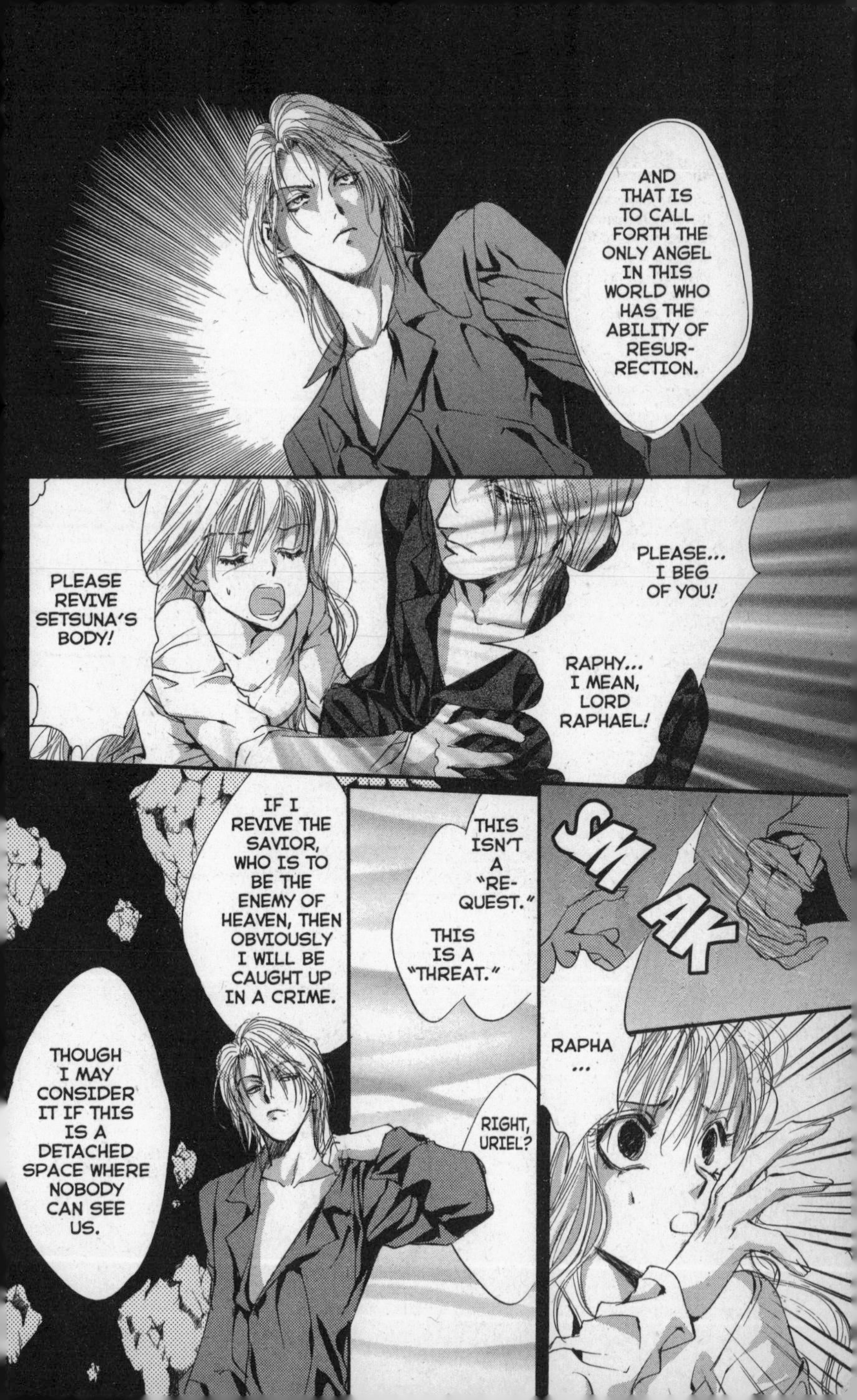
AND THAT IS TO CALL FORTH THE ONLY ANGEL IN THIS WORLD WHO HAS THE ABILITY OF RESUR-RECTION.
PLEASE... I BEG OF YOU!
RAPHY... I MEAN, LORD RAPHAEL!
PLEASE REVIVE SETSUNA'S BODY!
SMAK
RAPHA...
THIS ISN'T A "RE-QUEST."
THIS IS A "THREAT."
RIGHT, URIEL?
IF I REVIVE THE SAVIOR, WHO IS TO BE THE ENEMY OF HEAVEN, THEN OBVIOUSLY I WILL BE CAUGHT UP IN A CRIME.
THOUGH I MAY CONSIDER IT IF THIS IS A DETACHED SPACE WHERE NOBODY CAN SEE US.

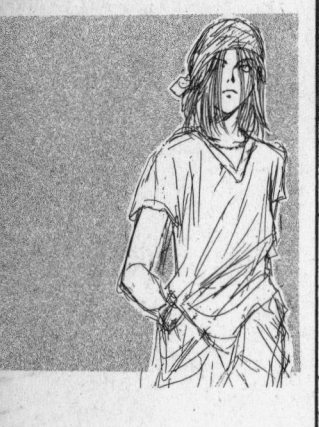

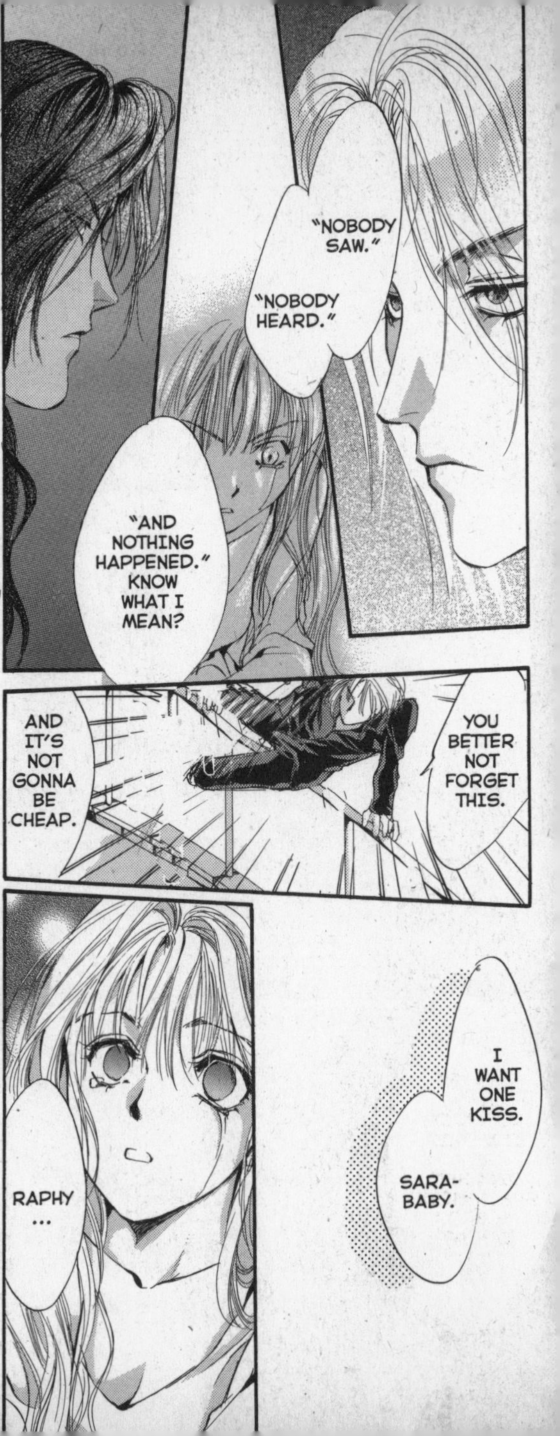
"NOBODY SAW."
"NOBODY HEARD."
"AND NOTHING HAPPENED." KNOW WHAT I MEAN?
YOU BETTER NOT FORGET THIS.
AND IT'S NOT GONNA BE CHEAP.
I WANT ONE KISS.
SARA-BABY.
RAPHY...

Just so you know, the bird-thingie talking to Asmodeus later on in this chapter is Mammon. That scene was kind of comical and lovely... Being a former Angel and rising up to the rank of Seven Satan shows that the power of money is pretty strong even in Hell, I guess. This chapter took a lot of time and effort... I just couldn't convey what I wanted to my assistants, and they had to work really hard too. The Hades saga is only two more chapters, so I was running out of pages and things were a mess. Kato and Uri show up but they had to get right down to business... I had to make the meeting between Hatter and Lucifer very simple. Well, you'll see more in book 11!

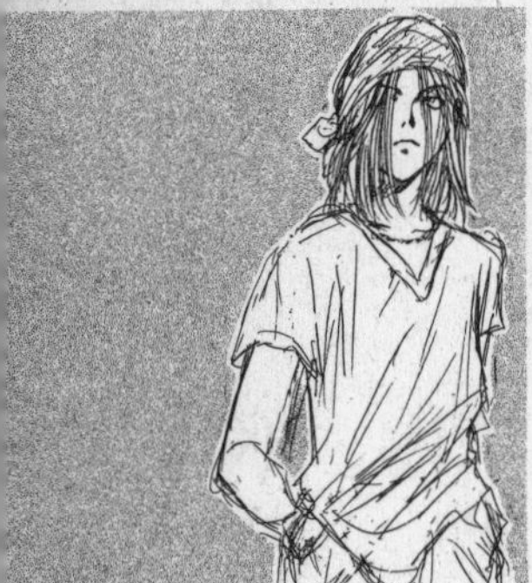

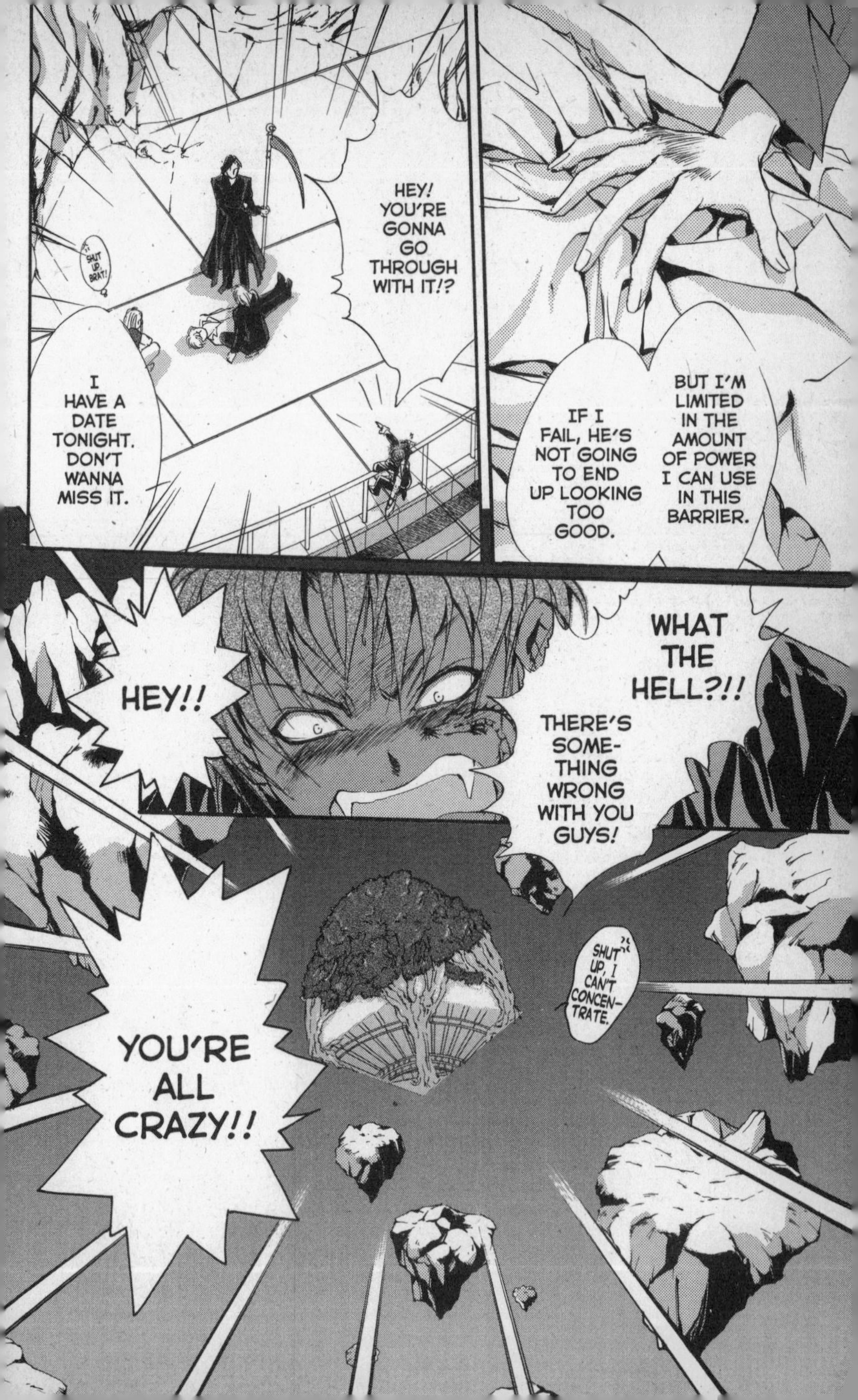
BUT I'M LIMITED IN THE AMOUNT OF POWER I CAN USE IN THIS BARRIER.
IF I FAIL, HE'S NOT GOING TO END UP LOOKING TOO GOOD.
HEY! YOU'RE GONNA GO THROUGH WITH IT!?
SHUT UP, BRAT!
I HAVE A DATE TONIGHT. DON'T WANNA MISS IT.
WHAT THE HELL?!!
THERE'S SOME-THING WRONG WITH YOU GUYS!
HEY!!
SHUT UP, I CAN'T CONCEN-TRATE.
YOU'RE ALL CRAZY!!

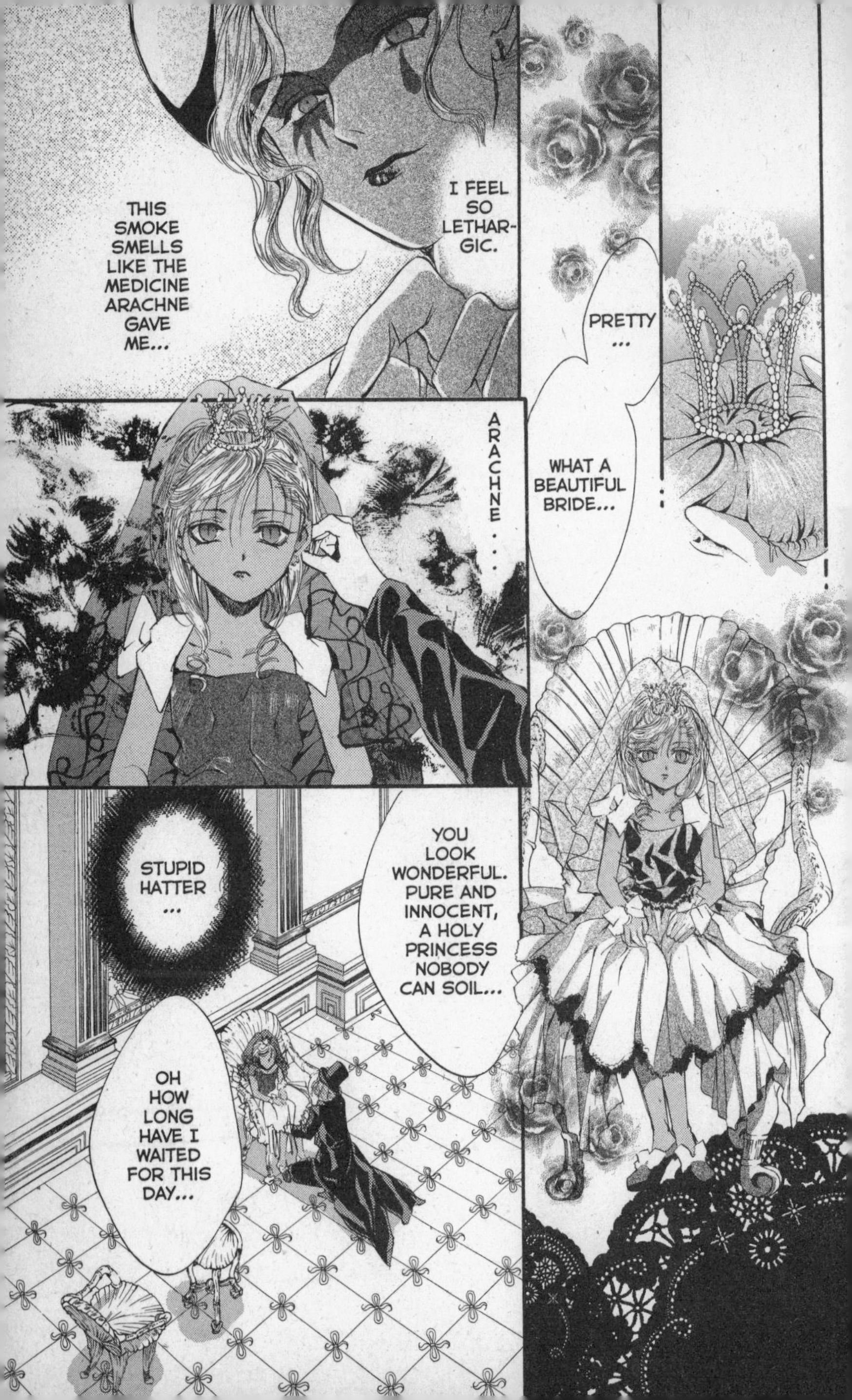
PRETTY...
WHAT A BEAUTIFUL BRIDE...
THIS SMOKE SMELLS LIKE THE MEDICINE ARACHNE GAVE ME...
I FEEL SO LETHAR-GIC.
ARACHNE...
YOU LOOK WONDERFUL. PURE AND INNOCENT, A HOLY PRINCESS NOBODY CAN SOIL...
STUPID HATTER...
OH HOW LONG HAVE I WAITED FOR THIS DAY...

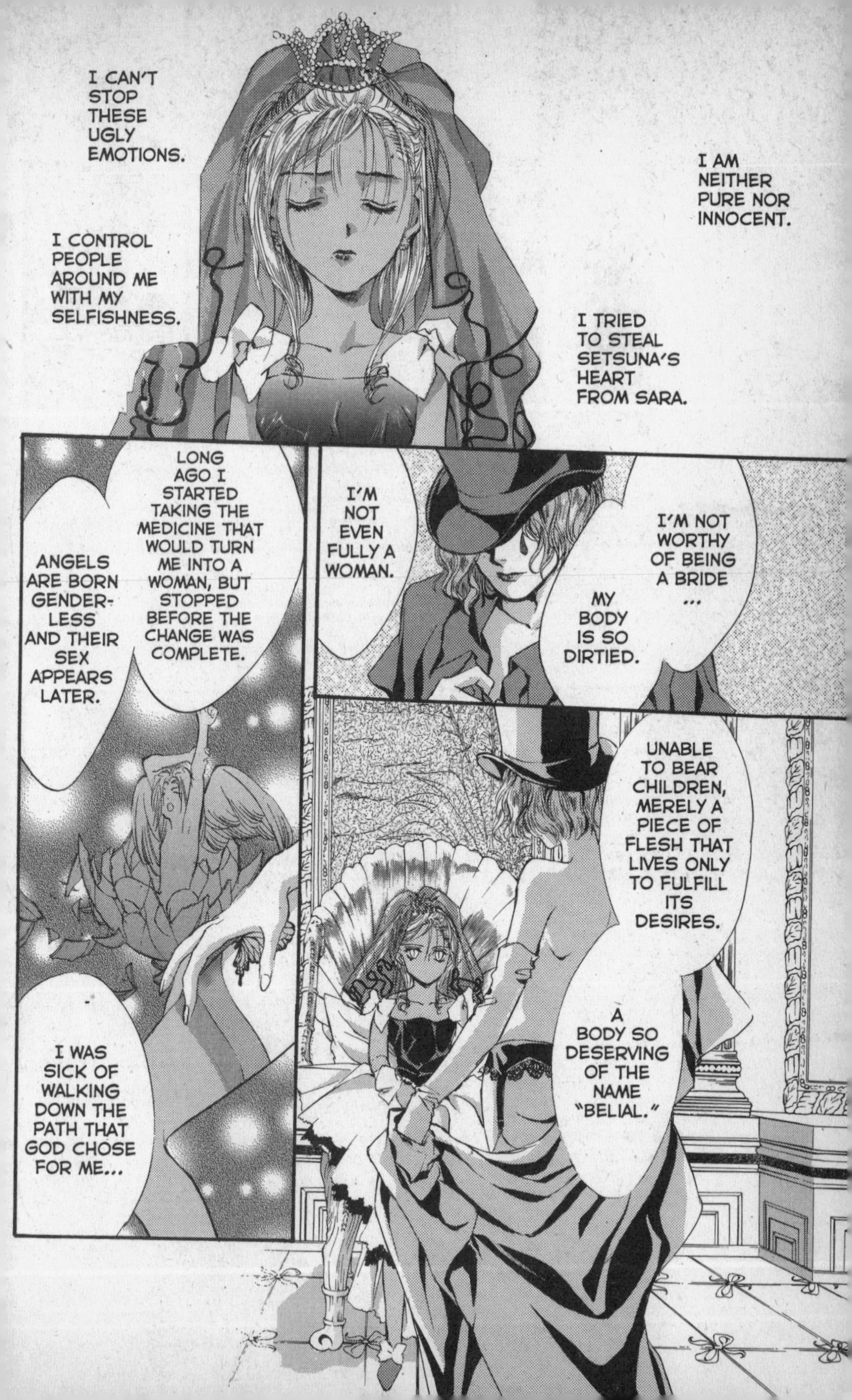
I AM NEITHER PURE NOR INNOCENT.
I TRIED TO STEAL SETSUNA'S HEART FROM SARA.
I CAN'T STOP THESE UGLY EMOTIONS.
I CONTROL PEOPLE AROUND ME WITH MY SELFISHNESS.
I'M NOT WORTHY OF BEING A BRIDE ...
MY BODY IS SO DIRTIED.
I'M NOT EVEN FULLY A WOMAN.
UNABLE TO BEAR CHILDREN, MERELY A PIECE OF FLESH THAT LIVES ONLY TO FULFILL ITS DESIRES.
A BODY SO DESERVING OF THE NAME "BELIAL."
LONG AGO I STARTED TAKING THE MEDICINE THAT WOULD TURN ME INTO A WOMAN, BUT STOPPED BEFORE THE CHANGE WAS COMPLETE.
ANGELS ARE BORN GENDER-LESS AND THEIR SEX APPEARS LATER.
I WAS SICK OF WALKING DOWN THE PATH THAT GOD CHOSE FOR ME...

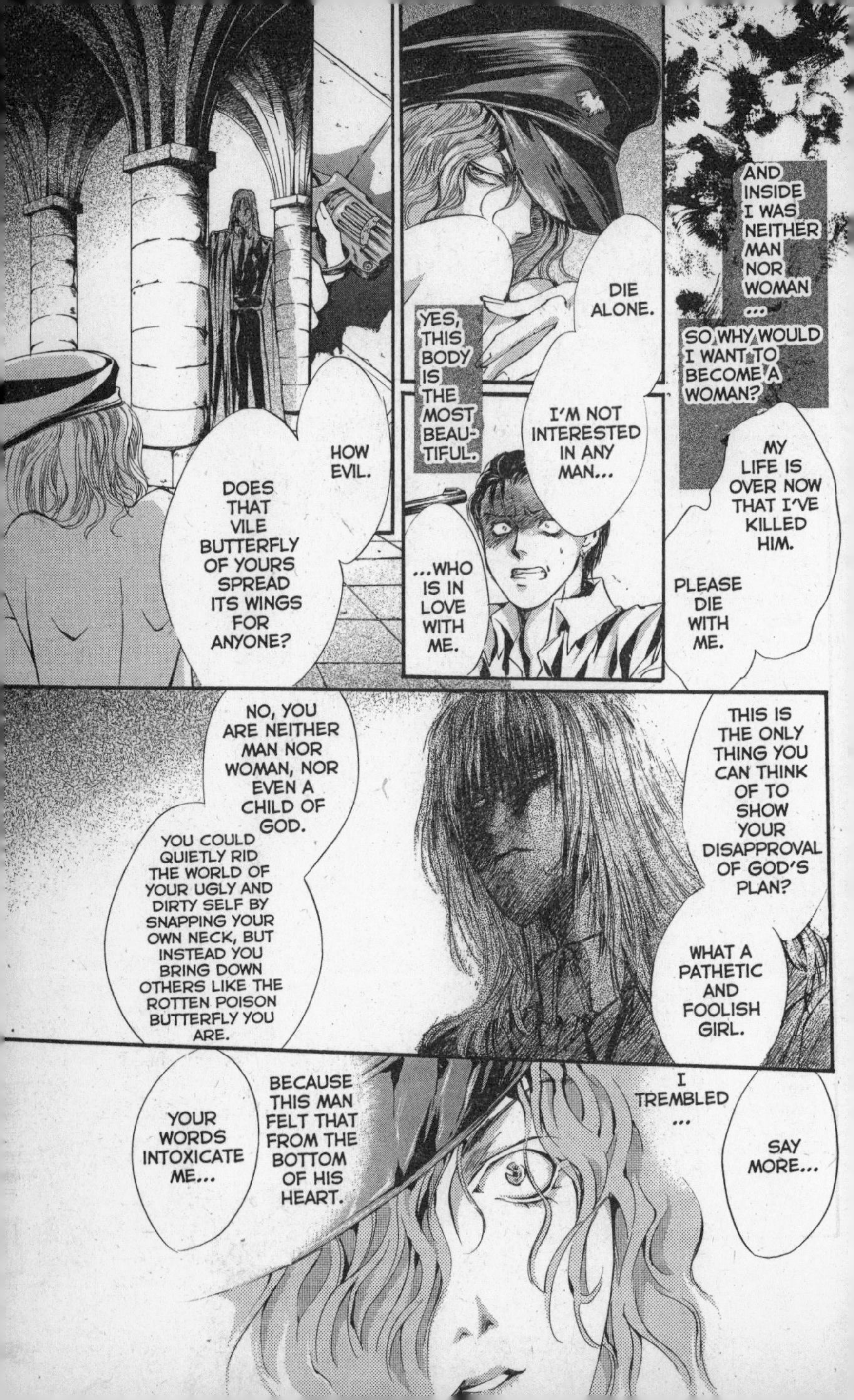
AND INSIDE I WAS NEITHER MAN NOR WOMAN ...
SO WHY WOULD I WANT TO BECOME A WOMAN?
MY LIFE IS OVER NOW THAT I'VE KILLED HIM.
PLEASE DIE WITH ME.
DIE ALONE.
YES, THIS BODY IS THE MOST BEAU-TIFUL.
I'M NOT INTERESTED IN ANY MAN...
...WHO IS IN LOVE WITH ME.
HOW EVIL.
DOES THAT VILE BUTTERFLY OF YOURS SPREAD ITS WINGS FOR ANYONE?
THIS IS THE ONLY THING YOU CAN THINK OF TO SHOW YOUR DISAPPROVAL OF GOD'S PLAN?
WHAT A PATHETIC AND FOOLISH GIRL.
NO, YOU ARE NEITHER MAN NOR WOMAN, NOR EVEN A CHILD OF GOD.
YOU COULD QUIETLY RID THE WORLD OF YOUR UGLY AND DIRTY SELF BY SNAPPING YOUR OWN NECK, BUT INSTEAD YOU BRING DOWN OTHERS LIKE THE ROTTEN POISON BUTTERFLY YOU ARE.
SAY MORE...
I TREMBLED ...
BECAUSE THIS MAN FELT THAT FROM THE BOTTOM OF HIS HEART.
YOUR WORDS INTOXICATE ME...

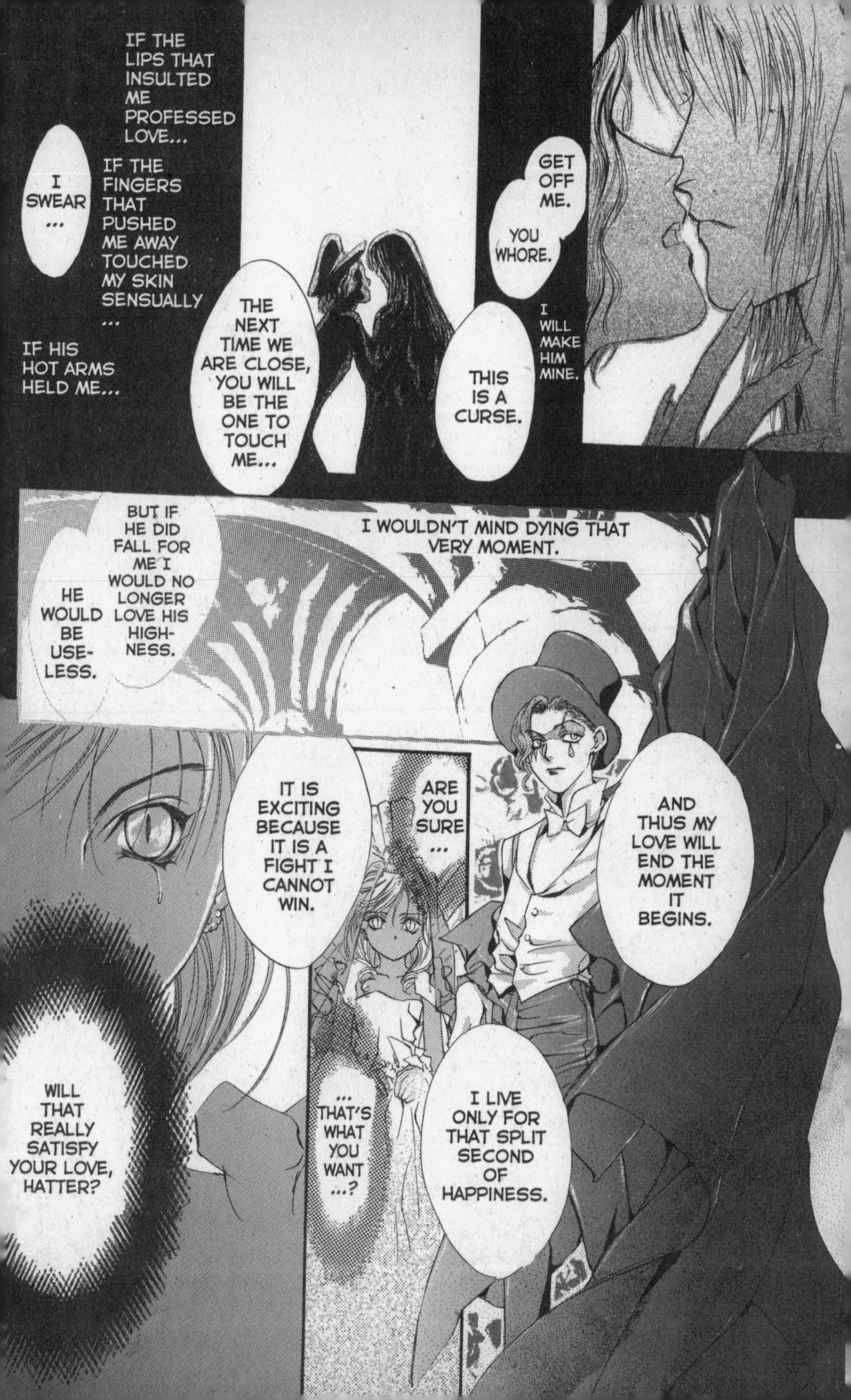
GET OFF ME.
YOU WHORE.
I WILL MAKE HIM MINE.
THIS IS A CURSE.
THE NEXT TIME WE ARE CLOSE, YOU WILL BE THE ONE TO TOUCH ME...
IF THE LIPS THAT INSULTED ME PROFESSED LOVE...
IF THE FINGERS THAT PUSHED ME AWAY TOUCHED MY SKIN SENSUALLY ...
I SWEAR ...
IF HIS HOT ARMS HELD ME...
I WOULDN'T MIND DYING THAT VERY MOMENT.
BUT IF HE DID FALL FOR ME I WOULD NO LONGER LOVE HIS HIGH-NESS.
HE WOULD BE USE-LESS.
AND THUS MY LOVE WILL END THE MOMENT IT BEGINS.
ARE YOU SURE ...
IT IS EXCITING BECAUSE IT IS A FIGHT I CANNOT WIN.
I LIVE ONLY FOR THAT SPLIT SECOND OF HAPPINESS.
... THAT'S WHAT YOU WANT ...?
WILL THAT REALLY SATISFY YOUR LOVE, HATTER?

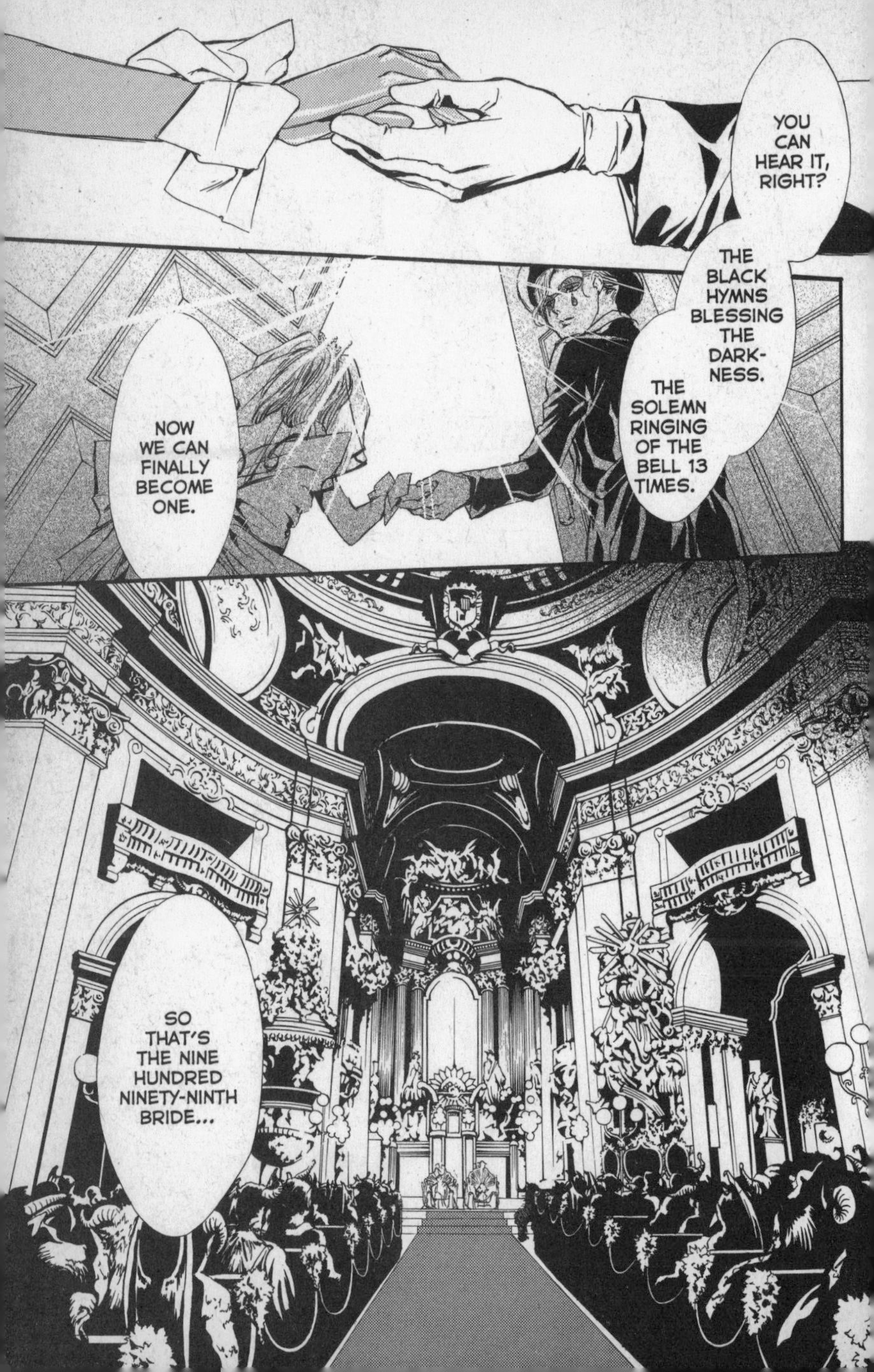
YOU CAN HEAR IT, RIGHT?
THE BLACK HYMNS BLESSING THE DARK-NESS.
THE SOLEMN RINGING OF THE BELL 13 TIMES.
NOW WE CAN FINALLY BECOME ONE.
SO THAT'S THE NINE HUNDRED NINETY-NINTH BRIDE...

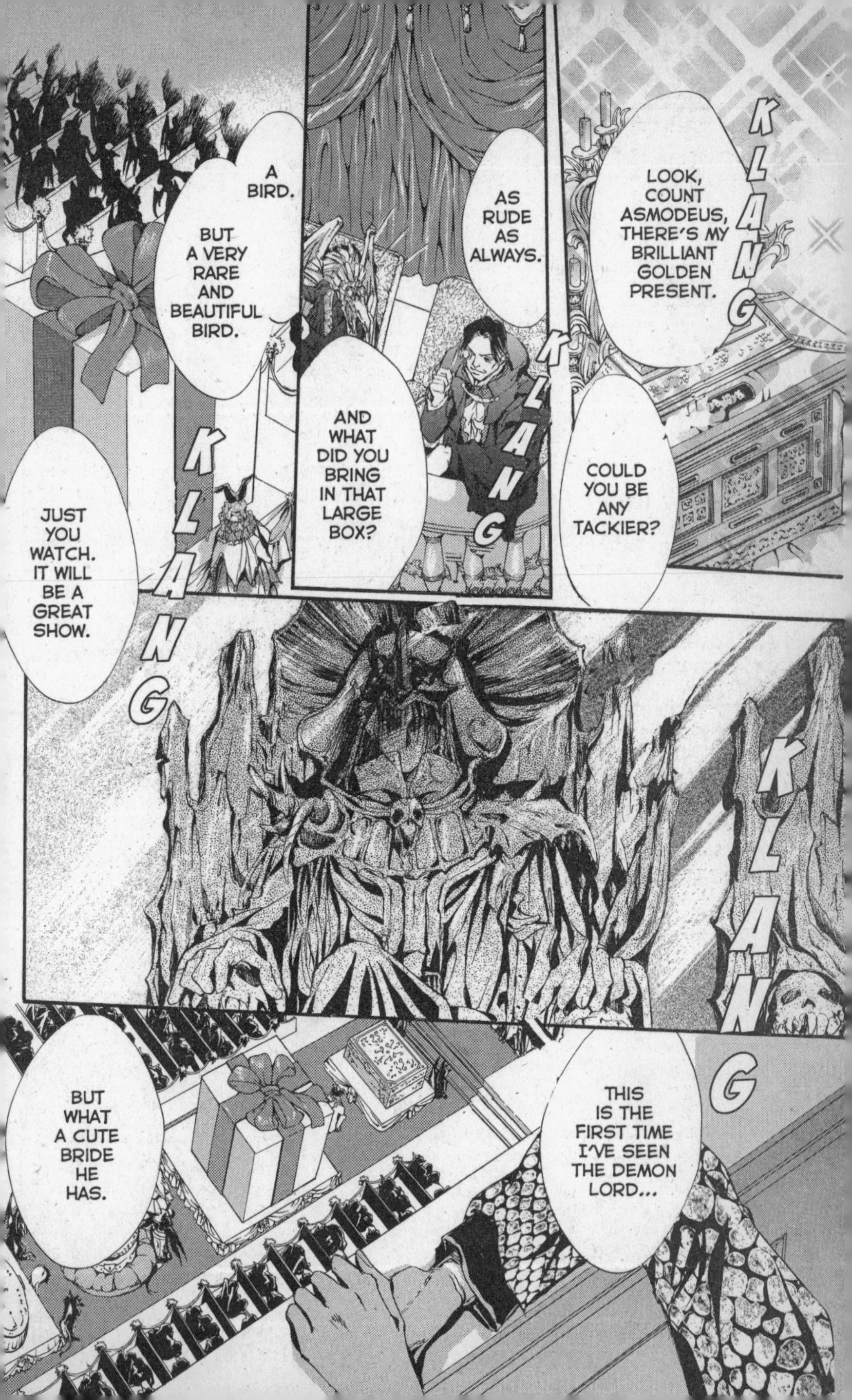
KLANG
LOOK, COUNT ASMODEUS, THERE'S MY BRILLIANT GOLDEN PRESENT.
COULD YOU BE ANY TACKIER?
AS RUDE AS ALWAYS.
KLANG
AND WHAT DID YOU BRING IN THAT LARGE BOX?
A BIRD.
BUT A VERY RARE AND BEAUTIFUL BIRD.
KLANG
JUST YOU WATCH. IT WILL BE A GREAT SHOW.
KLANG
THIS IS THE FIRST TIME I'VE SEEN THE DEMON LORD...
BUT WHAT A CUTE BRIDE HE HAS.

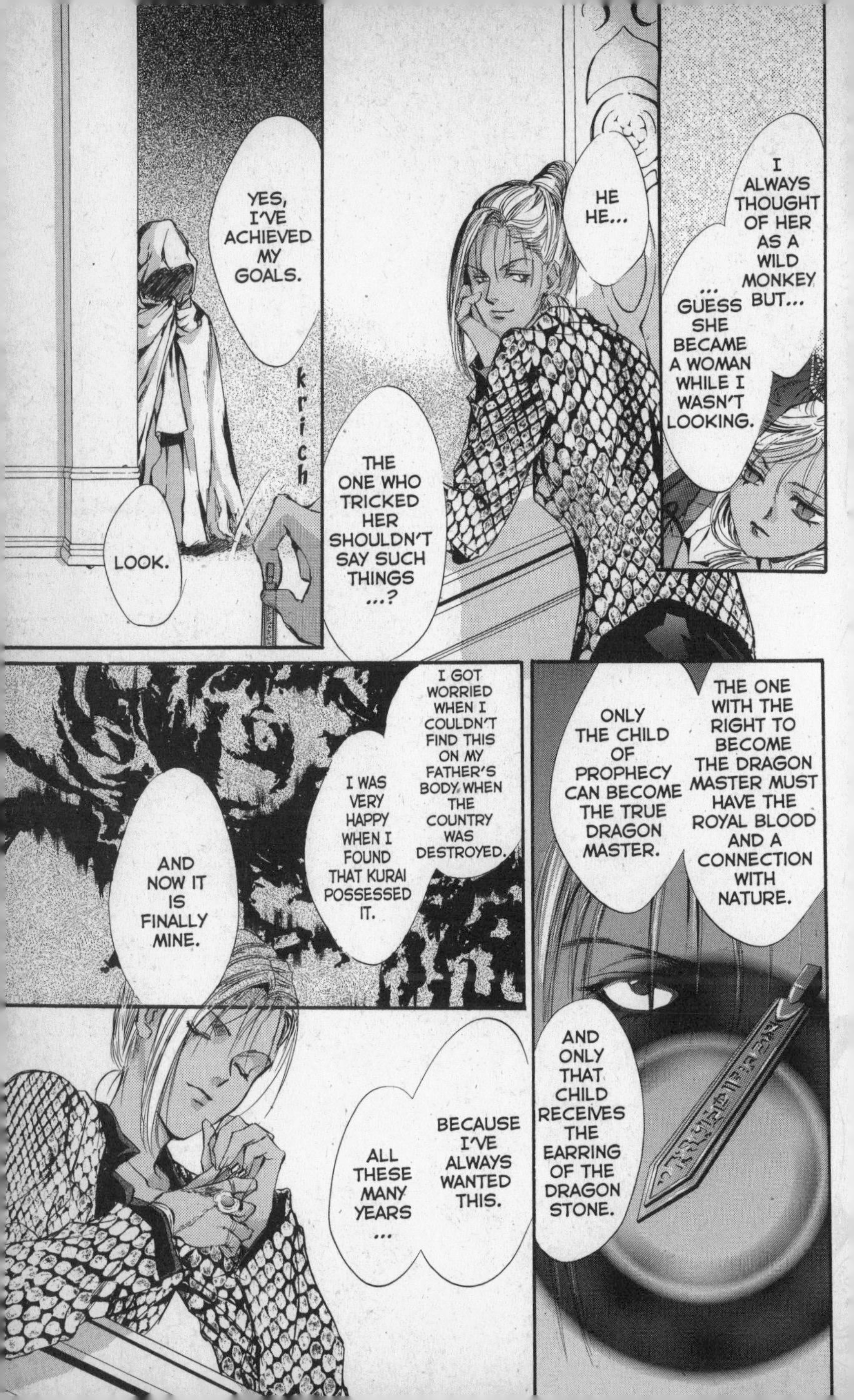
I ALWAYS THOUGHT OF HER AS A WILD MONKEY BUT...
...GUESS SHE BECAME A WOMAN WHILE I WASN'T LOOKING.
HE HE...
THE ONE WHO TRICKED HER SHOULDN'T SAY SUCH THINGS ...?
YES, I'VE ACHIEVED MY GOALS.
krich
LOOK.
THE ONE WITH THE RIGHT TO BECOME THE DRAGON MASTER MUST HAVE THE ROYAL BLOOD AND A CONNECTION WITH NATURE.
ONLY THE CHILD OF PROPHECY CAN BECOME THE TRUE DRAGON MASTER.
AND ONLY THAT CHILD RECEIVES THE EARRING OF THE DRAGON STONE.
I GOT WORRIED WHEN I COULDN'T FIND THIS ON MY FATHER'S BODY WHEN THE COUNTRY WAS DESTROYED.
I WAS VERY HAPPY WHEN I FOUND THAT KURAI POSSESSED IT.
AND NOW IT IS FINALLY MINE.
BECAUSE I'VE ALWAYS WANTED THIS.
ALL THESE MANY YEARS ...

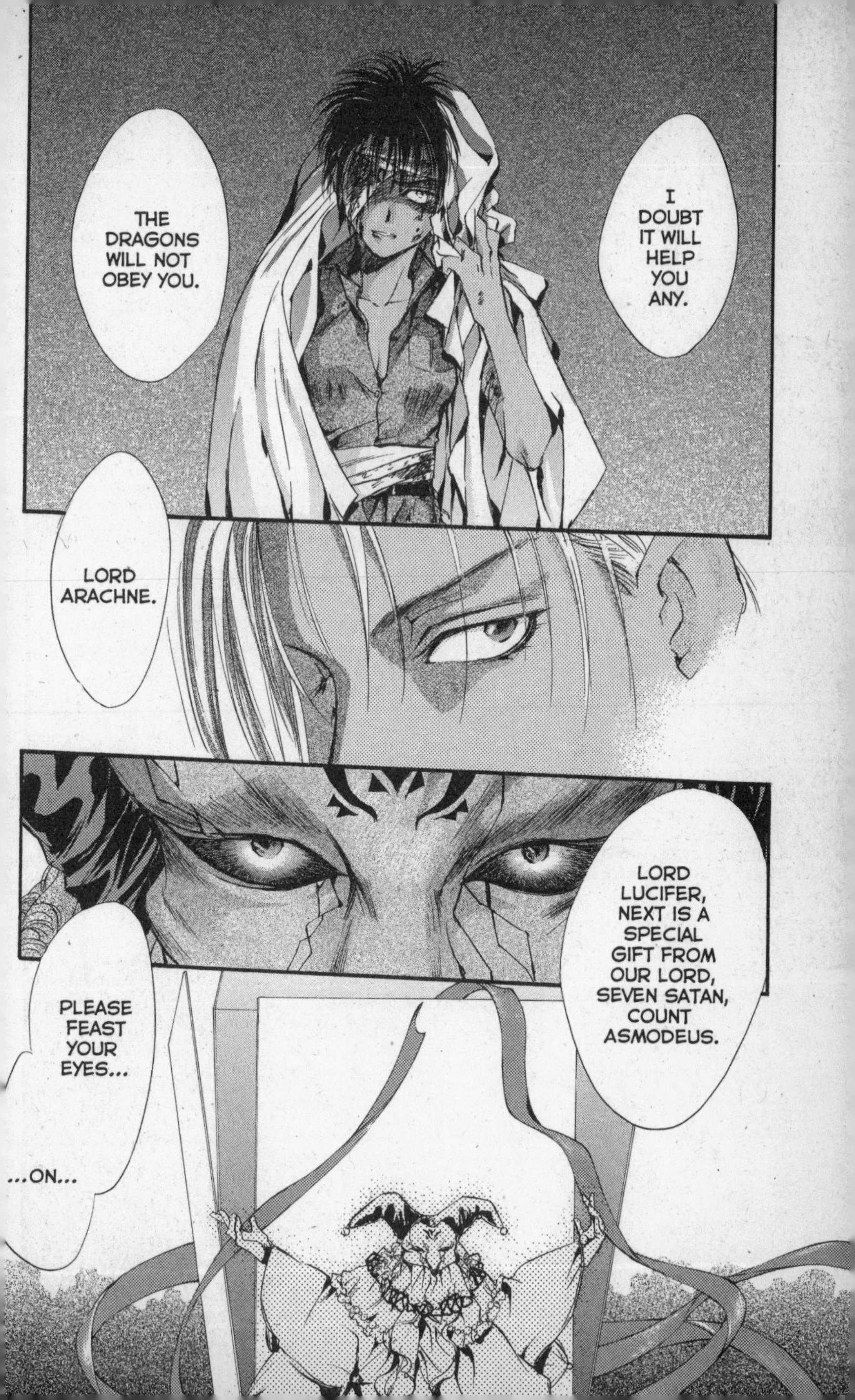
I DOUBT IT WILL HELP YOU ANY.
THE DRAGONS WILL NOT OBEY YOU.
LORD ARACHNE.
LORD LUCIFER, NEXT IS A SPECIAL GIFT FROM OUR LORD, SEVEN SATAN, COUNT ASMODEUS.
PLEASE FEAST YOUR EYES...
...ON...

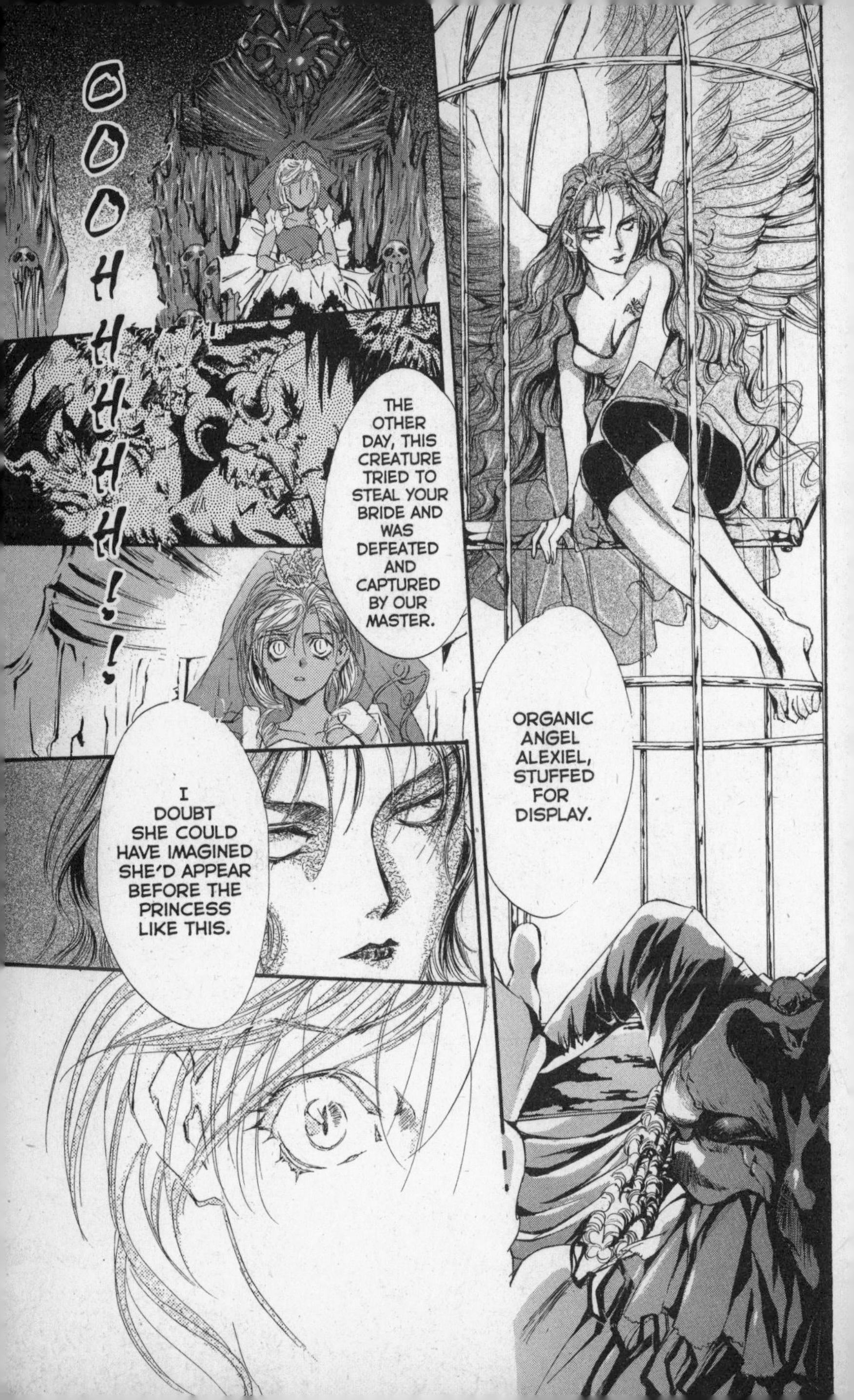
ORGANIC ANGEL ALEXIEL, STUFFED FOR DISPLAY.
OOOHHHHHH!!
THE OTHER DAY, THIS CREATURE TRIED TO STEAL YOUR BRIDE AND WAS DEFEATED AND CAPTURED BY OUR MASTER.
I DOUBT SHE COULD HAVE IMAGINED SHE'D APPEAR BEFORE THE PRINCESS LIKE THIS.

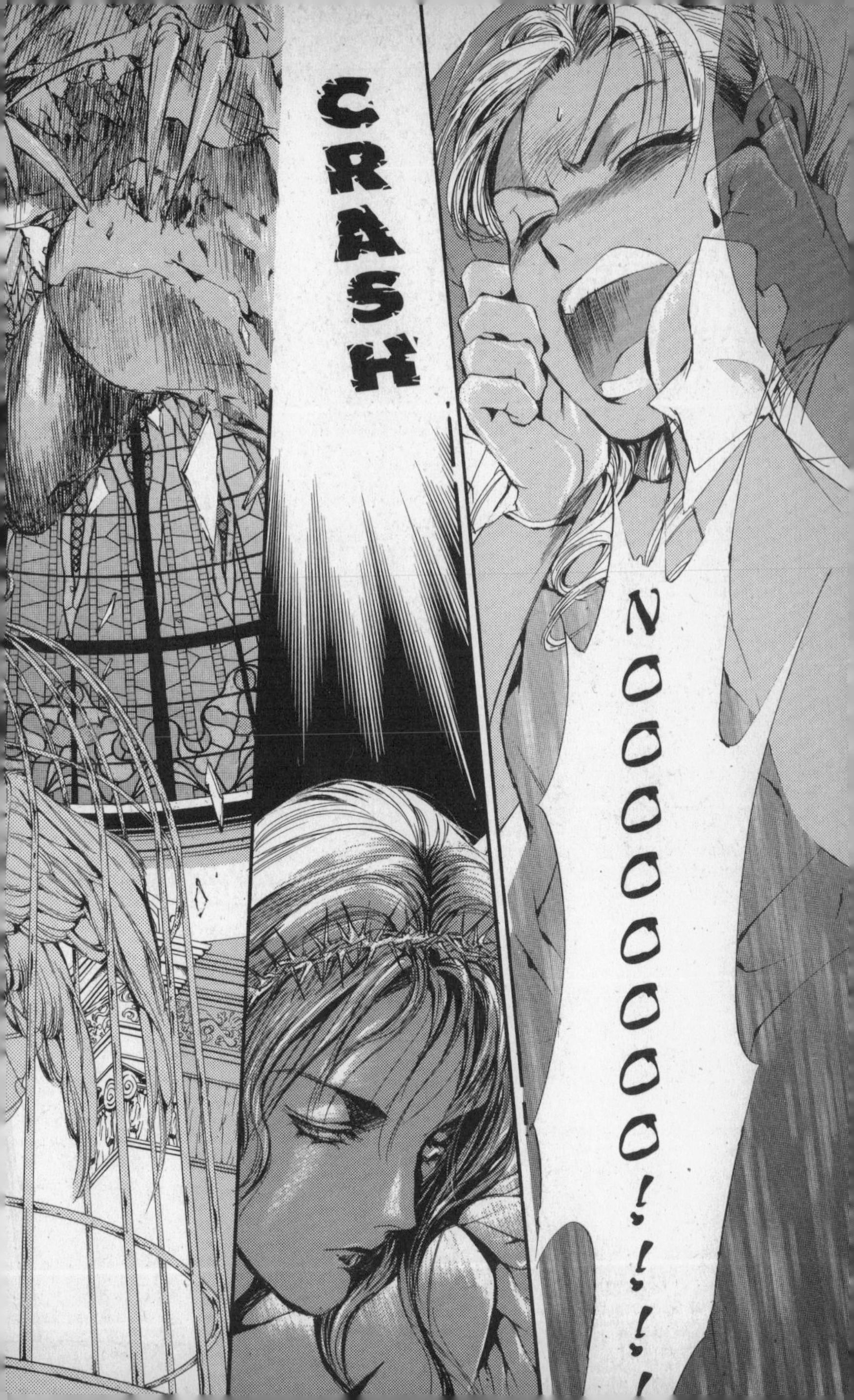
NOOOOOOOOOO!!!!
CRASH

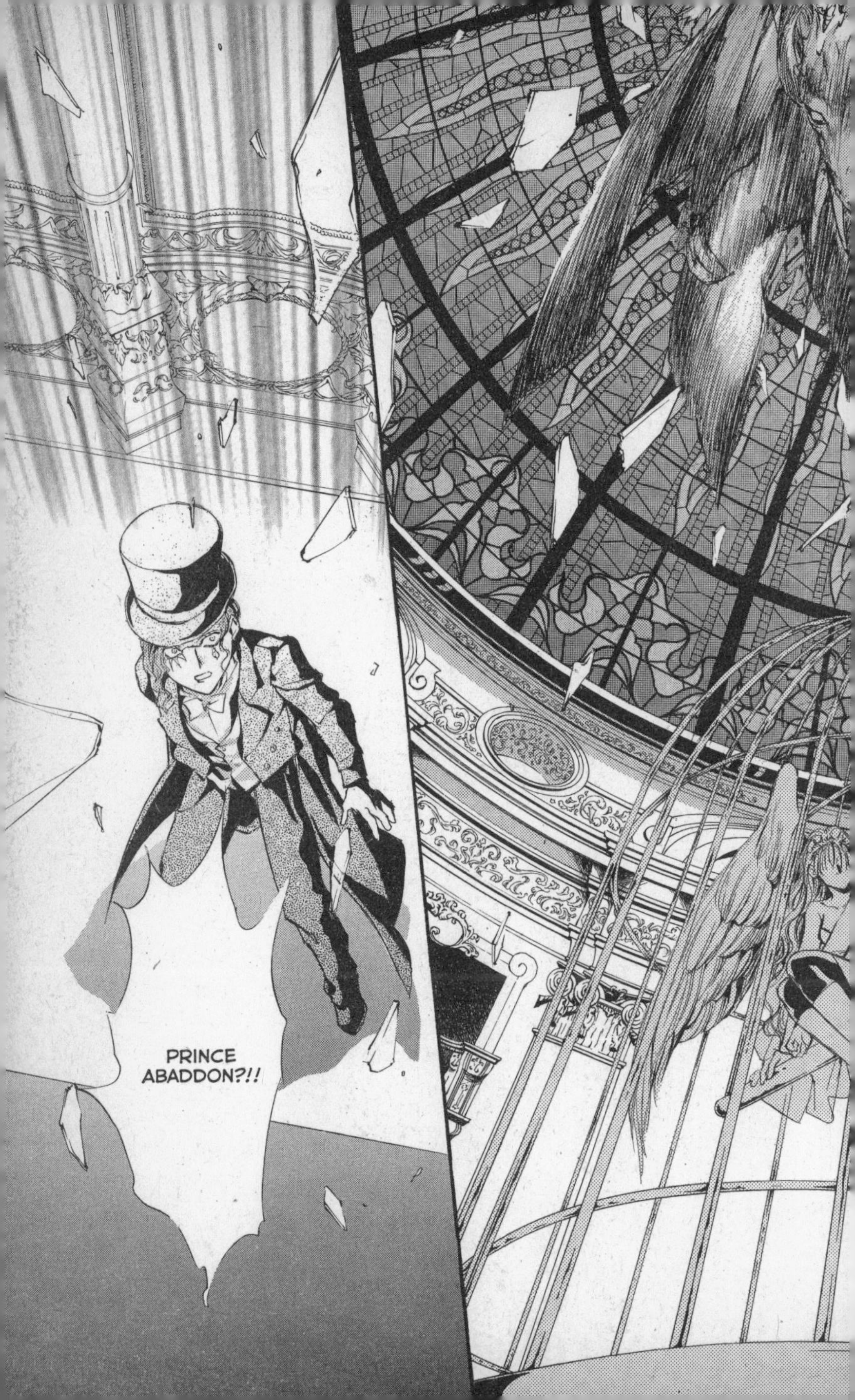
PRINCE ABADDON?!!

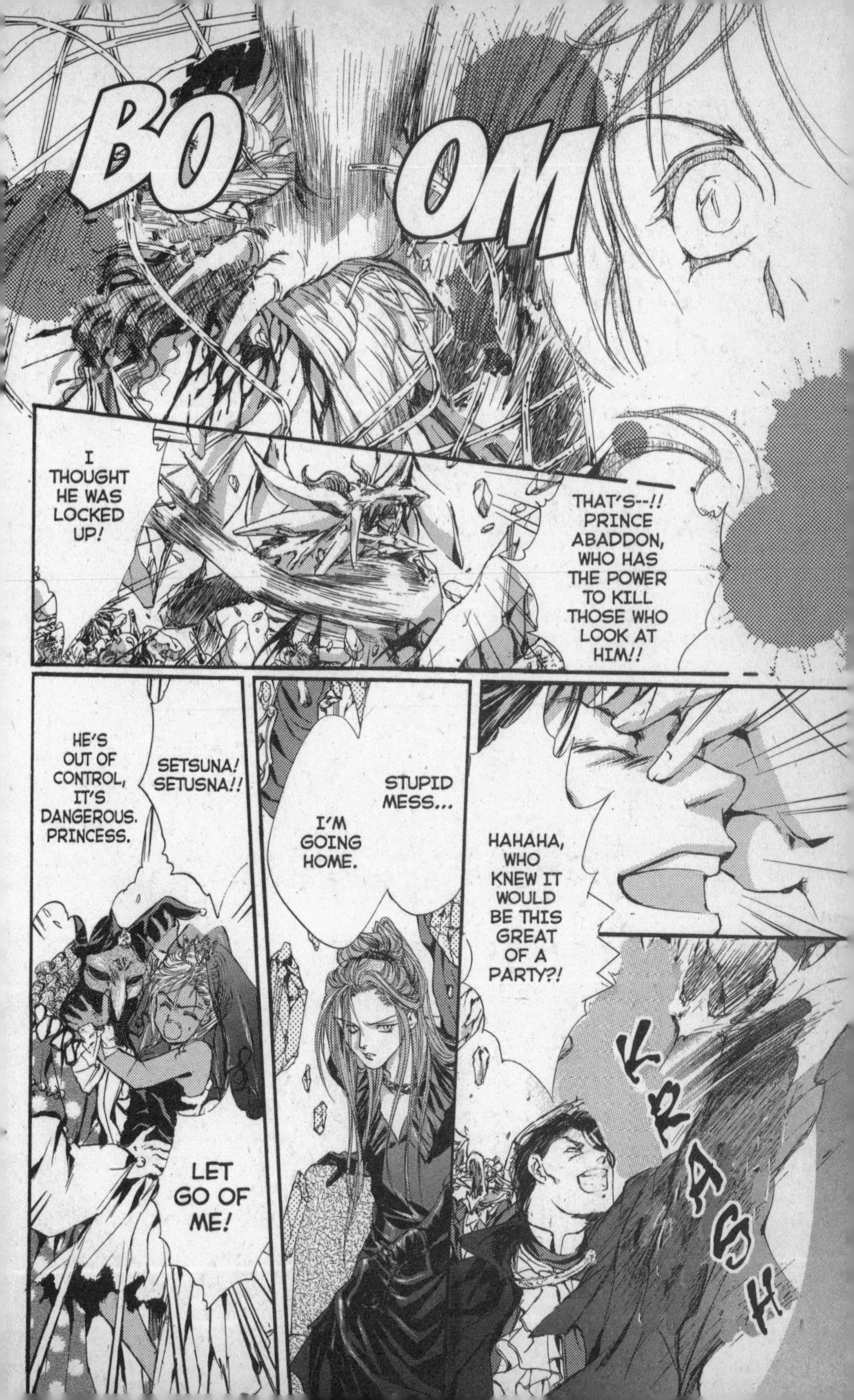
BOOM
THAT'S--!! PRINCE ABADDON, WHO HAS THE POWER TO KILL THOSE WHO LOOK AT HIM!!
I THOUGHT HE WAS LOCKED UP!
HAHAHA, WHO KNEW IT WOULD BE THIS GREAT OF A PARTY?!
KRASH
STUPID MESS...
I'M GOING HOME.
SETSUNA! SETUSNA!!
HE'S OUT OF CONTROL, IT'S DANGEROUS. PRINCESS.
LET GO OF ME!

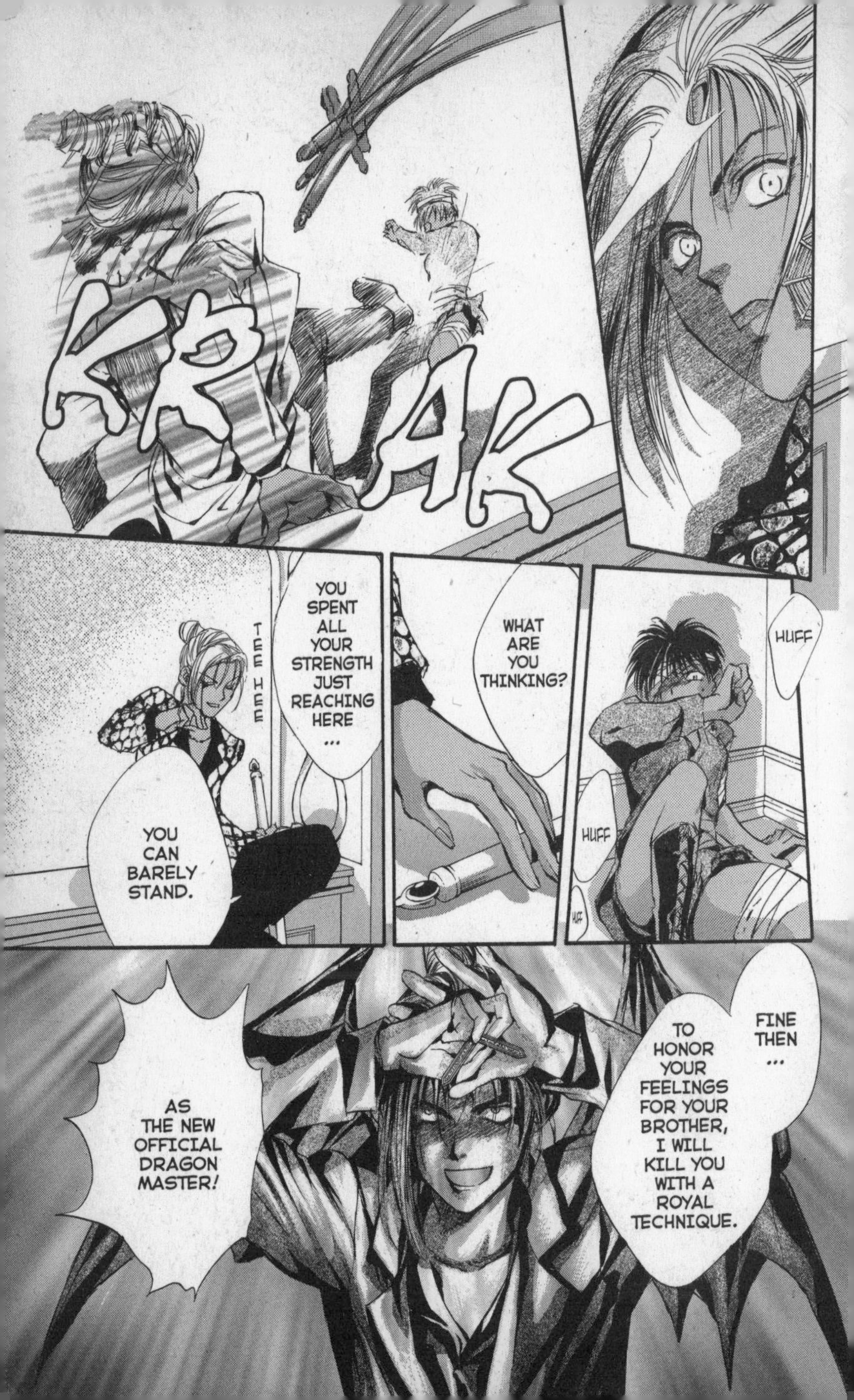
KRUAK
HUFF
HUFF
HUFF
WHAT ARE YOU THINKING?
YOU SPENT ALL YOUR STRENGTH JUST REACHING HERE ...
TEE HEE
YOU CAN BARELY STAND.
FINE THEN ...
TO HONOR YOUR FEELINGS FOR YOUR BROTHER, I WILL KILL YOU WITH A ROYAL TECHNIQUE.
AS THE NEW OFFICIAL DRAGON MASTER!

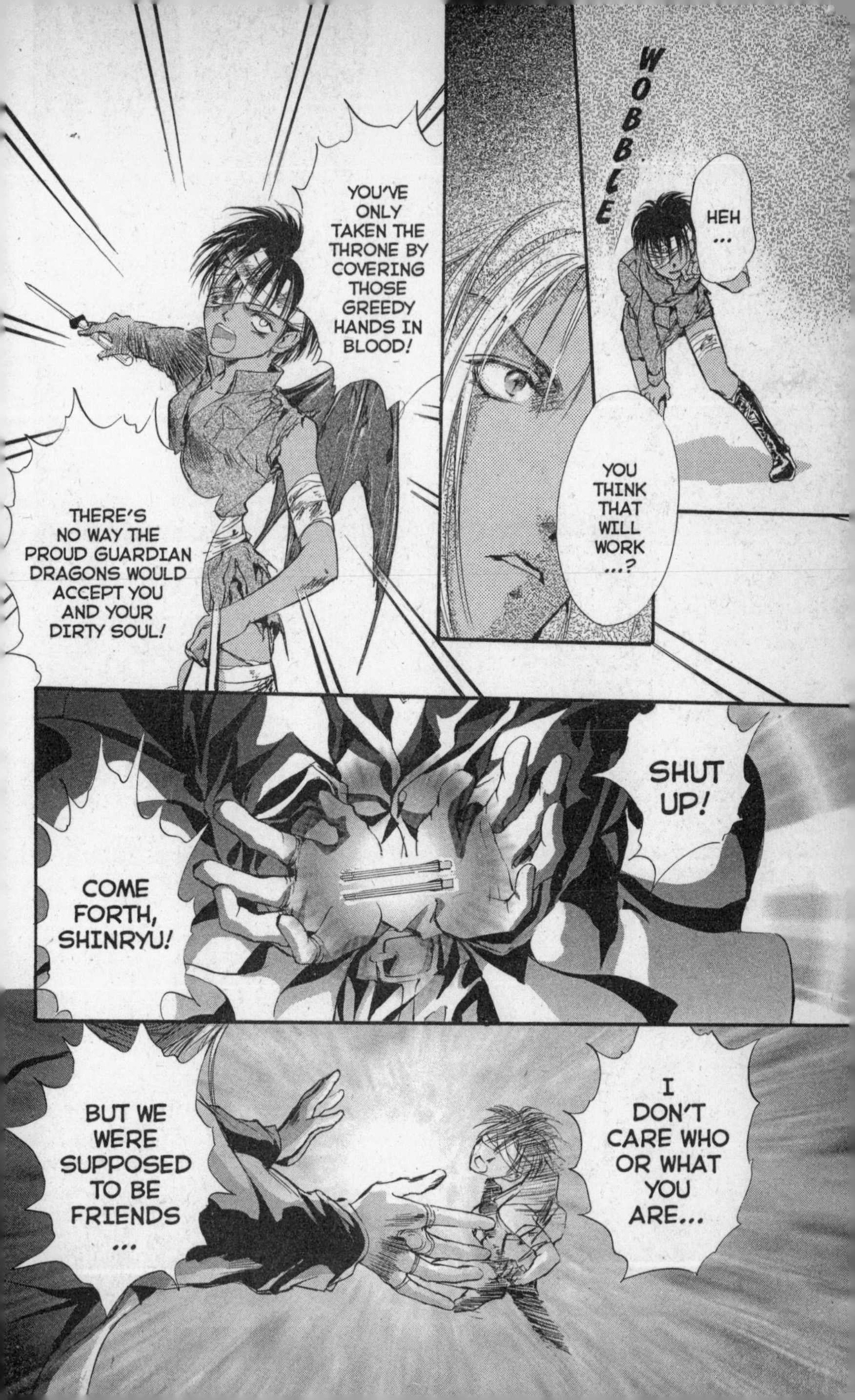
WOBBLE
HEH ...
YOU THINK THAT WILL WORK ...?
YOU'VE ONLY TAKEN THE THRONE BY COVERING THOSE GREEDY HANDS IN BLOOD!
THERE'S NO WAY THE PROUD GUARDIAN DRAGONS WOULD ACCEPT YOU AND YOUR DIRTY SOUL!
SHUT UP!
COME FORTH, SHINRYU!
I DON'T CARE WHO OR WHAT YOU ARE...
BUT WE WERE SUPPOSED TO BE FRIENDS ...

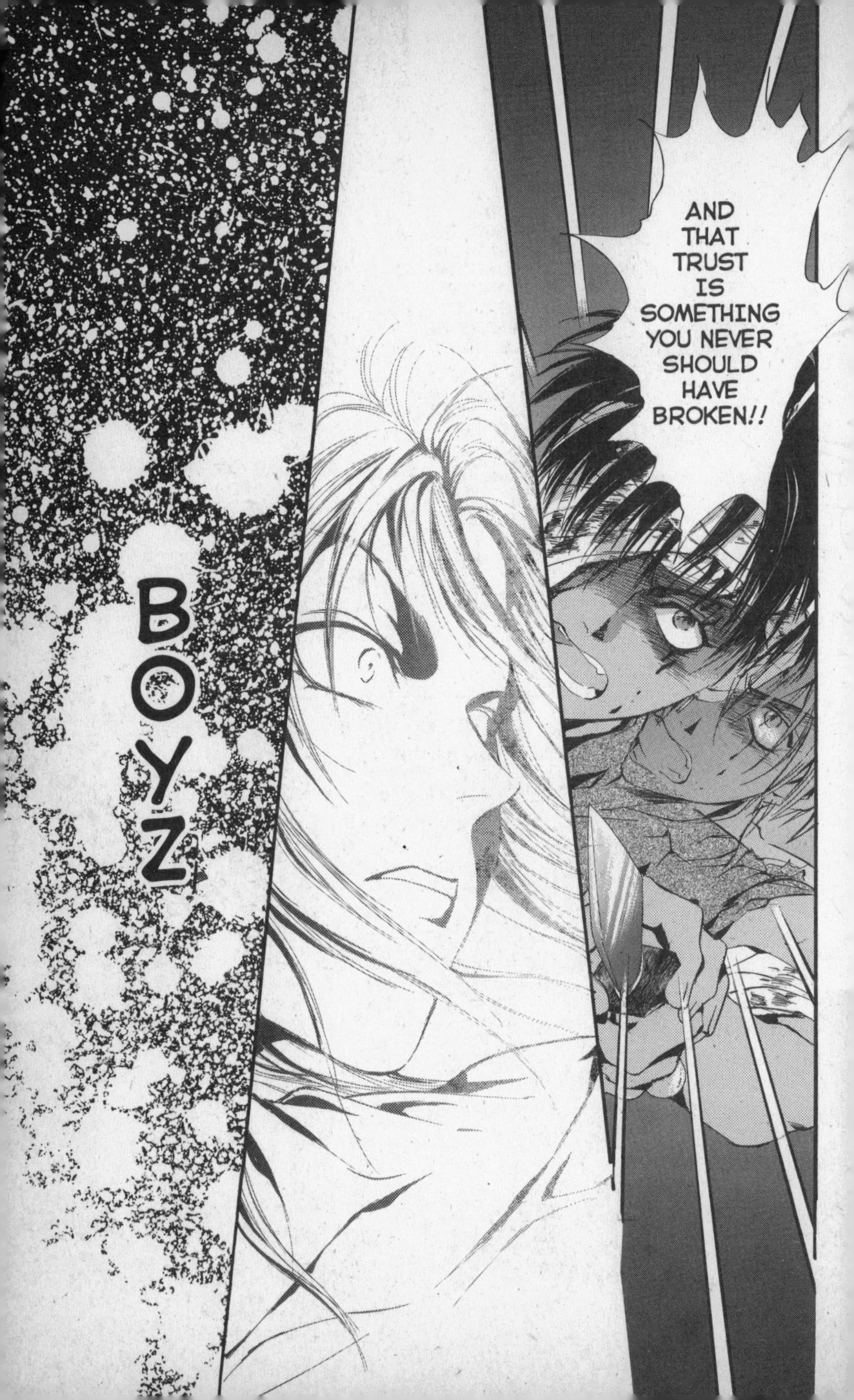
AND THAT TRUST IS SOMETHING YOU NEVER SHOULD HAVE BROKEN!!
BOYZ

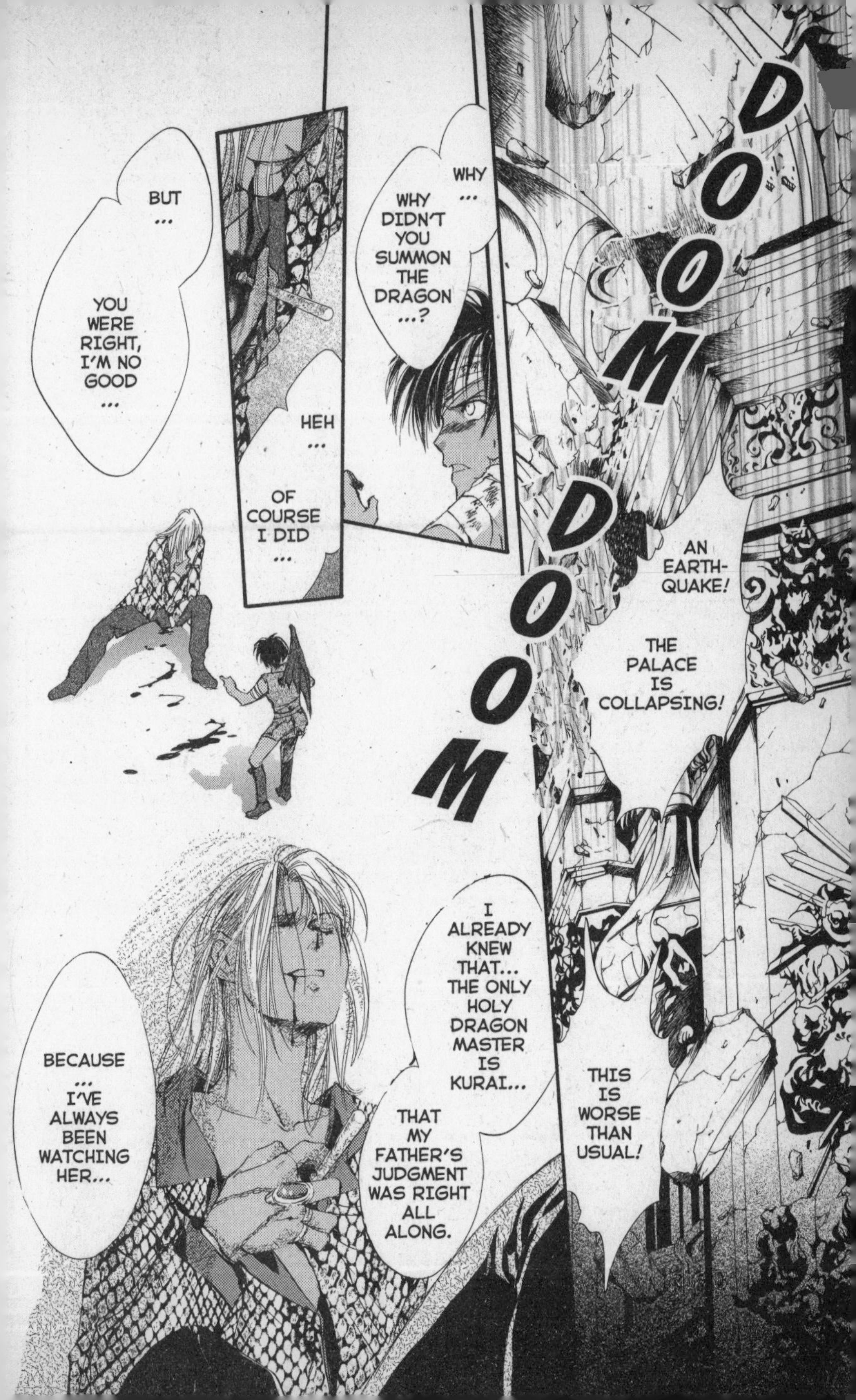
DOOM
DOOM
AN EARTH-QUAKE!
THE PALACE IS COLLAPSING!
THIS IS WORSE THAN USUAL!
WHY ...
WHY DIDN'T YOU SUMMON THE DRAGON ...?
HEH ...
OF COURSE I DID ...
BUT ...
YOU WERE RIGHT, I'M NO GOOD ...
I ALREADY KNEW THAT... THE ONLY HOLY DRAGON MASTER IS KURAI...
THAT MY FATHER'S JUDGMENT WAS RIGHT ALL ALONG.
BECAUSE ... I'VE ALWAYS BEEN WATCHING HER...

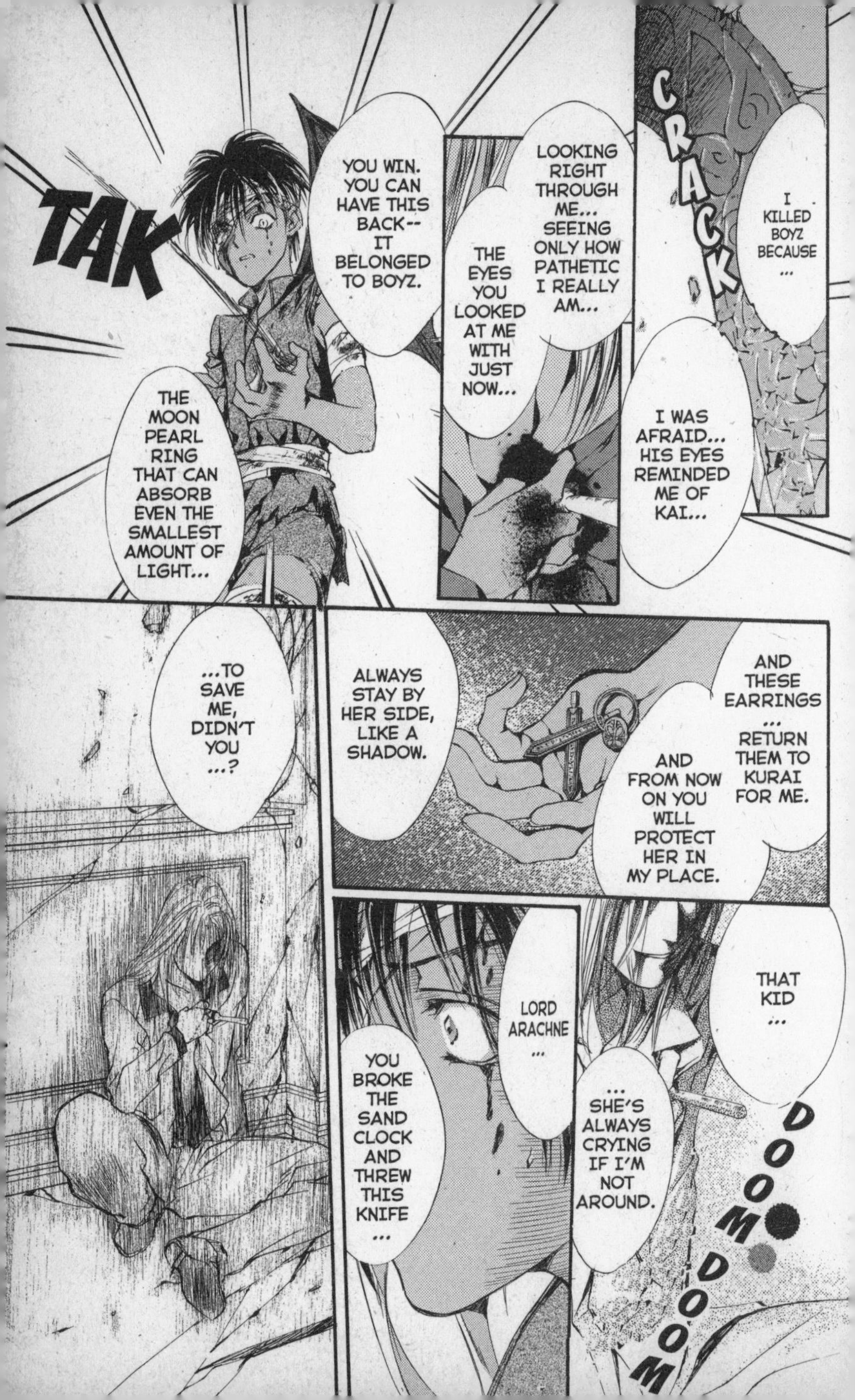
I KILLED BOYZ BECAUSE ...
CRACK
I WAS AFRAID... HIS EYES REMINDED ME OF KAI...
LOOKING RIGHT THROUGH ME... SEEING ONLY HOW PATHETIC I REALLY AM...
THE EYES YOU LOOKED AT ME WITH JUST NOW...
YOU WIN. YOU CAN HAVE THIS BACK-- IT BELONGED TO BOYZ.
TAK
THE MOON PEARL RING THAT CAN ABSORB EVEN THE SMALLEST AMOUNT OF LIGHT...
AND THESE EARRINGS ... RETURN THEM TO KURAI FOR ME.
AND FROM NOW ON YOU WILL PROTECT HER IN MY PLACE.
ALWAYS STAY BY HER SIDE, LIKE A SHADOW.
THAT KID ...
... SHE'S ALWAYS CRYING IF I'M NOT AROUND.
DOOM DOOM DOOM
LORD ARACHNE ...
YOU BROKE THE SAND CLOCK AND THREW THIS KNIFE ...
...TO SAVE ME, DIDN'T YOU ...?

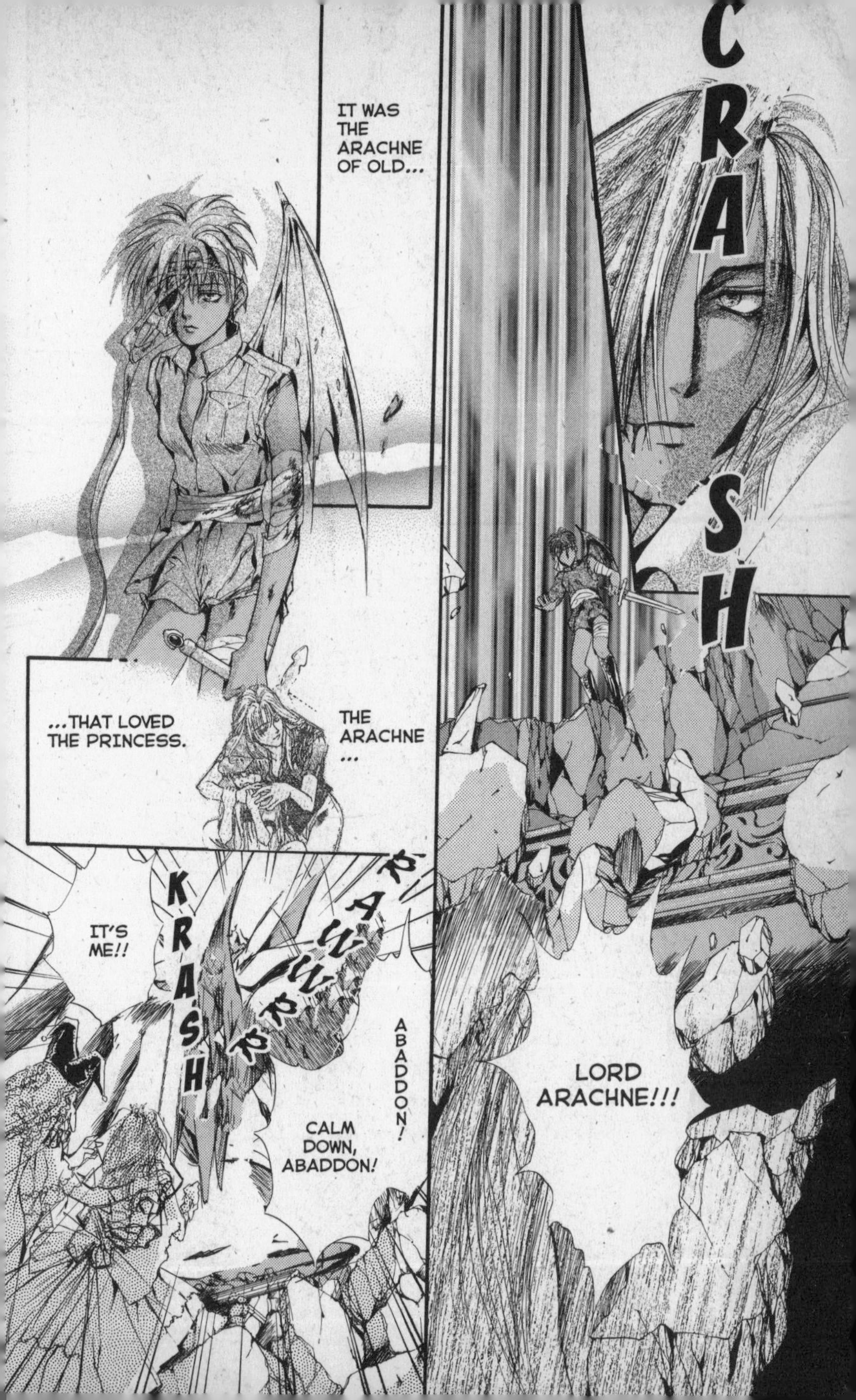
CRASH
LORD ARACHNE!!!
IT WAS THE ARACHNE OF OLD...
THE ARACHNE ...
...THAT LOVED THE PRINCESS.
RAWWRR
KRASH
IT'S ME!!
ABADDON!
CALM DOWN, ABADDON!

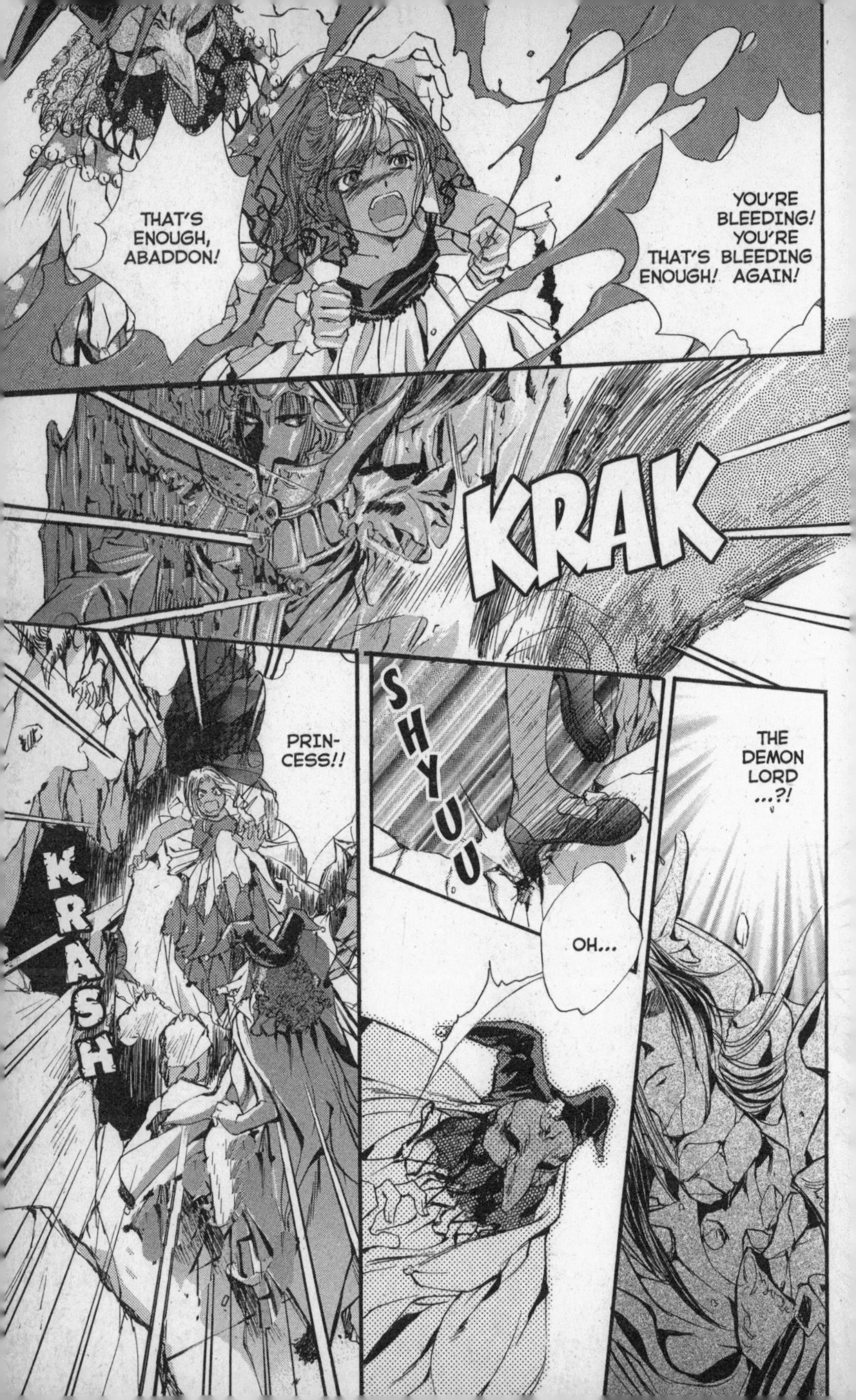
YOU'RE BLEEDING! YOU'RE BLEEDING AGAIN!
THAT'S ENOUGH!
THAT'S ENOUGH, ABADDON!
KRAK
THE DEMON LORD ...?!
OH...
SHYUU
PRIN-CESS!!
KRASH

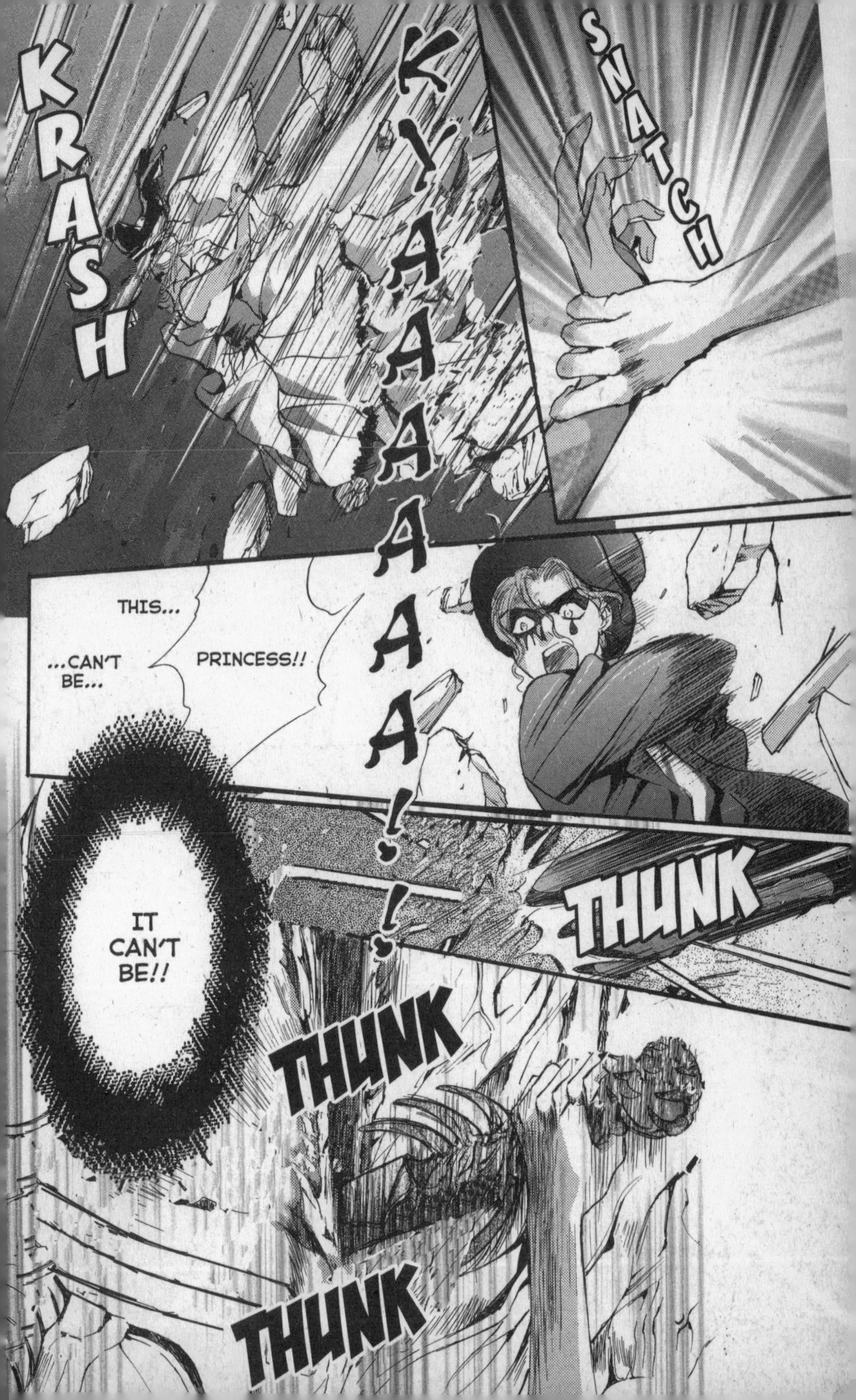
SNATCH
KRASH
KIAAAAAA!!
THIS...
...CAN'T BE...
PRINCESS!!
THUNK
IT CAN'T BE!!
THUNK
THUNK

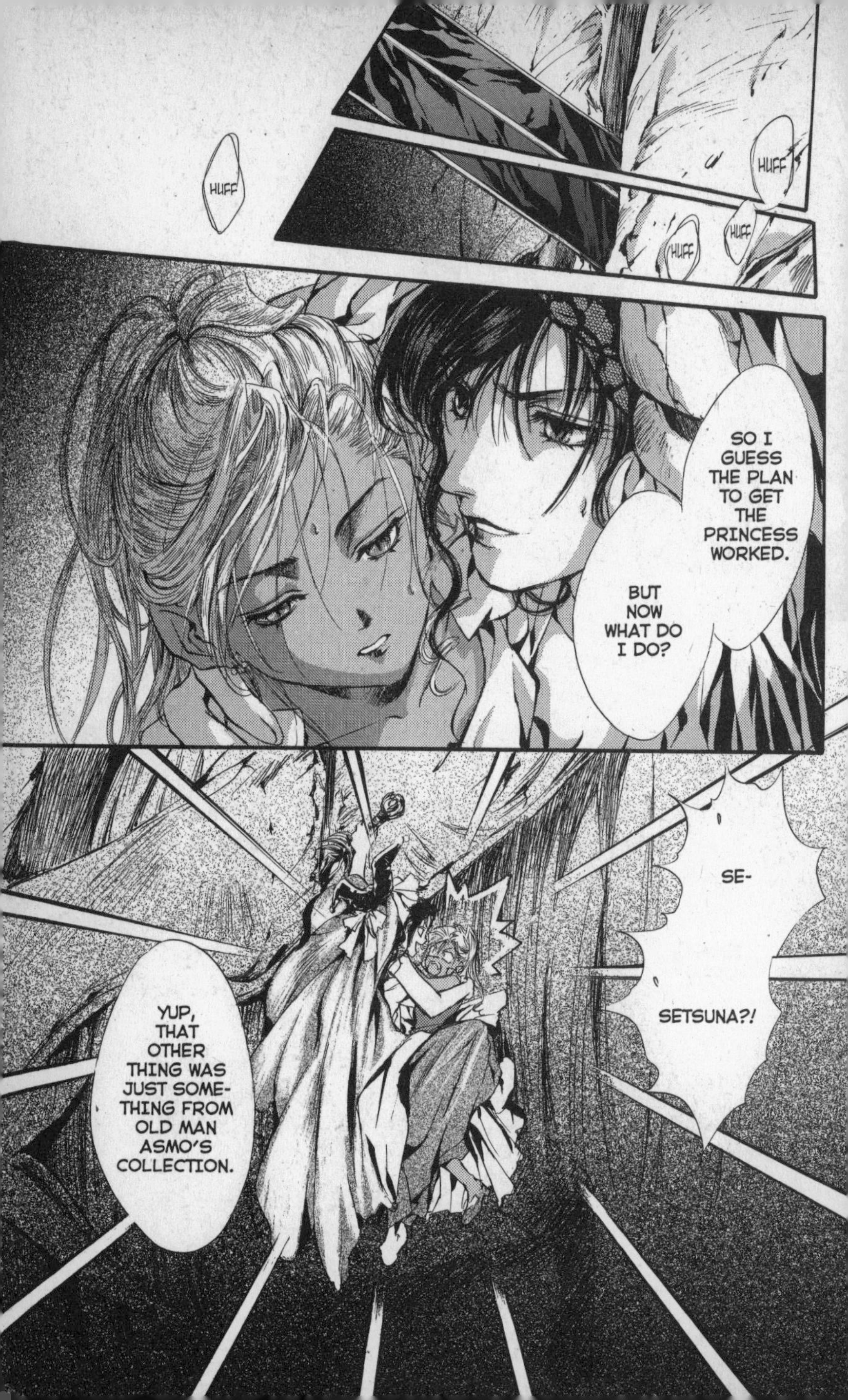
HUFF
HUFF
HUFF
HUFF
SO I GUESS THE PLAN TO GET THE PRINCESS WORKED.
BUT NOW WHAT DO I DO?
SE-
SETSUNA?!
YUP, THAT OTHER THING WAS JUST SOME-THING FROM OLD MAN ASMO'S COLLECTION.

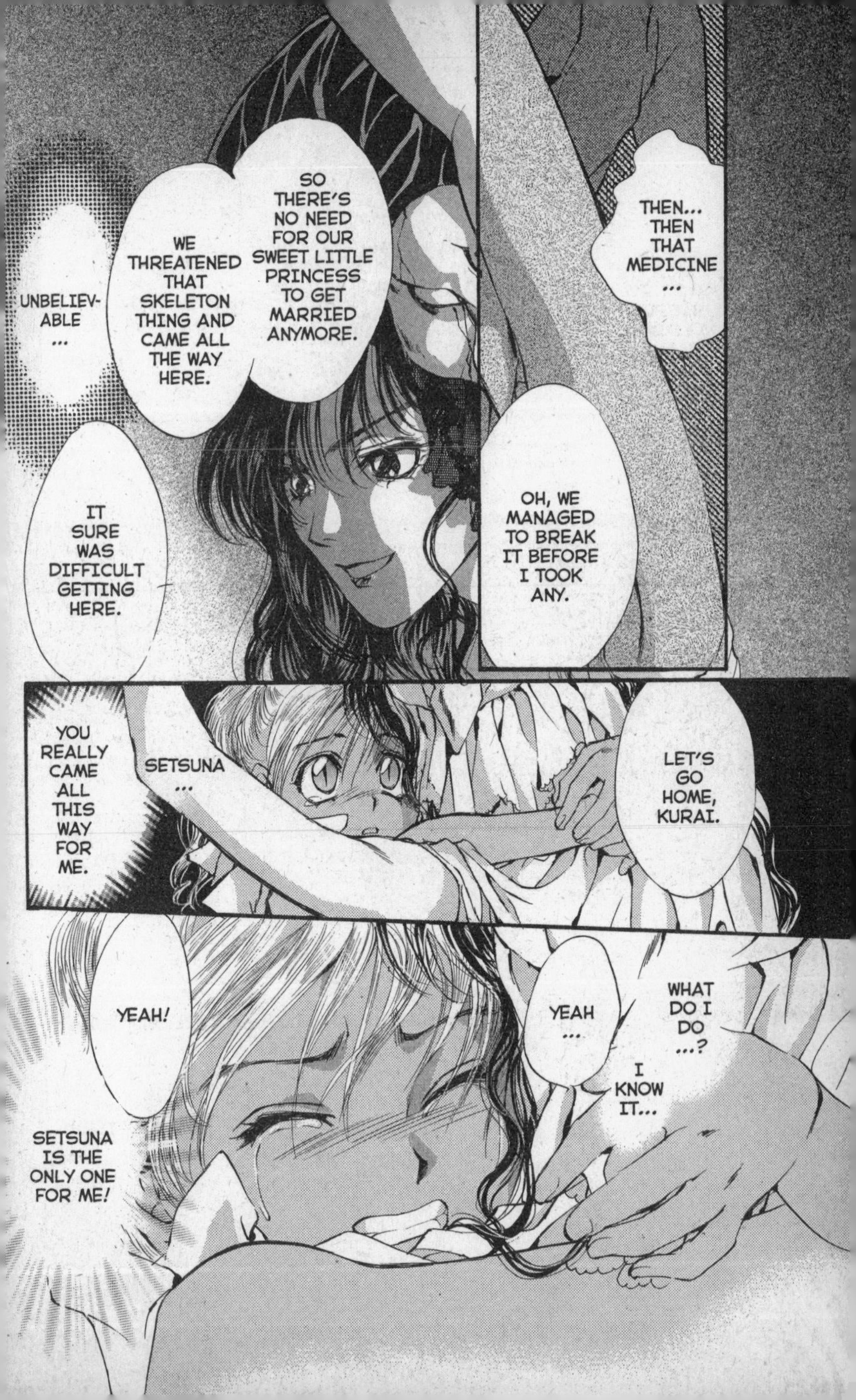
THEN... THEN THAT MEDICINE ...
OH, WE MANAGED TO BREAK IT BEFORE I TOOK ANY.
SO THERE'S NO NEED FOR OUR SWEET LITTLE PRINCESS TO GET MARRIED ANYMORE.
WE THREATENED THAT SKELETON THING AND CAME ALL THE WAY HERE.
UNBELIEV-ABLE ...
IT SURE WAS DIFFICULT GETTING HERE.
LET'S GO HOME, KURAI.
SETSUNA ...
YOU REALLY CAME ALL THIS WAY FOR ME.
WHAT DO I DO ...?
I KNOW IT...
YEAH ...
YEAH!
SETSUNA IS THE ONLY ONE FOR ME!

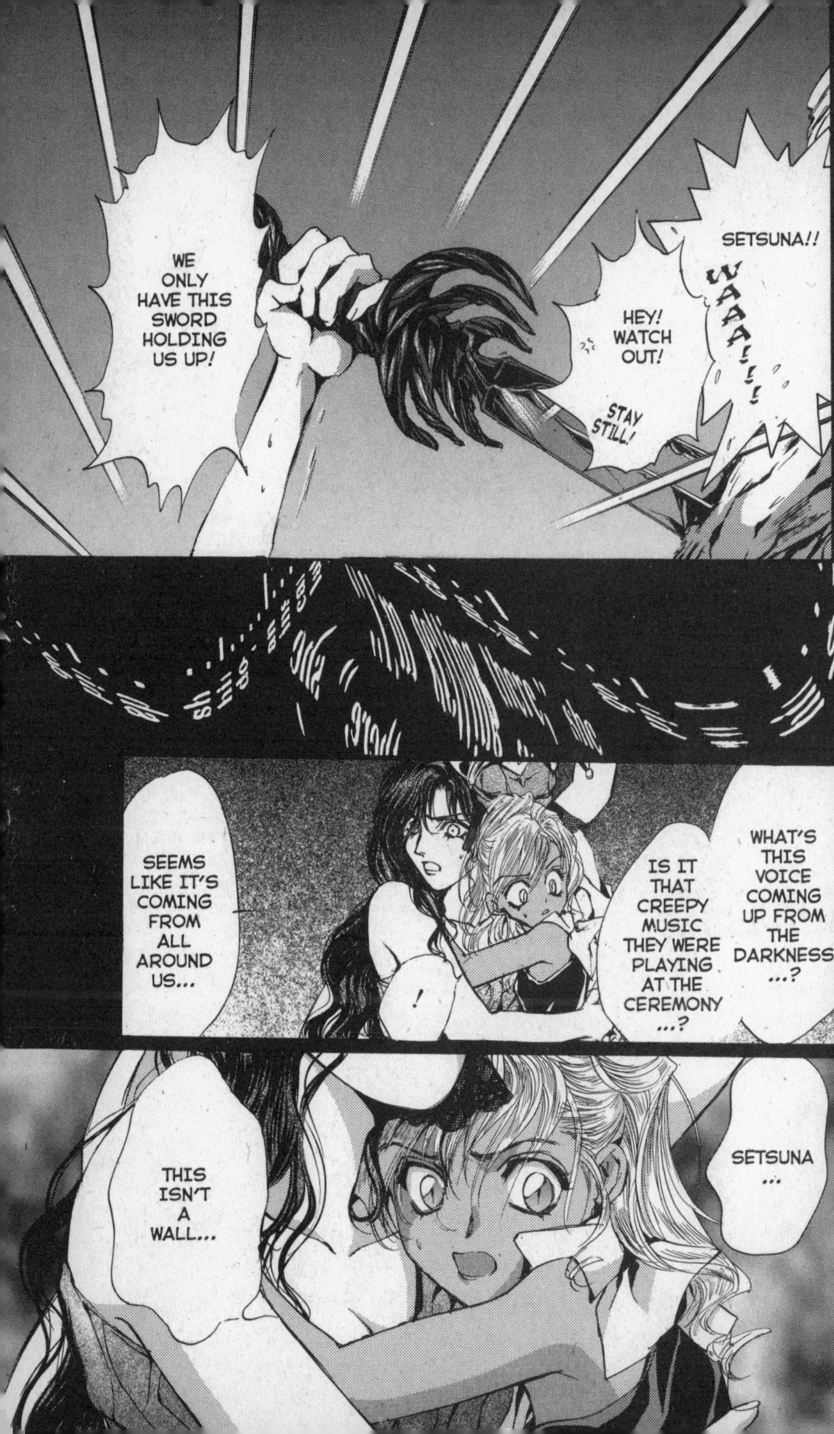
SETSUNA!!
WAAA!!!
HEY! WATCH OUT!
STAY STILL!
WE ONLY HAVE THIS SWORD HOLDING US UP!
WHAT'S THIS VOICE COMING UP FROM THE DARKNESS ...?
IS IT THAT CREEPY MUSIC THEY WERE PLAYING AT THE CEREMONY ...?
!
SEEMS LIKE IT'S COMING FROM ALL AROUND US...
SETSUNA ...
THIS ISN'T A WALL...

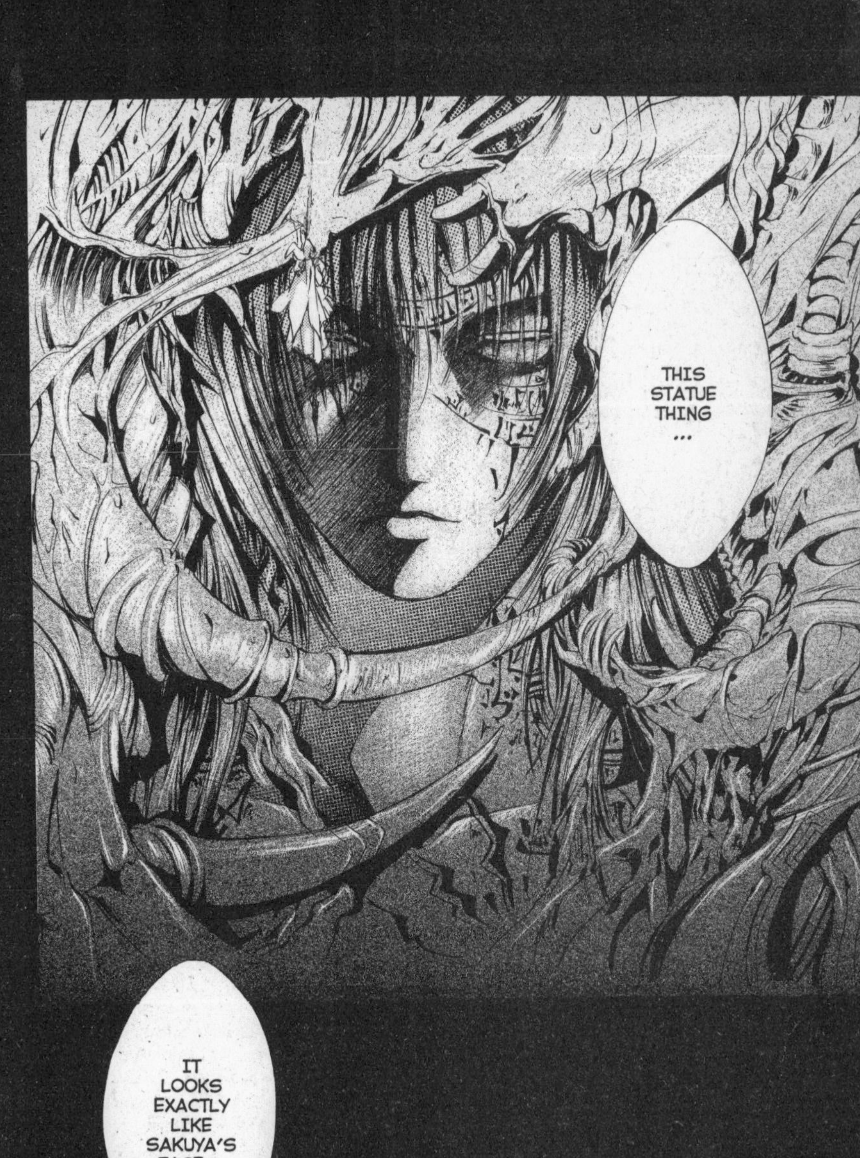
THIS STATUE THING ...
IT LOOKS EXACTLY LIKE SAKUYA'S FACE...

ANGEL SANCTUARY 10/END

angel lies and devil flattery

About the devil info I provided in this book. Since this was the devil saga, I added in research from actual sources. Though please understand that I took some liberties. Like with Astaroth. The demon corresponding to the sin of "sloth" is supposed to be Belphegor. And he's supposed to have breath so stinky that it's poisonous. And the way to defend against it is the silver nose ring... And he's ugly or looks like a snake. I made it so he was a beautiful former Angel who wears black. Very feminine and cold as ice.

It was written that he has both genders, but that's not accurate. When he is Astarte he has a woman's body and when he's Astaroth he has a man's body. I based his design off of someone in a band, but people think it's the bassist when it's not. Must be the fault of my art skills.... I'm sad nobody figured it out. The scenes when he shows his bare legs are sensual in a dangerous sort of way. He was very fun to draw and since he's not going to appear for a while, I drew the picture over on the left side of the page. One reason I didn't draw Belphegor is because they say that he's always sitting on a toilet.

That just didn't seem to go well with a shoujo manga.... Not that I have a problem with it... Anyway, with the Hell saga I get to draw lots of demons, and it's fun. The next book sees the climax of the Hell arc and the beginning of the Heaven arc. I'd like to be able to finish it by July 1998, but we'll see. Please keep reading till the end!

11/26/1997 Kaori Yuki!

Anael
NEXT ACCESS
Angel

...TO BE CONTINUED

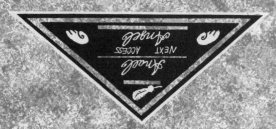

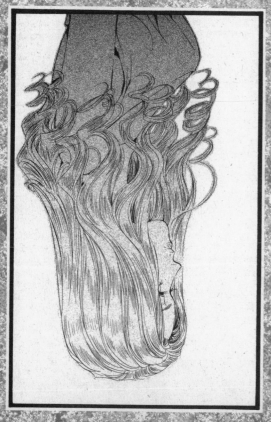

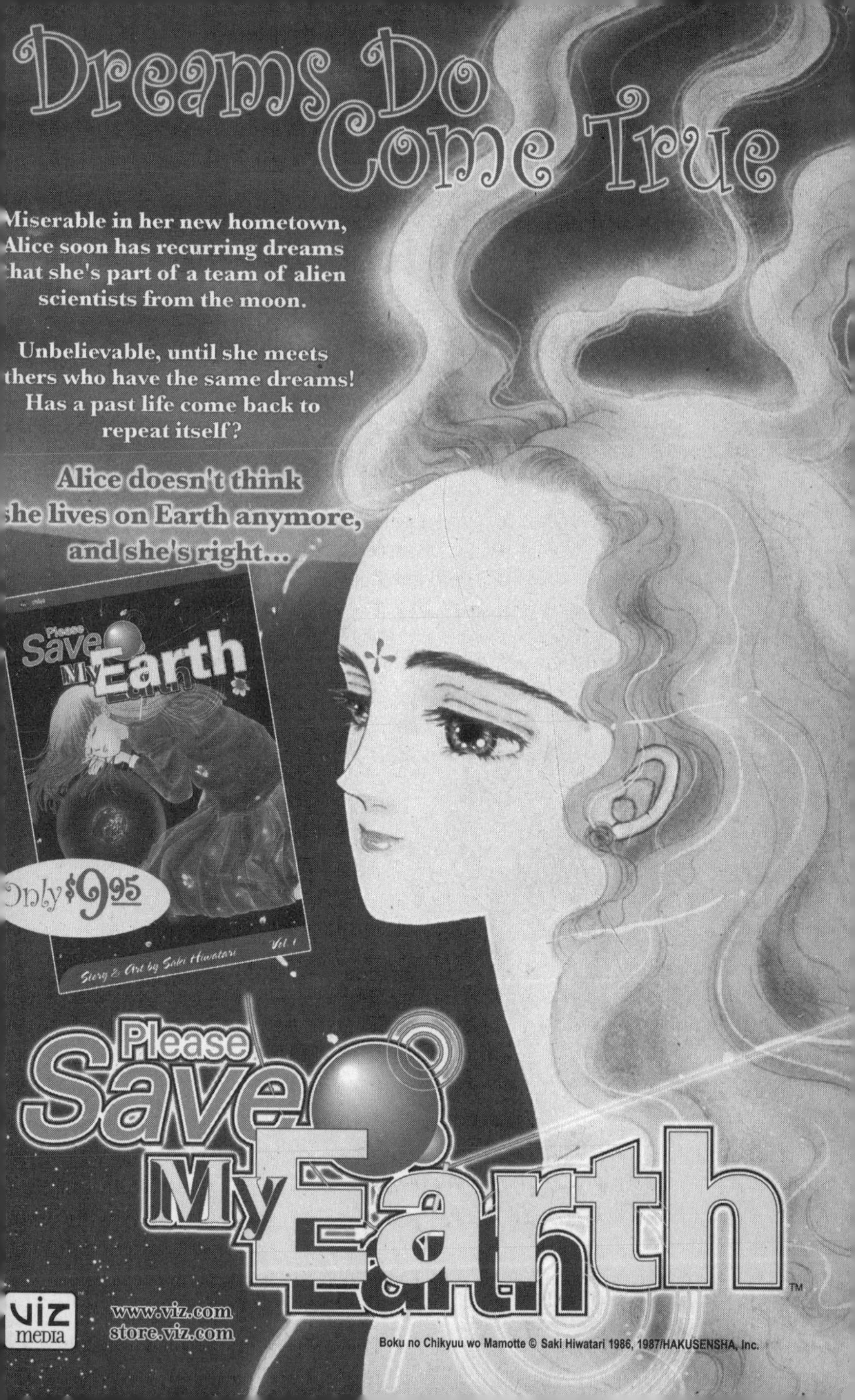

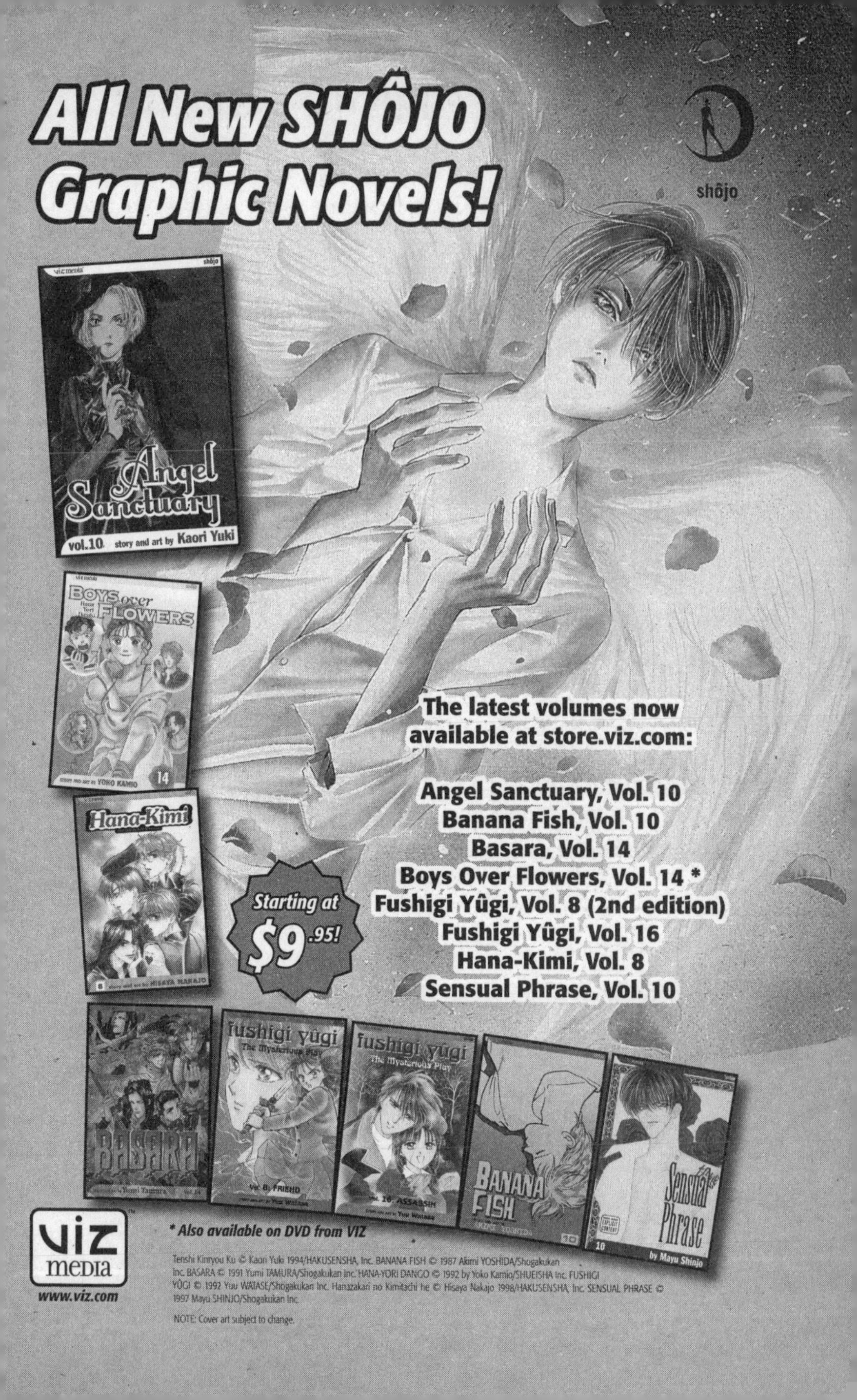
All New SHÔJO Graphic Novels!
shôjo
The latest volumes now available at store.viz.com:
Angel Sanctuary, Vol. 10
Banana Fish, Vol. 10
Basara, Vol. 14
Boys Over Flowers, Vol. 14 *
Fushigi Yûgi, Vol. 8 (2nd edition)
Fushigi Yûgi, Vol. 16
Hana-Kimi, Vol. 8
Sensual Phrase, Vol. 10
Starting at $9.95!
* Also available on DVD from VIZ
VIZ media
www.viz.com
Tenshi Kinryou Ku © Kaori Yuki 1994/HAKUSENSHA, Inc. BANANA FISH © 1987 Akimi YOSHIDA/Shogakukan Inc. BASARA © 1991 Yumi TAMURA/Shogakukan Inc. HANA-YORI DANGO © 1992 by Yoko Kamio/SHUEISHA Inc. FUSHIGI YÛGI © 1992 Yuu WATASE/Shogakukan Inc. Hanazakari no Kimitachi he © Hisaya Nakajo 1998/HAKUSENSHA, Inc. SENSUAL PHRASE © 1997 Mayu SHINJO/Shogakukan Inc.
NOTE: Cover art subject to change.

LOVE SHOJO? LET US KNOW!

☐ Please do NOT send me information about VIZ Media products, news and events, special offers, or other information.

☐ Please do NOT send me information from VIZ' trusted business partners.

Name: _____

Address: _____

City:_____ State:_____ Zip:_____

E-mail:_____

☐ Male ☐ Female Date of Birth (mm/dd/yyyy): ____ / ____ / _____ (Under 13? Parental consent required)

What race/ethnicity do you consider yourself? (check all that apply)

☐ White/Caucasian ☐ Black/African American ☐ Hispanic/Latino

☐ Asian/Pacific Islander ☐ Native American/Alaskan Native ☐ Other: _____

What VIZ shojo title(s) did you purchase? (indicate title(s) purchased)

_____

What other shojo titles from other publishers do you own? _____

_____

Reason for purchase: (check all that apply)

☐ Special offer ☐ Favorite title / author / artist / genre

☐ Gift ☐ Recommendation ☐ Collection

☐ Read excerpt in VIZ manga sampler ☐ Other _____

Where did you make your purchase? (please check one)

☐ Comic store ☐ Bookstore ☐ Mass/Grocery Store

☐ Newsstand ☐ Video/Video Game Store

☐ Online (site:_____) ☐ Other _____

How many shojo titles have you purchased in the last year? How many were VIZ shojo titles?
(please check one from each column)

SHOJO MANGA	VIZ SHOJO MANGA
☐ None	☐ None
☐ 1 – 4	☐ 1 – 4
☐ 5 – 10	☐ 5 – 10
☐ 11	11+

Wh phic novels? **(check all that apply)**

☐ Drama / conflict ☐ Fantasy
Real-life storylines ☐ Relatable characters

____

favorite shojo series?

____

/ artists? ______________________

____

islated and sold in English? ______________

____

pleted form to:

arch
Media Shojo Survey
ine Street
psie, NY 12601

Your privacy is very important to us. All information provided will be used for internal purposes only and will not be sold or otherwise divulged.